SCHAUM'S OUTLINE OF

UML

Second Edition

SIMON BENNETT
Systems Architect, Celesio AG

JOHN SKELTON
Architect Team Leader, Morse Professional Services

KEN LUNN
Interface Design Architect, National Health Information Authority

Schaum's Outline Series
McGRAW-HILL
New York San Francisco Washington, D.C. Auckland Bogotá Caracas
Lisbon London Madrid Mexico City Milan Montreal New Delhi
San Juan Singapore Sydney Tokyo Toronto

SIMON BENNETT is a Systems Architect with Celesio AG based in Coventry, UK. He was previously at Ericsson Intracom, and before that a Principal Lecturer in the Department of Information Systems at De Montfort University, where he was also a member of the Centre for Computational Intelligence. He is one of the authors of *Object-Oriented Systems Analysis and Design using UML*, published by McGraw-Hill.

JOHN SKELTON is the Team Leader for the Solution Architect and Technical Architect team within the Application Development group of Morse Professional Services. He is responsible for the architectural modelling, design and implementation of J2EE systems. He also engages in a wide variety of consultancy activities relating to J2EE services and modelling. Prior to this, he worked as a Senior Lecturer and Teacher Fellow in the Department of Information Systems, De Montfort University.

KEN LUNN is an Interface Design Architect for the National Health Information Authority, and has a Ph.D. in distributed computing. He has worked in industrial and academic research and development, developing, managing and consulting on advanced IT applications for over 25 years for major national and international companies. He is author of *Software Development with UML*, published by Palgrave MacMillan.

Schaum's Outline of UML, Second edition

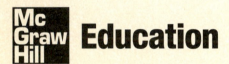 **Education**

ISBN 0-07-710741-1

Editorial Liaison: Elizabeth Choules
Senior Production Editor: Eleanor Hayes

Library of Congress Cataloguing-in-Publication Data

The LOC data for this book has been applied for and may be obtained from the Library of Congress, Washington, D.C.

Printed in the UK by William Clowes Ltd, Beccles, Suffolk

The McGraw-Hill Companies

PREFACE

Aim of the Book

This is the second edition of this book, which has been revised to cover Version 2.0 of the Unified Modelling Language (UML). In writing this book, we had three main aims: firstly, to provide a guide to UML that condenses the material in the UML Specification (Object Management Group, 2004a) and in the books by the main authors of UML; secondly, to do this by means of practical case studies that are developed throughout the book; and, thirdly, to provide plenty of practical examples and exercises for the reader. None of these is an easy task. The UML Specification has grown dramatically since it was first published and been split into several documents. The books by Rumbaugh, Booch and Jacobson (see Bibliography) together run to 1,500 pages, but have not been updated for UML 2.0 at the time of writing. Experienced practitioners know that a fully elaborated set of models for a system would be at least as much paper as in a copy of this book when printed out. A single case study does not always provide opportunities to develop all the rich notation of UML.

We have nonetheless tried to achieve all three. We have described the key features of the notation of each kind of diagram in UML. We have also provided a 'How To' section in each chapter in which we develop examples from one of our two case studies. We have used these case studies to provide worked examples, within and at the end of each chapter, and exercises, and believe that there is plenty of material in them that could be developed by a reader who wants more practical experience. We have tried, by using two case studies, to provide examples that cover business modelling, information system development and real-time system development. We hope that we have succeeded.

Structure

The first two chapters of the book introduce the case studies that we are using and provide background to UML. The next twelve chapters explain the notation of UML diagrams and how to produce them. For each type of diagram, there are sections on the notation, on how to produce the diagrams or of modelling guidance, on how each diagram is related to other diagrams, on how each diagram can be used in business modelling, and on how each diagram fits into the Unified Software Development Process. Within each chapter we introduce examples from the case studies. We also provide a set of review questions, with answers at the back of the book, solved problems and supplementary problems for the reader. Chapter 15 covers the ways in which UML can be extended. The final two chapters provide information on related topics: Software Tools for UML and Design Patterns. The book concludes with a summary of UML notation, answer pointers for the review questions, appendices, a glossary and a bibliography.

Changes in the Second Edition

In preparing the second edition of this book to cover UML 2.0, we have made some changes. The material in Chapter 2 on the UML metamodel has been removed to an Appendix, as we received comments from readers that it was off-putting to newcomers to UML. The chapter on Common Notational Conventions has been changed to one on Extending UML using profiles. The material on Common Notational Conventions, which was based on material in the UML 1.3 Specification, has been removed to an Appendix, as it is no longer part of the Specification, but we consider it useful. A new chapter has been introduced on Component Diagrams, as these are more significant in UML 2.0, and so the chapter that was formerly called Implementation Diagrams now just covers Deployment Diagrams. The chapters on Sequence Diagrams and what were formerly Collaboration Diagrams (now Communication Diagrams) have been swapped in order. This reflects the fact that Communication Diagrams are less significant in UML 2.0 than Collaboration Diagrams were in UML 1.X. Material on the new Timing Diagrams and Interaction Overview Diagrams is in the chapter that includes Communication Diagrams.

Conventions

All three authors are British and we have used British English spelling conventions (those of the Oxford English Dictionary) and punctuation throughout. We have tried to avoid terms that do not carry the same meaning in the varieties of English spoken around the world as they do in British English.

In the text, we have used an italic style to highlight new terms that have a special meaning in UML at the point where they are introduced, for example *classifier*, we have used a sans serif font for terms that are part of a UML model, for example CarSharer, and we have used a fixed width font for sample pieces of code and syntax, for example `sequence-term`. Examples within chapters and the solutions to solved problems at the end of each chapter are printed in a slightly smaller font than the main text.

In diagrams, we have used a sans serif font for labels that are part of the diagram and an italicized serif font for notes that describe elements of a diagram.

Acknowledgements

Our thanks go to David Howe, who provided invaluable help by reading every chapter of the first edition and making suggestions for improvements. All errors are nonetheless the responsibility of the authors.

All products, brand names or services that are referred to in this book are the trademarks or registered trademarks of their respective owners. No claim is made to these trademarks.

The OMG Unified Modeling Language Specification (Object Management Group, 2004*a*) is copyright of a number of organizations. Copyright © 2001–2003 Adaptive Ltd, Copyright © 2001–2003 Alcatel, Copyright © 2001–2003 Borland Software Corporation, Copyright © 2001–2003 Computer Associates International, Inc., Copyright © 2001–2003 Telefonaktiebolaget LM Ericsson, Copyright © 2001–2003 Fujitsu, Copyright © 2001–2003 Hewlett-Packard Company, Copyright © 2001–2003 I-Logix Inc., Copyright © 2001–2003 International Business Machines Corporation, Copyright © 2001–2003 IONA Technologies, Copyright © 2001–2003 Kabira Technologies, Inc., Copyright © 2001–2003 MEGA International, Copyright © 2001–2003 Motorola, Inc., Copyright © 1997–2001 Object Management Group, Copyright © 2001–2003 Oracle Corporation, Copyright © 2001–2003 SOFTEAM, Copyright © 2001–2003 Telelogic AB, Copyright © 2001–2003 Unisys, Copyright © 2001–2003 X-Change Technologies Group, LLC.

The names of towns, people, applications, companies, schemes and any other devices or services used for examples and case studies in this book are fictitious and do not refer to any real town, person, either living or dead, application etc., except where otherwise stated.

Simon Bennett, John Skelton, Ken Lunn
October 2004

CONTENTS

v

DEDICATION

To Helen, Joe and Laurie.   Simon

To Angela, Kate and Matthew. Thanks. Again.   John

To Simon, Charlotte and Nicole.   Ken

CHAPTER 1

Introduction to the Case Studies

1.1 INTRODUCTION

These two case studies are used throughout the book. The first one, CarMatch, is used for illustration of points and worked examples in each chapter. The second case study, VolBank, is used for worked examples and for problems for the reader. You should read the material in this chapter in order to understand the examples and complete the problems.

1.2 CASE STUDY 1—CARMATCH

1.2.1 CarMatch Background

CarMatch is a franchising company that is being set up to promote car sharing. In many cities, traffic congestion poses a threat to the quality of life as well as causing considerable pollution. This includes the release of carbon dioxide into the atmosphere. Many countries are trying to meet their obligations under international agreements to reduce carbon emissions in an attempt to prevent the worst effects of global warming. CarMatch is a response to this situation. In many areas, public transport has declined as car ownership has increased, and the public transport infrastructure is not available to take up the demand from people not using their cars to travel to work. Car sharing schemes offer one short-term way of reducing traffic without the immediate investment in public transport infrastructure that is required in the medium to long term.

CarMatch seeks to promote car sharing and to provide a service to potential car sharers by matching up people who both live and work near one another. While many people who work together share transport informally, it is more difficult for people who work near one another to find a suitable person to share transport with, and in some very large organizations, even people who work on the same site may not know one another.

CarMatch consists of three layers of structure: the global operation, which is a not-for-profit trust, the central operating company in each country and local franchise operations. Depending on the country in which it is operating, CarMatch's central operation will offer its services to local government and large corporations, which have legal obligations to reduce traffic in some countries or states. It will also publicize its services to the general public. People who join up will pay a small membership fee, which will be refunded if the local CarMatch franchise is unable to match them up with one or more other people who require or are offering transport. The CarMatch franchise will draw up model agreements between the participants, to prevent the money that changes hands to cover fuel costs being treated as taxable income, and advise on the insurance implications of car sharing. It will act as an agent for companies that sell insurance policies that specifically cover car sharing. Research has shown that car sharers are a good insurance risk.

Staff in the local franchises will undergo a comprehensive training course, which covers the consultancy that they must be able to offer to companies and local government, the legal situation in their own country or state, insurance requirements, safety considerations and how to operate CarMatch's systems. In some countries, regulation of the insurance industry means that franchise staff must also meet the requirements of regulatory bodies.

CarMatch expects to make its money from a combination of membership fees, consultancy income and the commission on insurance sales. A percentage of all income will be taken by the central operation, and the rest kept by the franchise. As road-pricing schemes based on radio communication between vehicles and road-side transponders become more widespread, CarMatch franchises will sell and install the necessary equipment and work with toll authorities and road-pricing schemes to negotiate discounts for members on the basis that they are reducing traffic demand.

1.2.2 CarMatch Computer Support

CarMatch has a requirement for a computer system that can be used by its franchisees. The aim is to launch the new service with computer support right from the start. In each country there will also be at least one web-server. These web-servers will provide up-to-date information and insurance brokerage services to franchisees as well as allowing members to register with CarMatch online. Information about members will then be downloaded to the franchisee's system in the relevant area. Where there is not a franchisee in an area, the central service will try to match members.

1.2.3 CarMatch Requirements

The requirements listed here are those of the systems that franchisees will use. The central system is the subject of a separate development process.

1 To develop a system that will hold information about members of the CarMatch scheme.

    1.1 To record the details of potential car sharers, whether they are offering transport, seeking transport or both, and the geographical location of their home and their work addresses.

    1.2 To transfer details of potential car sharers from the central web-server if they have registered online.

    1.3 To provide a web service interface to third parties who want to register car sharers.

    1.4 To provide an interface to credit card transaction systems and the Automated Bank Transfer System (ABTS) in order to process membership fee payments and refunds.

2 To match members up with other members as car sharers.

    2.1 On the basis of geographical locations and travel times to match up members who may be able to share transport.

    2.2 To record details of sharing arrangements that result.

3 To record insurance sales.

    3.1 To record details of the policies sold to members and to process renewals.

    3.2 To record the commission income from these policies.

4 To record details of potential and actual consultancy customers in the area of operation.

    4.1 To maintain a mailing list of potential customers.

    4.2 To record details of actual customers, contacts within the companies, addresses etc.

    4.3 To record visits made by the franchisee's staff and other contacts with consultancy customers.

5 The system must be capable of future expansion to incorporate information about toll and road-pricing schemes and equipment sold to and installed for members.

1.3 CASE STUDY 2—VOLBANK

1.3.1 VolBank Background

VolBank is a not-for-profit organization that matches volunteers with people and groups in need of help. Its overall aims are to promote citizenship and a sense of community by involving people in voluntary activities in their local area. It does this by maintaining a list of voluntary opportunities and a list of volunteers and seeking to match volunteers to the right opportunities. Part of VolBank's philosophy is that everyone has skills to offer and needs to be met. Because of this, it encourages volunteers to register their own needs and the recipients of help to offer their own skills. For example, Pete Duffield volunteered to help with painting and decorating. He was matched up with a local after-school centre for the under-tens whose centre needed repainting. The children offered their time to put on a show for a local old people's home. One of the elderly residents of the old people's home, Mrs Hernandez, offered her time to give someone a chance to practise Spanish conversation. Pete Duffield took her up on the offer so that he could brush up his Spanish before his holiday in Mexico.

The name VolBank comes from the idea that people can deposit the time that they are prepared to give, as well as a list of the skills that they are willing to offer. Information about VolBank is available through a number of sources, including local radio, television advertising and the Internet. VolBank has been set up in partnership with local voluntary organizations that put forward voluntary work that needs doing. They also act as local contact points for volunteers to put themselves forward.

Volunteers can register the skills they are offering with VolBank, by telephone to a volunteer organizer, in person through a local voluntary organization or by filling out their details on a web page. Once they are registered they can deposit time with VolBank by the same means. If the volunteer registers through a local voluntary organization, then the information is passed on in writing to VolBank, where it will be recorded by a volunteer organizer in the same way as if the volunteer had contacted VolBank directly by telephone.

Voluntary organizations and individuals (including volunteers) can register their needs for help by contacting a volunteer organizer. This volunteer organizer then tries to match up the people offering their time with the opportunities. This can happen in two different ways: a new volunteer can be matched against opportunities, or a new opportunity can be matched against a pool of volunteers. Matching is done on a geographical basis, using zip or postal codes, and by matching skills to needs.

Once volunteers have been matched to an opportunity, they are notified of the details, and, if they are interested, their details are passed on by the volunteer organizer to the voluntary organization or individual that requested the help. It is made clear to volunteers that this does not mean that they will automatically be accepted. For some kinds of work, such as work with children, there may be further vetting procedures or even police and social services checks. These are the responsibility of the organization requesting the help.

VolBank is in the process of setting up a computer system to handle all the business of registering and matching volunteers and opportunities, and notifying the participants.

1.3.2   VolBank Computer Support

VolBank needs a computer system to handle the matching of volunteers with opportunities and opportunities with volunteers. This computer system will need a link to the VolBank web-server. Member organizations will be notified whenever a match is made between an opportunity that they have registered and a volunteer. This will be done by fax or email. Volunteers will be notified by letter when a match has been made.

1.3.3   VolBank Requirements

The requirements listed here are for the system to handle registration, carry out the matching and notify participants. The web-server is a separate system.

1 To develop a system that will handle the registration of volunteers and the depositing of their time.

   1.1 To record the details of volunteers, including the skills and the address of each one.

   1.2 To record the time that each volunteer deposits in the system.

   1.3 To transfer from the web-server details of volunteers and the time they are depositing.

2 To handle the recording of opportunities for voluntary activity.

   2.1 To record details of member voluntary organizations.

   2.2 To record the needs of voluntary organizations for help.

   2.3 To record the needs of individuals (including volunteers) for help.

3 To match up donors and recipients of voluntary activity and record the results.

   3.1 To match a volunteer with suitable voluntary activities in his or her area.

   3.2 To match a voluntary activity with suitable volunteers in the same area.

   3.3 To record every match between volunteer and activity.

   3.4 To notify volunteers of matches.

   3.5 To notify voluntary organizations of matches.

   3.6 To record the success of each match and to produce a volunteering agreement for each successful match.

4 To produce statistical analyses of the number of volunteers and opportunities and the amount of time deposited.

CHAPTER 2

Background to UML

2.1 INTRODUCTION

The Unified Modeling Language (UML) is a visual language that provides a way for people who analyse and design object-oriented systems to visualize, construct and document the artefacts of software systems and to model the business organizations that use such systems. Rational Software Corporation and the Object Management Group (OMG) brought together elements of three significant object-oriented diagramming notations and aspects of many other notations to produce a standard modelling language that represents best practice in the software development industry. UML is still evolving as a standard, and the 2.0 version will almost certainly change again.

This chapter explains the history of UML, describes its current state and outlines its likely future development. It also summarizes the structure of UML and how it is documented. More detail about this is to be found in Appendix D.

2.2 ORIGINS OF UML

Object-oriented software development techniques have gone through three stages of evolution.

1. Object-oriented programming languages were developed and began to be used.

2. Object-oriented analysis and design techniques were produced to help in the modelling of businesses, the analysis of requirements and the design of software systems. The number of these techniques grew rapidly.

3. UML was designed to bring together the best features of a number of analysis and design techniques and notations to produce an industry standard.

These stages are described in the following three subsections.

2.2.1   Programming Languages

Simula-67 is usually credited as the first object-oriented language. Simula 1 was developed in the early 1960s as a language for writing discrete-event simulations. A simulation system is used to analyse and predict the behaviour of a physical system, such as a traffic intersection, a chemical reaction or an assembly line. A discrete-event simulation simulates the real system in terms of a set of discrete states that change over time in response to events that occur at specific instances in time. This distinguishes a discrete-event simulation from a continuous simulation in which the state is continuously evolving. Modelling a traffic intersection is a discrete-event simulation: vehicles arrive and the lights change at specific instants in time. A chemical reaction is normally modelled as a continuous simulation: the chemicals react together continuously and the rate of reaction is dependent on variables such as temperature and pressure.

Simula-67 was developed in 1967 by Kristen Nygaard and Ole-Johan Dahl from the University of Oslo and the Norwegian Computing Centre. It built on Simula 1 and is a general-purpose programming language. In 1986 the language became known just as Simula and it is still in use today. Simula introduced many of the features of object-oriented languages such as classes and inheritance (discussed in more detail in Chapters 4 and 5).

The first explicitly object-oriented language was Smalltalk which was developed by Alan Kay at the University of Utah and later with Adele Goldberg and Daniel Ingalls at Xerox PARC (Palo Alto Research Center) in the 1970s. It became more widely used in the 1980s with the release of Smalltalk-80. Smalltalk introduced the ideas of objects communicating by passing messages and of encapsulated attributes inside objects that are accessible to other objects only in response to a message.

Smalltalk was followed by the release of other object-oriented languages: Objective C, C++, Eiffel and CLOS (Common Lisp Object System). Since its release in 1996, Sun's Java has thrust object-oriented development into the limelight. The most recent addition to the world of O-O languages is Microsoft's C♯ (C-sharp), and the .Net Framework. Between Simula and C♯, many other object-oriented languages have been developed and continue to be developed, but it is Java with its relationship to the rapid growth of the Internet that has made object-oriented development more widespread.

2.2.2   Analysis and Design

A few years after the emergence of Smalltalk, books on object-oriented analysis and design began to appear. Some of these were closely tied to specific languages, such as Objective C and C++, while others were more general purpose. First among these were the work of Shlaer & Mellor (1988) and of Coad & Yourdon (1990, 1991). They were closely followed by Booch (1991), the team of Rumbaugh, Blaha, Premerlani, Eddy & Lorensen (1991) and, slightly later, Jacobson, Christerson, Jonsson & Övergaard (1992). These are just the most widely known and used; there were many others.

Different authors adopted different diagramming notations to represent classes and objects and the associations among them. Often different authors used the same notational element to represent different things. For example, Coad and Yourdon used a triangle to represent a whole–part association (aggregation in UML terms), while Rumbaugh and his co-workers used a triangle to represent inheritance. As well as providing a notation, all these authors also presented a method for using their notation, consisting of more or less clearly defined stages and activities and specifications of the analysis and design products.

The early 1990s were characterized by a confusing diversity of different object-oriented notations and methods, referred to by some authors as 'Method Wars'. Between 1989 and 1994, the number of modelling languages went from fewer than 10 to more than 50. In the mid-1990s this situation began to change. The methods of three key authors had become prominent: Rumbaugh, Booch and Jacobson. Rumbaugh had revised his *Object Modeling Technique* (OMT) as OMT-2; Booch had produced a second edition of his book outlining what is known as *Booch'93*; Jacobson's method was known either as *Object-Oriented Software Engineering* (OOSE) or as *Objectory*, the name of his company.

2.2.3 Emergence of UML

These three methods were also beginning to grow more similar as the authors incorporated the best features of other methods. In 1994 Rumbaugh and Booch began to work together at Rational Software Corporation to unify their two methods. In October 1995 they released the draft Version 0.8 of the *Unified Method*. In autumn 1995 Jacobson and his company, Objectory, joined Rational, and the three authors started developing both UML and the Unified Software Development Process, which was based largely on the Objectory method.

In June and October 1996 Versions 0.9 and 0.91 were released, incorporating feedback from people and organizations interested in the development of a standard object-oriented modelling language. At this time, the *Object Management Group* (OMG), an industry standards body, issued a Request for Proposal (RFP) for a standard object modelling language. Rational Software Corporation recognized that there was a need for wider involvement in the process and formed the UML Partners consortium with other organizations such as IBM, HP, Microsoft and Oracle, which were willing to commit resources to the further development of UML as a response to the OMG.

In January 1997 the UML Partners and a number of other companies and groups submitted proposals to the OMG. Subsequently, the others joined up with the UML Partners to produce Version 1.1 of UML. In November 1997, UML 1.1 was added to the OMG's list of Adopted Technologies, and the OMG took on the responsibility for the further development of UML.

The OMG set up a *Revision Task Force* (RTF) led by Cris Kobryn of MCI Systemhouse to take on the task of refining the UML specification—handling bugs, rectifying omissions, and resolving inconsistencies and ambiguities. The RTF produced an editorial revision of the UML specification (Version 1.2) in June 1998 and a full version (Version 1.3) in June 1999.

Version 1.4 was released in 2001, and 1.5, which added Action Semantics to 1.4, in 2003. However, in parallel, the OMG began work on a major new version, 2.0. 2.0 was adopted by the OMG in June 2003, but the specification still had many outstanding issues, and these have been resolved in a process that has carried on into mid-2004. In the rest of the book, where we need to refer to a specific earlier version of UML, we use its full version number, for example Version 1.4. However, where we are referring to the differences between Version 2.0 and features that were common to earlier versions, we use the shorthand 1.X to refer to all versions from 1.0 to 1.5.

2.3 UML TODAY

The current release of UML is Version 2.0. The responsibility for further development lies with the Revision Task Force set up by the OMG.

UML Version 2.0 is documented in the UML Specification (Object Management Group, 2004*a*). The specification in fact consists of a number of separate documents, including the UML Meta Object Facility 2.0, XML Metadata Interchange 2.0, UML Diagram Interchange 2.0, UML Object Constraint Language 2.0, UML 2.0 Infrastructure Specification and UML 2.0 Superstructure Specification.

(These documents can all be found on the OMG website at www.omg.org.) The key documents that describe UML are the UML 2.0 Infrastructure Specification (Object Management Group, 2004b) and the UML 2.0 Superstructure Specification (Object Management Group, 2004c).

The UML Specification is not written as a document for ordinary users of UML, but for members of the OMG, standards organizations, companies that produce UML modelling tools, authors of books and trainers, all of whom need to have a detailed understanding of UML. The Meta Object Facility describes the UML metamodel (see Section D.2) that is used to define UML and can be used to define other modelling languages. The XMI Specification and Diagram Interchange Specification in particular are written for modelling tool suppliers who need to work to standard formats for exchanging models between different tools. The XMI (XML Metadata Interchange) Specification uses XML (eXtensible Markup Language) to provide a specification for how data about UML models can be exchanged among applications. (Version 2.0 uses W3C (World-Wide Web Consortium) XML Schema (WXS) to define the XML, whereas previous versions used XML Document Type Definition (DTD).) The Object Constraint Language (OCL) Specification defines a language that is used to model constraints on model elements. OCL is explained in Chapter 13.

The UML Infrastructure Specification defines the core elements of UML; the UML Superstructure Specification defines the elements of UML that modellers use in UML diagrams. Although it includes some example diagrams, the Infrastructure does not define UML diagram types (class diagrams, sequence diagrams etc.); these are defined in the Superstructure. The way that UML is defined is explained in more detail in the next section.

The production of UML 2.0 had some specific aims, which were outlined in the Request for Proposal (RFP) that preceded it. These were as follows:

- **Architecture**—More rigorous specification of the metamodel, including a clearer separation between what is in the core of UML and what is defined in standard profiles.

- **Extensibility**—Improvement of the mechanisms for extending UML with notation for specific domains (see Chapter 15).

- **Components**—Better support for component-based development through the notation and semantics of component diagrams (see Chapter 8).

- **Relationships**—Better definition of the semantics of associations, including refinement and trace dependencies.

- **Statecharts and activity graphs**—Separation of the semantics of the two types of diagrams, so that activity graphs can be defined independently of statecharts (see Chapters 11 and 12).

- **Model management**—Better notation and semantics for model management.

- **General mechanisms**—Support for model version control and diagram interchange.

2.4   WHAT IS UML?

UML is a visual language that can be used in developing software systems. It is a specification language. The term 'language' confuses some people. It is not a language like a human language, nor is it a programming language. However, like both of these other kinds of language, it has a set of rules that determine how it can be used.

Programming languages consist of a set of elements and a set of rules that define how you are allowed to combine those elements to make valid programs. Formal specification languages like UML also consist of a set of elements and a set of rules that determine how you can combine the elements. Most of the elements of UML are graphical: they consist of lines, rectangles, ovals and other shapes, and many of these graphical elements are labelled with words that provide additional information. However, the graphical elements of UML are only a graphical representation of whatever is being modelled. It is possible to produce a UML model purely in terms of the data that describes the model. Nonetheless, the graphical representation helps people to understand the model or parts of the model, and it is the graphical representation that makes UML a visual specification language rather than a textual one.

2.4.1 UML Conformance

The rules about how the elements of UML can be combined are set out and explained in the UML Specification (Object Management Group, 2004a). To be conformant with UML, a model (or a modelling tool that is used to build UML models) must conform to the *abstract syntax*, the *well-formedness rules*, the *semantics*, the *notation* and the *XMI Schema*. The abstract syntax is expressed as diagrams and natural language (English), the well-formedness rules in Object Constraint Language (OCL) (see Chapter 13) and English, the semantics in English with some supporting diagrams, the notation in English with example diagrams, and the XMI Schema in XML. The rules that are expressed as diagrams use a subset of the notation of UML itself to specify how the elements of UML can be combined. This is an important feature of UML, but not one that you really need to understand in detail. It is called the *Four-Layer Metamodel Architecture* of UML and is shown in Figure 2-1. The metamodel is explained in more detail in Appendix D.

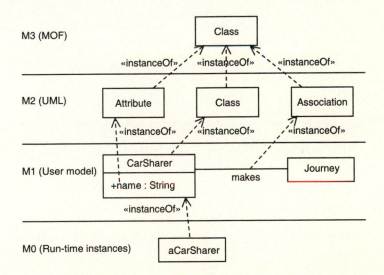

Figure 2-1: Layered architecture of UML

EXAMPLE 2.1   The following is an explanation of the notation of use case diagrams. It is not literally taken from the UML Specification, but is intended to illustrate the nature of the notation descriptions.

A UML Use Case Diagram is made up of ovals representing use cases and stick figures representing actors (the users of use cases). These are joined together by lines to show which actors use which use cases.

Which of the following is a valid use case diagram?

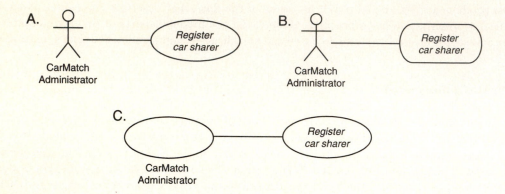

Solution

Only A is a valid use case diagram. B uses a round-cornered rectangle instead of an oval for the use case, and C uses an oval instead of the stick person for the actor.

EXAMPLE 2.2   Here are two rules from the definition of UML.

Names of stereotypes are delimited by guillemets and begin with lowercase (e.g., «type»). Names consisting of more than one word are concatenated together with no spaces. Initial embedded capital is used for names that consist of concatenated nouns/adjectives (e.g., ownedElement, allContents).

Which of the following stereotypes follow these rules?

«Type»   «new type»   «newType»   «longGreenDottedLine»

Solution

«Type» does not, as it begins with a capital letter. «new type» does not, as it has a space in it. The other two do follow the rules.

2.5   WHAT UML IS NOT

We have said that UML is a visual modelling language and explained its structure. It is worth stating briefly what UML is not.

UML is not a programming language. You cannot write a program in UML. Some software modelling tools can take a UML model and generate program code in different languages from it, but this will be little more than a framework. The developer will still have to write code to implement the methods. However, one of the aims of the Model-Driven Architecture (MDA) movement is to make it possible to build platform-independent models and to combine these with profiles for different platforms to produce platform-dependent models that can be transformed into executable code.

UML is not a software modelling tool. There are a number of software modelling tools that implement the UML standard to a greater or lesser extent, and the UML Specification has been written in part for software modelling tool developers to enable them to implement the standard and to exchange models between applications using the XMI Schema.

UML is not a method, methodology or software development process. The UML notation can be applied in projects that use different approaches to the process of software development and that break the system development life-cycle into different activities, tasks, stages and steps. One thing that has happened since the publication of the UML standard is that some of the many competing systems analysis and design methods have standardized their notation using UML. Their authors' views of what is the correct process to apply in developing systems are still different, but they can at least agree on how to represent system models in a visual notation. Closely associated with UML is the Unified Software Development Process (USDP), which has evolved from Jacobson's Objectory process. Section 2.10 explains how UML and USDP relate to one another and, in other chapters of this book, we have explained where each modelling technique fits into the USDP life-cycle.

2.6   NAMES OF UML ELEMENTS

All the model elements in UML are defined in the specification. Some of them have names that will be familiar to analysts, designers and programmers who have an understanding of object-oriented development, such as *Class*, *Attribute* and *Operation*. Many have been made up in order to give names to elements that are part of the UML metamodel but do not naturally relate to concepts that will be familiar to object-oriented professionals. Examples include *InteractionOccurrence*, *CombinedFragment* and *AddStructuralFeatureValueAction*. We use the former type of name throughout. We only use the latter where it is necessary to be specific about model elements that are not easily described in some other way. It remains to be seen which of these terms will make their way into the everyday language of object-oriented developers as UML 2.0 becomes more widespread.

2.7   THE FUTURE OF UML

The future of UML is in the hands of the Revision Task Force (RTF) of the OMG. The development of UML 2.0 has taken three years longer than planned. These plans were described in an article in the *Communications of the ACM* by Cris Kobryn, Chair of the RTF (Kobryn, 1999). Proposals for Version 2.0 were issued in September 2000, and it was planned for release in 2001. There is also information about the development of UML in the future on the RTF's website.

It is likely that there will be an editorial correction of Version 2.0, correcting errors and resolving ambiguous points in the specification. Much of this is based on feedback from users. Users of UML submit issues to the RTF's website for consideration, and the RTF examines each issue and decides what action to take. There are still a number of inconsistencies in Version 2.0, and these will need to be resolved.

2.8   UML PROFILES AND EXTENSIBILITY

Version 2.0 of UML continues the mainstream evolution of UML for general systems development. One of the features of UML is that it is capable of being customized for different kinds of applications and platforms. The mechanisms for doing this are *stereotypes*, *constraints* and *tagged values*. These extension mechanisms can be packaged together into *profiles* for different application domains, and profiles are described in more detail in Chapter 15.

2.9   WHY USE UML?

In this section we discuss why you should use UML. For those who are new to systems analysis and design, we first discuss the reasons for using a visual approach to designing systems. We then look at some of the benefits that are claimed for UML.

2.9.1   Why Use Analysis and Design Diagrams?

People who design all kinds of artefacts use pictures or diagrams to assist in the design process. Fashion designers, engineers, architects and systems analysts and designers all use diagrams to visualize their designs. Systems analysts and designers use diagrams to help them visualize the software systems that they are designing, despite the fact that the products of the design process—computer programs—are not themselves inherently visual. What advantages does using diagrams bring to the design process?

There are two main uses of diagrams in producing a design:

- to abstract features of the design;

- to show relationships between elements of the design.

Having chosen to use diagrams for these purposes, they are an important tool in communicating ideas to the other participants in the design process.

When an architect designs a building, he or she will produce a number of drawings with different purposes. These include diagrams that show an overall view of the building with very little detail, diagrams that show particular features of the design, such as the location of the pipework for the plumbing, and diagrams that show details of the design, such as the shape of wooden mouldings or the colour and texture of an external surface. No one diagram can embody every aspect of something as complex as a building, and no human can handle all the information about a building design in one go. It is the same with software systems: they are very complex, and the designer will represent different aspects of the design with different diagrams. Each of these diagrams picks out one or more specific aspects from the overall design. Even then, each diagram cannot represent every detail of those aspects of the design. A diagram of the plumbing in a building might simply use lines to represent each pipe rather than attempting to show the width of the pipe to scale. Similarly, a diagram showing communication between different elements in a software system might use lines to show the communication without attempting to represent the way that the communication is intended to take place, or technical aspects such as the bandwidth of the communication link.

This use of diagrams to simplify systems and to represent certain key features is known as *abstraction*. Abstraction is a mechanism that we use to represent a complex reality in simplified terms using some kind of model. The term abstraction can also be used to apply to the product of this process. More often, if the abstraction is represented in some physical way, such as a diagram on paper or a physical object, we use the term *model*.

In systems analysis and design, models are produced that abstract the important features of real-world systems. A UML class that describes a customer includes only those features of the customer that are of interest to a business information system. A UML class that models the behaviour of an aircraft in an air traffic control system models only those features of the aircraft that are of interest to a real-time control system. In both cases, part of the role of the systems analyst or designer is to decide which features are of interest and which are not.

EXAMPLE 2.3   In most business systems, the features of a customer that might be of interest include name, address, telephone number, fax number and email address. Hair colour, weight and height are unlikely to be relevant features. However, if the business system belongs to a slimming club then weight will be a relevant feature of clients that should be modelled. Abstracting the right features and building the correct model is part of the skill of systems analysis.

Systems analysts and designers use diagrams for all of these reasons and purposes. Computer systems are complex artefacts made up of hardware and software; diagrams provide a way of modelling these systems, how they are structured and how they are intended to work.

The relationships among elements of a design can also be shown graphically or in the supporting text that accompanies a model. In architecture, the relationships between elements can include the need to model the structural relationship between floors and the parts of the building (walls and joists) that support them. In modelling any subject, these relationships are as important as the things that they relate together. Relationships in models can include the following types:

- structural relationships between elements of a model that have some dependency on one another;

- organizational relationships between elements of a system that must be packaged together in the final system for it to work;

- temporal relationships between parts of the model in order to illustrate a sequence of events over time;

- cause and effect relationships between elements of a model, for example to show preconditions that must exist before something else will work;

- evolutionary relationships between models over time, showing how one element has been derived from another during the life-cycle of a project.

UML includes all these kinds of relationships between its elements. The following list gives an example of each:

- Structural relationships—associations between classes

- Organizational relationships—packages as a way of organizing model elements

- Temporal relationships—the time sequence of messages in an interaction sequence diagram

- Cause and effect relationships—states in statechart diagrams

- Evolutionary relationships—trace dependencies between diagrams in the design model and the analysis model

EXAMPLE 2.4   In a slimming club, each customer's weight will be recorded on a number of occasions, so a set of weight measurements will gradually be accumulated. There is a structural relationship between each customer and the set of weight measurements that belongs to that customer. This relationship can be abstracted into a relationship between the class Customer and the class WeightMeasurement. We may also want to model cause and effect relationships; for example, if a customer loses more than a certain amount of weight then the customer is awarded a certificate.

2.9.2   Why Use UML Specifically?

In an object-oriented system development project, UML is a candidate modelling language for the analysis and design of the product. (Note that not all development projects use object-oriented languages, despite the hype. For projects using procedural languages or functional languages and for projects that are to be implemented using a relational database, models in UML may be difficult to convert to an implementation. However, work on profiles that extend UML or on other metamodels such as the Common Warehouse Metamodel for modelling data warehouses means that the use of UML is becoming more widespread.)

The strongest reason for using UML is that it has become the *de facto* standard for object-oriented modelling. If it is necessary to involve a team of developers or to convey the information in models to other people, then UML is the obvious choice as it will facilitate communication among participants.

A second reason lies in the fact that it is a *unified* modelling language. It brings together the ideas of three leading players in object-oriented modelling and combines them into a single notation. Since the early versions, the organizations involved in the development of UML have also tried to incorporate the best features of other modelling languages, so it could be regarded as a combination of best practice in the field. However, there is a danger in this, namely that in trying to incorporate many views on object-oriented modelling, UML will become bloated with superfluous notation. The OMG's RTF has tried to avoid this by keeping the core of UML simple and using profiles and other extensibility mechanisms to extend it to new domains.

This is a third reason for using UML. Special profiles already exist to help the user to apply it to specific kinds of problem, and more are being developed. If a profile does not exist for a specific problem domain, then it is possible to extend the notation to apply to that domain. Jim Conallen's work on applying UML to modelling web-based systems is a good example of this, and one which we discuss in more detail in Chapter 15 (Conallen, 2002).

Finally, although UML itself does not include a specification of how it should be applied—a process— the Unified Software Development Process does provide guidance on how to develop a system using UML and is designed specifically to work with UML.

2.10   THE UNIFIED SOFTWARE DEVELOPMENT PROCESS

UML is a language for specifying systems in a formal way; it does not define a process for the analysis, design and implementation of systems. The developers of UML also produced a specification of a software development process that explains how they think developers should go about developing systems using UML (Jacobson, Booch & Rumbaugh, 1999). This software development process is known as the Unified Software Development Process, or simply the Unified Process (UP). Throughout the rest of this book we shall refer to it as the Unified Process. Rational Software Corporation (now part of IBM) also produced its own version of the Unified Process, the Rational Unified Process (RUP). While the UP is documented in a book, RUP has been turned into a product, consisting of a website that purchasers install on a server in their organization. The RUP contains descriptions of the process, activities, roles and guidelines on how to carry out the process. It can also be customized to an organization's requirements. We describe the UP here, as it is a generic process.

The Unified Process involves *people*, *projects*, *products*, *process* and *tools*. *People* are the participants and developers in one or more system development *projects*, which produce a software *product* or *products* following a *process* and using automated *tools* to assist in the development. The Unified Process is a use-case-driven process. This means that the users' requirements are captured in use cases, as sequences of actions performed by the system that provide some value for users. These use cases are used as the basis of subsequent work by developers to produce design and implementation models that implement the use cases. (The technique of producing use cases is explained in Chapter 3.)

The Unified Process is also architecture-centric, iterative and incremental. Architecture-centric means that the system architecture is developed to meet the requirements of key use cases in terms of the platform the system will run on and the structure of the system and subsystems. It is iterative in that the project is broken down into mini-projects. In each mini-project or iteration some part of the system is analysed, designed, implemented and tested. Each such part is an increment and the system is built up in increments. Iterations are not all the same; the kinds of activities involved in each iteration will change as progress is made through the overall cycle. In the Unified Process, the life-cycle is broken down into four phases: *Inception*, *Elaboration*, *Construction* and *Transition*. Each phase may consist of several iterations, and the balance of activities in each iteration will change as the project progresses.

The Unified Process produces more than just the finished system. A number of intermediate artefacts are produced; these are known as models. Each model specifies the modelled system from a particular viewpoint. As such, they are abstractions of the system, each one abstracting certain features of the system. The main models in the Unified Process are the *Use Case Model*, the *Analysis Model*, the *Design Model*, the *Deployment Model*, the *Implementation Model* and the *Test Model*. It should be possible to trace parts of each model back to its predecessor; for example, it should be possible to trace classes in the design model back to classes in the analysis model, and to trace these back to requirements in the use case model. This is known as a *trace dependency* between models.

2.11   MODEL MANAGEMENT IN UML

2.11.1   Packages

UML itself is organized into *packages*. Each package contains model elements and some contain the diagrams that make up UML. These are described in more detail in Appendix D.

The *Kernel* package contains the metaclass **Package** that provides the mechanism for the organization of models into packages. Packages can be used within a project to organize the different diagrams that are produced into coherent groupings. These packages are purely an organizational convenience and do not necessarily map to subsystems in the finished system.

The containment of one or more packages within another package can be shown using the notation of Figure 2-2, as a tree structure with a plus sign in a circle drawn at the end of the line that is attached to the container.

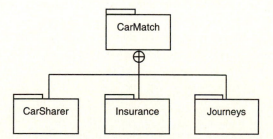

Figure 2-2: Tree-structured containment notation for packages in the CarMatch system

Alternatively, this can be shown by including packages within another, in which case the name of the containing package is displayed in the tab rather than the body of the package, as in Figure 2-3.

The relationships among packages can be stereotyped as «import», «merge» or «access».

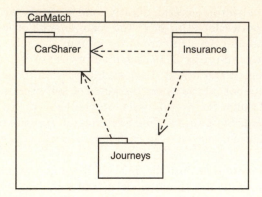

Figure 2-3: Alternative containment notation for packages in the CarMatch system

As we stated above, packages provide the mechanism for organizing model elements. Different views of a project, such as *Use Case View*, *Logical View* or *Component View*, can be represented as packages.

2.11.2   Subsystems

Subsystems represent units of the physical system that can be organized in stereotyped packages as in Figure 2-4. They are stereotyped either with the fork symbol shown or with the stereotype «subsystem».

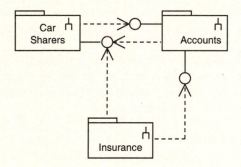

Figure 2-4: Example subsystems for the CarMatch case study

The subsystems in Figure 2-4 offer interfaces on which the other subsystems have dependencies. These elements of notation are explained in more detail later in the book.

2.11.3   Models

Models are abstractions of a physical system with a certain purpose. Typically models are used for the different stages in the development of a system. The top-level model of a system can be stereotyped as «systemModel» and contains other models, as in Figure 2-5. This also shows the use of a small triangle as a stereotype icon to distinguish models from packages and subsystems. The stereotype «model» can also be used.

The process aspect of the Unified Process is defined in terms of the *activities* that are needed to transform users' requirements into a working system. These activities are grouped together into *workflows*,

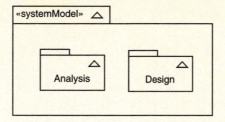

Figure 2-5: System model containing other models

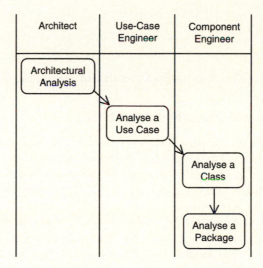

Figure 2-6: Analysis workflow as an activity diagram

and each workflow is represented graphically using an activity diagram. Figure 2-6 shows the analysis workflow.

Note that the authors of the Unified Process use a stereotyped form of the UML activity diagram to represent workflows. We have used standard UML activity diagrams. (Stereotypes are explained in Chapter 15 and activity diagrams in Chapter 11.)

Workflows also specify the workers who will carry out the activities. Workers are not specific people but abstract roles. More than one person may fill a particular worker role, or more than one worker role can be filled by the same person. The workers involved in the analysis workflow are shown in the activity diagram. Each activity is broken down into more detailed *steps*. Each activity is also specified in terms of the models and other project artefacts that are used as inputs in that activity and in terms of the artefacts that are produced as results of the activity. Figure 2-7 shows this for the activity *Analyse a Use Case*.

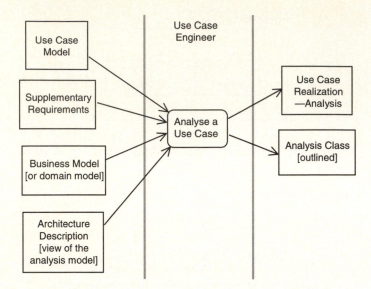

Figure 2-7: The inputs and results of analysing a use case

2.12   WHERE TO FIND MORE INFORMATION

The obvious source of information for anyone who wants to know more about UML is the UML Specification itself (Object Management Group, 2004a). However, it is written as a specialist reference manual, is heavy going and is now in several documents, although the Superstructure document (Object Management Group, 2004c) is the main one to read for the UML diagrams.

Addison-Wesley have published a number of books on UML, many in conjunction with people who worked for Rational Software and who now work for IBM. These include the original three books by the original authors of UML, Grady Booch, Ivar Jacobson and Jim Rumbaugh. There is a reference guide based closely on the Specification (Rumbaugh, Jacobson & Booch, 1999), a user guide with a case study (Booch, Rumbaugh & Jacobson, 1999) and a guide to the Unified Process (Jacobson et al., 1999). These three books are now seriously out of date, and have been superseded by many other books on UML.

McGraw-Hill have published a more general systems analysis and design textbook using UML notation co-authored by one of the authors of this book (Bennett, McRobb & Farmer, 2002).

Information on the current version of the specification and on the development of UML is available on the OMG website (www.omg.org). The OMG site has links to the UML Forum and pages maintained by the Revision Task Force members as well as other UML resources.

A good website with links to information about object-orientation and component-based development is Cetus (www.cetus-links.org).

Review Questions

2.1 Who were the three lead authors of earlier notations who joined Rational Software Corporation to develop UML?

2.2 Which organization is now responsible for the UML standard?

2.3 What is the purpose of the UML XMI Schema?

2.4 What must a UML model comply with in order to be conformant?

2.5 What are the four layers of the UML metamodel architecture?

2.6 How are well-formedness rules specified?

2.7 What are packages used for in UML?

2.8 What body within the OMG is responsible for the future of UML?

2.9 What are UML profiles used for?

2.10 Which of the following are abstractions?

      a A map that you draw using just a few lines on a scrap of paper for a friend to show the way to your home

      b A road atlas of London, England

      c London, England

      d A UML class diagram

2.11 Which of the following are models?

      a A UML class diagram

      b A set of UML class diagrams describing the classes in a software system

      c A 1:100 scale clay replica of a new sports car that will be used to test its aerodynamics in a wind tunnel

      d A full-scale, working prototype of a new sports car

2.12 Give three reasons for using UML.

2.13 What are the four phases of the Unified Process life-cycle?

2.14 Explain the relationships among workflows, activities and steps in the Unified Process.

Supplementary Problems

2.1 Investigate one of the notations that were the forerunners of UML (Rumbaugh's, Booch's or Jacobson's). Choose a UML diagram and its equivalent in the other notation and list what they have in common and what is different.

2.2 Investigate the three notations that were the forerunners of UML (Rumbaugh's, Booch's and Jacobson's). Choose one type of diagram and compare the notation in each.

2.3 Compare UML diagrams that have changed between Version 1.4 and Version 2.0 (collaboration/communication diagrams, sequence diagrams, activity diagrams and component diagrams). What benefits do you think the changes have brought?

2.4 One of the principles of human–computer interaction design is 'affordance'. This means that the form of an object should suggest its purpose. Based on your research for the previous two questions, do you think that the diagramming symbols used in UML have obvious affordances, or are they just an arbitrary set of symbols? Are there examples of both categories?

2.5 Find some case studies of the use of UML. (There are a number on the OMG UML site on the *UML Success Stories* page.) Identify any benefits that are claimed for using UML.

CHAPTER 3

Use Cases

3.1 INTRODUCTION

Many projects begin with use cases, as they provide a good way of getting an overall picture of what is happening in the existing system or is planned to happen in the new system. The *use case diagram* is very simple, with very little in the way of notation to remember. It is an effective means of communicating with users and other stakeholders about the system and what it is intended to do. Use cases can also be used as the basis of the test specifications that will be drawn up later in a project.

Use case diagrams show *use cases* and *actors* and the associations among them. Figure 3-1 shows what a simple use case diagram looks like. Use cases represent sequences of actions carried out by the system, and actors represent the people or other systems that interact with the system being modelled. Use case diagrams are supported by *behaviour specifications*, which define the interactions within a particular use case.

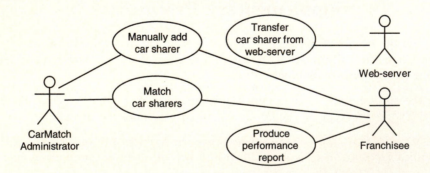

Figure 3-1: Example use case diagram

Use cases have come into UML from the work of Jacobson et al. (1992), originally carried out within Ericsson in Sweden. In Jacobson's approach, use cases are the starting point for the development of a new system.

Use cases are used to specify the behaviour of some entity such as a system or subsystem, known as the *subject*. Use cases do not specify the detail of how that behaviour is carried out. However, the detail will be elaborated using other models as the process of designing the system develops. Typically, how a use case will be realized in the eventual system is defined in one or more *communication diagrams* (see Chapter 10) that show the interaction between co-operating objects.

EXAMPLE 3.1   In a banking system, use cases define the interaction that takes place between customers and automated teller machines (ATMs). Figure 3-2 shows an example of a simple use case diagram for the ATM subsystem. The **Customer** actor represents the *class* of all customers who will use the ATM subsystem. When you use your local ATM to withdraw cash, you are an *instance* of **Customer** using a particular instance of the use case **Withdraw cash**. The person standing in line behind you is another instance of **Customer**, who will use a different instance of the use case **Withdraw cash**. Someone else may use an instance of the use case **Check balance** or **Print mini-statement**. You may successfully withdraw cash from the machine, but the person behind you may find that he or she does not have enough money deposited, and the use case instance will proceed along a different course from yours, rejecting the request.

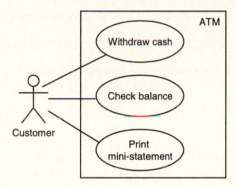

Figure 3-2: Example use case diagram for the ATM subsystem

The term *scenarios* is often used to refer to the different possible courses that different instances of the same use case might take. The use case diagram names only the use cases, but additional documents or diagrams may show the alternative scenarios that could occur.

EXAMPLE 3.2   What different scenarios might exist for the use case **Withdraw cash**?

Clearly, there could be many scenarios:

- The customer's card is not recognized and is rejected.
- The customer enters the wrong PIN and is asked to re-enter it.
- The customer enters the wrong PIN three times and the card is retained by the ATM.
- The customer enters an invalid figure for the amount of cash.
- The ATM attempts to connect to the bank's system but it is out of action or there is a network failure, so it cannot connect.
- The ATM does not have enough cash to meet the customer's request.
- The customer's account does not have enough funds to meet the request.
- The customer cancels the transaction part way through.

You may have thought of others. All these different scenarios are represented by the use case **Withdraw cash**. Eventually, the use case will have to be specified in enough detail for all these possible courses of events to be handled correctly by the objects that make up the subsystem. Initially, it is usual to specify the normal course of events (in which the customer successfully withdraws the amount of cash requested) and the most likely alternatives. As you will see later in Section 3.3, use case descriptions are often used to define the different scenarios. Other techniques can be used, including other UML diagrams.

3.2   PURPOSE OF THE TECHNIQUE

Use cases are created during the early stages of a project. Producing use case diagrams and the associated documents is an analysis technique rather than a design technique. Use cases can also be used later in the development process, for example to specify test cases. Use cases can be used to model what happens in the existing system (if there is one), or they can be used to model the new system that is going to be developed. The main purposes of producing use cases are as follows:

- They are used to model sequences of actions that are carried out by the system and that provide an observable result to someone or something outside the system, known as an actor.

- They provide a high-level view of what the system does and who uses it.

- They provide the basis for determining the human–computer and computer–computer interfaces to the system.

- They can be used to model alternative scenarios for specific use cases that may result in different sequences of actions.

- They use a simple diagrammatic notation that is comprehensible to end users and can be used to communicate with them about the high-level view of the system.

- They can be used as the basis for drawing up test specifications.

3.3   NOTATION

Use cases describe a sequence of actions that a system performs to achieve an observable result of value to an actor. They may be described informally in text, in a more structured form, for example using pseudocode, or through a behaviour specification represented by a link to another diagram, for example a communication diagram. The high-level view of the use cases in a system or subsystem is represented by use case diagrams.

3.3.1   Basic Notation—Use Cases, Actors and Relationships

Use cases are represented graphically in a use case diagram to allow the analyst to visualize each use case in the context of the other use cases in the system or subsystem and to show its relationships with actors and other use cases.

In a use case diagram use cases are drawn as an ellipse, as in Figure 3-3. The name of the use case is usually written inside the ellipse, but can be placed beneath it. Do not mix these two styles in the same model.

Use case names are text strings that contains letters, numbers and most punctuation marks—except for the colon, which is used to separate use case names from the names of packages (see Section 2.11 for an

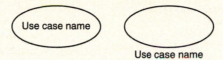

Figure 3-3: Use case notation

explanation of packages)—and it is a good idea to keep them short. Use case names are normally made up of an active verb and a noun or noun phrase that concisely describe the behaviour of the system that you are modelling, for example **Register car sharer**, **Match car sharers** or **Record sharing agreement**. Figure 3-4 shows examples.

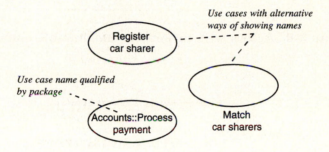

Figure 3-4: Use cases with suitable names

Actors are the people or systems that interact with use cases. For the most part, you will find that they are users of the system that you are modelling. In a use case diagram each actor is drawn as a stick person with the role name written beneath (see Figure 3-5).

Figure 3-5: Actor notation

When dealing with human actors, it is important to remember that the name of an actor is the name of the role that the actor performs in relation to the system and not just the job title. In a CarMatch office there may be people with different job titles (clerk, receptionist and supervisor) who can all register new car sharers in the system. Rather than drawing three different actors, we identify what is common to their jobs and create an actor for that role, in this case **CarMatch Administrator** (see Figure 3-6).

Actors are connected to the use cases with which they interact by a line that represents a relationship between the actors and the use cases (see Figure 3-7).

An example of this is shown in Figure 3-6. (There are other kinds of relationships between actors and other actors and between use cases and other use cases, which are described in Section 3.3.3.) The relationship indicates that there is an association between an actor and a use case. This means that particular people or systems in that actor role will communicate with particular instances of the use case; they will participate in the sequence of events that is represented by the use case. In practical

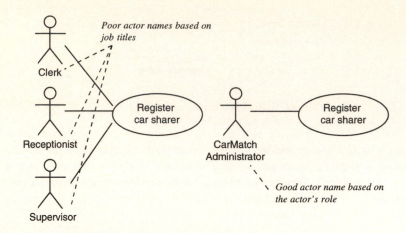

Figure 3-6: Actors with unsuitable and suitable names

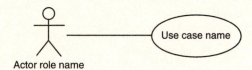

Figure 3-7: Relationship between an actor and a use case

terms, the use case will eventually be implemented as some kind of computer program and the actors will use the program by entering information, receiving information or both.

A single actor may be associated with more than one use case, and a single use case may be associated with more than one actor. Figure 3-8 shows this for part of the CarMatch system.

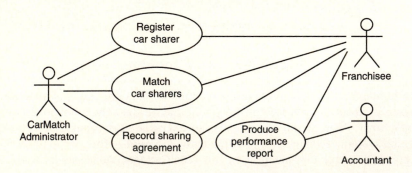

Figure 3-8: Actors and use cases

3.3.2 Behaviour Specifications

Each use case represents a sequence of activities that results in some observable outcome for the actor or actors who interact with it. This sequence of activities is documented in a *behaviour specification*. The link to a behaviour specification may be represented in a CASE tool by a link to a diagram that provides the specification. This could be a sequence diagram or a communication diagram, an activity diagram, a state machine diagram or text in a programming language. Often an informal specification is provided as a *use case description*. In a CASE tool it may be possible both to enter an informal description of a use case's behaviour and to specify it formally by linking it to another diagram. This makes it possible to 'zoom into' the specification by traversing this link.

Some UML diagrams have formal rules about the syntax of textual information. This makes it possible to execute the model and simulate the system, and eventually to translate the model into program code in a language such as Java or C++. However, use case descriptions do not have any formal syntax, and you can write the descriptions in the format that is most useful to you. Of course, you may be working in an organization that has its own rules or guidelines for how use cases are documented, in which case you should abide by those guidelines. The guidelines may include the use of a template for writing use case descriptions, and the sections of the template may include pre-conditions and post-conditions that can be formally specified in OCL (see Chapter 13).

There are three common approaches to writing use case descriptions:

- The first is simply to write one or a few statements or paragraphs that describe the typical sequence of activities that the use case involves.

- The second is to list in two columns the activities of the actor and the responses of the system.

- The third is to use a document template that contains sections for different aspects of the use case that you would want to record.

Figure 3-9 shows the first type of use case description for the use case **Register car sharer**, while Figure 3-10 shows the second type for the same use case. It may be that initially you produce the first type, and later when you have a better understanding of the requirements you produce the second type. Many organizations use the third type—a standard document template—often based on the approach described in Cockburn (2000). Examples can be found on the associated website (Cockburn, 2003).

> The user will enter the name, address and telephone number of the potential car sharer. For each journey that this person wants to share, the start address, the destination address, the start time and the finish time of the journey are entered.

Figure 3-9: Simple use case description for Register car sharer

Constantine (1997) classifies use case descriptions in a different way, according to whether they represent a logical view of the use case or a physical view. He distinguishes between 'essential' use cases and 'real' use cases. The word 'essential' here does not mean that these are somehow necessary use cases, but use cases that capture the essence of what is to be done. An essential use case describes the interaction in a way that is not dependent on the design of the eventual system. For example, Figure 3-10 is an essential use case description and contains no information about the physical implementation of the use case. Figure 3-11 is a real use case, as it includes information that defines the way that the physical interface will work.

The use cases within a use case diagram can be shown enclosed by a rectangle representing the subject. The rectangle maps either onto the complete use case model, which contains all the use cases and actors, or onto the system or subsystem to which the use cases belong. Figure 3-12 shows an early draft of the **Registration** subsystem of the CarMatch system.

	Actor	*System*
1	The user enters the name and address of the car sharer into the system.	The system confirms that the address can be matched against the geographical database.
2	The user enters the telephone number of the car sharer into the system.	The system prompts for the details of a journey.
3	The user enters the start time and start address.	The system confirms that the start address can be matched against the geographical database.
4	The user enters the finish time and destination address.	The system confirms that the finish address can be matched against the geographical database. The system prompts the user to indicate if another journey is to be entered.
5	The user either enters another journey (loop back to 3) or saves and exits.	The system either prompts for another journey (loop back to 3) or saves the car sharer and journey details and exits the use case.

Figure 3-10: Use case description for **Register car sharer** using columns

	Actor	*System*
1	The user enters the name and address of the car sharer in the Car Sharer entry window.	The system confirms that the address can be matched against the geographical database.
2	The user enters the telephone number of the car sharer into the Car Sharer entry window.	The system prompts for the details of a journey by displaying the Journey entry dialogue box.
3	The user enters the start time and start address.	The system confirms that the start address can be matched against the geographical database.
4	The user enters the finish time and destination address.	The system confirms that the destination address can be matched against the geographical database. The system prompts the user to indicate if he or she wants to enter another journey by enabling two buttons labelled Another and Done.
5	The user clicks on Another to enter another journey (loop back to 3) or clicks on Done to save and exit.	The system either clears the Journey entry dialogue box (loop back to 3) or closes the dialogue box, saves the car sharer and journey details and exits the use case.

Figure 3-11: Real use case description for **Register car sharer**

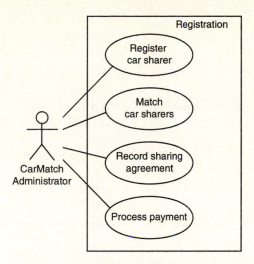

Figure 3-12: Use cases in a subsystem

3.3.3   Other Types of Association and Relationships

There are four other types of association or relationship that can be shown in a use case diagram. These are:

- generalization between use cases;

- generalization between actors;

- include relationship between use cases;

- extend relationship between use cases.

3.3.4   Generalization between Use Cases

Sometimes it becomes apparent that there is more than one version of a use case, and that the different versions have some actions in common and some that are unique to each one. Consider the use cases to add new car sharers to the system: there is one use case for adding new car sharers manually, one for the web service and another for transferring them in from the web-server. These three use cases all serve the same overall function, but they are different in some aspects of how they operate. We can consider the three use cases as specializations of the use case **Register car sharer**, and **Register car sharer** as the general case. This can be represented in a use case diagram through the use of *generalization*. The generalization association is drawn with a triangular icon on the line, which points towards the use case that is the general case, as in Figure 3-13.

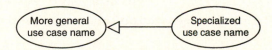

Figure 3-13: Use case generalization notation

An example of the notation for this is shown in Figure 3-14.

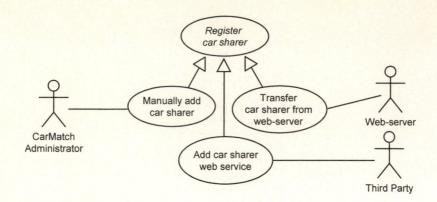

Figure 3-14: Use cases in a generalization association

This diagram indicates that the three use cases **Manually add car sharer**, **Add car sharer web service** and **Transfer car sharer from web-server** inherit some of the functionality from the use case **Register car sharer**, but that they differ from it in some way. In this case, it is because one will be linked to a user interface to allow the **CarMatch Administrator** actor to enter the details, the second will receive the details as an XML document from a third party, while the third will have an interface to the data on the web-server. Note that actors are not necessarily people, and can be other systems.

Sometimes the more general use case is one that will never exist in a real system; it is there only to define what is common to the specialized use cases. In this case, it is called an *abstract* use case, and its name is printed in italics. The specialized use cases are sometimes referred to as *concrete* use cases. In their book on the Unified Process Jacobson et al. (1999) call these 'real' use cases, but this is not part of the UML terminology and is likely to lead to confusion with Constantine's use of the word 'real' as described in Section 3.3.2.

Generalization is often implemented by the mechanism of *inheritance* and is covered in more detail in the case of classes in Chapter 5.

3.3.5   Generalization between Actors

It is also possible for a generalization association to exist between actors (Figure 3-15).

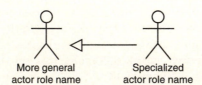

Figure 3-15: Actor generalization association notation

At CarMatch, the **Franchisee** can handle the registration of new car sharers, but can also be the recipient of management reports. Rather than show both the **Franchisee** and the **CarMatch Administrator** in association with every use case that they share as in Figure 3-8, it is possible to show the **Franchisee** as a specialization of the **CarMatch Administrator**. This means that the **Franchisee** can do everything that the **CarMatch Administrator** can do, and more. This is shown in Figure 3-16.

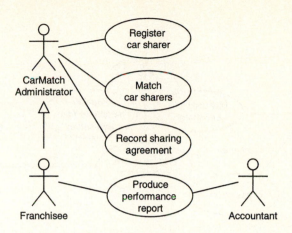

Figure 3-16: Actors in a generalization association

3.3.6   Include Relationship between Use Cases

Sometimes one use case includes the functionality of another use case. The *include* relationship is drawn as an open arrow with a dashed line that points towards the use case that is being included. The keyword **«include»** is written in *guillemets* («...») alongside the relationship arrow, as in Figure 3-17.

Figure 3-17: Include relationship notation

This happens at CarMatch, where there is a use case to process payments from car sharers. This can exist as a free-standing use case to deal with payments that come from members whose details were transferred from the web-server, but when a new car sharer is added manually, the membership payment is always processed at the same time. So the use case **Process payments** is both a use case on its own and included in the use case **Manually add car sharer**. This can be shown with an include relationship between the two use cases, as in Figure 3-18.

An include relationship can also be used when a particular use case is included in other use cases because it encapsulates some functionality that is used at several points in the system. This avoids having to define the same sequence of actions in multiple use cases. The including use case will continue up to the point where it includes the included use case, the full sequence of activities in the included use case will be carried out, and then the including use case will carry on at the point where it left off.

3.3.7   Extend Relationship between Use Cases

While an include relationship means that one use case always includes another, there are occasions where one use case may optionally be extended by the functionality in another use case. The relationship is drawn as an open arrow with a dashed line that points towards the use case that is being extended. The keyword **«extend»** is written in guillemets alongside the relationship arrow, as in Figure 3-19.

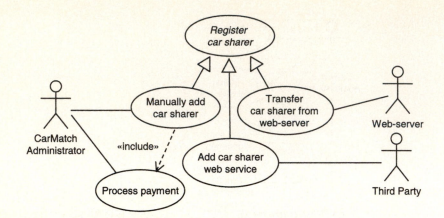

Figure 3-18: Use cases in an include relationship

Figure 3-19: Extend relationship notation

For example, if a car sharer is paying by cash or cheque, then the **Process payment** use case contains all the functionality that is required. However, if payment is by bank direct debit, or by credit or debit card, then the **Process payment** use case can be extended by either the use case **Process card payment** or the use case **Process direct debit**. An example of this is shown in Figure 3-20.

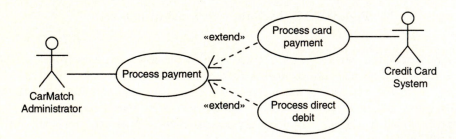

Figure 3-20: Use cases in an extend relationship

The names of the points in the use case at which the extension takes place can be shown in a compartment in the use case ellipse in the diagram. This compartment is headed *extension points* (even if there is only one) and is shown in Figure 3-21.

For the link to be followed into an extending use case and the sequence of activities in that use case to be carried out, some condition must evaluate to be true. In the example in Figure 3-21, there are three conditions, **paymentType = credit or debit card**, **paymentType = cash or cheque** and **paymentType = direct debit**. In this case, only one of these can be true, so at most one of the extending use cases will be used. If the member is paying by cash or cheque then neither of the extending use cases will be used. The condition and the extension point to which it refers can be shown in a comment attached to the extend relationship, as in Figure 3-21.

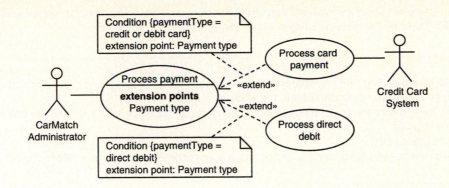

Figure 3-21: Use case showing extension points and conditions

3.4   HOW TO PRODUCE USE CASES

A systems analyst who is producing use case diagrams and descriptions will normally be working from source documents such as notes and transcripts of interviews. (A transcript is produced when an interview has been recorded on tape and the contents of the tape are then transcribed word for word into a word processed document.) The analyst may have carried out the fact-finding him or herself or may be working from someone else's notes.

Producing use cases involves the following steps:

- Find actors and use cases.

- Prioritize use cases.

- Develop each use case (starting with the priority ones).

- Structure the use case model.

This approach is based on the activities in the Unified Process (see Section 3.7).

3.4.1   Find Actors and Use Cases

The actors represent the roles that people perform in using the system and that other systems fulfil in interacting with the system. It is easier to find people and systems than actors to start with. Ask yourself these questions:

- Who are the people who will use this system to enter information?

- Who are the people who will use this system as recipients of information?

- What are the other systems that this system will interact with?

EXAMPLE 3.3   Here is a short excerpt from an interview transcript with one of the directors who is setting up CarMatch. Mick Perez is the systems analyst and Janet Hoffner is the director.

Mick Perez: So you're saying that car sharers will be able to register by telephoning the office and speaking to someone there who will enter their details into the system.

Janet Hoffner: Yes. Either the franchisee, or more likely one of the office staff will take the call and enter the details into the computer.

MP: Who are the office staff?

JH: Well, there's one or two clerks, a receptionist and a supervisor. They all have a role in the administration of the system.

MP: What will they be entering?

JH: Oh, the person's name and address, details of the journeys they want to share, any preferences they have, such as being a non-smoker.

MP: Is that the only way that this information will get into the system?

JH: No, it could also be transferred in from the national web-server.

MP: How will this information be used?

JH: Two ways. Firstly, it will be used to match up potential car sharers, and secondly, it will be used to produce a management report for the franchisee showing the number of registrations per week, whether they come from the web-server or by telephone and breaking them down by area.

If we ask these three questions about this description of the system being used, we can identify the franchisee, the clerks, the receptionist and the supervisor as people who enter information into the system. The franchisee is also a recipient of information from the system, and the web-server is another system that interacts with this one. Note that for this example, the car sharers do not interact directly with the system, and so they are not actors. There is nothing to distinguish the roles that the clerks, receptionist and supervisor play in this part of the system; they all administer the registration process, so we can use the actor role **CarMatch Administrator** to include all of them. **Franchisee** is also an actor, as the franchisee has a separate role as recipient of the management report. The final actor role is the **Web-server**, as this is another system with which the CarMatch system interacts.

Use cases represent sequences of actions carried out by the system, so to find use cases we need to look for the actions of the system. In this example there are four distinct use cases:

- Manually add car sharer.
- Transfer car sharer from web-server.
- Match car sharers.
- Produce management report.

These are shown in Figure 3-22. Note that we have not broken down the use cases into the level of detail that is described in the transcript. We are trying to group sequences of actions together into units that are meaningful in the context of the business. We do not create use cases with names like Take call or Enter details. The detail will be in the behaviour specifications.

3.4.2   Prioritize Use Cases

The next step is to prioritize the use cases. The purpose of this is to ensure that the important use cases are developed in early iterations of the next activity.

EXAMPLE 3.4   Of the use cases listed in the previous example, getting the details of car sharers into the system in the first place and matching them up are probably more important than producing management reports, and they would be the priorities for further elaboration.

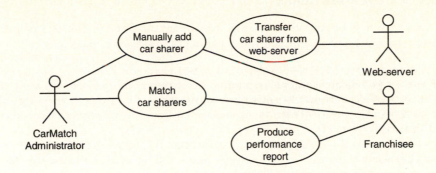

Figure 3-22: First-cut use cases and actors

3.4.3   Develop each Use Case (Starting with the Priority Ones)

The purpose of this activity is to produce the detailed specification of each use case along the lines of the use case descriptions in Section 3.3.2. This activity may also result in new use cases coming to light. In the Unified Process there is a staff role for *Use-Case Specifiers*, people who produce the detailed step-by-step specification of use cases. In most projects, it is likely to be a systems analyst who is carrying out this role.

EXAMPLE 3.5   Here is another brief excerpt from an interview with Janet Hoffner describing in more detail what happens when a new car sharer is entered into the system.

Janet Hoffner: Whether we are entering a new car sharer manually or by transferring the data from the web-server, the processing is the same apart from how we deal with membership payments. If we are entering a new car sharer into the system manually, then we need to process their membership payment at the same time. If their data is being transferred from the web-server, then we process it separately later. When we process the payment, the person can pay either by a regular direct debit or using a credit or debit card. If it's a direct debit payment, then the data about the payment is stored, and we transfer a batch of payment details to the ABTS system at the end of the month.
Mick Perez: What's ABTS?
JH: The Automated Bank Transfer System. It handles electronic payments, okay. If it's a card payment, it's processed there and then.
MP: What about the matching process?
JH: That'll be based on several factors, mostly it's geographical...

At this point, the analyst will begin to produce use case descriptions to define the use cases informally. The transcript on page 32 can be used to draw up a use case description like the one in Figure 3-9. The information in the transcript above also tells the analyst a number of things:

- Manually entering car sharers and transferring them from the web-server are two versions of the same thing.

- When a car sharer is entered manually, payment details are always processed, but this needs to be a separate use case because it can also happen on its own.

- The Process payment use case can be extended in two different ways: to handle payment by credit or debit card, or to handle payment by bank debit.

These aspects of the use cases can be used to add further structure to the use case model.

3.4.4   Structure the Use Case Model

In this activity structure will be added to the use case diagram through the use of generalization, include and extend relationships and through the grouping of use cases in packages.

EXAMPLE 3.6   There are two different ways of registering car sharers. Both perform the same core function, but one responds to the **CarMatch Administrator** entering data through a user interface, while the other happens in response to the data about a new **Car Sharer** being transferred from the web-server. Generalization can be used to represent this part of the model.

The use case **Process payment** is a use case in its own right but is also included in the use case **Manually add car sharer**. This can be represented by an include relationship.

The use case **Process payment** can optionally be extended in one of two ways, depending on the payment type. This can be represented by an extend relationship.

We have also already noted that the **Franchisee** is a specialization of the **CarMatch Administrator**, so we can use generalization to represent this.

Figure 3-23 shows the combination of all these structural aspects of the use case diagram for this Registration subsystem.

3.5   BUSINESS MODELLING WITH USE CASES

UML includes special *profiles* that can be used to apply the notation of UML to particular aspects of system development. One of the profiles that is described in the UML 1.3 Specification is the UML Profile for Business Modelling. In this profile, use case diagrams can be applied to the activity of business modelling.

The use cases that have been given as examples in this chapter have all been use cases within a system that communicate with actors who are direct users of the system.

It is possible to draw use case diagrams to represent business processes and their interaction with people and systems that are external to the business.

EXAMPLE 3.7   CarMatch as a business interacts with a number of external actors. These can be identified from the material in Chapter 1. They include **CarMatch Member**, **Credit Card Company** and **ABTS**.

The use cases in a business model are the functions with which these people and organizations interact. For example, a **CarMatch Member** interacts with the business use cases **Register with CarMatch**, **Agree to car sharing arrangement** and **Pay membership**. These business use cases are shown in Figure 3-24.

3.6   RELATIONSHIP WITH OTHER DIAGRAMS

As was stated in Section 3.3.2, the behaviour of a use case may be specified using another UML diagram: a communication diagram, a sequence diagram, an activity diagram or a state machine diagram. In a CASE tool, this would be handled by a hyperlink from the use case to the related diagram that specifies its behaviour.

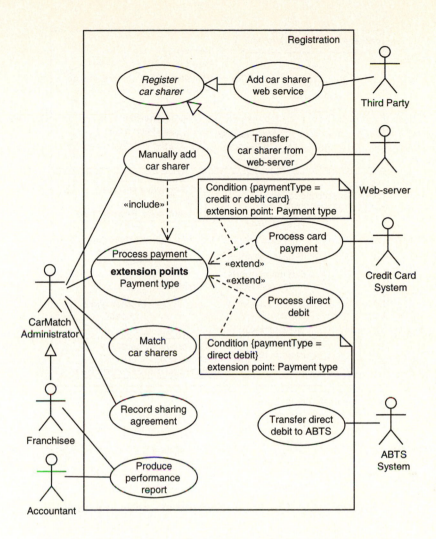

Figure 3-23: Structured version of use case diagram

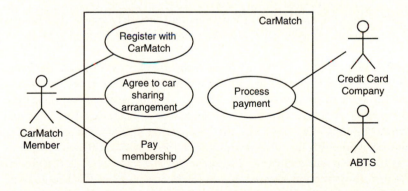

Figure 3-24: Business profile use case diagram

Like all other UML models, the use case model is organized in packages as part of the *Model Management View*. Use cases belonging to a single subject may belong to different packages. Figure 3-25 shows this for the use cases of Figure 3-23.

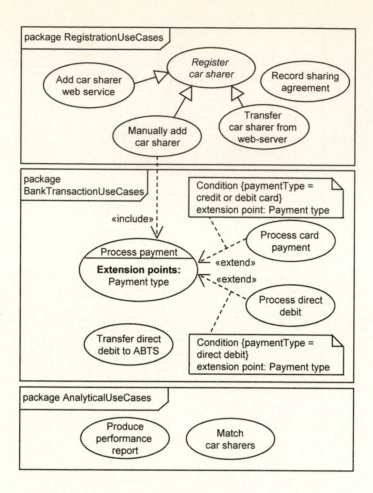

Figure 3-25: Use case diagram showing packages

3.7   USE CASES IN THE UNIFIED PROCESS

Jacobson et al. (1999) describe the Unified Process as use-case-driven, and use cases are central to the way that users' requirements are identified and documented in the Unified Process.

In Chapter 2 we explained how the Unified Process comprises five workflows. Each workflow consists of a number of related activities that are carried out by different workers. By carrying out the activities in each workflow, the workers produce models, which are elaborated as the development proceeds. In the Unified Process, the first of these workflows is the Requirements Workflow, and the *Use Case Model* is one of its outputs. Figure 3-26 shows the workflow as an activity diagram (see Chapter 11) using stereotyped icons (see Appendix C) to represent the workers and activities. The one activity that we have not discussed in the current chapter is *Prototype User-Interface*. This activity involves producing a prototype of the user interface for selected use cases. It does not use UML notation but is part of the Unified Process workflow.

In the Unified Process, use cases are *realized* by a collaboration with a *trace* dependency between the use case and its realization. A trace dependency is a special kind of dependency between elements of different models that make it possible to trace the requirements through to their final implementation. It is shown in a diagram as a «trace» stereotype in guillemets. The trace represents a relationship between elements of two models that is either historical or based on some process that has resulted

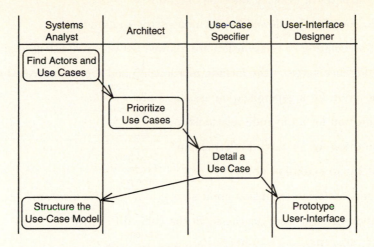

Figure 3-26: Requirements workflow as an activity diagram

in one being derived from the other. Figure 3-27 shows the trace dependency between the use case **Manually add car sharer** and its realization. (In the figure, UI is an abbreviation for user interface.) The notation of the dependency will be explained in Chapter 7.

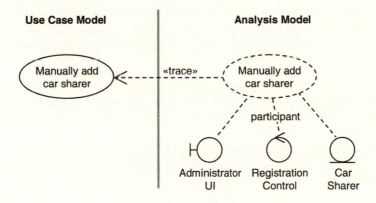

Figure 3-27: Trace dependency between use case and realization

Review Questions

3.1 Define what is meant by a use case.

3.2 What is the notation for a use case?

3.3 Define what is meant by an actor.

3.4 What is the notation for an actor?

3.5 Define what is meant by a scenario.

3.6 At what stage in a project would use cases first be used?

3.7 What are the purposes of drawing use case diagrams?

3.8 What kind of association is allowed between one actor and another?

3.9 What kinds of association or relationship are allowed between one use case and another?

3.10 What is the difference between the include relationship and the extend relationship?

3.11 What is the notation for a generalization association?

3.12 What is the notation for an include relationship?

3.13 What is the notation for an extend relationship?

3.14 What is meant by an extension point?

3.15 How is the condition for an extension point shown in a use case diagram?

3.16 In which workflow are use cases developed in the Unified Process?

3.17 What are the Unified Process activities to produce use cases?

Solved Problems

3.1 In the insurance subsystem for CarMatch, staff will search for suitable policies for a member based on the member's age and occupation and where he or she lives. They will then recommend one or more policies to the member. If the member wants to buy a policy, then they will sell it to him or her. What use cases are involved here? What should they be called?

There are three activities carried out by the staff using the system: searching for the policies, recommending the policies to the member and selling a policy. The names should be kept simple: Search for policy, Recommend policy and Sell policy.

3.2 In the CarMatch system, there will be an insurance supervisor and an insurance assistant in each franchise office. Their role will be to deal with insurance sales to CarMatch members. They will both use the same use cases in the system. How many actors are involved and what should their name or names be?

Because both the assistant and the supervisor use the same use cases, there is no need to differentiate between them as actors, so one actor is all that is required. The exact name is not important, but Insurance Administrator would be suitable.

3.3 Here is a transcript of an interview with Janet Hoffner.

Janet Hoffner: When we are selling insurance, the first thing is to get the details of the member: their age and occupation, where they live and their insurance history, that is, whether they've had any recent accidents.

Mick Perez: Where does that come from?

JH: Some of it comes from their membership details in the system, some of it we'll get from them over the 'phone.

MP: What happens next?

JH: We'll try to find a suitable policy. We'll be searching for the best policy for them, based on the information we have. The system could come up with more than one policy. We'll recommend the ones that best meet the member's needs.

MP: Do you always get a sale?

JH: No, obviously sometimes the person will decide to buy a policy, but sometimes they won't.

MP: So you set out to recommend a suitable policy. You always do a search for a suitable policy, and sometimes you sell a policy.

JH: Yep! That's about it.

Using extend and include, represent the relationships among the three use cases here.

The key factors here are that the overall task is to recommend a policy to a member. This always includes the functionality of searching for suitable policies. We have made Search for policy into a separate use case already, so it is linked to the use case Recommend policy by an include relationship: Recommend policy always includes Search for policy. However, the use case Sell policy only happens sometimes, so the link between it and Recommend policy is an extend relationship: sometimes it is extended by the additional functionality. This is shown in Figure 3-28. Note the direction of the arrows for extend and include relationships.

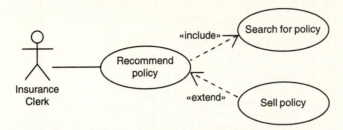

Figure 3-28: Use cases for selling insurance

3.4 What do you think is the condition on the extension point for the use case Sell policy to be invoked from Recommend policy?

The condition will be Member agrees to purchase policy. At this stage we do not know how this will be implemented. Later it could be specified in terms of a specific piece of data being entered in a field on screen.

3.5 Here are some other requirements for the Insurance subsystem. Draw a use case diagram to include them as well as the use cases from the examples above.

- To notify the insurance company system of all sales.
- To receive notification of new policies and the criteria that enable them to be matched to members' needs from the insurance company system.
- To receive notification of premium changes from the insurance company system.
- To generate on a weekly basis renewal notices for all policies one month before they are due for renewal. (These will be mailed out to the policy holders.)
- To renew a policy.
- To notify the insurance company system of all renewals.
- To calculate the insurance premium for recommendations, sales and renewal notices.

Note that all the transfers of information between the insurance company system and CarMatch are intended to be automatic transfers between the two computer systems.

A possible solution is shown in Figure 3-29. Note that this solution assumes that notifying the insurance company system happens as part of the use cases to sell and renew policies. If the use case Notify insurer happens at a later time, say once a week on a Friday, then the include relationships from Sell policy and Renew policy to Notify insurer would not be required.

Supplementary Problems

3.6 The first three problems apply to the CarMatch consultancy subsystem. Draw a use case diagram showing the actor Consultant with an association with each of the use cases Record consultancy visit and Record consultancy expenses.

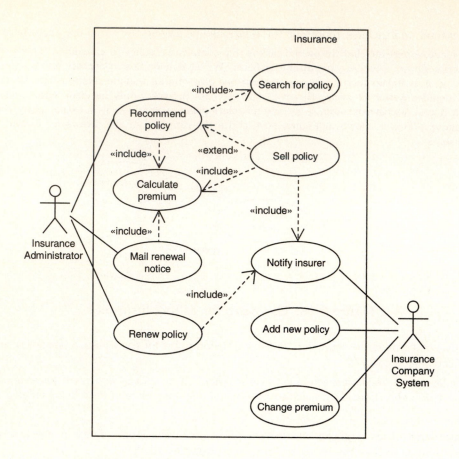

Figure 3-29: Use case subsystem for insurance

3.7 Add the actor Senior Consultant and a generalization association between the actors Consultant and Senior Consultant to the diagram from the previous problem. A Senior Consultant can do all that a Consultant can do, as well as the use cases Initiate consultancy project, Conclude consultancy project and Invoice customer. Add these three use cases to your diagram.

3.8 The use case Record consultancy visit is sometimes extended by the use case Record consultancy expenses. The use case Conclude consultancy project always includes the use case Invoice customer. Add the necessary relationships to the diagram from the previous problem. (Take care which way the arrows point.)

3.9 Read the case study material for VolBank in Chapter 1. (All the following problems use this case study material. Each problem builds on the previous ones.)

List the actors that you think are involved in this system.

3.10 List the use cases that you think are involved in the VolBank system.

3.11 Which actors have an association with which use cases? (Note that every actor should be associated with at least one use case, and every use case should be associated with at least one actor.)

3.12 Which are the priority use cases for elaboration?

3.13 Here is a short transcript of an interview between Said Hussain, a systems analyst, and Martin Page, Recruitment Director of VolBank.

Said Hussain: So, how will you get information about volunteers into your system?

Martin Page: Well, most volunteers will call into a local voluntary organization, and their information will be passed on by 'phone to one of our volunteer organizers, some will ring us directly, and some will use our web-server, and then we'll transfer the data from the web-server.

SH: What about the voluntary time they're banking in the system?

MP: They can either do that at the same time as they register, or they can do it separately.

SH: So, that data needs to be transferred from the web-server or entered manually by a volunteer organizer as well?

MP: Yes.

Develop and structure your use case diagram based on the information in the transcript.

3.14 Here is some additional information about VolBank. Use this to complete your use case diagram.

- Some local voluntary organizations will have their own computer systems, and will transfer details of opportunities into VolBank's computer system. Others will telephone or send in a paper form with the details.

- There are two processes for matching volunteers and opportunities. The first process takes place when someone volunteers, and matches the volunteer against all the unfilled opportunities on file. The second takes place when a new opportunity is registered, and matches the opportunity against all the volunteers with available time. In both cases the matching is done on the basis of the geographical location of both the volunteer and the opportunity, and by matching the skills and interests of the volunteer against the needs of the organization.

- Once a volunteer is matched with an opportunity, the volunteer will be notified and, if he or she is interested, the voluntary organization that requested help will then be notified. If they accept the volunteer, then an entry will be made in the system recording a successful match.

- The recruitment director requires a statistical report of numbers of volunteers, how they registered, how much time they have deposited and how much time has been used.

3.15 Write a use case description for each of the use cases that you have found for the VolBank system in the previous problems.

CHAPTER 4

Class Diagram: Classes and Associations

4.1 INTRODUCTION

The class diagram shows the building blocks of any object-oriented system: the classes that make up a system. The potential for collaboration among those classes, through message passing, is shown in the relationships between these classes.

The range of concepts that can be represented through the UML class diagram notation is extensive. Non-technical participants in the development process are less likely to understand the more detailed concepts and notation of a class diagram than the other, more intuitive, 'problem domain' diagrams such as use case diagrams (Chapter 3) and activity diagrams (Chapter 11). In this chapter the basic elements of the class diagram notation will be covered, with subsequent chapters introducing further notational elements.

A class diagram shows a static view of the classes in a model, or part of a model. The attributes and operations of classes can be shown along with the various different kinds of relationship that bind the classes together. The analogy of a class diagram as a road map or atlas could be used. The classes are the towns or cities with the relationships being the routes between those places.

The interactions and collaborations that actually take place to support any one particular functional requirement represent one specific route across the map. That route will navigate from class to class, traversing the relationships between those classes. It is only possible to navigate between two points by following valid relationships from the start point, via intermediate points to the intended destination.

42

The class diagram itself does not show the specific route through the class model to be taken to satisfy any one use case. Instead the class diagram shows all points available and the possible routes between them. The actual route taken for any one specific 'journey' through the class model is shown on interaction diagrams such as sequence diagrams (Chapter 9) or communication diagrams (Chapter 10).

For example, the class diagram in Figure 4-1 for a banking system shows the static structure of the core model components from the problem domain. In this instance, the class diagram shows only the name of each class and the relationships between the classes. In the diagram, the **Customer** class represents a general *type* or *class*, of which there will be many *objects* or *instances*. The association between the **Customer** and **Account** classes indicates that there is some kind of collaboration between these two classes. From the label on the association, it can be seen that the nature of the association is that a customer **Holds** an account.

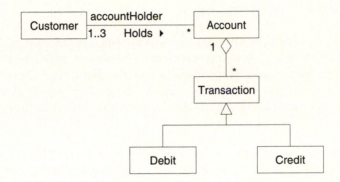

Figure 4-1: Example class diagram for banking system

By inspection of the class diagram in Figure 4-1, it may be possible to infer other aspects of the class diagram notation. However, as already mentioned, the complete notation set for class diagrams is extensive. In order to approach the complete notation in a structured and coherent manner, the notation will be covered in Chapters 4 to 7.

In this chapter we will introduce the basic class diagram notation for showing classes, their features and the basic associations among them. In subsequent chapters the more detailed and advanced aspects of the notation will be introduced to build up a complete understanding.

4.2   THE CLASS DIAGRAM THROUGH THE DEVELOPMENT PROCESS

The classes that are shown on a class diagram will depend on the phase of the development process and the level of detail being considered.

In the analysis phase, the classes apparent in the problem domain are of primary interest. The end-user stakeholder would recognize many of these problem domain classes. At this stage, the classes that may be used in the implementation of a solution are of little interest or may not have even been considered yet.

As the development moves into the design phase, classes and relationship structures that reflect the solution model will be introduced. These classes may not be part of the understanding of the end-user community but are necessary in order to produce a coherent and well-structured model.

Classes that allow us to move towards an implementable solution will be added. Such classes may relate to the interface of an application or to the persistent data management for an application. The relationship structure between classes may be amended to reflect implementation considerations. Additional attributes and operations may be added to classes in order to enhance the quality or performance of the implemented solution.

The contents of a class diagram will reflect this change in emphasis during the development process. As the class diagrams for a solution model will include many implementation classes they can quickly become very large. As with other UML notations, model management can be used to help deal with these issues of complexity and size (Appendix C).

4.3 PURPOSE OF THE TECHNIQUE

As mentioned above, class diagrams are used throughout the development process. Class diagrams show the static structure of the classes that make up a system or subsystem. The static structure of classes includes the classes of interest themselves and the features of those classes—that is, their attributes and operations, and the relationships among them. The classes of interest in a system or subsystem will provide the capabilities for fulfilling some part of the functional requirements for the system.

Class diagrams do not show how different components of a class model interact with each other. That is the purpose of techniques such as interaction sequence diagrams (Chapter 9) or communication diagrams (Chapter 10).

Class diagrams show the behavioural and data management responsibilities of each class, and thus how this responsibility is delegated across the class model. They do not show the functional requirements of a system (or subsystem) from the perspective of the end-users of a system. That is the purpose of use case diagrams (Chapter 3).

The main purposes of producing class diagrams are as follows.

- They are used to document the classes that constitute a system or subsystem.
- They are used to describe the associations, generalization and aggregation relationships among those classes.
- They are used to show the features of classes, principally the attributes and operations of each class.
- They can be used throughout the development life-cycle, ranging from the specification of the classes in the problem domain to the implementation model for a proposed system, to show the class structure of that system.
- They can document how the classes of a particular system interact with existing class libraries.
- They can be used to show individual object instances within the class structure.
- They can show the interfaces supported by a given class.

4.4 CLASS DIAGRAM—BASIC NOTATION

The class model for a system may consist of a large number of classes and relationships between those classes. The complexity of such a large model can be managed by showing fragments of the class model on different class diagrams. A class diagram may correspond to a specific (sub)system, package or model. Alternatively, a class diagram may show the relationships that exist among classes from different (sub)systems, packages or models. Any contextual relationship between a particular class diagram and a specific (sub)system, package or model must be clearly asserted by the developer producing the class diagram in the documentation associated with a class diagram.

4.4.1 Classes

The basic building block for class diagrams is the class. Classes are shown as rectangles, with the name of the class centred in the rectangle. The class name should start with a capital letter. By convention a class's name should have no spaces between multiple words in the name, but should start each subsequent word with a capital letter. For example, **BankAccount**, not **Bank account**, **CustomerInvoice**, not **Customerinvoice**. This minimal form of a class is shown in Figure 4-1.

Each class symbol may also include list compartments for attributes, operations and either none, one or more predefined compartments for other features. A list compartment is an area containing a list of whichever class features are contained by that compartment. (Attributes and operations are referred to collectively as the *features* of a class.) The list compartments for attributes and operations can be independently omitted. In other words it would be acceptable to show a class as:

- a class name only;
- a class name and a list of attributes;
- a class name and a list of operations;
- a class name, a list of attributes and a list of operations.

These four cases are shown in Figure 4-2.

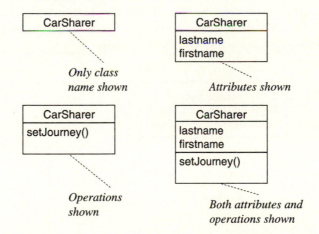

Figure 4-2: Classes with basic compartments

Each list compartment may be named, though the names for the attribute and operation compartments are usually assumed (that is, they are not normally named). It is, however, good practice to name the list compartments that are used in addition to the attribute and operation compartments. Additional list compartments are commonly used for the events to which a class may be subject, or the functional responsibilities of a class (Figure 4-3).

As shown in Figure 4-4, the class name compartment can also be used to show the *stereotype* or generic type to which the class conforms and any properties of the class as a list of tagged values enclosed in curly braces ({...}, see Appendix C).

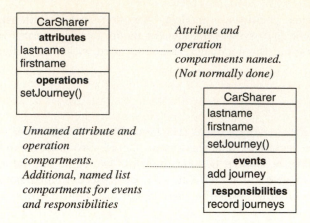

Figure 4-3: Named class list compartments

In the context of the class diagram, stereotypes would typically be used to show where a model component conforms to a well understood behaviour. Figure 4-4 indicates that the RegisterCarSharerController conforms to the pattern of behaviour understood by the «controller» stereotype.

> **Aside**
>
> A controller class can be used to co-ordinate the interaction between classes in the core class model of an application and the interface of that application. Structuring the implementation in this way shields the interface implementation from many types of change to the underlying class model. Similarly, different interfaces can be commissioned without requiring reworking of the underlying class model. The controller stereotype is not a core stereotype of UML.

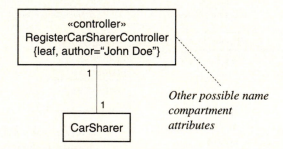

Figure 4-4: Information shown in the class name compartment

Class properties provide descriptive information about the class to other people involved in the modelling process. The class properties are listed in curly brackets, that is {property [',' property]*}. Class properties could include:

- modelling management information such as: author, dateCreated, dateLastModified, and status;
- class information with a boolean (true/false) type, such as: isAbstract, isLeaf, and isRoot.

The terse form of the class information properties isAbstract, isLeaf and isRoot (for example, abstract) is identical to the more verbose property string property-name=true (for example, isAbstract=true). The property-name=false setting has no direct terse form, that is, there is no notAbstract form. However, omission of a property specification is generally taken to imply the property-name=false setting.

Abstract classes are never instantiated, that is, there will never be an object instance of an abstract class. isAbstract=false is the assumed status if the isAbstract property is omitted.

The isLeaf property can be used to specify whether or not a class can be subtyped through a generalization structure. See Chapter 5 for a discussion of generalization. Setting isLeaf to true (isLeaf=true or isLeaf) means that a class may not be specialized (or subtyped). Setting isLeaf to false (isLeaf=false) means that a class may be specialized. The property isLeaf=false is the default if the isLeaf property is omitted.

One last notation of the class name compartment is the ability to include the path name, or package structure, for a class. This can be useful when it is necessary to make clear the lineage of a class. The *class pathname* takes the form `path-or-package-names::className`. Where a list of package names is used (package—subpackage, etc.), each package name in the package hierarchy is separated by double colons, '::', for example java::sql::Connection. The pathname context of a class is known as the *namespace* of a class. Class names must be unique within a namespace.

This notation is useful where model management principles have been used to organize a large class model into a series of packages (subsystems, etc.). Some class diagrams will need to show the associations between classes from different packages. Figure 4-5 shows the class pathname being used to show two classes from different packages.

Figure 4-5: Using class pathnames

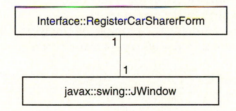

Figure 4-6: Using class pathnames to access an external class library

Figure 4-6 shows the class pathname being used to show access to a class from an external class library (in this case, the Java Swing interface library).

4.4.2   Object Instances

The UML class diagram notation allows for class instances, that is, objects, to be shown on a class diagram. In this chapter, only the most basic object notation will be introduced. A more thorough treatment of object notation is provided in Chapter 7.

The basic object notation is very similar to the basic class notation. The name compartment of the object shows the name of the object instance and its class type. The name of an object is of the form `objectName : ClassName`, all underlined. For example, aDocument : Document, salesReport : Document. As with classes, the class name can be preceded by the class pathname, for example newPolicy : Insurance::Policy (Figure 4-7).

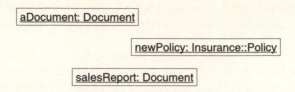

Figure 4-7: Object instances

4.4.3   Attributes and Operations

The other two common components of a class symbol are the attribute and operation lists. Both attributes and operations are listed, one per line, in the appropriate compartment. Each attribute and operation listed in its respective list compartment may be suffixed with a property list in the form of a list of tagged values enclosed in curly braces ({...}). Properties are discussed in more detail in Section 4.4.3.5.

Each attribute and operation name should start with a lower-case letter. The exception to this is for the set of constructor operations of a class, which will have the same name as the class itself in exactly the same upper- and lower-case format. Constructors are not always shown in class diagrams, as their existence may be assumed. By convention, attribute and operation names should have no spaces between multiple words in the name, but should start each subsequent word with a capital letter. For example, **setSharingAgreement**, not **SetSharingAgreement**, and **addRequirement**, not **add requirement**.

The level of detail known or displayed for attributes and operations will vary depending upon the phase of the development life cycle in which the class diagram is being used. In the analysis phase, only general information may be known or shown. For example, the parameters of an operation may not yet have been clearly established. In the design phase, levels of detail necessary to allow successful implementation will have been established. For example, not only will the parameters required for an operation be known, but also the data types of each of those parameters.

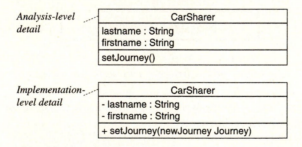

Figure 4-8: Attribute and operation lists

4.4.3.1   Attribute and Operation Types

Examples of analysis- and implementation-level representations for attributes and operations are shown in Figure 4-8. Both attributes and operations take the basic form `feature-name : type`, where type is the data type of the attribute or the data type returned by the operation.

Omitting the return type of an operation, as in Figure 4-8, has different connotations depending on the perspective from which the class diagram has been drawn. This is discussed further in Section 4.5.

Both attributes and operations can be typed with a class type from the implementation environment class libraries. For example, dateOfBirth could be typed as Date (a class commonly found in the class library of object-oriented development environments and languages). Attributes and operations could also be typed as a class from the class model currently being specified. For example, a getHomeAddress() operation on CarSharer could be typed as Address (Figure 4-9).

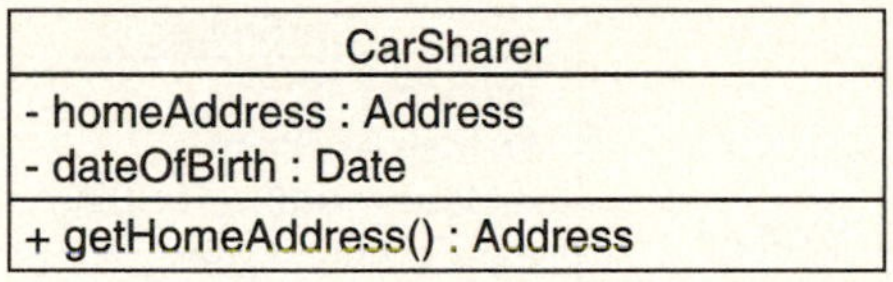

CarSharer
- homeAddress : Address
- dateOfBirth : Date
+ getHomeAddress() : Address

Figure 4-9: Features typed with a class

The implication of using this typing is that the attribute or value returned by a feature will provide all the operations available on the class it was typed as. So, an attribute typed as Date could provide formatting and internationalization operations that could be used by the class containing the Date-typed attribute.

It is quite normal to use both primitive types and class types in class models. Primitive types such as int can be used to represent an integer value where only simple arithmetic operations are carried out on that value. Languages such as Java often provide class representations of these primitive values. For example, the Java class Integer acts as a wrapper around an int value, providing additional operations such as comparisons (for example, equals) and conversion to other types (for example, floatValue). Thus type names such as String, int and Date reflect the use of both primitive and class types.

4.4.3.2   Attribute and Operation Visibility

Attributes and operations can be assigned a level of visibility shown on the class diagram with a *visibility* indicator. The visibility of a feature can be defined by either a keyword or a symbol. There are four specific types of visibility, private (with the symbol -), public (+), protected (#) and package (~).

The visibility of an attribute or an operation relates to its availability to other classes. *Private* visibility means that a feature is available only within the class that owns that feature. *Public* visibility means that the feature is available to any class associated with the class that owns that feature. *Protected* visibility means that the feature is available within the class that owns that feature and any subtype of that class. Protected visibility relates to the concepts of generalization covered in Chapter 5. Finally, *Package* visibility means that the feature is available only to other classes in the same package as the declaring class (and the declaring class itself).

EXAMPLE 4.1   What is the visibility of each of the attributes and operations shown in Figure 4-9?

SOLUTION   homeAddress and dateOfBirth are private. getHomeAddress is public.

By convention, attributes are normally private and operations predominantly public. Private operations can be used, however, for internally delegated responsibilities. Insofar as basic attributes and operations are concerned, there is no default value for visibility. The omission of a visibility indicator simply means that the visibility is not shown or has not yet been defined.

4.4.3.3   Attributes in Detail

There are three other properties of attributes that will be discussed here, namely: default values, derived attributes and multiplicity. The notation for all three properties is shown in Figure 4-10.

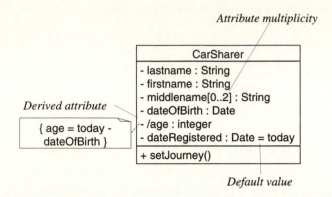

Figure 4-10: Attribute properties: default value, derived value and multiplicity

Default Values

The default initial value for an attribute can be specified as part of a class diagram by including the clause = `default-value` after the attribute type. The specification in the example given in Figure 4-10 is that the default value for the **dateRegistered** for a **CarSharer** should be set to **today** (the current system date). This specification comes into effect when an instance of the object is created. The methods that implement the creation operations should take account of this specification and make sure that the **dateRegistered** is set to the current system date. Subsequent processing in a constructor operation may overwrite this default value, but the initial value must be set to start with.

Derived Attributes

The value for a derived attribute can be determined from the values of other attributes (or features of other classes). Given that the value for a derived attribute can be determined from other feature values, there is no inherent need to implement an attribute for a specified derived attribute. The presence of a derived attribute in a conceptual or specification model conveys a requirement and is provided to improve the clarity of the model. In reality, a derived attribute could be implemented as part of an operation, as an explicit operation or by implementing a real attribute to hold the derived value. In UML a derived attribute is annotated by the inclusion of a forward slash (/) immediately before the attribute name. The specification for the derivation of a derived attribute can be shown as a constraint in a note attached to the derived attribute.

In Figure 4-10, the attribute **age** is indicated as being derived. The derivation is shown as a constraint based on the current system date and the value of the **dateOfBirth** attribute.

Multiplicity

A multiplicity clause can be used immediately after the attribute name to indicate the number of separate values that an attribute could hold. The multiplicity of an attribute takes the form of a multiplicity clause, which consists of a lower and upper bound range, enclosed in square brackets, [m..n]. Here m specifies the lowest number of values and n the highest number of values that an attribute can hold.

The lower bound of a multiplicity (m) can be any non-negative integer, that is, a whole number that is greater than or equal to 0. The upper bound of a multiplicity (n) can be any integer that is greater than or equal to m, or it can be the character *, meaning 'many' (an unspecified and unlimited number greater than the lower bound, m). There are some conventions for multiplicity clauses:

- 1..1 is truncated to 1.
- 0..* is truncated to *.
- If no attribute multiplicity is specified it is assumed to be 1 (the truncated version of 1..1).

A single integer value (for example, 7) can be used to indicate a fixed number of attribute values, for example in an array (dayName[7]). Some valid occurrences of an attribute's multiplicity would be:

1. 'telephoneNumber[1..3]'—this definition says 'at least one value will be held for telephone number, and possibly up to three values';
2. 'telephoneNumber[0..1]'—this definition says 'a telephone number can be null or alternatively a single telephone number can be held'. A null value means no value at all. Null is different to either 0 for an integer or '␣' (space) for a string, for example;
3. 'telephoneNumber[1..*]'—this definition says 'at least one value will be held for telephone number, and possibly up to an unlimited number of values'.

A case may arise where it is clear that an attribute will have a range of values. The specific multiplicity may not yet be known, beyond the fact that it will not be [1]. In such a case using a multiplicity of [*] would provide for the general case of multiple values for an attribute.

A multiplicity clause can be augmented with properties to define whether the set of values bound by that clause is ordered and/or unique. For example, telephoneNumber[1..*] identifies a set or one or more values for the telephoneNumber attribute.

By adding {ordered}, the designer specifies that the set of values is ordered. For example, telephoneNumber[1..*] {ordered} might be used where telephone numbers are listed in the preferred sequence for contacting a car sharer.

By adding {unique}, the designer specifies that the set cannot contain duplicated values. For example, telephoneNumber[1..*] {unique} indicates that no duplicated telephone numbers can be held in the set of telephone numbers.

Finally, these two properties can be used together, yielding telephoneNumber[1..*] {ordered, unique}.

4.4.3.4   Operations in Detail

The basic specification of operations has already been outlined. Each operation shown in a class node on a class diagram can include a comma-separated list of the parameters accepted by that operation. The main extensions to the specification of an operation on a class diagram relate to the level of detail shown for these parameters.

Parameters

Each parameter in the list has the basic form parameter-name : parameter-type. For example, setNextOfKin(name : String), setFirstMatched(firstDate : Date) or equals(testAddress : Address).

Omitting the `parameter-name` : part of the clause, leaving `parameter-type` for a parameter, is a valid shorthand. For example, setNextOfKin(String), setFirstMatched(Date) or equals(Address).

As with the specification of default values for attributes, the default value for a parameter can be specified by suffixing a parameter with the clause = `default-value`. For example, an operation approveApplication that takes a date as a parameter may use the current system date as the default value for a parameter and thus be specified as approveApplication(dateApproved : Date = today).

Parameters may be prefixed with a *parameter kind* clause. The parameter kind can be in, out, or inout. If an explicit parameter kind is omitted, then the default kind is assumed to be in. The parameter kind is of specific use in implementation environments where parameters may be passed by reference instead of by value.

Where a parameter is passed by value, the value of a parameter (a variable) is held as a separate value (that is, it has a separate memory allocation). This means that any modifications made to the value of that parameter by the called operation do not affect the original variable unless those modifications are passed back to the method of the calling operation (using a return value) and explicitly written back to the original variable. This mode of behaviour is illustrated in the pseudocode shown in Figure 4-11.

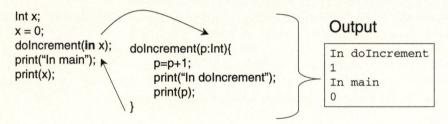

Figure 4-11: Parameters passed by value

In this example, an integer variable is created and then instantiated to the value 0 (zero). The variable is then passed by value (in) as a parameter to the doIncrement operation. The doIncrement operation then increases the value of the variable passed as a parameter by 1 and prints the context, In doIncrement, and the value of the variable within the operation (1, one). The doIncrement operation then ends and the processing flow returns to the main routine. The doIncrement operation does not return any value (that is, it has the default return type of void). The main routine then prints the context, In main, and the value of the variable in the main routine. This value (0) was unaffected by the processing within the doIncrement operation. The values of the variable x and the parameter p had different memory allocations and the change made to p did not affect x.

In contrast, where a parameter is passed by reference, the memory location of a variable is passed to the called operation. The original variable and the parameter therefore share the same memory allocation. Any modifications to the variable within the called operation will alter the value of the variable held at the memory location passed to the operation. The effect of this is that the value of the original variable is changed by the processing of the operation. This mode of behaviour is illustrated in the pseudocode shown in Figure 4-12.

In this second example, an integer variable is again created and instantiated to the value 0 (zero). The variable is then passed by reference (inout) as a parameter to the doIncrement operation. The doIncrement operation then increases the value of the variable passed as a parameter by 1 and prints the context and the value of the variable within the operation (1, one). The doIncrement operation then ends and the processing flow returns to the main routine. This main routine then prints the context and the value of the variable within the main routine. This value (1, one) was amended by the processing within

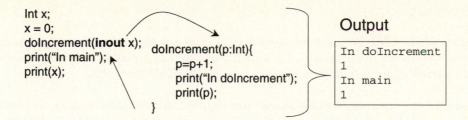

Figure 4-12: Parameters passed by reference

the **doIncrement** operation. The values of the variable **x** and the parameter **p** had the same memory allocation and the change made to **p** was, in effect, a direct change to the value of **x**.

So, **in** parameters are passed by value, **out** and **inout** parameters are passed by reference. An **out** parameter does not actually provide information to an operation but is passed simply as a means of retrieving data from the operation once it has completed.

Method Note

The specification of a method body for an operation may be included as a note attached to an operation on the class diagram (Figure 4-13). (A note is called a *Comment* in UML 2.0, although the term *Note* can still be used.) This would normally be done only where the specification for a method is relatively small, and the specification for that method will make a useful contribution to the information documented on the class diagram.

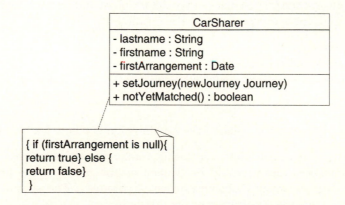

Figure 4-13: Note showing method specification

It is important to note that the method note does not specify how the method should be implemented. Instead, the method note provides a specification of what the method should do. This specification will normally take the form of a constraint, which can be written using the Object Constraint Language (Chapter 13).

Grouping Operations

One final aspect of the UML notation for operations in classes is the ability to group operations by an arbitrary feature of the set of operations. Operation grouping will probably be encountered only in the use of certain modelling tools (Chapter 16) that support this UML notation.

The types used for this grouping include named stereotypes («constructor», «query», and «update») and visibility. The named stereotypes that are used in this example are not part of UML. Figure 4-14 shows an example of operation grouping.

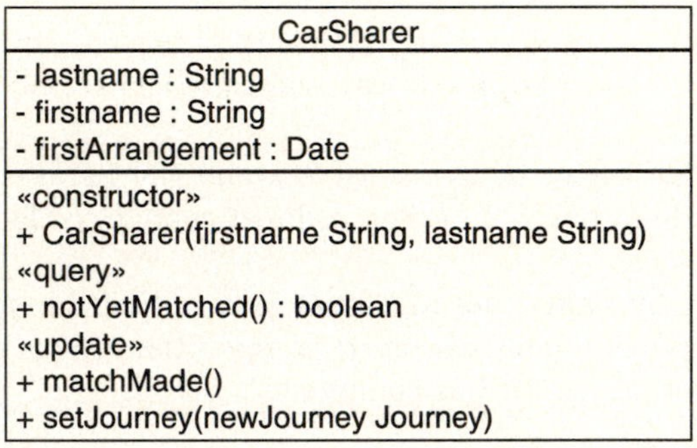

CarSharer
- lastname : String
- firstname : String
- firstArrangement : Date
«constructor»
+ CarSharer(firstname String, lastname String)
«query»
+ notYetMatched() : boolean
«update»
+ matchMade()
+ setJourney(newJourney Journey)

Figure 4-14: Operations grouped by operation stereotype

4.4.3.5   Properties

As with classes, attributes, operations and the parameters for operations can be annotated with a property string. This property string is used to add descriptive information about the attribute to the class model.

The property string is always the last element in the definition of an attribute, operation or parameter. The format is `definition {property-string}`. For example:

- /age : integer {readOnly}
- telephoneNumber[0..3] : String {sequence}
- dateRegistered : Date = creationDate {redefines dateStarted}

The valid property strings for an attribute are:

{readOnly} Which indicates that the value of the attribute cannot be set after initialization.

{union} Which indicates that the attribute represents a union of other attribute values. For example, /contactTelephoneNumbers {union} could be defined as the union of the homeTelephoneNumber, workTelephoneNumber and mobileTelephoneNumber attributes. The specific definition could be added as part of the general description of the attribute.

{subsets *property*} This property string indicates that the attribute is defined as being limited to a subset of the values which could be obtained from the other named property. For example, if the attribute Constants.validTitles : String[*] holds values 'Ms', 'Miss', 'Mrs', 'Mr' and 'Dr', then FemaleMember.validTitles {subsets Constants.validTitles} could hold 'Ms', 'Miss', 'Mrs' and 'Dr'.

{redefines *property*} To provide a meaningful example of the use of the {redefines...} property string, we need to cover the concepts of inheritance and aggregation. For this reason, an example of redefines is deferred until Section 5.4.1.

{ordered} This property would be applied to an attribute which is capable of holding a set of data. The use of this property indicates that the values of that set are ordered.

{bag} Again, this property would be applied to an attribute which is capable of holding a set of data. The use of this property indicates that a given value would be allowed to repeat within the set of values. For example, previousNicknames : String[*] {bag} could hold 'Bazza', 'Baz' and 'Bazza' again.

{sequence} or {seq} This property combines the {ordered} and {bag} properties. In other words, a sequence is an ordered bag.

{composite} This property string indicates that the attribute represents a composite value, aggregated from other values. For example, /fullAndFormalName {composite} may be defined as being made up of title, firstName, familyName and nameSuffix.

The UML version 2.0 Specification does not explicitly define the valid property strings for operations or parameters. However, it seems reasonable to assume that the property set identified above could be applied to parameters and operations, on the assumption that all but the {redefines...} property applies to the returned type of an operation.

4.4.4   Associations

An object-oriented system is built from class types that collaborate with each other by passing messages and receiving responses. When running, an object-oriented system is populated with instances that conform to their class type. Where instances of one class pass messages to instances of another class, an *association* is implied between those two classes.

4.4.4.1   Association Names

UML shows an association between two classes as a solid line. The association can be labelled with a name to indicate the nature of the association. The name of an association must begin with a capital letter. If an association is labelled then an arrow-head should be used with the association name to indicate the direction in which the text of the association name should be interpreted.

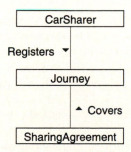

Figure 4-15: Named associations

Figure 4-15 illustrates two simple associations, one between Journey and SharingAgreement and a second between CarSharer and Journey. These associations indicate that a CarSharer **Registers** a Journey and that a SharingAgreement **Covers** a Journey.

An association between two classes is also called a 'binary' association. However, as this is the most common form of association, the more concise term (association) is used.

4.4.4.2 Multiplicity

The next thing that can be added to an association is information about the multiplicity of the association. Multiplicity as applied to attributes has already been discussed in this chapter. In terms of an association, multiplicity indicates the number of object instances of the class at the far end of an association for one instance of the class at the near end of an association. This concept of association multiplicity is illustrated in Figure 4-16. (It should be noted that the notation used to show instances of the classes and the association in Figure 4-16 are not part of the UML notation set.)

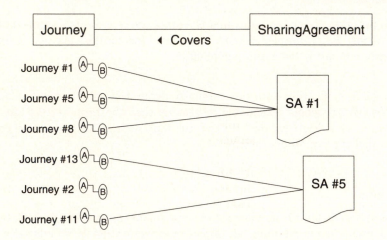

Figure 4-16: Occurrences of an association between instances of classes

It might be said that there must be at least two **Journeys** covered by a **SharingAgreement**, otherwise they are not shared. CarMatch might set five **Journeys** as the working maximum for the number of **Journeys** covered by a **SharingAgreement** as that is the maximum capacity of most cars. This gives the multiplicity of between two and five **Journeys** per **SharingAgreement**.

Looking the other way along this association from **Journey** to **SharingAgreement**, it might be established that a **Journey** can be covered by a minimum of zero **SharingAgreements**. That is to say that there will be **Journeys** that have not yet been matched and covered by a **SharingAgreement** or whose participation in a **SharingAgreement** has ended. To avoid potential complications or conflicts of interest, CarMatch might wish to limit a **Journey** to be part of only one **SharingAgreement** at a time. This gives a multiplicity of between zero and one **SharingAgreement** per **Journey**.

> **Aside**
> Words like 'might' are being used here to indicate that arbitrary choices are being made about the specific lower and upper bounds for the multiplicity. In practice, these bounds will be established from information gathered from the problem domain. At this point the bounds being used are illustrative.

In summary then, the association between **Journey** and **SharingAgreement** has the following multiplicity: a **SharingAgreement** Covers 2..5 **Journeys** and a **Journey** is covered by 0..1 **SharingAgreements**.

This information can now be shown on an association on a class diagram. As the phrases above indicate, the multiplicity clause is shown at the end of the association for the direction in which it is being read. When reading from **Journey** to **SharingAgreement** the 0..1 is shown at the **SharingAgreement** end.

In class diagrams, the notation for multiplicity on associations is the same as the notation introduced for attributes on page 50. The full notation of the multiplicity for the **Covers** association is shown in Figure 4-17.

Figure 4-17: Multiplicity of an association

If the multiplicity of an association end is not shown it is assumed to be currently not known or not specified. This is different from attribute multiplicity. If attribute multiplicity is omitted then it is assumed to be '1'.

4.4.4.3   Role Names

On occasions it is necessary to clarify the role played by a class in an association. Figure 4-18 shows three examples of roles: **homeAddress**, **startAddress** and **destinationAddress**.

Remember that the association multiplicity **1** is short for **1..1**, that is, a minimum of **1** and a maximum of **1** and that ***** is short for **0..***, that is, a minimum of zero and an unlimited maximum. The multiplicity of the **Journey** end of the **StartsAt** and **EndsAt** associations was not known and therefore omitted from this class diagram.

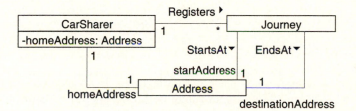

Figure 4-18: Role names on associations

In the unnamed association between **CarSharer** and **Address**, **Address** plays the role of the **homeAddress** of a **CarSharer**. From the multiplicity of the association between the **CarSharer** and **Address** classes, it can be seen that a **CarSharer** will always have a **homeAddress** and will never have more than one **homeAddress**. The implementation of this association as a private attribute of type **Address** in **CarSharer** is also shown.

The one-to-one association between the **CarSharer** and **Address** classes implies that, even if two car sharers have exactly the same home address, those home addresses will be held as two separate and distinct instances of **Address**. Those instances will have the same attribute values, but will be different instances of **Address**.

EXAMPLE 4.2   Discuss the role played by **Address** in the context of the two associations **StartsAt** and **EndsAt** between the **Journey** and **Address** classes shown in Figure 4-18.

SOLUTION   From the multiplicity of the two associations, it can be seen that a **Journey** starts at one **Address**, and ends at one **Address**. Instances of **Address** can then play the roles of the **startAddress** of a **Journey** and the **destinationAddress** of a **Journey**. This could be shown as the implementation attributes **startAddress : Address** and **destinationAddress : Address** respectively.

Role names can be useful when specifying method notes as the body of the method note can use the role name to refer to an instance of an associated class (Figure 4-19).

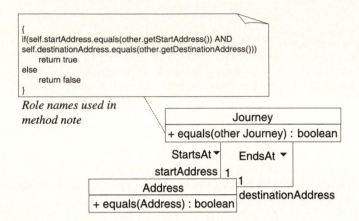

Figure 4-19: Use of role names in operation specifications

4.5 MODELLING GUIDANCE

The production of a class model, and hence class diagrams, is an iterative process. At the outset, only a rudimentary 'wire-frame' class diagram may be produced. This diagram will almost certainly dispense with implementation details while striving to capture the essential structure of the required class model.

A model (and diagram) produced in the early stages of the modelling process, and thus reflecting the requirements of the problem domain being modelled, will consist both of classes apparent to the problem domain and of classes that represent insights into that problem domain. Such a model can be constructed from the products of the initial information-gathering activity undertaken at the outset of a project. These products may include, among other sources, interview transcripts, sample documents, pro-formas and manuals. The model and diagram can then be refined through an iterative process of critical review and further information gathering.

Models and diagrams produced later on in the development process will reflect the intended design or implementation, respectively, of a software system. These models may well draw on the classes in a conceptual model (see above). However, specification- and implementation-oriented models also suit modelling approaches based on the principles of functional delegation (see Section 4.5.2).

Section 4.4.3 introduced the notation for the return type of an operation. At this point it should be noted that the perspective from which a class diagram is drawn will affect the interpretation of an omitted return type. In a conceptual diagram, the omission of a return type may be interpreted as being no more significant than saying that the return type of the operation is not yet known or has not yet been finalized. In a specification or implementation class diagram the omission of the operation return type implies that the operation does not return a value (equivalent to a return type of **:void**).

4.5.1   Conceptual Modelling

In the modelling process, producing a class diagram will require the modeller to iterate over a series of activities. These activities will each contribute to the overall picture and specification being produced.

- Find classes and associations.
- Identify attributes and operations and allocate to classes.
- Identify generalization structures (see Chapter 5).

It is not necessary to work through the steps in rigorous sequence. Instead, early iterations in conceptual modelling may involve iterations around the identification of classes, attributes and associations. In later iterations, class operations and generalization structures may begin to emerge.

4.5.1.1   Find Classes and Associations

Classes and associations can be identified from use case descriptions (Chapter 3), directly from the products of information-gathering activities, or by inspection of and insight into the class model itself (thinking about it and bringing experience to bear).

Nouns, that is, the names of kinds of things, and noun phrases used in use cases and interview transcripts often indicate classes. Bennett et al. (2002) suggest some categories of classes that may be identified.

Specific occurrences of a general type, such as people ('John Doe'), organizations ('Bald Eagle Insurance'), and organizational units ('The sales team').

Structures, which are things mentioned in the problem domain, such as 'car sharers', 'volunteer team'.

Abstractions of things such as:

    People and roles 'Car sharer', 'Volunteer', 'Account holder', 'Insurance sales advisor';

    Physical artifacts 'car', 'cover note', 'insurance policy';

    Concepts 'sale', 'skill', 'requirement'.

Enduring relationships between other identified classes, such as 'agreement', 'registration'.

Verb phrases can indicate associations between classes. In other cases, inherent logical associations between classes might become apparent as the class model is refined. Examples to indicate the type of phrase to be considered as an association might include 'Customer holds account', 'Car sharer registers journey', or 'Volunteer holds particular skills'.

EXAMPLE 4.3   Here is a another excerpt from an interview transcript with one of the directors who are setting up CarMatch. Remember, Mick Perez is the systems analyst and Janet Hoffner is the director. Identify any classes and associations mentioned in the transcript.

Mick Perez: Can we look at the way car sharing is actually organized now. I'd like to find out a bit more about the ideas you work with.

Janet Hoffner: Sure. I guess at the heart of everything there is the car sharer. That's a person who has registered with us so that they can share journeys with other registered car sharers.

MP: Tell me more about how you keep details of the journey that someone wants to share.

JH: Well, a car sharer can actually register several journeys with us. They do not have to limit themselves to just one journey to share.

MP: I guess they would have to want to share at least one journey to be classed as a car sharer though?

JH: That's right. Remember that they can register as many journeys as they want. When we find other car sharers that want to share a similar journey we match up the sharers and formalize things with a sharing agreement.

MP: . . .

SOLUTION   Mick Perez has gone through the transcript, using his experience to pick out possible classes and associations for a conceptual class diagram. Mick has underlined probable class nouns or noun phrases, and drawn a box around probable association verbs or verb phrases.

Mick Perez: Can we look at the way car sharing is actually organized now. I'd like to find out a bit more about the ideas you work with.

Janet Hoffner: Sure. I guess at the heart of everything there is the <u>car sharer</u>. That's a <u>person</u> who has <u>registered</u> with us so that they can <u>share journeys</u> with other registered car sharers.

MP: Tell me more about how you keep details of the journey that someone wants to share.

JH: Well, a car sharer can actually <u>register several journeys</u> with us. They do not have to limit themselves to just one journey to share.

MP: I guess they would have to want to share at least one journey to be classed as a car sharer though?

JH: That's right. Remember that they can register as many journeys as they want. When we find other car sharers that want to share a similar journey we match up the sharers and formalize things with a <u>sharing agreement</u>.

MP: . . .

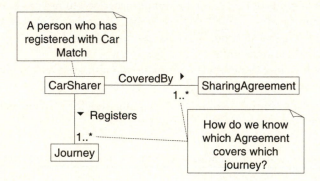

Figure 4-20: A first draft conceptual class diagram

Mick's first draft class diagram for the interview fragment above is shown in Figure 4-20. The classes **CarSharer**, **Journey** and **SharingAgreement** that were identified in the transcript are included in the class diagram; moreover, the fact that it has been possible to identify associations that relate the classes together encourages Mick that the classes themselves are reasonable.

Mick is not so sure about the associations though. As the note in Figure 4-20 indicates, Mick has identified that the structure of the associations does not seem to make sense. Queries such as this could be resolved, either by further consideration of the concepts being modelled or by taking the diagram (and notes) back to the interviewee and clarifying the conceptual relationships. In this particular case, the notion of a sharing agreement actually relates shared journeys, rather than the car sharers themselves (Figure 4-21).

4.5.1.2   Identify and Allocate Attributes and Operations

The items of data held for each instance of a class are the attributes of that class. As with classes, in conceptual modelling attributes should be reasonably straightforward to identify from the available information sources.

Operations describe the processing capabilities of a class. In conceptual modelling it may not be easy to identify the detailed operations for each class until more detailed work on the interaction diagrams

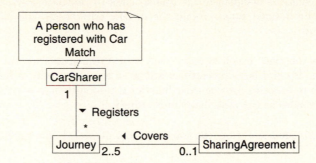

Figure 4-21: The second draft conceptual class diagram

has been completed (see Chapters 9 and 10). However, some operations may be apparent from the available information sources and these should be noted.

EXAMPLE 4.4   Consider another extract from the transcript of the interview between Mick Perez and Janet Hoffner. From this extract, identify any attributes and operations that can be added to the class model.

Mick Perez: What kind of information do you hold about the journeys that car sharers will register with you?
Janet Hoffner: Well, I'm sure that you realize it will primarily be 'where from' and 'where to'. We need to know where each journey will start from and where it will end. We will also want to know travel times for each direction of the journey. That is to say, the desired departure and arrival times for both the outward and return journeys.
MP: What kind of things do you need to know about the start and destination of each journey? Will that information need to be used to match up possible shared journeys?
JH: Good point. Yes, I guess that however we hold the start and destination address, we'll need to be able to use that information to automate the matching of car sharers. The home address of a person might also be used in some journey matching.
MP: ...

SOLUTION   From this transcript it can be seen that some time-based attributes are required for departure and arrival times. There are three mentions of address information as well. There are the start and destination addresses. There is also the home address of a car sharer. These addresses could be held as text strings, but this will probably not allow anything more than crude matching for sharing purposes.

One way of modelling addresses in this early iteration might be to create an **Address** class. The **Address** class has responsibility for maintaining information relating to an address and also for matching two addresses with each other.

To support this last notion, a **matches** or **equals** operation could be defined. This operation returns a **boolean true** or **false** value depending on whether two compared addresses would enable car sharing.

If this separate **Address** class proves to be an unnecessary split of functional responsibility, because address handling and matching could have been modelled within **CarSharer**, then the **Address** class could be replaced in subsequent iterations. If the existence of the **Address** class begins to look more certain then the specification of the **Address** class can be refined and improved in subsequent iterations. Things that would make the existence of a class look more certain would be the identification and allocation of attributes and operations to that class or the participation of the class in further associations.

A similar **equals** operation could be assigned to the **Journey** class to calculate whether two journeys are close enough in requirements to be deemed equal. Again the specific criteria and specification for 'close enough' would need to be established.

Attributes are allocated to the class which is most likely to be responsible for the particular item of data represented by an attribute. By and large, operations will go in the same class as the attributes upon which, or with which, they operate in order to provide their functional responsibility. Attributes and operations may need to be moved to other classes as the class diagram is refined.

The attributes and operations identified from the transcript and discussed above are shown in Figure 4-22.

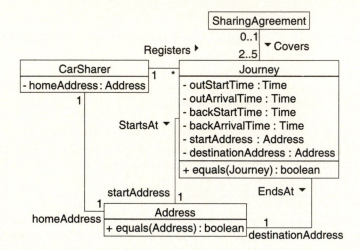

Figure 4-22: Identification and allocation of attributes and operations

In the next iteration, the **Address** class may well be assigned suitable attributes to represent address information (for example, **street**, **town**, **state** or **county**, **zipcode** or **postcode**). In Figure 4-22 the implementation of the **StartsAt** and **EndsAt** associations has been shown as attributes of type **Address** in the **Journey** class. The unnamed association between **CarSharer** and **Address** has also been implemented as the **homeAddress: Address** attribute on **CarSharer**. These implementations are shown to illustrate a possible interpretation of the class model. Associations would not normally be implemented at this early stage.

Modelling in this way can continue until the analyst is satisfied that a comprehensive model exists. The model should incorporate the major classes that exist in the problem domain, their attributes and some of the operations that will be apparent in the solution.

4.5.2   Modelling using Functional Delegation

When generating models and diagrams produced from a specification or implementation perspective, it can be more fruitful to use principles of functional delegation. Specification and implementation class diagrams will reflect the intended design or implementation of a software system respectively.

The principle of functional delegation is that responsibility for data ownership and processing of that data should be delegated to the most appropriate class. We have already seen a simple illustration of this in the section on identification and allocation of operations. The **Journey** class had responsibility for establishing whether its requirements were the same as (or very similar to) another instance of **Journey** (the **equals(Journey) : boolean** operation). As part of determining this, the **equals** operation on the **Journey** class will probably need to establish whether start and destination addresses are the same between two journeys. The responsibility for checking that one address is geographically the same as (or very similar to) another address does not lie with **Journey** though. That responsibility is delegated to the **equals(Address) : boolean** operation on the **Address** class.

Modelling by functional delegation is based on the examination of the interactions that will take place between classes in order to fulfil some required, usually externally visible, function in the required system. Given that interactions between classes are being modelled, this implies that three primary components of class models can be investigated using this modelling approach:

- Classes
- Operations
- Associations

Clearly interactions could not happen without classes. Any interaction will be initiated by some kind of probe or message from an external source. This initiation could be an event in an interface, a message passed from a class in another system, an interrupt trigger (for example, from a sensor), and so on. By establishing how a class will react to this initiation, the operations of a class begin to emerge. The operation that handles the initiation will probably not deal with all the processing within the method of that one operation. Instead other methods on the same class may be called to assist in processing the initiating message.

At some point it will probably be established that an operation in this first class needs to obtain information or trigger processing that is not part of the responsibilities of this class. The operation will therefore pass a message to the class that is responsible for that information or the operation required in order to delegate that functional responsibility. This passing of messages from one class to another indicates the presence of an association between those two classes. Thus a picture emerges of a set of classes collaborating through each other's operations to achieve some larger functional goal.

Arguably the most popular technique for simulating this collaboration between classes is the Class–Responsibility–Collaborators (CRC) card technique ((Beck & Cunningham, 1989) and (Wirfs-Brock, Wilkerson & Wiener, 1990)). A CRC card is a small piece of card or paper (say 15 cm by 8 cm). The name of a class is written at the top of the card. Down the left-hand side of the card, the responsibilities of the class are listed. Down the right-hand side the other classes with which this class collaborates are listed (Figure 4-23).

Journey	
Responsibilities	**Collaborations**
Check if another Journey is the same as this one	Address supports checking for equality between one address and another
Maintain details of a journey	

Figure 4-23: CRC card for Journey class

The analysts involved in the development of a system take one or more CRC cards. The collaborations necessary to fulfil a requirement under analysis are enacted by the team of analysts, with each analyst playing the part of the classes they hold. As this enaction continues, the need for a new functional responsibility or collaboration may be identified. A negotiation then takes place to agree the most appropriate existing or new class to be responsible for the identified responsibility.

Modelling with the functional delegation approach begins to blur the starting point in terms of UML notations. The interactions between classes that are captured through enacting techniques such as CRC cards should be modelled in notations such as the UML communication diagram or interaction sequence diagram (Chapters 9 and 10 respectively).

A class diagram could be produced first, using a conceptual modelling approach, to act as a foundation for interaction-based techniques. Alternatively, using functional-delegation-based modelling, the class diagram could be drawn as an abstraction of the static structure of the classes identified through the modelling of the interactions necessary to support a particular functional requirement.

4.5.3 Summary of Modelling Approaches

The modelling approach taken will depend upon whether the analyst intends to produce a conceptual class model or a specification or implementation model. For specification and implementation models, a modelling approach based on the dynamic interaction of classes and the functional delegation that takes place as part of that interaction may be appropriate. Producing a conceptual model clearly suggests a conceptual modelling approach. In the former case, a class diagram may be produced as an abstraction of the classes identified during the modelling of the dynamic behaviour required in the system.

In practice, the two approaches may be used alternately or side by side. The conceptual modelling identifies the key classes for the area of the system to be modelled in the CRC exercise, thus creating a set of class (CRC) cards with which to begin the functional delegation modelling.

In practice, the experienced analyst will use whichever modelling approach most suits the particular problem or subproblem in hand. It would not be unusual or unreasonable for the analyst to switch between approaches demanded by the task in hand. It is important, however, that the end product of the modelling phase, the class diagram, is a clear and consistent representation of the concepts modelled. There should be a clear distinction between a version of a class diagram that represents a conceptual model of the problem domain, and a class diagram that represents the specification or implementation of the required software to fulfil the requirements of the problem domain.

4.5.4 Object-Oriented Concepts

At this point it will be useful to identify and discuss some of the fundamental object-oriented concepts that are exemplified by the notational elements covered in the preceding sections.

4.5.4.1 *Operation Signature*

Collectively the name, parameter list and return type of an operation are referred to as its signature. It is quite possible (and not uncommon) to have several operations with the same name and return type in one class provided that each of those operations has a different parameter list from the other same-name operations. The different parameter lists can reflect the different contexts in which the operation can be called.

The ability to specify the signature of an operation without having to specify its method is a useful feature in object-oriented modelling. Knowing the name of the operation to pass a message to, the type to expect in return and the arguments that must be passed as parameters provides a clear specification for the collaboration between operations.

4.5.4.2   Encapsulation

The notion of an operation's signature and visibility leads to another key object-oriented concept, that of encapsulation. By specifying attributes as private and operations as public and by requiring correct use of operation signatures, a class hides the method (the implementation) of an operation from the calling operation.

This encapsulation has the significant benefit of limiting the scope of effect of changes to the implementation of an operation. So long as an operation continues to provide its specified functional capability and continues to conform to its signature then the implementation of the operation can be changed without having to change any of the other operations that call this operation. For example, the algorithm for performing a calculation or the data types used for the data items in that calculation could be changed without effect on the signature of the operation.

4.5.4.3   Object State

Objects are instances of classes. As classes have attributes and participate in associations it follows that, at any instant in time, an object will hold specific values for those attributes and will participate in specific occurrences of the associations with other objects.

Collectively, the set of attribute values and instances of associations with other objects is referred to as the state of an object. If the value of an attribute of the object changes or an association with another object is made or broken, then the state of the object may change. Not all changes to attribute values or associations result in a change of state. As part of the analysis process, the attributes whose values are significant to the state of an object will be identified. Modelling of the effect of state changes can be done in UML using the state machine diagram notation (see Chapter 12).

4.6   RELATIONSHIP WITH OTHER DIAGRAMS

The class diagram shows the static structure of the classes in a system. The class diagram can be used to describe the class model from three primary perspectives; conceptual, specification, and implementation. The modelling approach taken may depend on the particular perspective being modelled.

In an object-oriented system, the operations defined in the class diagram will interact with each other to fulfil the functional requirements of the system. The class diagram therefore relates to the functional requirements by virtue of the dynamic use of the static class and operation structure described by the class diagram (Figure 4-24).

The dynamic use of operations and hence classes is documented in communication diagrams or interaction sequence diagrams (Chapters 9 and 10 respectively). The functional requirements of the system are described by the use case diagram described in Chapter 3.

4.7   CLASS DIAGRAMS IN THE UNIFIED PROCESS

Chapter 3 discussed how the Unified Process is use case driven. Given this fundamental approach, the use of the class diagram in the Unified Process is heavily influenced by functional delegation concepts.

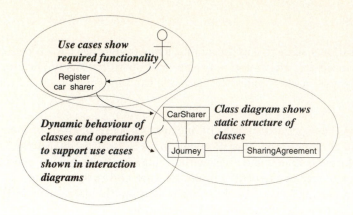

Figure 4-24: Class diagram relationships with other diagrams

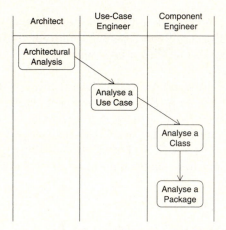

Figure 4-25: Analysis workflow as an activity diagram

In the analysis model, a conceptual class diagram is produced from the use case analysis (Figure 4-25). The class model produced in this activity can be structured using model management concepts such as packages.

The collaborations required between classes to provide the functional capability necessary to support requirements (in the form of use cases) will be examined in more detail as the design progresses. The consideration of these collaborations will clarify the specification of the classes in the class model (and hence class diagrams, Figure 4-26). As the specification becomes more and more firm, classes can be organized into subsystems of coherent and cohesive functional capability.

As the transition is made from specification to implementation, the subsystems act as a framework for identifying discrete functional components. These components can be built together to provide an identifiable and testable increment to the functional capability of the implemented system (Figure 4-27).

As components are implemented, they are incorporated into incremental builds of the implemented system for system testing.

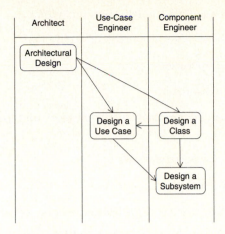

Figure 4-26: Design workflow as an activity diagram

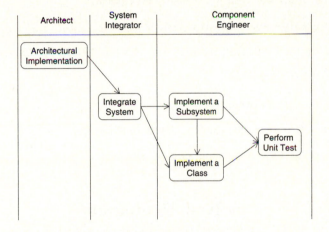

Figure 4-27: Implementation workflow as an activity diagram

Review Questions

4.1 What are the basic notational elements of class diagrams?

4.2 What are the purposes of drawing class diagrams?

4.3 Define what is meant by a class.

4.4 What is the most basic notation for a class?

4.5 Define what is meant by a class pathname.

4.6 What is the notation for showing a class pathname?

4.7 Define what is meant by an attribute.

4.8 What is the basic notation for an attribute?

4.9 What other properties can an attribute definition include?

4.10 What is the notation for these other properties of attributes?

4.11 Define what is meant by an operation.

4.12 Define what is meant by a parameter.

4.13 Define what is meant by 'passing parameters by reference' and 'passing parameters by value' and the difference between them.

4.14 What is the basic notation for an operation?

4.15 What is the notation for parameters of operations?

4.16 Define and illustrate how the phase of a project influences the level of detail shown for classes.

4.17 How can initial values for attributes be specified on a class diagram?

4.18 How can default values for parameters be specified on a class diagram?

4.19 Define the meaning of an association between two classes.

4.20 What is the basic notation for a labelled association?

4.21 What is the notation for indicating the role played by a class in an association?

4.22 What is meant by multiplicity?

4.23 What is the notation for multiplicity?

4.24 Which two elements of a class diagram can have multiplicity?

4.25 What are the two main ways of drawing class diagrams?

Solved Problems

4.1 In the Insurance subsystem for CarMatch, car sharers can take out an insurance policy. Each insurance policy will be part of a particular insurance company's scheme. What classes might there be here?

With the outline, conceptual information presented here, producing a conceptual approach seems to be the most sensible course of action. No class is needed for CarMatch. CarMatch is the context of this conceptual class model, rather than a component in it. The concepts mentioned in this example that could be modelled as classes seem to be: insurance policy, insurance company, insurance scheme and car sharer.

The insurance scheme was a slightly tricky concept to spot. The phrase '... *insurance policy will be part of a particular insurance company's scheme*' implied that a policy is part of a scheme run by a company. The mention of 'company's' was possessive, that is the company 'owns' the scheme.

4.2 The previous example identified classes as part of the Insurance subsystem. What should the proper UML names of the classes be? Use class pathnames to qualify where each class comes from.

As a first attempt, the class names might be InsurancePolicy, InsuranceCompany, InsuranceScheme and CarSharer. However, CarSharer has already been modelled as part of (what might be labelled) the CarSharer package. Thus a suitably qualified class name should be CarSharer::CarSharer.

Given that the other classes are part of the Insurance subsystem, then writing the names of the classes with their pathnames would give, for example, Insurance::InsurancePolicy. This replicates the subsystem context and it might be better to use the names Policy, Scheme and Company (Insurance::Policy, Insurance::Scheme and Insurance::Company when the class pathname is included).

4.3 The premium due for a policy will, in part, be based on the home address of the car sharer taking out the policy. The payment schedule for a policy will generate a number of transactions. The transactions are really part of the **Accounts** subsystem. Draw a class diagram that incorporates the classes from the **Insurance** subsystem, along with those just described. Include suitably labelled associations in your class diagram.

See Figure 4-28.

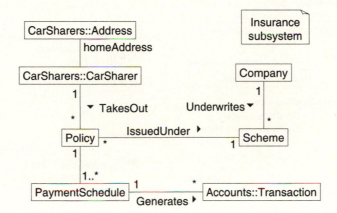

Figure 4-28: Class diagram showing classes and associations

4.4 The following questions test your understanding of multiplicity notations and have 'Yes' or 'No' answers. Answer the questions based on the multiplicities shown in Figure 4-28.

1. Can a policy be issued under three schemes?
2. Could we hold the details for a scheme without holding details for a policy issued under that scheme?
3. Does a car sharer have to take out an insurance policy?
4. Could a car sharer take out more than one policy?
5. Could we hold details of a policy that has not been taken out by a car sharer?

1. No, a policy can be issued under one and only one scheme.
2. Yes, a scheme does not have to have any policies issued under it (*=**0..***).
3. No, again *.
4. Yes, *.
5. No, a policy must be issued for a (1=1..1) car sharer.

4.5 For each insurance policy, it will be necessary to know the policy number, the start date of the policy, when it is due for renewal and the commission rate due on the premium for that policy. The start date is when the policy was first taken out. The renewal date is when the policy next expires. We also need to know how much money has been paid in total as payments against the policy (in the current year of the policy). The current year of the policy is defined as the renewal date minus one year.

Identify any attributes and operations here. Allocate them to appropriate classes. Suggest suitable types for the attributes, operations and any parameters for the operations. Add all these to your class diagram showing the visibility of both attributes and operations.

Clearly there are some attributes for Policy here. policyNumber, startDate, renewalDate, premium and commissionRate are all reasonably easy to identify and allocate to Policy. A derived attribute, startOfCurrentYear, has also been included for the start of the current payments year. The specification for this derived attribute can be given in a note. All these attributes could be private. Figure 4-29 shows all these attributes along with their visibility and the derived attribute specification.

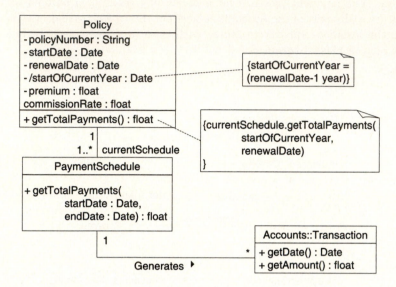

Figure 4-29: Class diagram showing attributes and operations

In terms of the operations, policy now has a getTotalPayments operation. The note which is included on the diagram indicates that the method for this operation should call the getTotalPayments operation on the instance of PaymentSchedule that is fulfilling the role of the currentSchedule. This call will use the values of startOfCurrentYear and renewalDate as the two Date values passed to currentSchedule.getTotalPayments when it is called.

The class diagram has been specified on the premise that each Transaction made against the currentSchedule PaymentSchedule will be polled to see if it falls into the specified year (using the getDate operation and comparing the value to startOfCurrentYear and renewalDate). If the Transaction does fall in the current year, then the value of the Transaction will be retrieved using the getAmount operation and will be added to a running total.

In terms of the getTotalPayments operation on Policy, the class diagram shows a specification of class functionality required to support that operation. The attributes and other possible operations needed to support this function are not shown. For example, Transaction will probably need to include attributes to represent the date and value of a transaction. These are not shown, yet.

Supplementary Problems

4.6 Read the case study material for VolBank in Chapter 1. List any classes that may exist in the description. Sketch out a first draft class diagram.

4.7 Here is part of a transcript of an interview between Said Hussain, a systems analyst, and Martin Page, Recruitment Director of VolBank. (Other excerpts from the same interview are used in subsequent exercises.)

Said Hussain: Can you tell me a little more about the information you need to hold about volunteers please?

Martin Page: Well, we need to know stuff like their name, and contact details. . .

SH: Contact details?

MP: Yes, their telephone number and email address. We also find it useful to know how old our volunteers are.

SH: So do you hold a volunteer's date of birth?

MP: Yes. That can be useful if we get two people with the same name.

SH: . . .

Identify any attributes (derived or otherwise) in this transcript and allocate them appropriately to your list of classes. If there are any derived attributes, include the specification of the derivation as a method note. Suggest and add to your diagram suitable types for each attribute.

4.8   From the interview excerpt that follows, identify suitable associations between the classes you have identified thus far. You should be able to work out the multiplicity of most of the associations as well. (Some of the classes identified in your answer to the previous question may not have attributes, but you should still include those classes in this question.)

Said Hussain: So how are volunteers related to volunteering opportunities?

Martin Page: Well, volunteers will bank time with us. That is time that they are available to work on volunteering projects. Based on their availability we can match them to suitable opportunities.

SH: OK. I can see how you have banked time for volunteers, what about the 'projects' end?

MP: Well, there's a similar set-up there with organizations banking time on the various different projects that they need help with.

SH: I see. Do you ever get projects that are set up by more than one organization?

MP: No, but an organization may have several projects on our books at any one time. Volunteers with banked time can work on several different projects. Each time they do some volunteer work it will only be for one project at a time though.

SH: . . .

Hint: Part of the last comment by Martin Page actually covers a couple of associations in one phrase. See if you can unpick the multiplicity of all the associations from it.

4.9   Based on the excerpt below, identify and allocate operations to support the functional requirements suggested in the transcript.

Said Hussain: How do you intend to match volunteers and volunteering opportunities?

Martin Page: Well, we'd like to be able to start with a volunteer and find the volunteering opportunities that they match against. We'd also like to be able to start with a volunteering opportunity and find any matching volunteers.

SH: Is the matching done on a time basis?

MP: At this stage, yes. I'd like to explore other possibilities later, but let's stick to just time matching for now.

SH: So you need to check whether the banked time for a volunteer is the same as the time required for a project?

MP: That would do it.

SH: . . .

4.10   Extending the operations you identified in the Problem 4.9, see if you can add a method note to specify how the operation to find volunteers for a project might work. You may need to use role names to clarify the roles played by classes in associations.

4.11 To match the banked time of a volunteer with the required time of a project, some kind of 'matches' operation will be needed. If you do not have such an operation already, add it to the most suitable class. What parameters might the operation take? What might its return type be?

4.12 If you have not done it already, add visibility indicators to all your attributes and operations.

CHAPTER 5

Class Diagram: Aggregation, Composition and Generalization

5.1 INTRODUCTION

Chapter 4 introduced the basic UML class diagram notation. Two elements of class diagrams, classes and associations, were covered. The creation of an association between two classes implies collaboration between those classes, achieved through message passing. In this chapter, the UML notation for some extensions to these basic modelling concepts is introduced.

5.2 PURPOSE OF THE TECHNIQUES

When drawing associations between classes on a class diagram, associations are sometimes created where the name of the association is something like **consists of** or **is made up of**. While there is clearly an association between the classes, it is desirable to be able to express the more subtle 'objects of this class consist of objects of that class' semantic. This is the purpose of *aggregation* and *composition*. Another notation for showing composition is also discussed in this chapter, namely the *composite object*.

73

The concept of *generalization* allows the inheritance of properties between classes. Properties inherited can be attributes, operations and participation in associations. Generalization within object-oriented systems is a very powerful construct that can promote the reuse of pre-written, pre-tested code with the resultant benefit of reduced code duplication.

5.3   AGGREGATION AND COMPOSITION NOTATION

In some cases, the associations between classes indicate that objects of one class are made up of, or consist of, objects of another class. UML has two special kinds of association that are part of the class diagram notation to show this: the aggregation association and the composition association. Both forms of relationship add a notational element to the existing notation for associations covered in Chapter 4. The general concept of aggregation is often referred to as being a *whole–part* or *part of* relationship. One class is a part of another class.

In effect, the aggregation and composition notations convey a property of the association they are used on. An aggregation (or composition) association is not a different type of class-to-class relationship. Rather, it is that the nature of the association being aggregation or composition is something that might be known and expressed about an association.

5.3.1   Aggregation

An aggregation association is used to indicate that, as well as having attributes of its own, an instance of one class may consist of, or include, instances of another class. The actual number of 'part' instances will depend on the multiplicity at the part end of the association. The use of aggregation does not override multiplicity specifications.

A typical example of aggregation would be in a manufacturing system where an assembly is made up of components. This association can be shown in the class diagram as an aggregation association rather than just as a plain association. (See Figure 5-1.)

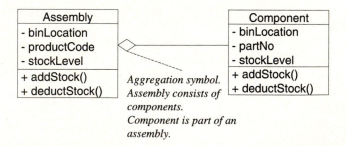

Figure 5-1: Example of aggregation notation

UML uses a unfilled diamond shape at the end of the association to show that this is an aggregation association. The diamond is always connected to the class that is the aggregate; the class that is made up of something else. The term *whole–part* is sometimes used to refer to aggregation associations. Instances of the class at one end of the association are the *wholes* and they are made up of *parts*, the instances of the class at the other end of the association. The aggregation diamond is always at the whole end of the association. In Figure 5-1, the **Assembly** is the *whole*, or aggregate, and the **Component** is the *part*.

5.3.2   Composition

Aggregation, then, implies a whole–part structure between two classes. This is also the job of the composition notation. However, a composition association also implies that the life-cycle of the 'part' cannot extend beyond the life-cycle of the 'whole'. For example, when the 'whole' end is deleted, any remaining 'part' components must also be deleted. In other words, in composition a part cannot exist without being part of a whole.

In aggregation this is not so. In aggregation a part is capable existence outside of whole–part association. In Figure 5-1, a component can exist without being part of an assembly. Similarly, an assembly could be created from components that exist prior to the creation of the assembly. Composition is, then, a stricter form of aggregation.

In UML, there are two notations for composition. The first notation is very similar to aggregation, except that the diamond is filled to show composition. This notation is arguably the more commonly used notation. Figure 5-2 shows an example of this notation, using classes from a publishing system. As the class diagram shows, a **Document** is composed of one **FrontMatter** component, one or more **Sections** and one **Index**. As the composition form of aggregation implies, the **FrontMatter**, **Section** and **Index** components do not exist without being part of a **Document**. Moreover, if a **Document** is deleted then all the constituent parts of that document will also be deleted.

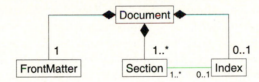

Figure 5-2: Composition in a publishing system

Where a component class (for example, **FrontMatter**, **Section** or **Index** in Figure 5-2) has a multiplicity with a lower bound of 1 (1..) then an instance of the component should be created when an instance of the composing whole is created. Where a component class has a multiplicity with a lower bound of 0 (0..) then an instance of the component may be created sometime after an instance of the composing whole has been created (but before the composing whole is deleted).

EXAMPLE 5.1   In the class diagram shown in Figure 5-2, does a **Section** have to be created when a **Document** is created? What about an **Index**?

SOLUTION   With a multiplicity of 1..* at least one **Section** must be created when a **Document** is created.

With a multiplicity of 0..1 it is not necessary to create an **Index** automatically when a **Document** is created.

The second notation for showing composition is by graphical containment; drawing one node inside another. This graphical containment can be used with either classes or instances of classes (objects).

Figure 5-3 shows the portrayal of composition using graphical containment. In general terms, the nature of the composition is the same as that shown in Figure 5-2. The multiplicity of the component objects in the composition is shown as a multiplicity clause after the class name (e.g. **Section** [1..*]).

The multiplicity of the component classes could also be shown as a number in the top-right corner of the class box. This approach may be more commonly used where the multiplicity upper and lower bounds

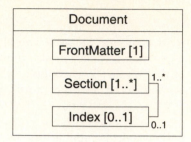

Figure 5-3: Composition using graphical containment

are the same. For example, using **4** as shorthand for **4..4**. For multiplicity shown in the top-right corner of the class box, the square brackets are not omitted.

Class composition shown using graphical containment can have association either within the composition or to other nodes outside the composition.

With containment-based composition (as shown in Figure 5-3) associations connecting the contained classes have additional constraints imposed upon them. Consider the association between **Section** and **Index**, for example. The association in Figure 5-3 links classes (and hence instances of classes) contained by the same document. In this context, the association could not be used to link a section to an index item which was held for a different document. However, this cross-document indexing would be perfectly permitted using the association-based composition shown in Figure 5-2. Thus modelling composition using graphical containment provides stronger constraints upon the model produced. As such, this approach should be used with care and attention.

Finally, object instances can be shown using graphical containment to define how those instances are structured and linked. Figure 5-4 illustrates this notation.

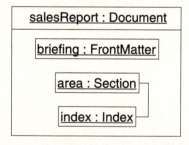

Figure 5-4: Object instances shown using graphical containment

5.3.3   Shared Paths

Where more than one association from a class shares the same aggregation or composition, those associations can be drawn using converging paths with a shared aggregation or composition symbol. Figure 5-5 illustrates an alternative way of drawing Figure 5-2 using converging paths.

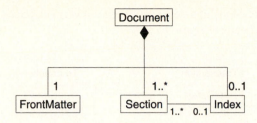

Figure 5-5: Aggregation with converging paths

5.4 GENERALIZATION NOTATION

Generalization is a different type of relationship between two classes. Generalization relationships therefore do not use the association notation considered in Chapter 4 (nor the aggregation and composition notations covered in this chapter).

The generalization relationship is sometimes described as being a *kind of* relationship. One class is a kind of another class. This is perhaps best illustrated with an example. Figure 5-6 shows an extended version of the ATM class diagram first used at the start of Chapter 4.

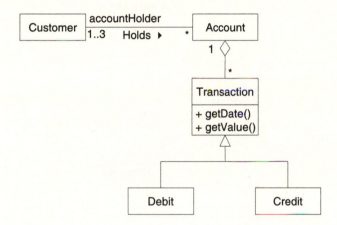

Figure 5-6: Extended ATM example with generalization

Generalization is shown in UML as a line ending with a triangular arrowhead at the class which is the more general type. For example, in Figure 5-6 there is a generalization relationship between **Debit** and **Transaction** and **Credit** and **Transaction**. These two generalizations have converging paths. These generalizations indicate that both **Debit** and **Credit** are kinds of **Transaction**. Every **Debit** is a kind of **Transaction**, every **Credit** is a kind of **Transaction**. **Transaction** is a generalization of **Debit** and **Credit**. Conversely, **Debit** and **Credit** are *specializations* of **Transaction**.

In a generalization relationship, the specializations are known as *subclasses* (or *subtypes*). In Figure 5-6, **Debit** and **Credit** are subclasses. The generalized class is known as the *superclass* (or *supertype*). In Figure 5-6, **Transaction** is a superclass.

Generalization allows the inheritance of the attributes and operations of a superclass by its subclasses. In the example shown in Figure 5-6, the **getDate** operation could be invoked on an instance of the **Debit** class as this operation is inherited from the **Transaction** class.

UML allows generalization relationships to have either convergent paths with a shared arrowhead or independent paths and arrowheads (Figure 5-7).

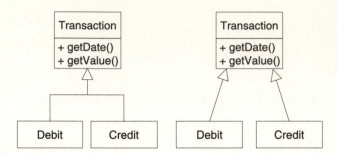

Figure 5-7: Different ways of drawing paths for generalization relationships

Generalization relationship structures are sometimes referred to as hierarchies, reflecting their tree-like structure. There is no reason why a generalization hierarchy cannot have several layers. In such a case a subclass could also be a superclass. Figure 5-8 illustrates a generalization hierarchy with an example taken from the Java graphics class library.

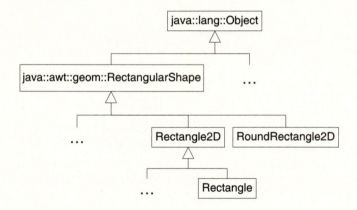

Figure 5-8: Generalization hierarchy in Java

As Figure 5-8 demonstrates, the subclass to superclass relationship could extend over several generalization relationships.

Any class that is a generalization of a class, regardless of the number of generalization relationships between the two classes, is known as an *ancestor* of that class. For example, in the generalization hierarchy shown in Figure 5-8, Object, RectangularShape and Rectangle2D are all ancestors of Rectangle. The immediate ancestor of a class may also be referred to as the *parent class* of that class.

Any class that is a specialization of a class, regardless of the number of generalization relationships between the two classes, is known as a *descendant* of that class. For example, in the generalization hierarchy shown in Figure 5-8, Rectangle, Rectangle2D and RectangularShape are all descendants of Object.

Where one class is a direct subclass or superclass of another class, then it is more appropriate to use the more specific term subclass or superclass (or parent class) than the more general term descendant or ancestor.

Figure 5-8 also illustrates that a class in one package can be a specialization of a class in a different package. For example, the **Object** class exists in the **java::lang** package whereas the **RectangularShape** class and its descendants exist in the **java::awt::geom** package.

The interpretation of generalization depends on the perspective of the class diagram. In a conceptual diagram, generalization shows that an instance of one class is also (and at the same time) an instance of another class. In a class diagram drawn from either a specification or implementation perspective, generalization implies a specification of the operations that must be supported by the subtype. For example, in Figure 5-6, the **Transaction**, **Debit**, **Credit** generalization structure implies that **Debit** and **Credit** must support the **getValue** and **getDate** operations. How they will implement these operations is not specified. The inheritance simply specifies that they must provide those operations. This means that the implementation of an operation and indeed the attributes used in that implementation may vary from subclass to subclass or between subclass and superclass.

As well as the inherited properties and participation in associations of the superclass, subclasses may extend the superclass with subclass-specific responsibilities. For example, for the Java classes shown in Figure 5-8, the **RoundRectangle2D** class from the Java environment provides a rectangle with rounded corners. The rounding arc to be used at the corners of the rectangle is supported by specific operations such as **getArcHeight()** and **getArcWidth()**, which return information about the size of the rounding arc used at the corners of the rectangle, as well as supporting operations, such as **getBounds()**, inherited from **RectangularShape**.

In Section 4.4.3 the idea of protected visibility for attributes and operations was introduced. The protected attributes and operations of a class can be accessed by any of the descendants of that class. Protected properties cannot be accessed by classes that are not part of this descendant 'family tree'. Where an ancestor class has private properties, these properties are not available to descendant classes, or any other class.

It should be noted that, while the *kind of* notion serves a useful purpose as an introductory way of thinking about generalization, it is potentially misleading. It may be a little too vague when considering the more precise specifications of the behaviour of operations on a class. A more correct and formal notion is one of substitutability. As this book is primarily about the UML notation, rather than object-oriented modelling *per se*, substitutability is not considered any further here.

5.4.1   Attribute redefinition

In Section 4.4.3.5, the use of property strings for attributes, operations and parameters was introduced. One of these properties was {**redefines**...}.

In the context of inheritance, the intention of this property becomes a little clearer. Figure 5-9 illustrates the use of the **redefines**... property string.

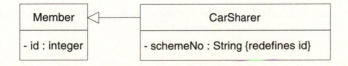

Figure 5-9: Use of {redefines...}

In this example, the **schemeNo** attribute redefines the **id** attribute of Member to become the identifier for instances of the subclass.

Where the name of a subtyped attribute or operation is the same as in the parent class, then the redefinition is implicit and does not need to be annotated.

5.5   MODELLING GUIDANCE

5.5.1   Aggregation and Composition

It is important not to use aggregation and composition too freely. For example, in the first edition of *UML Distilled*, Fowler & Scott (1999) discussed the example of an association between an organization and the employees of that organization. Is this relationship an aggregation? Should a class diagram suggest that an organization is an aggregation of employees?

The answer to the question of whether or not to use aggregation probably lies, in part, with the context of the whole and part ends of the association. What other associations do they participate in? What is the overall intention of the use of the classes in the intended system? Are they to be processed together (as an aggregation) or separately?

For example, the case of an assembly and components used earlier, where both assembly and components are processed together, suggests a closer, aggregation association rather than a 'normal' non-aggregated association. When modelling concepts such as the employees in a department or organization, where employees or departments may be processed independently of each other, a non-aggregated association might be more appropriate.

It should be remembered that aggregation is a conceptual notion. The way in which an association is implemented may be guided by the information represented on a class diagram for an association, but the implementation does not necessarily have to be ruled by that information. For example, Figure 5-10 shows two different ways of modelling an association, one with aggregation, one without. A possible implementation of the association as an attribute of **Assembly** is also shown. The implementation of the **Component** end as an attribute of type **Component** with multiplicity of * is valid for both associations.

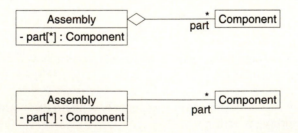

Figure 5-10: Implementation of associations with and without aggregation

Remember that the composition association implies coincident life-cycles, with the part object instances being deleted when the whole object is deleted. Given this coincident life-cycle and the discussion of aggregation above, it should be clear that composition should be used with even more caution than aggregation. If composition is used on an association, then it will carry very specific and more tightly constrained connotations for the implementor of the class model.

5.5.2   Generalization

When developing a class diagram, any generalization structures within the class model will need to be identified and modelled. This is desirable because, as stated above, generalization promotes reuse and improves specification and implementation consistency.

From the discussion in Section 5.4, it should be clear that the perspective of a class diagram will affect interpretation of the generalization used. When working on a conceptual model, an instance of a subclass will at the same time be an instance of the generalized superclass. On a specification- or implementation-level diagram, use of generalization represents a specification or description of the operations to be implemented in a subclass.

The modelling of generalization structures implies certain features in the code implemented for the specified model. Before modelling approaches are considered, it is worth reviewing these implications so that they can be borne in mind in the subsequent modelling discussion:

Extending class properties Subclasses will inherit the properties of their superclass(es). This means that an instance of a subclass will inherit all the attributes and operations of its superclass. This inheritance iterates up through to the top of the generalization tree. In addition to the inherited properties, a subclass can also possess attributes and operations specific to the subclass. In this way, the subclass can extend the specification of the superclass. Section 5.4 gave an example of this extension of inherited properties for the Java **RoundRectangle2D** class.

Redefining operations Operations can be inherited 'as is'. In other words, both the operation signature and the method of the operation are inherited from the superclass. It is also possible, and often desirable, for a subclass to redefine the method of an inherited operation in terms of the semantics of the subclass. The signature of the inherited operation remains the same, but the method of the operation is redefined by the subclass.

'Placeholder' operations In some cases, operations on a superclass may be included simply to ensure that subclasses provide that operation. The superclass itself has no method for the operation, but expects subclasses to provide a suitable method for the operation themselves. On the superclass, the operation in effect has the property **abstract**, though it is not normal to show this property explicitly in the class diagram. In this context, it would be normal to specify the whole superclass as being abstract. This would mean that there would be no instances of the class.

In certain circumstances generalization may be used where only one subclass is apparent in the class model at the time the model is developed (Figure 5-11). This can be done to promote future flexibility in the class model.

Figure 5-11: Generalization with a single subclass

For example, for Figure 5-11 the analyst may be reasonably sure that, in the future, it will be necessary to introduce other subclasses of **Employee**. Each of these subsequent subclasses will specialize the general behaviour of **Employee** in a suitable way. However, the analyst does not invent other subclasses that are not present or required in the current problem domain.

When producing a class model, generalization structures may be identified in either a 'bottom-up' or 'top-down' manner. These terms refer to the means of identifying generalization structures rather than the actual drawing of a generalization structure on a diagram.

5.5.2.1 Bottom-up Generalization

As class models are produced, classes that share properties, responsibilities and collaborations may become apparent. The common properties of those classes can be generalized into a suitable superclass and generalization relationships created between the new superclass and the original classes, which are now subclasses.

EXAMPLE 5.2   In the class model shown in Figure 5-12, both Car and Truck have shared responsibilities (the getRoadLicenceDue(): Date and renewRoadLicence() operations) and collaborations ('Fleet consists of cars' and 'Fleet consists of trucks'). How could the shared features be suitably generalized?

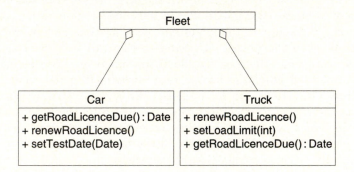

Figure 5-12: Classes sharing common responsibilities and collaborations

SOLUTION   The analyst infers that there is a high degree of commonality between Car and Truck and experiments with a superclass of Vehicle as a generalization of both of those classes. The result of this experimentation is shown in Figure 5-13.

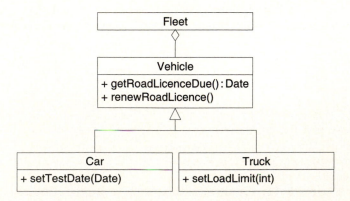

Figure 5-13: Common responsibilities and collaborations generalized into superclass

In this example, the generalization seems to be reasonable. Common responsibilities and collaborations can be generalized to the Vehicle class without compromising the semantics of the model. Care should be taken with this approach that generalization is not introduced simply as a means of graphical tidying of a complex diagram.

Generalization can be driven by the identification and appropriate abstraction of shared behaviour. Shared behaviour can be defined as the properties of classes (their attributes and operations) or participation in associations.

5.5.2.2   Top-down Generalization

As a class model develops, the analyst may become aware of the need to model classes that have common properties and share common participation in associations. Rather than modelling these classes with the associations seen in Chapter 4, the analyst can use generalization to show the inherent substitutability of one class for another.

EXAMPLE 5.3   Based on the following short transcript extract, identify any necessary classes and construct a suitable generalization relationship.

Janet Hoffner: We would like the system to be able to log which administrator changed records in a system. Is that possible?
Mick Perez: Sure. We are talking about administrators making changes to records here, aren't we?
JH: That's right...
MP: Oh, but there will be other users of the system who could change records in the future, won't there?
JH: I guess so, yes. Our initial plan is to have administrators do all the keyboard work, but I guess that won't always be the case.

SOLUTION   Mick's first thoughts on modelling the above requirements are shown in Figure 5-14. In this model fragment, the **AuditRecord** class is associated directly with the **Administrator** class. Mick has also shown an implementation of this association as an attribute on **AuditRecord**.

Figure 5-14: Possible class structure without generalization

Mick then realized that this structure would not be as resilient against future extension as it might be. If, in future, audit records need to be kept for other types of user, then both the **AuditRecord** and **Administrator** classes might need changing.

Mick decided that a better way to model this aspect of the model was to generalize the properties, responsibilities and collaborations of **Administrator** as an **Employee** class. Figure 5-15 shows the result of this enhancement.

Future changes to the class model, to add other **Employee** subclasses (for example, **Manager**, **Agent**), should not necessarily require amendments to the **AuditRecord** class.

5.5.3   Object-Oriented Concepts

As with the previous chapter, it will be useful to draw out some of the fundamental object-oriented concepts that are exemplified by the notational elements covered in the preceding sections.

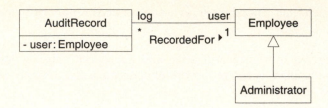

Figure 5-15: Class structure with generalization

5.5.3.1   Object State Revisited

In Chapter 4 the concept of object state was introduced. To recap, object state depends on the values of certain key attributes and the instances of associations with other objects. Changes to these attributes or associations may result in a change in the state of the object.

Generalization hierarchies are sometimes used to manage state-specific object behaviour. Consider the class diagram shown Figure 5-16. The **Booking** class delegates responsibility for handling how it behaves in any particular state to the **BookingStatus** class. The **BookingStatus** has two subclasses, **Provisional** and **Confirmed**.

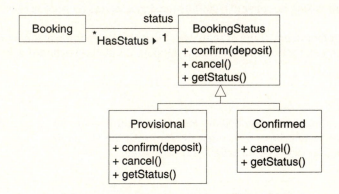

Figure 5-16: Illustration of state tracking using generalization

All the **BookingStatus** subclasses support the **getStatus** and **cancel** operations. The **Provisional** subclass also provides a **confirm** operation that allows a provisional booking to be confirmed (for example, with the payment of a deposit). The method of the **confirm** operation would replace the instance of **BookingStatus (Provisional)** with another instance (**Confirmed**). The **Confirmed** class does not provide this operation so a **Booking** in the **Confirmed** state cannot confirm itself again. The old instance would copy across all its attribute values to the new instance (barring any values affected by the state change) and then link the **Booking** object to the new state object (the new **Confirmed** object).

For more information on this object state pattern, see Chapter 17.

5.5.3.2   Polymorphism

The class diagram shown in Figure 5-16 also illustrates the object-oriented notion of polymorphism. Polymorphism is the ability of two operations with identical signatures to fulfil the same abstract functional requirement in different ways. For example, the **cancel** operation in **Provisional** might simply place the resource allocated to the booking back on an available list (for example, tables in a restaurant or seats in a cinema). However, the **cancel** operation on **Confirmed** must also handle the deposit that has been paid. For example, the **cancel** operation on **Confirmed** might free up the resource but be specified so as to require another customer to book (and pay a deposit upon) the resource before the deposit can be returned.

5.6 ADVANCED GENERALIZATION NOTATION

UML provides additional generalization notations that can be used to extend the commonly encountered generalization notation covered in Section 5.4.

5.6.1 Generalization Annotations

Generalization structures can be annotated with both constraints and set names. Constraints can be used in generalization structures where subclasses of the generalization are subject to certain semantic conditions. Set names can be thought of as role names for generalizations, either clarifying the semantics of the generalization or allowing multiple generalizations from one superclass.

5.6.1.1 Constraints

Generalization constraints can be either predefined or user-defined. The abstract UML notation for constraints is shown in Figure 5-17. The constraint itself is shown in curly braces ({...}). Where a shared path generalization is used, the constraint can be placed next to the superclass end of the generalization, near the triangular arrowhead. This notation is shown in the left-hand illustration in Figure 5-17. Where separate generalization paths are shown, a dotted line is drawn across the generalization paths for the subclasses to which the constraint applies. The name of the constraint is then written near the end of the dotted line. This notation is shown in the right-hand part of Figure 5-17.

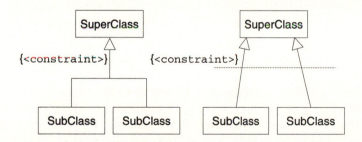

Figure 5-17: Generalization constraint notation

UML has predefined the following four common constraints.

incomplete The {*incomplete*} constraint indicates that, while some of the subclasses may have been specified, it is known that not all subclasses that exist in the problem domain have been specified. For example, Figure 5-18 shows how the specialization of **Mammal** into **Dog** and **Cat** does not specify all the specializations of **Mammal** that exist.

complete The {*complete*} constraint specifies that all the subclasses in that generalization have been defined within the class model. Remember, though, that not all those subclasses may be shown on one class diagram.

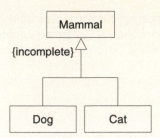

Figure 5-18: Illustrative example of incomplete constraint

disjoint In a disjoint generalization, an instance can only be an instance of one of the subclasses. If any of the subclasses acts as a superclass in a further generalization then the subclasses of that further generalization (the subsubclasses) cannot inherit from more than one of the disjoint subclasses.

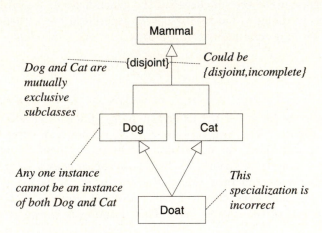

Figure 5-19: Illustrative example of disjoint constraint

The subclasses in a disjoint generalization have no commonality. An instance of one of the subclasses cannot be an instance of one of the other subclasses in the same disjoint constrained generalization.

Figure 5-19 illustrates this using **Mammal**, **Dog** and **Cat** again. The {disjoint} constraint specifies that one instance cannot be an instance of both **Dog** and **Cat**. The subclasses constrained to be disjoint are mutually exclusive. Given this disjoint nature, the constraint also specifies that no further class should inherit from both **Dog** and **Cat** (nor any other classes covered by the {disjoint} constraint).

The **Doat** class, which specializes **Dog** and **Cat** as shown in Figure 5-19, is incorrect as it specializes two classes governed by the same disjoint constraint.

overlapping An overlapping generalization is an approximate opposite of a disjoint generalization. An instance may be an instance of more than one subclass in the generalization. If any of the subclasses acts as a superclass in a further generalization then the subclasses of that further generalization (the subsubclasses) can inherit from more than one of the disjoint subclasses (Figure 5-20).

The {overlapping} constraint specifies that one instance can be an instance of both **WindPoweredBoat** and **MotorPoweredBoat**. The subclasses constrained to be overlapping are not mutually exclusive. Given this overlapping nature, the constraint also specifies that it is acceptable for

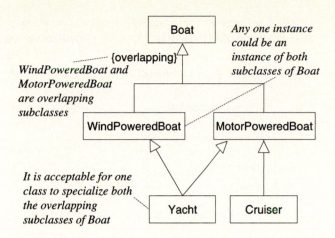

Figure 5-20: Illustrative example of overlapping constraint

further subclasses to inherit from both **WindPoweredBoat** and **MotorPoweredBoat** (and any other classes covered by the {**overlapping**} constraint).

The **Yacht** class, which specializes both **WindPoweredBoat** and **MotorPoweredBoat** as shown in Figure 5-20, is perfectly acceptable as it specializes two classes governed by the same overlapping constraint.

5.6.1.2   Set Names

Set names on generalization relationships are similar to the notion of role names of associations. The set name provides a name for the generalization. The name of a set must be different from the following properties of the superclass:

1. the names of any associations starting at or ending at the superclass;
2. the attributes of the superclass.

The set name for a generalization is shown near the triangular arrowhead for a shared path, or near each generalization relationship for separate paths. Figure 5-21 shows set names for two different generalization structures, one for separate paths, one for shared paths.

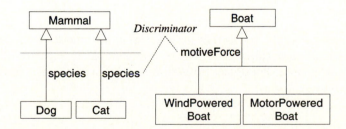

Figure 5-21: Notation for generalization set names

Set names can be particularly useful where a class is the superclass for two or more different generalization structures. In this situation, the set name allows the different generalizations to be identified.

Figure 5-22 illustrates the use of set names and constraint names together. The Product class is a superclass for four subclasses, PremiumProduct, StandardProduct, OrderProduct and StockProduct.

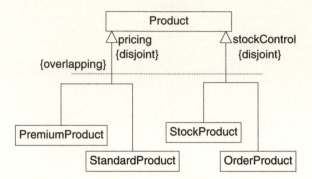

Figure 5-22: Use of set names with multiple generalizations

The implication might be that the pricing subclasses will introduce properties related to processing price-based functionality (for example, discount, markup, calculateProfit). Similarly, the stockControl subclasses might introduce properties related to processing stock-based functionality (for example, stockLevel, reorderLevel, leadTime, reorderStock).

Both the pricing and stockControl generalizations are constrained as disjoint. This means that a Product can be either a PremiumProduct or a StandardProduct, but not both. Similarly, a Product can be either a StockProduct or an OrderProduct, but not both.

The two generalizations, however, have an overlapping constraint specified across them. This constraint indicates that a Product can be one of the pricing products and one of the stockControl products at the same time. Thus an instance could be:

1. an instance of Product, but not specialized as either a pricing product or a stockControl product;
2. a PremiumProduct, but not specialized as a stockControl product;
3. a StandardProduct, but not specialized as a stockControl product;
4. a StockProduct, but not specialized as a pricing product;
5. an OrderProduct, but not specialized as a pricing product;
6. a PremiumProduct and a StockProduct;
7. a PremiumProduct and an OrderProduct;
8. a StandardProduct and a StockProduct;
9. a StandardProduct and an OrderProduct.

Finally, it should be noted that the convergent path notation for inheritance relationships can only be used for relationships which share the same set name. For example, in Figure 5-22 it would be incorrect to draw the StandardProduct and StockProduct inheritance relationships with convergent paths as they represent different set names.

5.6.2   Abstract Superclasses

In a generalization structure it may be possible for an object to be an instance of one or more of the subclasses of the generalization, or an instance of the superclass of the generalization. For example, an organization may employ a person without assigning that person a particular role or job function. Thus, for the generalization structure shown in Figure 5-23, it would be possible to have instances of both subclasses (**Administrator** and **Manager**) and instances of the superclass **Employee**. The latter would represent employees with no specific role as either **Administrator** or **Manager**.

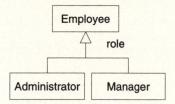

Figure 5-23: Generalization with instances of superclass permitted

If the opposite were true, and the organization insisted that all staff were allocated a role, then there would be no direct instances of the **Employee** superclass.

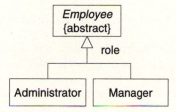

Figure 5-24: Generalization with abstract superclass

To reflect this requirement in the class diagram, the {**abstract**} property in the class name compartment can be used to indicate that the *Employee* class will never have any direct instances (Figure 5-24). The name of an abstract class is shown in italics.

Review Questions

5.1 Define what is meant by aggregation.

5.2 How do aggregation associations differ from 'normal' associations?

5.3 Define what is meant by composition.

5.4 How does composition differ from aggregation?

5.5 What is the UML notation for aggregation?

5.6 What are the two UML notations for showing composition?

5.7 Why might aggregation (or composition) be referred to as a *whole–part* relationship?

5.8 Why might generalization be referred to as a *kind of* relationship?

5.9 What is the UML notation for generalization?

5.10 What are the two UML path notations that can be used for generalization?

5.11 What are generalization constraints? What four generalization constraints are pre-defined by UML? Give your own example of a generalization constraint in use.

5.12 Give your own example of the use of a generalization set name.

5.13 What, arguably, is a more concise way of showing a constraint on a generalized association?

5.14 Why might aggregation and composition associations be misleading on a class diagram?

5.15 Describe the process of top-down identification of generalization structures.

5.16 Describe the process of bottom-up identification of generalization structures.

Solved Problems

AGGREGATION AND COMPOSITION

5.1 Here is an excerpt from a transcript of an interview between Mick Perez and Janet Hoffner. Based on the transcript, identify any aggregation associations.

Mick Perez: Just remind me, what kind of things do you need to know about the start and destination of each journey?

Janet Hoffner: We'd want to know the building name and number, the apartment number, the street, locality, town or city, county and postal code or zip code. We'd also want to hold similar information for the home address of a car sharer as well.

MP: OK. Didn't you say that the journey start and destination address will be used to match up possible shared journeys?

JH: Yes—interesting point that. I'm not quite sure how you'll do this. We want to be able to establish whether two addresses are close enough to each other to be able to consider them a match for a shared journey. For example, two people may want to get from a start destination on adjacent corners of two different blocks to destination addresses in different floors of the same building. A person looking at the addresses would know that the addresses are similar enough to be a match, but in terms of just text of the addresses, they look completely different.

MP: ...

Mick could see that address information was needed for car sharers. An address would need to be held as a car sharer's home address and for the start and destinations of each journey. Given that address information would be kept for these three requirements, Mick modelled an **Address** class with associations to **CarSharer** and **Journey**. Mick assigned all the address attribute information required by CarMatch and an **equals** operation, to establish whether one **Address** could be considered the same as another, to the **Address** class. Figure 5-25 shows Mick's class diagram for this part of the class model.

In terms of processing, the home address (**Address**) of a **CarSharer** would always be processed with the **CarSharer** for which the **Address** was created. Similarly, the **startAddress** and **destinationAddress** of a **Journey** would always be processed as part of the processing carried out on a **Journey**. Given this, Mick decided that **Address** was a part of **CarSharer** (whole) in the form of the **homeAddress** of a **CarSharer**. Similarly, **Address** was a part of **Journey** (whole) in the form of the **startAddress** and **destinationAddress** of a **Journey**. For this reason, Mick modelled the associations from **Address** as aggregations in Figure 5-25.

To support the required functionality **Address** would be accessed from **CarSharer** and **Journey**. It would not be necessary to navigate from an **Address** back to either the **CarSharer** or the **Journey** to which the **Address** relates. Mick used association navigability to show this.

To indicate the implementation of these associations, Mick put **startAddress** and **destinationAddress** attributes in **Journey** and a **homeAddress** attribute in **CarSharer**. All these address attributes were of type **Address**. His class diagram for this part of the system is shown in Figure 5-25. Figure 5-25 includes both the aggregation associations and the implemented attributes (**homeAddress**, **startAddress**, **destination-Address**).

5.2 Mick then considered the nature of the **Address** class more carefully. Was the intention to create a new address for every car sharer or journey? If a car sharer registered one or more journeys

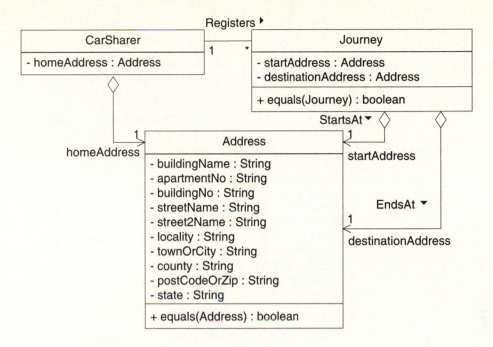

Figure 5-25: Class diagram with Address aggregation

from his or her home address, would that count as the same occurrence of an address or different occurrences of addresses that happen to have the same state (attribute values)?

(As Mick knew he had not considered this in enough detail yet, he had left the multiplicity of the Journey–Address associations blank at the Journey end in the class diagram in Figure 5-25.)

Mick decided that each address would probably be a different occurrence. The address matching would work in much the same way regardless of whether addresses were shared or not.

If addresses were shared, that is, if one address occurrence could be used by more than one car sharer or journey, then look-up facilities would be needed in the Address class. This would be necessary to allow new instances of CarSharer and Journey to find out if there was an existing address that was their address. Thus Mick deduced that the most straightforward approach would be to use different occurrences of Address for every car sharer's home address and the start and destination of each Journey.

Given this decision, Mick then knew that the life-cycle of an Address instance would be coincident with the CarSharer or Journey for which the Address instance was created. An instance of Address would only come into being when created by the CarSharer or Journey that used that Address and would cease to exist when the CarSharer or Journey that used it was deleted.

Thus, the aggregations could actually be shown as compositions. Furthermore, the multiplicity of the associations between Journey and Address was now clear. These clarifications are shown in Figure 5-26.

GENERALIZATION

Mick then turned his attention to modelling some of the specification for how one Journey might be matched against another. Reviewing his class model thus far, Mick noted that the Journey class delegated responsibility for working out whether one address was the same as another to the Address class. This delegation gave rise to the equals operation on Address.

Mick now had to establish how an address would work out whether it is the same as another. It has already been mentioned that a simple String match is neither accurate enough, nor powerful enough, to match similar addresses with each other. Mick therefore decided to look at bringing in some Geographical

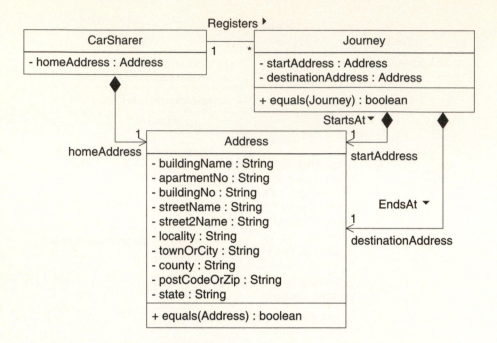

Figure 5-26: Class diagram with address composition

Information System (GIS) capability. A GIS would give Mick the ability to work out when one address is geographically close to another.

5.3 Mick discussed processing addresses with Jan Cusack, a member of his team who knew about Geographical Information Systems (GIS).

Jan Cusack: I've been looking at the address matching you were talking about.

Mick Perez: Great—do you have any pointers for me?

JC: Well, there are three 'standard' geolocating standard class libraries that you might need to work with. One is the United Kingdom Ordnance Survey (OS) map reference-based system, another is based on latitude and longitude, and the third is the 'Tiger' referencing system.

MP: Do they all do the same kind of thing?

JC: Broadly speaking, yes. What you'd need to do is wrap up access to each of those class libraries with your own subclasses.

MP: I guess that when it comes to matching locations with each other, I've got to look at converting between a format I can use in the CarMatch system and the format used in one of the standards you mentioned.

JC: I guess so, you'll probably want to provide an 'equals' to do the checking between one location and another.

MP: Great, I'll have a go at modelling that. Can I bounce my model back off you later on?

JC: No... Only joking—of course you can.

Mick knew that he could create his own classes that inherited functions from classes available in the three different GIS class libraries. His own classes could then extend that functionality to provide the operations he needed to match one address with another. However, Mick also realized that he would probably need to manage the conversion between the internal representation formats used by each of the different GIS systems and an external format, and vice versa. Mick sketched out some thoughts based on this discussion (Figure 5-27).

This diagram is quite complex. Looking at the different aspects of it, a number of features are of interest. Mick has used a model management notation to show use of other packages by his own (Figure 5-28).

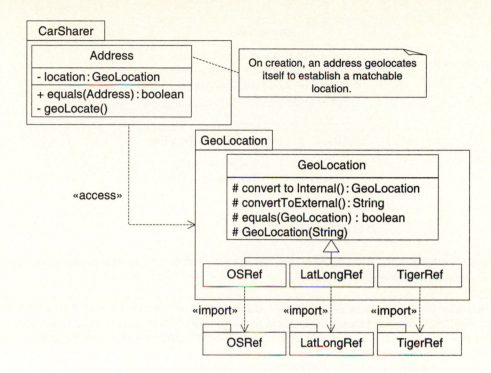

Figure 5-27: **Address** modelling with generalization

Three different class libraries (packages) are imported. Mick's three classes GeoLocation::OSRef, Geo-Location::LatLongRef and GeoLocation::TigerRef will eventually be specializations of suitable classes in each of the three imported packages. These classes have not been identified yet. Mick is assuming that they are available based on what Jan told him.

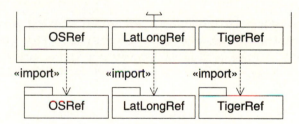

Figure 5-28: **Package imports**

Mick's GeoLocation package is accessed by the CarSharer package (the «access» dependency). This indicates Mick's intention to create an association between the Address class and the GeoLocation class. The access dependency indicates that classes in the CarSharer package will be able to access the publicly available classes within the GeoLocation package.

Within the GeoLocation package, OSRef, LatLongRef and TigerRef are specializations of GeoLocation. Geo-Location specifies three operations with protected visibility. The three subclasses will inherit these operations (Figure 5-29).

Mick's intention is that the equals operation will use the convertToInternal and convertToExternal operations inherited by the OSRef, LatLongRef and TigerRef subclasses to hide the system-specific details of each of the three different GIS systems. Each subclass, OSRef, LatLongRef and TigerRef, will implement convertToInternal and convertToExternal so as to encapsulate the attributes and other operations inherited from the specific GIS system (of the same name) indicated by the «import» dependency.

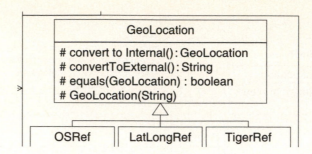

Figure 5-29: Generalization

Supplementary Problems

5.4 Here is another excerpt from the interview between Said Hussain, a systems analyst, and Martin Page, Recruitment Director of VolBank.

Said Hussain: Can we go back to this idea of banked time you mentioned earlier? You seem to be saying that banked time is recorded for both volunteers and organizations with volunteering opportunities.
Martin Page: That's right. We want to be able to match up the banked time for a volunteer with the required time that has been banked for a volunteering opportunity.
SH: So does banked time exist for anything else?
MP: No, only for volunteers and opportunities. We really consider a volunteering opportunity in terms of the time requirements it has.
SH: What about volunteers?
MP: Yes, I guess volunteers are considered to be of interest to us in terms of the volunteering time that they have banked.
SH: ...

Reconsider the associations you developed in Problem 4.8. What potential is there for adding the aggregation concept and notation to those associations? What about composition? Justify any decision you make between aggregation, composition and no aggregation at all. Amend your class diagram to include aggregation or composition where you have decided to include it.

5.5 The transcript below moves on to address some of the issues of generalization in the VolBank case study.

Said Hussain: Can we move on from the recording of details for volunteers, banked time and volunteering opportunities? I'd like to look at what you do in terms of assigning volunteers to opportunities.
Martin Page: OK. Well, once we've got a match, we allocate volunteers to projects, I mentioned that already.
SH: Project?
MP: A volunteering opportunity.
SH: OK, could there be a team of people working on a project?
MP: A team, yes. Though we do also have individuals working on other projects. Oh, and on some projects, we have a team large enough to warrant having one or more team leaders.
SH: Go on.
MP: Well, we need to know what role a volunteer is playing in a project.
SH: So you're saying that there are different kinds of assignment?
MP: Just so. There is no reason why one volunteer could not work on one project as an individual or team leader, and on another as a team member. It varies from project to project.

From the transcript above, identify a possible generalization. Amend your class diagram appropriately.

5.6 VolBank are considering introducing a profile points scheme. In the scheme, volunteers build up a points profile. The more volunteer work they do, the more points they get. The points can be redeemed as a discount on prices at certain retail outlets that are supporting the scheme. All assignments to volunteering opportunities will need to support profile points calculation. The way in which profile points are calculated will vary depending on the type of assignment. Team members on a project will have profile points calculated based on hours worked and the 'team member rate', which is the same for all team members. For team leaders, profile points will be calculated based on hours worked, team size and the 'team leader rate'; again, this will be the same for all team leaders. Finally, for volunteers working as individuals on a project, profile points are to be calculated on hours worked, the 'individual bonus adjustment' and the 'individual rate'.

Amend your generalization superclass and subclasses to include the responsibilities indicated in the passage above.

5.7 Consider the generalization you have created in Problem 5.5. Could you apply any of the predefined UML constraints to the generalization? Explain your reasoning.

5.8 For the generalization you have created in Problem 5.5, suggest some suitable set names for the generalization structure.

5.9 In the generalization you have created in Problem 5.5, is the superclass abstract? If so, why? If not, why not? What circumstances affect your conclusion?

CHAPTER 6

Class Diagram: More On Associations

6.1 INTRODUCTION

The basic notation and semantics of UML associations were introduced in Chapter 4. Two types of textual labelling can be used with associations: the association name, which indicates the basic nature of the association, and role names, which can be used explicitly to describe the nature of the participation of a class in an association.

Examples of association names used in this book included the **Holds** association between **Customer** and **Account** (Figures 4-1 and 5-6), and the **Registers** association between **CarSharer** and **Journey** (Figure 4-18). Example role names used in this book up to this point include the **accountHolder** role played by **Customer** in the **Customer–Account** association (Figures 4-1 and 5-6).

Association multiplicity was introduced as a means of indicating the range of participation of a class in an association as viewed from the other end of the association. Common multiplicity clauses on associations are 1 and *, short for 1..1 and 0..* respectively.

Chapter 5 extended the basic association notation with aggregation and composition. Both these extensions to the association are used to indicate that the nature of the association between two classes is one of *whole–part*. The composition association is a more strict form of association, implying coincident life-cycles. In a composition association, when the whole class in the association is destroyed, then any association part classes are also destroyed.

This chapter covers the remaining UML notations for associations. These notations represent more specialized semantics which may be used to a greater or lesser extent in the modelling process. All the notations in this chapter are, arguably, less common than the notations covered thus far. This lower rate of use is the primary reason for considering these notations in this separate chapter.

In order to illustrate these notations, the examples used in this chapter may present elements of the common case studies in a slightly differently way to other chapters. Where this has been done, every effort has been made to point out those differences.

6.2   ASSOCIATION END NOTATIONS

The notations covered in this section are all used to add specific meanings to the end of an association where it joins a class. Role names are one such association end notation that has already been covered in Chapter 4. A role name specifies the role played in an association by the class at the end of the association where the role name appears. Figure 6-1 shows an example that was used earlier in this book.

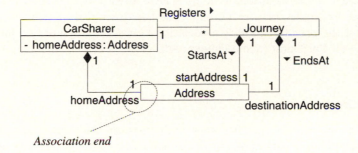

Figure 6-1: Role name notation

Figure 6-1 shows how the **Address** class plays the role of **homeAddress** in the unnamed association with **CarSharer**. **Address** also plays the roles of **startAddress** and **destinationAddress** in the **starts at** and **ends at** associations, respectively, between the **Journey** and **Address** classes.

6.2.1   Visibility

A role name can be prefixed with a visibility indicator. Visibility was introduced in Section 4.4.3. Remember that visibility can be shown with the keyword **package** (~), **private** (or the symbol -), **public** (+), or **protected** (#).

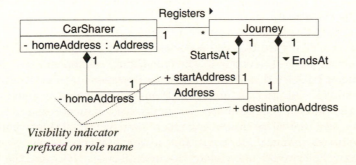

Figure 6-2: Association visibility shown with role names

The visibility annotation on an association end can be used only as a prefix to a role name. That is to say, association visibility can be used only where a role name has been added to the association end. Figure 6-2 shows an example of the association visibility notation.

EXAMPLE 6.1   What visibility indicators are used in Figure 6-2?

SOLUTION   The Address class has private visibility as viewed from CarSharer in the CarSharer–Address association (- homeAddress). The Address class has public visibility as viewed from Journey in both the starts at and the ends at associations between Journey and Address (+ startAddress and + destinationAddress).

The indicator specifies the visibility of the class as perceived when traversing the association towards the role name and visibility indicator. For example, in Figure 6-2, the homeAddress (Address) for a CarSharer should be considered as private. The visibility indicator provides guidance to the designer about how to implement the association. Examples have already been given of the implementation of associations. In those examples, private visibility has been assumed. For example, Figure 6-2 shows the implementation of the private visibility association between CarSharer and homeAddress (Address) as a private attribute on CarSharer (homeAddress : Address).

6.2.2   Changeability

The changeability of an association specifies whether an instance of a class can add or delete instances of the class at the changeability constrained end of the association after it has been created or initialized. The changeability can be **changeable**, **frozen** or **addOnly** and is shown as a constraint. Figure 6-3 illustrates the changeability notation, using the document publishing example seen in Section 5.3.2.

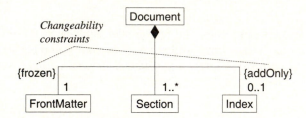

Figure 6-3: Association changeability constraints

If no changeability constraint has been specified, then a default value of {changeable} is assumed. For example, in Figure 6-3 the composition association between Document and Section has no changeability constraint and so is assumed to be {changeable}. This association is constrained only by the composition and the multiplicity specifications.

The class diagram shown in Figure 6-3 also specifies that an instance of a Document should create one FrontMatter component when it is created. The FrontMatter component created when the Document instance is created cannot be deleted without deleting the Document instance itself. No other FrontMatter components can be added. At first, it might be thought that there is some overlap between the multiplicity of 1 and the {frozen} changeability. The multiplicity indicates that a Document must have a FrontMatter component, and that there can never be more than one FrontMatter component per Document. However, without the frozen changeability constraint, it would be permissible to replace one FrontMatter instance with another. This would not violate the multiplicity. However, the frozen changeability constraint specifies that the FrontMatter instance created with the Document instance cannot be replaced. The association between the two original instances is {frozen}.

Finally, the association between **Document** and **Index** has an {**addOnly**} changeability constraint. Taken in conjunction with the multiplicity and composition, this specifies that a **Document** instance can be created without an instance of **Index** being created at the same time. The **0..** part of the multiplicity allows this. When the **Document** instance is destroyed, then the **Index** instance must also be destroyed. The coincident life-cycle of the composition association specifies this. The {**addOnly**} changeability constraint specifies that an **Index** component can only be added to a **Document**. Once that component has been added, it cannot be removed. Taken together with the upper bound of the multiplicity (**..1**), this means that once an **Index** component has been added for a **Document**, it cannot be replaced with another **Index** component.

6.2.3   Ordering

Where the target of an association has a multiplicity with an upper bound greater than one, it may be necessary to specify whether or not those associated instances have an explicit order.

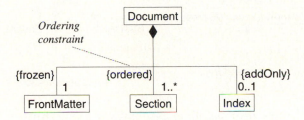

Figure 6-4: Association ordering constraint

Figure 6-4 shows that the **Sections** within a **Document** should be ordered. If an ordering constraint is omitted then the association end is assumed to be {**unordered**}.

As with other constraints that have already been covered, the ordered constraint should be considered as a specification. The specific mechanism used to implement the ordering is left to the designer of the implementation classes.

Another constraint, {**sorted**}, may be used in a class diagram drawn from an implementation perspective. The sorted constraint refines the ordered constraint. The sorted constraint implies that the ordering is based on the state of the ordered instances. Again, the actual sorting mechanism is not specified by the {**sorted**} constraint.

6.2.4   Navigability

It is usually assumed that associations can be followed in either direction (indeed this is the UML guideline). This implies that messages can be passed in either direction between two classes connected by an association. For example, in Figure 6-5, the association between **CarSharer** and **Address** specifies a path for **CarSharer** to send a message to **Address** and also a path for **Address** to send a message to **CarSharer**.

This open and general interpretation is fine at the conceptual level, and provides for a general understanding of the class model. However, the design and implementation of a bi-directional association carries an overhead compared to the implementation of an association that is only ever navigated in one direction. This overhead is discussed in more detail in the modelling guidance section for navigability (Section 6.7.4).

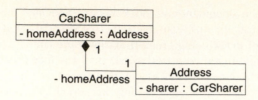

Figure 6-5: Unspecified association navigability

In UML, an association can be annotated as being navigated in a particular direction by adding an arrowhead to an association to indicate the direction of navigation. Figure 6-6 illustrates this notation.

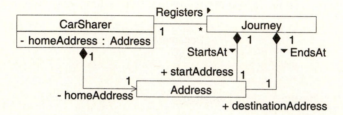

Figure 6-6: Explicit association navigability

In Figure 6-6 the analyst has indicated that the association between **CarSharer** and **Address** is navigated only from **CarSharer** to **Address**. More significantly, the annotation shows that it is not necessary to implement navigability from **Address** to **CarSharer**.

Navigability arrows can be shown on neither, one or both ends of an association. By convention, omission of navigability implies bi-directional navigability. However, in some software development teams it may be standard practice to implement associations with multiplicity of 1–* (for example, the **registers** association between **CarSharer** and **Journey**) as navigable only from the 1 end (**CarSharer**) to the * end (**Journey**). If such a practice is the standard interpretation, then showing navigability arrows for both directions of an association can be used to require explicit bi-directional navigability.

Conversely, association ends can also be annotated as being non-navigable. This notation places a cross on the end of the association which cannot be navigated to, as shown in Figure 6-7.

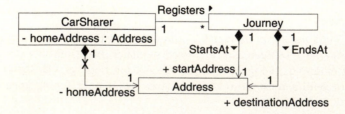

Figure 6-7: Prohibited association navigability

In Figure 6-7, the analyst has indicated that the association between **Address** and **CarSharer** must not be navigated in that direction.

6.2.5 Properties

As with attributes, an association end can be annotated with a property string. The following properties can be applied to an association end:

- {subsets *name*}
- {redefines *name*}
- {union}
- {ordered}
- {bag}
- {sequence}, or {seq}

The meaning of each of these property strings is analogous to the corresponding attribute property string (Section 4.4.3.5). If the association end is navigable (i.e. can be treated as an attribute) then the {readOnly} and {composite} properties of attributes can also be applied to the association end.

6.3 QUALIFIERS

An association qualifier at the source end of an association specifies a means of identifying zero, one or more of the class instances at the target end of an association.

The UML notation for a qualifier is shown in Figure 6-8. An association qualifier is an attribute list consisting of one or more attributes. Each attribute can be listed as the attribute name on its own, or in the form **name : type**. The qualifier appears in a box that should be slightly smaller than the class symbol and placed adjacent to the class symbol.

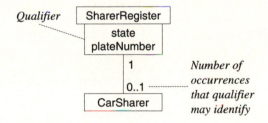

Figure 6-8: Illustration of notation for qualifiers

The multiplicity at the target end of the qualified association indicates the number of instances that the qualifier may identify. In Figure 6-8, the multiplicity at the target (**CarSharer**) end of the association is **0..1**. The qualifier consists of two attributes, **state** and **plateNumber**. If values are known for both of these attributes then, according to the multiplicity given, the qualifier will identify either none or one **CarSharer**.

The interpretation of the none (**0..**) depends on the context of the model. In this case it might suggest that state and plate number may not be constrained to be the state and plate number of a car owned by a registered car sharer.

6.4   ASSOCIATION CLASSES

In the previous section, the notion of a qualifier being an attribute of the association was introduced. This is not the only case in which it might be necessary to hold information about the association between two classes. The need to hold contextual information about an association between two classes is not uncommon. Indeed, in an object-oriented system, it may be necessary to delegate functional responsibility, in the form of operations, to an association.

In UML, attributes and operations can be added to an association using the association class notation. Figure 6-9 shows the UML notation for an association class. Association classes are shown with the same notation as other classes on a class diagram (see Chapter 4).

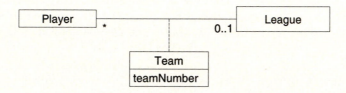

Figure 6-9: Association class notation

An association class and the association it represents are semantically the same thing. The association class and the association itself are, however, shown separately in the UML notation. The association class is attached to the association that it represents by a dashed line.

As the association class is the same model artefact as the association, the name of the association class and the association itself are the same. The name of the association can be shown on the association or on the class (as a valid class name).

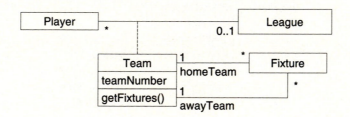

Figure 6-10: Association class participating in an association

In terms of the underlying semantics of UML, an association class is a specialization of a class and an association. As a specialization of class, association classes may participate in the same types of relationships as other classes (for example, as a superclass in a generalization or in an association). Figure 6-10 illustrates this with the Team association class playing the roles of homeTeam and awayTeam in two associations with Fixture.

6.5   DERIVED ASSOCIATIONS

The notation for derived attributes was discussed in Chapter 4. The UML notation also allows the specification of derived associations. The notation for derived associations is illustrated in Figure 6-11.

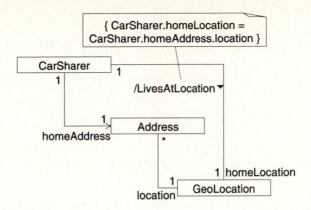

Figure 6-11: Derived association notation

As with derived attributes, the name of a derived association is prefixed with a / character. The derivation of the association can be shown as a constraint on the class diagram. Figure 6-11 shows a derived association labelled **/LivesAtLocation** between **CarSharer** and **GeoLocation**. The specification of the derivation is shown in a method note, which is attached to the association label.

The specification in Figure 6-11 shows that the **homeLocation** role in the **lives at location** association can be derived from the associations between **CarSharer** and **Address**, and **Address** and **GeoLocation**. As with derived attributes, the appropriate use of role names can be helpful in formulating a derivation specification.

EXAMPLE 6.2   How does the multiplicity of the associations traversed in the specification of a derived association affect the multiplicity of the derived association itself?

SOLUTION   Looking from the class at the start of the derived association, and traversing to the class at the end of it, the upper and lower bounds of the multiplicity should reflect the highest and lowest multiplicity bounds encountered across all steps of the derivation. For example, in the example shown in Figure 6-11, the lowest multiplicity found in both the **CarSharer–Address** and **Address–GeoLocation** associations is 1... Similarly, the highest multiplicity bound encountered is ..1. Therefore, the multiplicity at the **homeLocation** end of the **lives at location** association is 1..1 (or 1). The same multiplicity is derived by traversing the associations from **GeoLocation** to **CarSharer**.

If the specification had traversed an association with an upper bound of ..* and an association with a lower bound of 0.. then the multiplicity would have been 0..* (or *).

6.6   N-ARY ASSOCIATIONS

The associations that we have considered thus far are binary associations. Binary associations link two classes together. UML also provides a notation for *n-ary associations*, which link three or more classes together.

The UML notation for an n-ary association is a diamond symbol connected to the classes that participate in the association. The notation is illustrated in Figure 6-12.

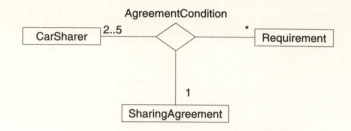

Figure 6-12: N-ary association notation

Figure 6-12 shows an n-ary association. The association is labelled **agreement condition**. In the present example, requirements have been taken to exist independently of **CarSharer**s and are therefore represented by a class. One instance of the **agreement condition** association would relate instances of **CarSharer**, **Requirement** and **SharingAgreement** with each other.

For an n-ary association, any one instance of the association could relate any combination of the associated classes that is permitted by each classes multiplicity.

For example, in Figure 6-12:

- A given occurrence of an agreement condition may relate two instances of **CarSharer**, one instance of **SharingAgreement** but no instances of **Requirement**. Saying that more colloquially, an agreement condition may relate two car sharers, one sharing agreement, but no requirements. (For an informally arranged, but formally agreed share.)
- Another agreement condition may involve 15 requirements, five sharers and one agreement.

EXAMPLE 6.3   Would it be possible for an occurrence of an agreement condition to involve four requirements, one car sharer and two sharing agreements?

SOLUTION   It would not. **SharingAgreement** has a multiplicity of 1 (that is, 1..1). Thus the maximum number of **SharingAgreement**s in an agreement condition association must be 1. Also, the multiplicity of **CarSharer** is 2..5 so it would not be valid for an agreement condition to have a minimum of just one **CarSharer**.

6.7   MODELLING GUIDANCE

This chapter covers relatively specialist annotations that can be used on class diagrams. Given this context, some of the modelling guidance given in this section focuses on the implications of using or not using the annotations. This is particularly true of the following section on association ends.

6.7.1   Association Ends

Visibility

The visibility of an association end can be considered in a way similar to that regarding the visibility of attributes in a class. In object-oriented systems, it is arguably better practice to restrict access to the internal structure of a class. Consider the implications of making an association end public. Figure 6-13 shows an example class diagram used earlier in this chapter.

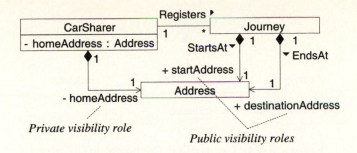

Figure 6-13: Association end visibility

The startAddress and destinationAddress roles are publicly available. Consider the case where there is a requirement to add a printStartAddresses operation to the CarSharer class. The operation should return the set of addresses that are the start addresses for all the journeys registered by a car sharer.

As startAddress is publicly available, CarSharer could access the instance of Address that is the start-Address of a Journey directly. A specification of this operation might include some code like:

```
forAll(Journey){
    Journey.startAddress.print();
}
```

In other words, for all journeys registered by a car sharer, the printStartAddresses operation will call the print() operation on the instance of Address playing the role of startAddress for that Journey.

At first sight, this approach might seem attractive. The alternative would be to pass a printStartAddress message to each Journey which in turn sends a print() message to its startAddress. This latter approach involves two messages whereas the former approach calls Address.print() directly from CarSharer.

However, this direct calling has a drawback. What would happen if the interface (the set of publicly available operations) on Address were to change, or the method of the print() operation were to change? In this situation, having direct calls to Address operations in classes not directly associated with Address becomes a liability. Tracking down these classes and ensuring that all possible interactions have been re-coded and tested becomes a significant overhead. Instead, it is arguably better practice to keep association end visibility private.

6.7.2   Changeability and Ordering

Changeability constraints can be useful when a class structure has a predefined form that must be adhered to. An illustration of this notion, as applied to document structure, was used when the notation was introduced in Section 6.2.2. A slightly amended version of this example is shown in Figure 6-14.

EXAMPLE 6.4   What is the interpretation of the Document–FrontMatter and the Document–Index associations and constraints?

SOLUTION   For Document–FrontMatter, a document must have one and only one front matter component. One front matter component cannot be replaced with another ({frozen}). For Document–Index, a document need not

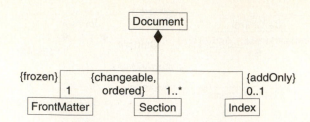

Figure 6-14: Controlled Document structure

have an index when it is created. Once an index is added it cannot be replaced. A document cannot have more than one index.

The {changeable} constraint on Document–Section, taken together with the 1..* multiplicity, implies that:

- a document must have one section when it is created (from the multiplicity);
- sections can be added, removed or replaced (from the changeability constraint) so long as the document always has at least one section (from the multiplicity).

The {ordered} constraint can be useful where the existence of an inherent or explicit order exists across the instances of a class. In Figure 6-14, the ordered constraint on the Document–Section association specifies that the sections that make up a document have an inherent order. The nature of this ordering is not specified. It could, for example, relate to the internal structure of the document within an editor environment, or perhaps to a section number allocated to each section.

6.7.3   Derived Elements

The principles of derivation constraints have already been discussed in the context of derived attributes (Section 4.4.3.3). Taken together with the example discussed in Section 6.5, there is no more to add by way of modelling guidance here.

6.7.4   Navigability

Figure 6-15 shows one possible implementation of a bi-directional association between CarSharer and Address. In this case the association has been implemented as two attributes on the two classes. The homeAddress attribute on CarSharer allows identification of the associated Address instance. The sharer attribute on Address allows the associated CarSharer instance to be identified. Thus two attributes were needed to implement one association. In effect, one attribute is needed for each navigation direction. (It should be noted that different designs could be used to implement the same association.)

As well as this design overhead, there will be a run-time overhead in supporting bi-directional associations. When an Address instance is created as the homeAddress of a CarSharer instance, the Address instance will need to be instructed to point back to the CarSharer instance that created it. If the home address of a CarSharer changes (one instance of Address is replaced by another), then the new Address will need to be associated with CarSharer and the new Address instance will again have to be instructed to point back to the CarSharer. This association maintenance becomes more complicated where the multiplicity is not 1..1.

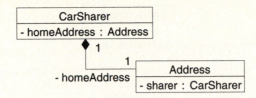

Figure 6-15: Unspecified association navigability

Specifying navigability for an association can simplify the design and implementation of an association. For example, if the association between **CarSharer** and **Address** is specified as navigable only from **CarSharer** to **Address**, then it is no longer necessary to implement the **sharer : CarSharer** attribute on **Address** (Figure 6-16). Putting a crude metric to this, compared to the example discussed above for Figure 6-15, the specification of uni-directional navigability will halve the design and run-time overhead.

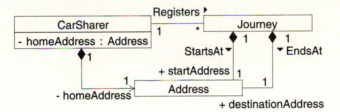

Figure 6-16: Explicit association navigability

EXAMPLE 6.5   Identify any other associations in the class diagram shown in Figure 6-16 that you think could be uni-directional.

SOLUTION   Figure 6-17 shows a probable solution.

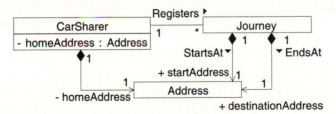

Figure 6-17: Other uni-directional associations

It might be reasonable to assume that the **StartsAt** and **EndsAt** associations between **Journey** and **Address** will only ever be navigated in the direction from **Journey** to **Address**.

6.7.5   Qualifiers

Qualifiers can be useful as a means of specifying how a class may search a set of associated objects using attribute values from the problem domain rather than using specific object identifiers. There are three common variations on the use of qualifiers.

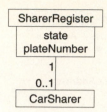

Figure 6-18: A qualifier with two attributes

Figure 6-18 shows an association between a **SharerRegister** and a **CarSharer**. The **SharerRegister** is CarMatch's list of registered **CarSharer**s. The qualifier consists of two attributes, **state** and **plateNumber**. Taken together, this qualifier and the multiplicity of **0..1** at the **CarSharer** end of the association indicate that, given values for the two qualifier attributes, it would be possible to identify either none or one **CarSharer**. The lower bound of the multiplicity (**0..**) indicates that a **state** and **plateNumber** might not identify a **CarSharer**. The upper bound of the multiplicity (**..1**) indicates that at most one **CarSharer** will be identified.

Figure 6-19: Unique qualifier

The class diagram in Figure 6-19 shows how the parties that are covered by a **SharingAgreement** can be identified by their party number (**party#**). In this example, **party#** is defined as being of type **int**.

As the lower bound of the multiplicity at the **CarSharer** end of the association is **1**, the association specifies that a given **party#** will always identify (at least) one **CarSharer**. Similarly, as the upper bound of the multiplicity is also **1**, no more than one **CarSharer** will be identified by a given **party#**. Putting the upper and lower bounds of multiplicity together, the association specifies that a given **party#** will always identify one and only one **CarSharer** in a **SharingAgreement**.

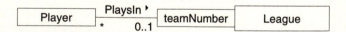

Figure 6-20: Partitioning qualifier

Finally, Figure 6-20 shows an example of how a qualifier can be used to identify a group of instances. In this case, a **teamNumber** can be used to identify zero, one or more players in a league. The **teamNumber** qualifier may not identify any players or it may identify a group of players.

The attribute(s) that make up the qualifier of an association are not attributes of the classes at either end of the association. For example, in Figure 6-20, **teamNumber** is not an attribute of **League** or **Player**. Instead, **teamNumber** is an attribute of the **plays in** association between **League** and **Player**.

It is intuitively clear that the qualifier attribute is not an attribute of the class at the association end at which the qualifier is placed. For example, if **teamNumber** were an attribute of **League**, it would hold multiple values for all the teams in a league. Some kind of link to the actual teams, or the players in those teams, would need to be created to instantiate links between leagues and players.

It is perhaps less intuitive that **teamNumber** is not an attribute of **Player**. However, the multiplicity of the **plays in** association allows for players that do not play in a league. In this situation, a **teamNumber** attribute on **Player** would not be applicable and would have a null value.

Instead, the **teamNumber** value is data that is known about the context of a player playing in a league. In other words, it is an attribute of the association itself. If a player is not playing in a league then there is no instance of an association between **Player** and **League** and hence no **teamNumber** value to be held. If a player changes leagues then the context of the association changes, so it is reasonable that the attribute whose value changes is an attribute of the association.

6.7.6   Association Classes

In essence, association classes are used when the association itself has attributes or operations that need to be represented in the class model. One common situation in which association classes are used is to capture the historical or time-based nature of a relationship. Table 6-1 illustrates some examples of possible association classes.

Table 6-1: Examples of historical or time-based association classes

Association	Association class	Possible attributes
Contractor–Project	Assignment	startDate, role, contractRate
CarSharer–RequirementType	Requirement	priority, comment, fromDate, untilDate

One potential indicator that an association class may be required is where it proves difficult to assign attributes to the classes at either end of an association with a *–* multiplicity.

As the association and the association class are one and the same concept, there can only be one occurrence of an association class per occurrence of an association. For example, consider the **Contractor–Project** association and **Assignment** association class suggested in Table 6-1. This association is shown in Figure 6-21.

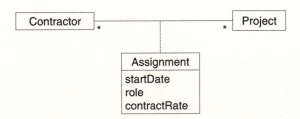

Figure 6-21: Assignment association class between Contractor and Project

Each assignment of a contractor to a project will result in one occurrence of the association and hence one set of values for **startDate**, **role** and **contractRate**. Where a contractor works on different projects, these three attributes on the association class will hold different values for the different associations. Where a contractor is assigned to the same project a second (or subsequent) time, there can still be only one occurrence of the association between **Contractor** and **Project** and hence association class. Thus, the values for startDate, role and contractRate would hold only the latest values for the assignment of a contractor to a project and not a set of historical values.

Modelling this association class as an equivalent set of normal classes and associations would require this 'one association class per association' constraint to be enforced by the multiplicities used. The class diagram shown in Figure 6-22 is not equivalent to Figure 6-21 as it would be possible to create different occurrences of the Assignment class for the same occurrences of Contractor and Project.

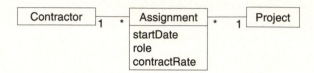

Figure 6-22: Assignment modelled as class

Thus an association class can be used where the 'one association occurrence, one association class instance' constraint should be enforced. If this is not the case, for example if a history of assignments of one contractor to one project is required, then the association class should be modelled as a normal class with appropriate associations to the other classes.

6.7.7   N-ary Associations

Section 6.6 introduced the notation for n-ary associations using the example of requirements covered by sharing agreements between car sharers. An investigation of the modelling process that resulted in the use of this notation will illustrate where this notation is useful.

Consider the situation when the analyst begins to model the associations between CarSharer, Requirement and SharingAgreement. Figure 6-23 illustrates some possible occurrences of the associations that need to be modelled.

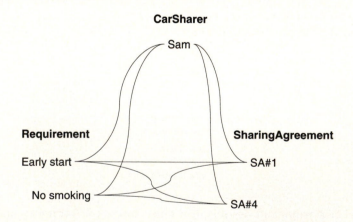

Figure 6-23: Occurrences of three way association

Figure 6-23 shows that Sam: CarSharer has two requirements, Early start: Requirement and No smoking: Requirement. Sam participates in SA#1: SharingAgreement and SA#4: SharingAgreement. Both sharing agreements cover the two requirements that Sam has.

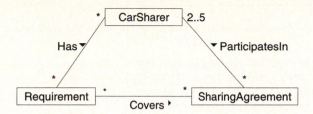

Figure 6-24: Modelling association occurrences from Figure 6-23

Figure 6-24 shows an initial attempt at modelling these association occurrences. The analyst has modelled three binary associations between the three classes. These binary associations are adequate for the occurrences shown in Figure 6-23. However, if more illustrative occurrences are added, the problem with this binary association structure will begin to become apparent.

Figure 6-25 shows additional occurrences of the associations between the three classes. Lou: CarSharer with requirements of No smoking: Requirement and Allergen filter: Requirement. Lou participates in SA#4: SharingAgreement with Sam and also in SA#7: SharingAgreement. Both of these sharing agreements cover the requirements of Lou.

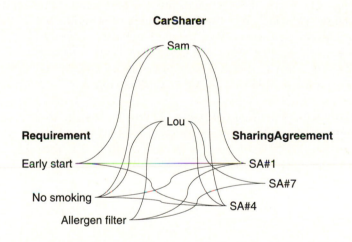

Figure 6-25: Additional association occurrences

The problem with modelling these occurrences as three binary associations is that it is not possible to preserve the original integrity of the original occurrences when navigating across the associations.

Consider what can happen when navigating from **CarSharer** around the three binary associations. If the integrity of the association occurrences is maintained then two things should be true. First, it should be possible to navigate across all three associations and get back to the starting point of that navigation. Second, it must not be possible to navigate to an association or class occurrence not covered by the original association occurrences. An example will be used to illustrate these points. Figure 6-26 shows most of the occurrences shown in Figure 6-25.

Aside

To make the diagram less cluttered with lines, the following association occurrences have been omitted from Figure 6-26:

- the occurrence linking Sam to Early start
- the occurrence linking Sam to No smoking
- the occurrence linking Lou to SA#7
- the occurrence linking Lou to SA#4

These occurrences have only been omitted to make the diagram in Figure 6-26 easy to read. These omitted occurrences do not affect the explanation that follows.

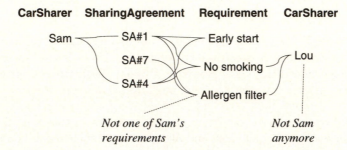

Figure 6-26: Navigating association occurrences from Figure 6-25

Starting with Sam, it is possible to traverse to the **SharingAgreements** in which Sam participates (SA#1 and SA#7). From these occurrences of **SharingAgreement**, it is possible to navigate to the **Requirements** satisfied by those **SharingAgreements**. Here the first problem is encountered. At this point it is possible to navigate from Sam's SharingAgreement SA#1 to the Requirement Allergen filter. This **Requirement** was met by SA#1, but it was not one of Sam's requirements. Thus it is not possible to navigate from Allergen filter on to Sam, the starting point of this navigation. Continuing with the navigation from SA#1 to No smoking it is then possible to navigate to CarSharer Lou.

The context of this navigation was Sam: CarSharer. Following the occurrences it was possible to get to a **Requirement** that was not one of Sam's. It was also possible to follow the occurrences through to Lou: CarSharer, a different context to the one the navigation started under. The same loss of integrity will occur regardless of where the navigation starts around the three-association structure.

EXAMPLE 6.6   Navigate around the binary associations in Figure 6-25, starting at SA#4: SharingAgreement and the Allergen filter: Requirement in turn. What integrity problems do you encounter?

SOLUTION   In brief, it is possible to navigate as follows:

- SA#4–Lou–Allergen Filter (not covered by SA#4)—then to SA#1 or SA#7 (not starting context).
- Allergen filter–SA#1–Sam (does not have Allergen filter as requirement)—then to Early start or No smoking (not starting context).

The conceptual problem here is one of interpretation. Each of the binary associations is valid in its own context. For example, the **covers** association between the **Requirement** and **SharingAgreement** classes is valid as an association between those two classes. It is only when those three separate associations are interpreted as something that links occurrences of all three classes involved that the integrity problems arise.

If there is a conceptual requirement to be able to associate instances of all three classes with each other in one association instance, then an association structure that allows just that is needed. Figure 6-27

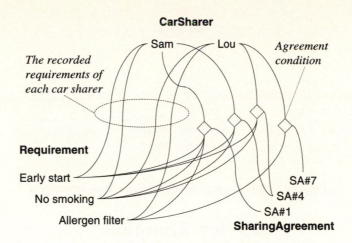

Figure 6-27: N-ary association occurrences

illustrates the occurrences of such a three-way association, along with the occurrences of the requirements for each car sharer.

What Figure 6-27 shows is that there is a hidden type representing occurrences of the association. Each of those occurrences will be associated with occurrences of CarSharer, Requirement and a SharingAgreement. Figure 6-28 models these association and class occurrences as a class diagram.

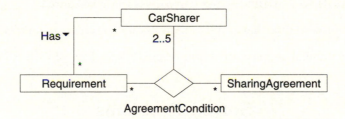

Figure 6-28: N-ary association on class diagram

The has association between CarSharer and Requirement in Figure 6-28 allows the capture of the requirements for each CarSharer. Those requirements may not yet be satisfied, but they will guide the establishment of sharing agreements to make sure that only those car sharers with the same requirements are put together.

For the sake of clarity it was necessary to limit the number of occurrences shown in these figures. Although it might be inferred from the class and association occurrences used here that all the requirements of a car sharer are met by every agreement in which they participate, this is not the intention. The intention is that each occurrence of the n-ary association will meet some, but not necessarily all of the requirements of the car sharers involved in the association. Thus the requirements that are covered will need to be included in the association. The agreement condition association relates car sharers and their requirements to sharing agreements.

The need for attributes and operations of n-ary associations may also be identified during the modelling process. An association class can be added to an n-ary association for these attributes and operations. The notation for an association class on an n-ary association is shown in Figure 6-29. Association classes have already been discussed in Section 6.4.

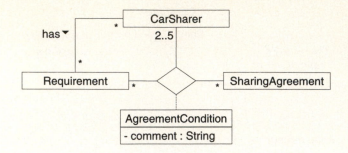

Figure 6-29: N-ary association class notation

Review Questions

6.1 How is the visibility of an association end shown on a class diagram?

6.2 Identify and describe the changeability constraints defined in UML.

6.3 What is the notation for specifying that the objects involved in an association should be ordered?

6.4 How is association navigability shown in UML? Under what circumstances might it be necessary explicitly to specify an association as having bi-directional navigability?

6.5 Discuss the meaning of qualifiers as used on a class diagram.

6.6 What features do derived attributes and derived associations share?

6.7 How can a single association that involves more than two classes be modelled in UML?

6.8 If an association is found to have attributes or operations, how can these be modelled in UML?

Solved Problems

6.1 Figure 6-30 shows a class diagram first used for Problem 4.3.

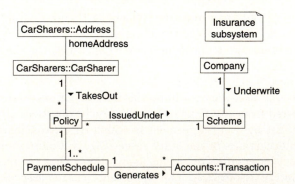

Figure 6-30: Core Insurance package class model

Annotate the class diagram shown in Figure 6-30 with the changeability and ordering constraints and the navigability suggested in the following transcript. (For the purposes of this question, assume that bi-directional navigation needs to be explicitly specified.)

Mick Perez: Can you tell me a little bit more about these insurance classes? [Mick shows Janet the class diagram in Figure 6-30]. I'd like to clarify how some of the information represented here is used. What kind of cross-referencing will you want to do?

Janet Hoffner: Well, when we're analysing our sales figures we'll need to know which policies were sold under each scheme.

MP: What about needing to know the scheme that a policy was issued under?

JH: Oh yes, we'll need to know that whenever we look at the details of the policy. We'll also need to know the payment schedules for a policy.

MP: While we're in that area—I assume that the scheme that a policy is issued under doesn't change?

JH: That's right. Payment schedules can change though. Sometimes people need to change or amend the way they're paying.

MP: Do you ever need to be able to look up the policy for a payment schedule?... or the payment schedule that a transaction was paid under?

JH: No and no. Of course we do need to be able to list the payment schedules for a policy as I just said. We'll also need to list the payment transactions made under a payment schedule.

MP: OK—just to finish this bit off, can we look at the transactions? We're into financial regulation territory here. Is it a case of 'normal rules apply'?

JH: Depends what you mean by 'normal rules'. We aren't allowed to delete or amend paid transactions. We can archive them after five years, but not delete them. That means they build up over time. When we list transactions we do it in date order.

MP: OK, that's great. Thanks very much.

Figure 6-31 shows the portion of the model which has been annotated.

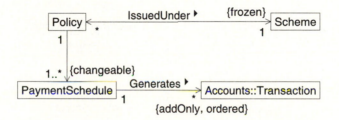

Figure 6-31: Association end annotations for core Insurance package class model

In Figure 6-31 the following annotations have been made:

- The issued under association between Policy and Scheme has been annotated as bi-directional. This means that navigation support will be implemented in both directions for the association.
  Furthermore, the Scheme end of the association has been annotated as {frozen}. This constraint implies that the scheme under which Policy was issued cannot be changed.
- The unlabelled association between Policy and PaymentSchedule has been annotated as navigable from Policy to PaymentSchedule. This means that it will not be necessary to directly support navigation in the other direction along the association in the implementation model.
  Furthermore, the PaymentSchedule end of the association has been annotated as {changeable}. This constraint specifies that payment schedules can be added, changed and removed within the confines of the 1..* multiplicity. The multiplicity specifies that a minimum of one payment schedule must be in force for a policy.
- The generates association between PaymentSchedule and Accounts::Transaction has been annotated as navigable from PaymentSchedule to Transaction.
  Furthermore, the association end has been annotated with the {addOnly, ordered} constraint. The addOnly component specifies that new transactions can be added, but old transactions cannot be deleted or changed. This might seem reasonable in order to comply with financial record-keeping regulations. The ordered component of the constraint suggests that the transactions for a PaymentSchedule will be ordered. The fact that the ordering is date based has not been shown, but could be mentioned in a note attached to the ordered constraint.

6.2 One interpretation of the **+getByName()** operation on **Collection** in Figure 6-32 is that name is a qualifier of the association between **CarSharerCollection** and **CarSharer**.

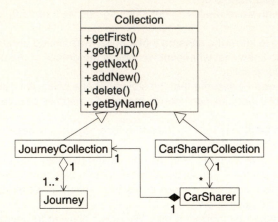

Figure 6-32: Collection classes for Journey and CarSharer

Redraw this association to include name as a qualifier. Assume that a value for name might not identify any car sharers, or that it might identify several.

Figure 6-33 shows the **CarSharer.name** attribute as a qualifier.

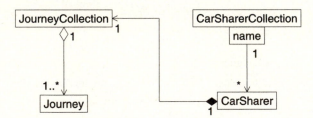

Figure 6-33: Qualifier and interface specifier annotations added

6.3 (This problem extends the CarMatch case study by introducing elements that are not used elsewhere. Do not worry about integrating this class model with others already produced.)

One member service that CarMatch are considering offering is evening talks. The talks would be led by an invited speaker. Occasionally two speakers are used for one talk. The talks will require booking a set of venues. For example, a talk on defensive driving might involve one of CarMatch's seminar rooms for a talk and the parking lot for a hands-on session. Other talks, such as driving to maximize fuel economy, would be purely classroom based. Registered car sharers can book a place on a talk. When a talk is first scheduled, a speaker and venue will be known but no car sharers will be booked on it yet. CarMatch want to be able to extend the proposed system to support a diary of these talks.

Model these requirements as an n-ary association with an association class, adding suitable attributes and operations to any new classes.

Figure 6-34 shows a basic class model showing the multiplicity of the n-ary association.

One occurrence of **talk** could involve:

    1. Between zero and many **CarSharers**. A talk can be set up with no **CarSharers** booked on it. CarMatch did not indicate that there was a maximum number of people that could be booked on a talk but there probably is. Even if a specific upper bound to the multiplicity of, say, 24 is established,

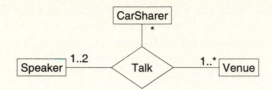

Figure 6-34: N-ary association for CarMatch evening talks

the association will probably be implemented in the same way as for *. If the upper bound were relatively low, that is, only two or three, then the implementation might be different.

2. One or two **Speakers**. The scenario indicated that a talk has a speaker when it is arranged. It was also suggested that two speakers is the normal limit. Care should be exercised in specifying an upper bound of 2 here though. A legitimate implementation of an upper bound multiplicity of 2 would be to have two attributes of type **Speaker**. In such an implementation a third speaker could not be added under any circumstances. It is wise to check carefully with the stakeholders in such cases.

3. One or more **Venues**. In line with the discussion about upper bounds in the previous paragraph, the upper multiplicity bound has been modelled as * to allow for a talk with more than the normally envisaged number of venues (for example, a roaming talk on map reading). The lower bound is one, as a talk has at least one venue arranged when it is set up.

Figure 6-35 shows a second draft of the class model.

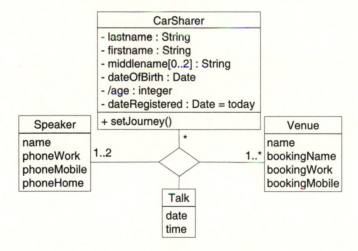

Figure 6-35: N-ary association class for CarMatch evening talks

Possible attributes have been added for **Speaker**, **Venue** and **Talk**. The attributes and operations of the **CarSharer** class used in an earlier chapter have been included here. The **Talk** association is now represented by an association class.

Supplementary Problems

6.4 VolBank have asked you to model the structure of their (dynamic) HTML form-based interface for registering and banking time via the Internet. The form will have one section relating to the volunteer. This will include the **Volunteer** class attributes. This section must be present and cannot be removed from the HTML form. The next section will allow the entry of time availability as banked time. To begin with, the HTML form will have no slots for banking time. It must be possible to add further entries (slots) to the form to bank more time. It will not be possible to remove time entries (slots) from the HTML form. In terms of the underlying classes to process the HTML form, it will be necessary only to navigate from the form object down to the volunteer section and each of the banked time entries.

Model the above requirements as a class diagram showing changeability and ordering constraints and navigability.

6.5 Problem 5.5 introduced the notion of an **Assignment** of a **Volunteer** to a **Project** (**Volunteering Opportunity**). Figure 6-36 shows one possible structure for this part of the class model (attributes and operations have been suppressed).

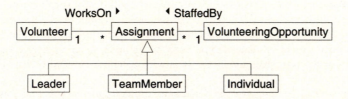

Figure 6-36: Assignment of Volunteer to VolunteeringOpportunity modelled as class

Redraw Figure 6-36 using an n-ary association and association class. Add the attributes and operations you identified in Problem 5.6.

CHAPTER 7

Class Diagram: Other Notations

7.1 INTRODUCTION

The previous three chapters have introduced the major notational elements of class diagrams and certainly those most commonly encountered. This chapter covers the remaining notational elements provided by UML to model class structures. These notations represent specialized semantics that, with the exception of the object notation, may well be encountered only rarely.

As with the previous chapter, the examples used in this chapter may present elements of the common case studies slightly differently to other chapters in order to illustrate the notations covered here. Where this has been done, every effort has been made to point out those differences.

7.2 OBJECT-RELATED NOTATIONS

7.2.1 Object Instances

The basic notation for showing object instances on a class diagram has already been introduced in Chapter 4. The name compartment of the object shows the name of the object instance and its class type. The name of an object is of the form `objectName : ClassName`, all underlined.

Figure 7-1 shows some examples of the basic object notation. For example, <u>aDocument : Document</u>, or <u>salesReport : Document</u>. As with classes, the class name can be preceded by the class pathname, for example <u>newPolicy : Insurance::Policy</u>. The name of the object instance can be omitted, resulting in an anonymous object such as <u>:CarSharer</u>.

From a conceptual perspective and in implementation environments that support multiple inheritance, it is quite possible for an object to be an instance of more than one class at the same time. In UML,

119

aDocument : Document
newPolicy : Insurance::Policy
salesReport : Document
: CarSharer

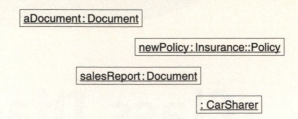

Figure 7-1: Notation for object instances

multiple class names can be specified for an object in a comma-separated list. Thus the object name compartment can contain a value of the form `objectName : ClassNameA, ClassNameB, ...`. For example, aYacht : WindPoweredBoat, MotorPoweredBoat.

As objects represent occurrences of a classes, some or all of the attributes will hold values reflecting the properties of the object instance. Figure 7-2 shows the notation for specifying the attribute values of objects. The basic notation is of the form `attributeName : type=value`. Figure 7-2 shows two attributes in this form, lastname and age. The age attribute is also a derived attribute. The type of an attribute value must be compatible with the type of the attribute on the class. As such the attribute type in an object can be omitted as it is not needed. The other attributes in Figure 7-2 use the more concise `name=value` notation.

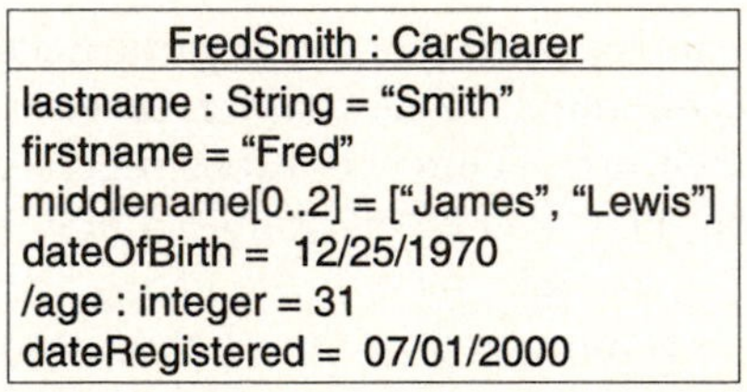

FredSmith : CarSharer
lastname : String = "Smith"
firstname = "Fred"
middlename[0..2] = ["James", "Lewis"]
dateOfBirth = 12/25/1970
/age : integer = 31
dateRegistered = 07/01/2000

Figure 7-2: Notation for object attributes

7.2.2 Links

As well as showing instances of classes, in the form of objects, instances of associations can be shown between objects. This concept has already been introduced informally in the discussion of multiplicity and n-ary associations in preceding chapters.

Figure 7-3 illustrates the UML notation for links between objects. A link is shown as a solid line between the objects that it connects. For n-ary associations, links are shown as a small diamond connected by a solid line to each object participating in the link (Figure 7-4).

Multiplicity is not shown for links as each link connects single instances of objects (the multiplicity would always be 1–1). Navigation annotations may be shown so long as they are consistent with the association of which the link is an instance.

Qualifier instances can also be used at an instance level. Figure 7-5 illustrates the use of qualifier instances with objects.

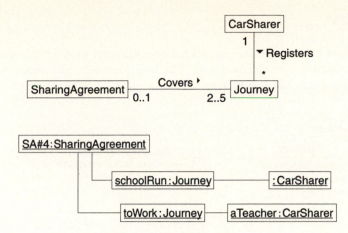

Figure 7-3: Links between objects

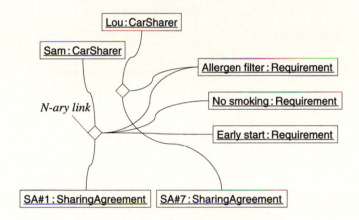

Figure 7-4: N-ary links

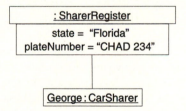

Figure 7-5: Instance of association qualifiers

7.2.3 Object Diagram

An object diagram can be constructed from objects and links. Figures 7-3, 7-4 and 7-5 are all illustrations of simple object diagrams. The objects and links in an object diagram can incorporate any of the notational elements discussed here in Section 7.2 (for example, attribute values, link role names, class state). Such a diagram might be useful during the elaboration phase of the development process to examine the state of classes and associations between them.

7.3   DEPENDENCY

Dependencies can be used to specify relationships between different model elements. The UML notation for a dependency is a dashed, arrowheaded line. The line goes from the dependent model element to the model element upon which the dependency exists. Figure 7-6 illustrates this notation.

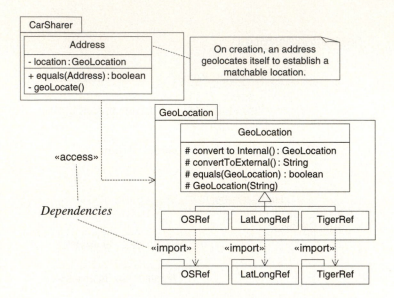

Figure 7-6: Dependency relationships

In Figure 7-6, the access dependency between the **CarSharer** and **GeoLocation** packages indicates that the public classes in the **GeoLocation** package will be available to classes in the **CarSharer** package. Not all the classes in the **GeoLocation** package may be publicly available. Associations cannot be created between **CarSharer** classes and non-public classes within the **GeoLocation** package.

7.4   CLASS-SCOPE FEATURES

Attributes and operations are normally assumed to be the features that will be manifested by object instances of a class, in other words, they have instance-scope. Different objects will hold different attribute values for the same class attribute. Two different objects could both have a name attribute set to **Fred** but those two strings are two different instances of a string that happen to have the same string value.

Sometimes it is desirable to have a class attribute that has the same value across all object instances of a class. Such attributes are referred to as being *static*. Figure 7-7 shows an example of this. In Figure 7-7, three instances of the **CarSharer** class, sharerFred, sharerBert and sharerFred2, are shown. These instances were created one after another.

In this example, the **CarSharer** class also specifies a class-scope attribute, **nextIDNumber**, and a class-scope operation, **setIDNumber**. The class-scope attribute holds the same value over all instances of **CarSharer**. The **nextIDNumber** is used by **setIDNumber** to assign an incrementing **idNumber** to each instance of a class on creation. As each instance is created and fires the **setIDNumber** operation, the value of **nextIDNumber** is incremented ready for access by the next instance of **CarSharer** to be created.

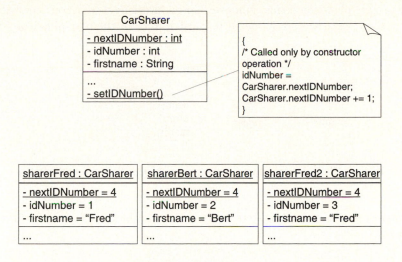

Figure 7-7: Class-scope features

Figure 7-7 shows the instances after the creation of <u>sharerFred2</u>. At this point in time, <u>**nextIDNumber**</u> has a value of 4. When <u>**sharerFred**</u> was created, <u>**nextIDNumber**</u> had a value of 1, which was assigned to this instance. At the later point in time that is shown in Figure 7-7, <u>**nextIDNumber**</u> has been incremented through the creation of <u>**sharerBert**</u> then <u>**sharerFred2**</u>.

In UML, class-scope attributes and operations, whose scope encompasses all instances of a class rather than individual instances, are underlined. Other uses of class attributes might include: setting default sizes for graphical components such as shapes, windows and panels or providing default values for text strings that can be changed in a running system, rather than being coded into an operation.

7.5   STEREOTYPES

Stereotyping is used in UML as a means of extending the core modelling concepts provided by the UML metamodel (or other metamodels). By defining a stereotype for a model component, the analyst is specifying that a modelling element conforms to the well-defined pattern of behaviour or existence of the named stereotype.

The basic UML notation for specifying a stereotype is to add the name of the stereotype enclosed in guillemets above the class name. This textual annotation can be augmented with, or replaced by, an iconic representation of the stereotype. For example, Figure 7-8 shows the representation of a «component» class in textual and text-plus-icon form.

Figure 7-8: Textual and text-plus-icon representation of a stereotyped class

The permissible forms of iconic representation will vary depending upon the particular stereotype being employed. For example, with the «component» stereotype illustrated above, the icon-only representation of the stereotype has been dropped from the specification. Component classes are now only shown using either the textual or text-plus-icon forms. However, for an interface stereotype (interfaces are coming up in Section 7.5.5), either the textual or iconic form is used, but not the text-plus-icon form (Figure 7-9).

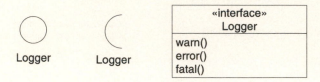

Figure 7-9: Stereotype representations for an «interface»

There are a number of predefined UML stereotypes which can be used to add detail to a model.

7.5.1   Enumeration

It is sometimes useful to be able to specify a limited and predefined set of values from which the value of a particular attribute can be set. Figure 7-10 shows the notation for the enumeration stereotype in UML.

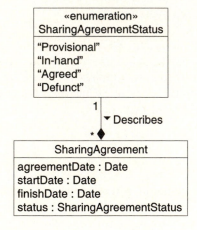

Figure 7-10: The «enumeration» notation

The basic notation for an enumeration is a named class symbol. The inclusion of the «enumeration» stereotype above the class name indicates that this class represents an enumeration of values. The literal values for the enumeration are placed in the middle list compartment of the class symbol.

In Figure 7-10, SharingAgreementStatus is an enumeration that contains the literal values "Provisional", "In-hand", "Agreed", and "Defunct". The enumeration is associated with the SharingAgreement class and the probable implementation of the association as an attribute of type SharingAgreementStatus on SharingAgreement is shown.

An enumeration can have operations. The operations would be listed in the lower list compartment in the normal way as for classes.

7.5.2 Data Type

Sometimes it is desirable to model explicitly the data types in a class diagram. Such data types will have no inherent identity. For example, in Java, calling **new String("Hello World!")** in two separate commands would yield two different instances of the **String** class, but those instances would be indistinguishable from each other.

Data type classes can be shown using the «datatype» stereotype for a class, as shown in Figure 7-11.

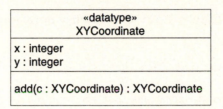

Figure 7-11: The «datatype» notation

It is quite possible for a «datatype» class to have both attributes and operations. The **XYCoordinate** class shown in Figure 7-11 has attributes for the x and y coordinates of the instance and an operation to add another coordinate to this one, yielding a coordinate as a result (none of the «datatype» class attribute values will be altered by this operation).

7.5.3 Primitive Types

UML supports the representation of primitive data types, which may have operations modelled inside or outside of UML, but which have no internal structure. Examples of such primitive types are: **String**, **Integer** and **Boolean**.

Primitive types are shown as illustrated in Figure 7-12.

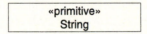

Figure 7-12: The «primitive» notation

7.5.4 Utility

UML provides a notation for modelling a collection of global attributes and operations as a «utility» stereotype. As with an enumeration, the notation for a utility is based on the class symbol. Figure 7-13 illustrates the utility notation.

In Figure 7-13, the **InsuranceTools** utility provides attributes and operations that can be used throughout the CarMatch system. It is not necessary to associate a utility with the classes that use the utility attributes or operations, as they are globally available.

7.5.5 Interfaces

An interface is a specialized type of class that cannot be instantiated. An application could never create object instances of an interface. Interfaces are used to define either:

Figure 7-13: The «utility» notation

- a set of public attributes and operations that must be provided by the classes that implement a given interface; or
- a set of public attributes and operations that are required by the classes that depend upon a given interface.

(For Java practitioners out there, it should be noted that this definition of an interface differs from the Java definition of an interface. The Java definition of an interface does not allow an interface to have attributes, nor hence state.)

The operations of an interface class have no behaviour; no method. They are not implemented. So the interface itself defines no specific behaviour. The behaviour of an operation is provided by the classes that implement a given interface, in accordance with the operations (and attributes) defined by the interface.

Using a trivial example, an interface may specify a **toString():String** operation, without providing any method to implement the **toString()** behaviour. Classes that implement this interface must provide a **toString():String** operation with method behaviour appropriate to their attributes and state. Classes that depend upon the **toString()** operation can assume that an appropriate **String** will be returned from a call to **toString()**; for error logging purposes, for example.

The concept of the implementation or realization of an interface is similar to that of generalization covered in Chapter 5. The key difference is that a class that realizes an interface is responsible for implementing the operations of the interface rather than inheriting and then specializing existing methods as in generalization.

Figure 7-14 illustrates the use of interfaces in UML using classes taken from the Java class library. (Remember that in Java, interfaces cannot have attributes or state.) The **List** class in Figure 7-14 illustrates the notation for specifying an interface stereotype in UML using the **«interface»** keyword.

(Figure 7-14 shows an alternative UML notation for the **«realization»** dependency as a generalization relationship drawn with a dashed line rather than a solid line.)

The **List** interface class specifies an ordered collection of objects. The **List** interface class provides operations to support:

- insertion of objects into a list (for example, **add(Object)**, which should allow an object to be added to the end of the list);
- interrogating a list regarding its contents (for example, **isEmpty()**, which should return a boolean true value if the list has no elements in it);
- handling the list of objects (for example, **toArray()**, which should return an object of type **Array** containing all the elements of the list);

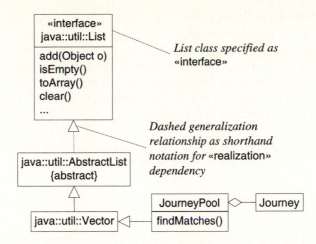

Figure 7-14: Class-based and association-based interface notation

- removing objects from a list (for example, **clear()**, which should remove all the elements from the list).

Just to labour the point, the **List** class itself does not implement these operations, as it is an interface class. As shown in Figure 7-14, the **AbstractList** class realizes the **List** interface and thus provides methods to support the operations specified in the **List** interface class.

The example shown in Figure 7-14 shows the refinement in the Java class library down from **List**, through **AbstractList** to **Vector**. The example also illustrates how a class in the **CarSharer** package, **JourneyPool**, might use the inherited behaviour of its ancestors. In the example, the **JourneyPool** class provides **Vector**-like operations plus the **findMatches** operation. The intention is that as instances of **Journey** are registered with **CarMatch** they are added to the **JourneyPool** collection, using **Vector** (and hence **AbstractList** and hence **List**) behaviour. The **JourneyPool** class then provides a specific operation **findMatches** to match up similar journeys that could be shared. The **findMatches** operation might well utilize **Vector**, **AbstractList** (and hence **List**) operations to provide the matching capability.

As a simpler notational form, UML allows a realized (or *provided*) interface to be represented by a small circle labelled with the name of the interface. Figure 7-15 illustrates this notation, again using the **List** class first introduced in Figure 7-14.

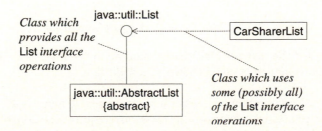

Figure 7-15: Alternative notation for interface class

The **AbstractList** class *provides* the operations of the **List** interface and is thus attached by a solid line to the **List** interface element. The example shown in Figure 7-15 also introduces the **CarSharerList** class to illustrate the dashed arrow notation to link a class that requires some (though not necessarily all) of the operations on the interface.

7.5.6   Required and Provided Interfaces

In the notations shown in the previous section, the nature of the relationship between the interface and other classes was indicated by the type of dependency used to connect the class and interface. If the dependency from class to interface had a «realization» stereotype (as with java::util::AbstractList in Figure 7-14), then the class implements, or *provides*, the interface [to other classes]. However, if the dependency is not otherwise stereotyped (as with CarSharerList in Figure 7-15), then the class assumes the presence of, or *requires*, the interface to be present.

UML provides an alternative notation for indicating the different natures of these provided and required dependencies. Figure 7-16 illustrates the required interface notation.

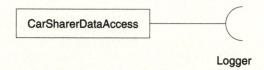

Figure 7-16: The required interface notation

The model shown in Figure 7-16 indicates that the CarSharerDataAccess class requires the availability of the Logger interface. As interfaces cannot be directly instantiated, this implies that a class which implements (or provides) the Logger interface must be made available to the CarSharerDataAccess class.

Thus the UML notation for a required interface for a class is to use a semi-circle icon to show the interface and a solid line to indicate the required dependency.

It may be that a number of different classes all implement (or provide) a particular interface. This is illustrated in Figure 7-17 where the FileAppender, ConsoleAppender and JDBCAppender classes all implement (or provide) the Logger interface.

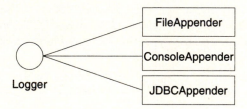

Figure 7-17: The provided interface notation

In this case, the notation for the provided interface is similar to the interface stereotyped icon that we have already seen. The dependency is again shown as a solid line.

Thus putting the two notations together, the resultant appearance (Figure 7-18) gives a clear indication of the strong, but indirect relationship between the class that requires the Logger interface and the class which provides that interface.

7.5.7   Type versus Implementation Class

UML allows a distinction between «type» classes and «implementationClass» classes. A «type» class is similar in concept to an interface insomuch as it defines the operations to be provided for the class

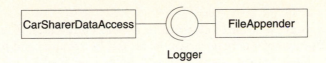

Figure 7-18: The required and provided interface together

without implementing the methods for those operations. However, a type class is used to show how a modelling concept in one aspect of a model or phase of modelling maps to a different concept in another aspect of the model or phase of modelling. For example, a **«type»** class identified in the analysis phase of a project might be implemented as a different **«implementationClass»** type in the design or implementation phase of that project.

The UML notation for a type class is based on the class symbol, augmented with a **«type»** stereotype. The class **GatherCarSharerDetails** shown in Figure 7-19 illustrates this notation.

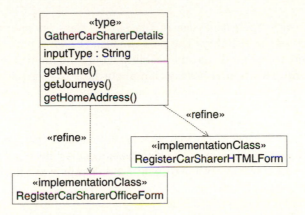

Figure 7-19: Notation for «type» and «implementationClass» classes

From the preceding discussion it should not be too surprising to learn that an **«implementationClass»** is a class that refines a type class by implementing the methods of the type class. Figure 7-19 shows two implementation classes, **RegisterCarSharerOfficeForm** and **RegisterCarSharerHTMLForm**. The office form would allow CarMatch staff to gather car sharer details for sharers who come into a CarMatch office. The HTML form would be served over the Internet to allow car sharers to register online. Figure 7-19 shows the two refinement dependencies between the implementation classes and the type class.

The example shown in Figure 7-19, the **GatherCarSharerDetails** type class, illustrates the generic functionality that might be expected in any system interface that will be used to input car sharer details. As well as the operations, an attribute **inputType** is shown. The intention here is that whichever medium is used to input the car sharer details will be noted through the **inputType** attribute. With the class model shown, this would enable CarMatch to track online versus office-based registrations.

The implementation of **GatherCarSharerDetails** will be tailored through the two implementation classes to suit the requirements of the particular environment in which the implementation class runs (via the Internet or as a desktop window). Each implementation class might introduce additional functional capability to meet the requirements of its environment or to provide added-value to the look and feel of the interface. For example, the desktop form implementation might make direct use of desktop functionality (and hence class libraries), such as drag and drop of icons on the form, that are simply not available within an HTML-based form.

7.6   PORTS

Accurate definition of the means by which a class can be accessed is essential to avoid excessive coupling between the internal realizations of different classes. Notations for required and provided interfaces have already been introduced. These notations and concepts can be combined in order to help to define the *ports* on a class. Figure 7-20 illustrates the port notation.

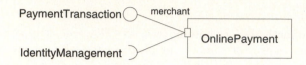

Figure 7-20: Ports on a Class

The UML notation for a port is a small box placed at the side of the class whose port(s) are being defined. Required and provided interfaces are connected to the port, thus defining which services the class provides or which services the class expects from its environment.

The port can be shown overlapping the edge of the ported class (as shown in Figure 7-20), which indicates that the port has *public* visibility. The port can also be shown entirely inside the ported class, indicating that it is a hidden port and that its visibility should be defined as part of the name clause of the port. (The UML Specification is not specific about how the visibility of such a 'hidden' port should be shown. The use of a visibility definition on the name clause is a supposition on the part of the author.)

For example, in Figure 7-20, the **OnlinePayments** class provides a port (named **merchant**) which provides the **PaymentTransaction** interface and requires the **IdentityManagement** interface. The contract this makes is that, given appropriate interaction with the required and provided interfaces, the **OnlinePayments** class will function correctly.

At an object instance level, when an instance of a class is created, then any required and/or provided interfaces identified by a port on that class will also be created.

Ports are identified with a name, optional class type and multiplicity (`name : Class [multiplicity]`). In Figure 7-20 the port on **OnlinePayments** is named **merchant**. This port's definition could be extended to (for example) **merchant : MerchantBroker** [1]. This would specify that the port for the **OnlinePayments** class is implemented by a single (1..1, or 1) instance of the **MerchantBroker** class, which is referred to as **merchant**.

In the case where the port definition identifies a class (as in **merchant : MerchantBroker**), then that class takes responsibility for fulfilling the required and provided interfaces on behalf of the 'ported' class. By naming and typing a port we are able to specify the service that the port supports.

7.6.1   Forwarding and Filtering

Ports connect to the required and provided interfaces on the *outside* of the ported class. They can also connect to the classes that the ported class is composed of, and which will interact with the external system through those interfaces.

Figure 7-21 shows the notation for connecting ports with the elements of a ported class. In this case, the **merchant** port (which has been defined as being of type **MerchantBroker**) is connected to the **HameksPayment** and **DynasTeamPayment** classes.

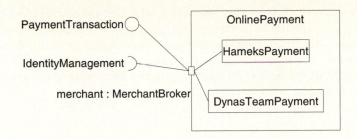

Figure 7-21: Ported Class Composition

This raises the question of how a message arriving at a port from one of its interfaces is passed on to the *internal* classes connected to that port. Possible options may include:

- filtering the incoming message to see whether it should be handled at all, and if so forwarding it;
- inspecting the content of the incoming message to determine which internal class should handle that message;
- multi-casting the incoming message to some or all of the internal classes, again depending upon the content of the incoming message;
- load-balancing incoming messages to the internal classes by forwarding, for example, on a round-robin basis.

Where the port has been typed, as in the example used in Figure 7-21, it is reasonably clear that the behaviour of the class type used for the port would define the behaviour of the port in the face of these incoming messages. The UML specification describes this concept as 'semantic variation'. Where the port has not been typed, the behaviour of the port is taken to be not explicitly specified.

7.6.2   Behaviour Ports

Ports can also be connected to a state symbol, in order to define the conceptual behaviour of the port. Figure 7-22 shows an example of this usage.

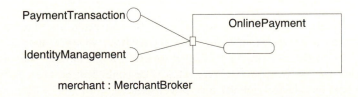

Figure 7-22: Behaviour Port Notation

This connection to a state symbol defines that messages in and out of the port will be handled by the ported class itself and not by a component of that class. With this notation, the state symbol is not named. Its presence alone is enough to define the port as being a behaviour port (and the ported class as handling the message traffic on the port).

The specification of behaviour ports in this way, along with the use of graphical containment to show the composition of a class, should be combined with the use of composite structure diagrams (Section 17.4.1). Composite structure diagrams use graphical containment to show how a classifier is composed of subelements. These subelements will collaborate in order to fulfil the externally visible functionality of the composite classifier. In other words, the behaviour of the port can be described by a composite structure diagram.

7.7   TEMPLATE CLASSES AND BOUND CLASSES

The UML notation for a *template class* is similar to the basic class symbol, with the parameters for the class being identified in a dashed box in the top right corner of the class symbol. Figure 7-23 illustrates the template class notation for two different classes, **PCSet** and **PCArray**.

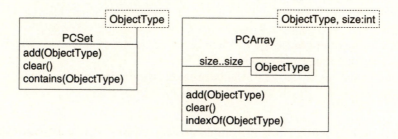

Figure 7-23: Template class notation for two different classes

UML also permits the graphical modelling of the parameter components of a template class. For example, in Figure 7-23 the **PCArray** class illustrates that it (the **PCArray** class) has a composite association with the **ClassType** that is passed as a parameter. (The composition is shown using graphical containment.) The multiplicity of this association is defined by the **size** parameter. In summary, the class definition in Figure 7-23 specifies that the **PCArray** class will include between **size** and **size** (the **size..size** multiplicity) occurrences of the **ObjectType** class, in other words, an array of size **size**.

Aside
The UML Specification does not appear explicitly to permit the range definition **size..size** to be abbreviated to **size**. This is permitted where a specific value is known; for example, **1..1** may be truncated to **1** or a single integer value such as **7** may be used to specify a range of one value. This simplification has not explicitly been extended to a logical definition such as **size..size**.

What is a template class though? Arguably, the most common use of template classes is to support sets or collections of objects. Figure 7-24 illustrates this usage, showing two instantiations of the template classes shown in Figure 7-23.

In Figure 7-24, the **JourneyList** class is bound to the **PCSet** template class with the «bind» dependency. This binding also instantiates the **ObjectType** parameter to **Journey** (shown as a mapping →). Thus, the operations of **PCSet** would actually be realized as, for example, **add(Journey)**. So, the final effect of instantiating **PCSet** as **JourneyList** is that **JourneyList** will behave as a set with elements of type **Journey**.

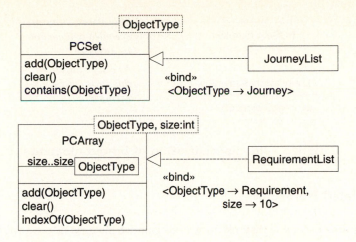

Figure 7-24: Instantiation of template classes

EXAMPLE 7.1   What is the meaning of the binding between RequirementList and PCArray?

SOLUTION   RequirementList binds to PCArray setting ObjectType to Requirement and size to 10. The effect of this is to instantiate RequirementList as an array that can hold up to 10 occurrences of type Requirement.

For the example shown in Figure 7-24, JourneyList and RequirementList are referred to in UML as *bound elements*. Bound elements can be shown using the notation in Figure 7-24. An alternative notation is shown in Figure 7-25.

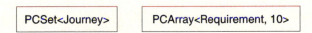

Figure 7-25: Alternative notation for showing bound elements

This alternative notation is graphically more concise than the notation used in Figure 7-24. The name of the class is of the form `TemplateName<ParameterList>`. However, the alternative notation does not allow the bound element to be named in the class diagram.

As a bound element is fully specified by the template class of which it is an instantiation, the bound element cannot extend the functionality of the template class by introducing further attributes or operations. Nor can the bound element change the functionality of the template class beyond the instantiation to the particular bound element parameters. However, it is perfectly acceptable to specialize a bound element and then to extend or refine those specializations in line with the principles of generalization. Figure 7-26 illustrates this principle.

7.8   MODELLING GUIDANCE

As with the previous chapter, this chapter covers relatively specialist annotations that can be used on class diagrams. Given this context, some of the modelling guidance given in this section focuses on the implications of using or not using the annotations.

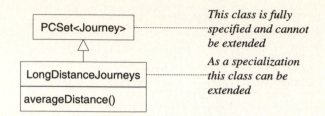

Figure 7-26: Specialization of bound elements

7.8.1   Object-Related Notations

Drawing object diagrams can be a very useful way of gaining insights into a problem domain. Objects and links can be used to explore potential association structures by illustrating possible configurations of those objects and links. Figure 7-27 illustrates a first attempt at modelling the core classes and associations in the CarMatch case study.

Earlier chapters have already presented a class model for **CarSharer**s, **Journeys** and **Address**es. However, the purpose of this section is to illustrate the usefulness of object diagrams in the early stages of modelling. As such, this aspect of the model is being treated as though it is being encountered for the first time.

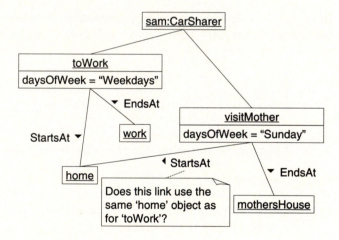

Figure 7-27: First draft object diagram for core CarMatch model

This first draft object diagram has highlighted a problem in the interpretation of the object that a trip goes from or to. The analyst has used a note to indicate that he or she is unsure whether the same **home** object can be used for the **from** link for two different trips.

The analyst redraws the object model, using a slightly different structure. Figure 7-28 shows this second draft.

The second draft shows the **from** and **to** locations as components of each trip using the graphical containment representation of composition. Using this notation, it becomes necessary to use separate objects for the two occurrences of the **home** location for the two different trips. Redrawing the objects in this way causes the analyst to think about the nature of the existence of different locations, clarifying their role in the problem domain and their representation in the solution domain. In this case, based on

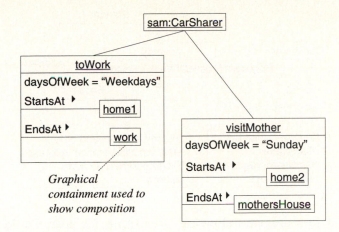

Figure 7-28: Second draft object diagram for core CarMatch model

this clarification, the analyst decides that this second draft more accurately describes the true nature of the relationship between trips and locations.

The next step is to think about suitable type (class) names for the instances represented in the model. The analyst already has the type name **CarSharer** and has thus far been using the informal terms **trip** and **location**. Having discussed the object diagram further with the client and using the language of the client (CarMatch) the analyst decides upon appropriate formal (class) type names for the objects. In this case study, trip becomes **Journey** and location becomes **Address**. Figure 7-29 shows the amended object diagram, which now includes the class type of each object. In Figure 7-29 the analyst has also added notes about the multiplicity of the associations represented by the links on the object diagram.

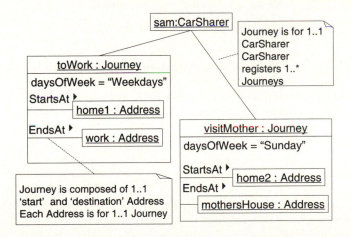

Figure 7-29: Object diagram showing class types for core CarMatch model

Finally, the analyst switches from an instance-based perspective to a type-based perspective, that is, from an object diagram to a class diagram. The analyst draws a class diagram that reflects the general types illustrated on the object diagram. Figure 7-30 shows the class diagram drawn from the object diagram shown in Figure 7-29.

So, objects and links, drawn as an object diagram, can be an extremely useful tool in the process of analysis to investigate particular aspects of the problem domain. Using an object diagram to give

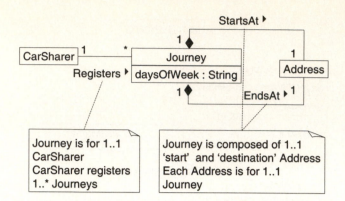

Figure 7-30: Class diagram showing class types for core CarMatch model

examples of possible structures in the problem domain can be an extremely useful tool to enable more effective communication with members of the user community.

7.8.2 Dependency

A dependency specifies that one model element requires the presence of another model element in order to function or be implemented. The implication of the dependency is that, if the model element upon which the dependency is specified is changed, then the dependent model element may also need to be changed (Figure 7-31).

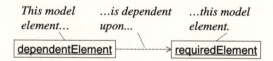

Figure 7-31: Illustration of dependency between model elements

The nature of that dependent requirement is specified by the stereotype of the dependency relationship. Dependencies fall into four main categories, binding, abstraction, usage and permission.

Many of the dependencies discussed here are arguably of more relevance to process modelling concepts than to the static structures represented in class or object diagrams.

Binding Binding dependencies have one stereotype, «bind». This dependency relates a bound element to the template class that will complete the definition of the resultant class. The dependency should also include a list of values passed as parameters to the template. Figure 7-32 illustrates a «bind» dependency.

Abstraction An abstraction dependency defines a relationship between two elements or sets of elements that represent the same concept at different levels of abstraction.

«**derive**» A derived element is a redundant specification within the model as the value(s) of the derived element can be worked out from the required element(s). The specification of a derived element must be provided as part of the dependency. A derived element may be implemented to improve the efficiency or clarity of the solution. Figure 7-33 illustrates a derived specification.

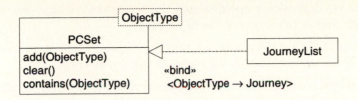

Figure 7-32: Binding dependency

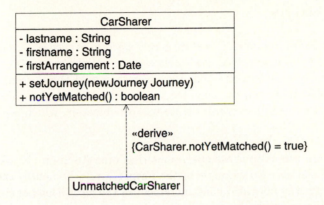

Figure 7-33: Derivation dependency

«realization» A realization dependency specifies the relationship between an element in the implementation model and an element in the specification model.

«refine» A refinement dependency specifies the relationship between model elements at different levels of abstraction, for example analysis-level and design-level elements.

«trace» A trace dependency specifies the relationship between two elements that represent the same concept in different models.

Usage Usage dependencies specify a requirement that one model element has for the presence of another model element.

«call» A call dependency specifies a collaboration between two operations; one operation will call the other operation.

«create» A create dependency implies that creation of an instance of the dependent class will result in the creation of an instance of the class that is the target of the dependency.

«instantiate» An instantiate dependency implies that the operations on the dependent class will create instances of the class that is the target of the dependency.

«send» A send dependency is specified between an operation and a signal. The dependency specifies that the operation sends the signal.

«use» A use dependency indicates that one class is dependent upon another class in order to realize its complete implementation.

«substitute» A substitute dependency is used to indicate where one class may be substituted for another, but where there is no direct inheritance relationship between those classes. The UML specification requires that the class being substituted in implements the same, or more specific, interfaces as the class being replaced.

Permission Permission dependencies are used to specify the accessibility of model elements in one namespace to model elements in a different namespace.

«access» An access dependency specifies that the dependent package can utilize the elements of the package that is the target of the dependency.

«import» An import dependency specifies that the dependent package incorporates model elements from the package that is the target of the dependency.

«permit» The «permit» dependency overrides normal visibility constraints, allowing the dependent element to access the target element regardless of the specified visibility.

7.8.3   Class-Scope Features

Class-scope features are useful in monitoring state across a group of classes. An example of this was used in Figure 7-7 on page 123. This example used a class-scope attribute **nextIDNumber** as an incremental count. As new object instances were created, they were assigned the current value of **nextIDNumber**. The value of **nextIDNumber** was then incremented, ready for assignment to the next instance. Class-scope attributes can also be useful to control state-based behaviour, which is discussed in more detail in Chapter 12.

Class-scope operations are typically those operations that operate upon class-scope attributes or that manipulate instances of classes. An example of the former would be **setIDNumber** in Figure 7-7. This operation is responsible for the allocation and increment of the **nextIDNumber** count. An example of the latter would be a constructor method, which is a class-scope operation to create instances of a class.

7.8.4   Class Types

Use of stereotyping will not be a primary concern for novice analysts. As their understanding of object-modelling, patterns and object-technologies improves, stereotyping can be introduced as a means of enriching the information content of class diagrams.

Stereotyping provides a useful shorthand specification for the type conformance of a model element. The two principal uses of stereotyping that have been discussed here are for classes and dependency relationships. The usage of stereotyping to define dependencies has already been discussed in Section 7.8.2. By specifying a class as having a particular stereotype, the analyst is identifying the nature of the role played by a class in the overall model. For example, specifying a class as «interface» clearly indicates the purpose of the class as specifying a pattern of structure without providing any operational implementation of that structure.

Template classes and bound elements are again of primary relevance to the more experienced analyst. The notation has been covered in this book primarily for the sake of completeness. Template classes offer the means of defining reusable harnesses. However, the disadvantages of design and code bloat may outweigh the advantages.

Review Questions

7.1   Discuss a situation where object diagrams can be useful during the analysis process.

7.2   On an object diagram, which association annotations are permitted for links?

7.3   The 'shorthand' notation for **«realization»** dependencies is derived from two other UML notations. What are they?

7.4 On a class diagram, how are class-scope features distinguished from instance-scope features?

7.5 What is the semantic difference between class-scope features and instance-scope features?

7.6 What are the three general notations covered in this chapter for specifying stereotypes in UML?

7.7 What is the purpose of an «enumeration» class?

7.8 What is the purpose of a «utility» class?

7.9 What stereotype notations can be used to identify an «interface» class.

7.10 What is the semantic difference between a required and provided interface?

7.11 In what way does an «implementationClass» differ from a «type» class?

7.12 What notation is used to relate «implementationClass» to its «type» class?

7.13 What is the basic notation for a template class?

7.14 What are the two notations for showing bound elements? What is the key semantic difference between the two notations?

Solved Problems

7.1 Draw an object diagram to illustrate the 'evening talk' class diagram shown in Figure 6-35 in Problem 6.3 on page 117.

Three variant object diagrams are shown. Clearly there are many possible choices of object instances.

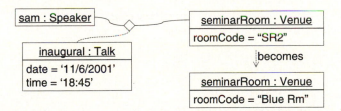

Figure 7-34: A talk with no attendees registered yet

Figure 7-34 shows a talk that has been arranged for an identified date and time. The speaker has been identified, as has the venue. As the object diagram suggests, the change of roomCode reflects a change in the state of the SeminarRoom : Venue object. It is still this same object instance that is involved in the association instance though.

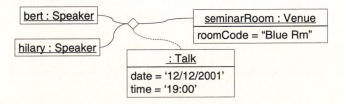

Figure 7-35: A talk with two speakers

Figure 7-35 shows a talk with two speakers. Finally, Figure 7-36 shows a talk with two venues and several registered car sharers.

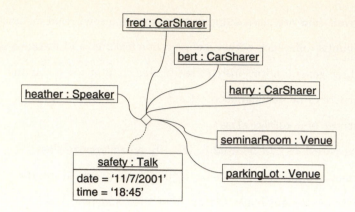

Figure 7-36: A talk with three registered car sharers

7.2 Add an «enumeration» class to the 'evening talk' class model used in Problem 7.1. The enumeration class should be used to set the status of a Talk. A talk can be "Provisional", "Confirmed" or "Cancelled".

Figure 7-37 shows the relevant classes.

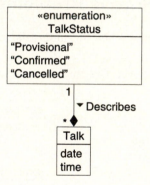

Figure 7-37: Enumeration class for evening talk status

7.3 Draw a class diagram that shows the following requirements as a template class with two bound elements. Use the more verbose notation with the template class and «bind» relationships.

Janet Hoffner: We will need to keep a list of the requirements a car sharer has. A car sharer could have no requirements, but we want to be able to list up to 10 requirements per car sharer. That '10' is a strict limit. We will also need to keep a list of the next of kin for a car sharer; we'll need to keep at least one and no more than three.

Figure 7-38 shows a possible solution. Other annotations have been suppressed.

Supplementary Problems

7.4 Draw an object diagram to illustrate the classes, n-ary association and association class in the class model you constructed for Problem 6.5.

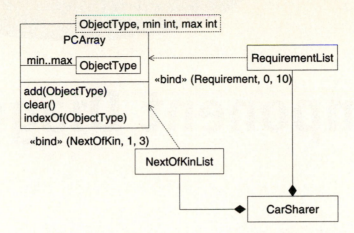

Figure 7-38: Template class and bound elements

7.5 The VolBank system will make use of two operations, getTimeInterval(fromTime : Time, toTime : Time) and **getDateInterval(fromDate : Date, toDate : Date)**, in many different operations throughout the system. For example, to calculate time worked on an assignment, time available as banked time, length of time a volunteering opportunity has been registered, length of time a volunteer or organization has been registered. How could these two operations be modelled so as to specify that they should be globally available? Model a suitable class to show the notation in use.

7.6 Rather than holding a single contact for an organization, VolBank want to hold a list of contacts. Show how this could be modelled using both the 'terse' and 'verbose' UML notations for template classes and bound elements.

CHAPTER 8

Component Diagrams

8.1 INTRODUCTION

When constructing software systems there are two practices (among many others) that can be used to mitigate some of the risks typically associated with the software development process. These are:

- reducing and clearly defining the coupling between the software components of the application;
- reusing existing components, whose functionality is already proven (perhaps including open source or commercial-off-the-shelf (COTS) components).

Both of these practices depend upon an ability to define accurately the boundary and make-up of coarse-grained software components.

Components may be as granular as individual classes (i.e. a component is a class) or they may represent a collection of classes (i.e. one component represents several classes). However complex the internal structure of a component, it must define its externally accessible functionality in terms of the interfaces that it either provides or requires. The concept of, and notation for, required and provided interfaces was introduced in Chapter 7.

8.2 PURPOSE OF THE TECHNIQUE

Component diagrams can fulfil several purposes within the modelling process.

- They can be used to model envisaged software components and the interfaces between them at the outset of a project, thus providing a means of deferring consideration of detailed design to a more appropriate time.
- They can be used to hide the specification of underlying detail and instead focus on the inter-relationship between components as specified by the interfaces between those components.
- They can be used to show how previously proven components are integrated into the current system design.

142

8.3   NOTATION

8.3.1   Components

Figure 8-1 introduces the basic notation for a component.

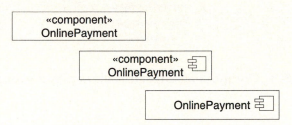

Figure 8-1: Basic notations for a component

A component is shown as a rectangle containing the name of the component. The **«component»** stereotype is shown along with an optional iconic representation of the same stereotyping. Previous versions of UML use the icon seen here as the main shape of component nodes. However, this has been simplified to a rectangular node to make diagrammatical support easier to provide in modelling tools.

8.3.2   Component Interfaces

As mentioned above, a key notion in the use and modelling of components is that each component must adhere to the specification of the interfaces that it either provides or requires. Naturally then, we need to be able to link a component to the interfaces that define its boundary. Figure 8-2 shows the **OnlinePayment** component and the fact that this component provides the **PaymentTransaction** interface and requires the **IdentityManagement** interface.

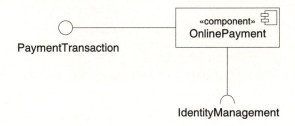

Figure 8-2: Provided and required interfaces for a component

(**OnlinePayment** was shown as a class in the previous chapter. It is shown in its more likely guise as a component here.)

The interfaces upon which a component depends can also be shown in the form of a list, grouped by dependency stereotype. This notation is shown in Figure 8-3.

At this point we can examine in more detail the basic notion of components and their use. In Figures 8-2 and 8-3, we have a means of specifying that there will be an **OnlinePayment** component that must provide a **PaymentTransaction** interface. This provided interface of the component will support the attributes and operations (along with their parameters and return types) defined for the **PaymentTransaction** interface. Our system will only interact with the provided and required interfaces for this component. We will know what those attributes and operations are as the **PaymentTransaction** is well defined. Similarly,

Figure 8-3: Component interfaces shown as a grouped list

we know that our application must provide the **IdentityManagement** interface that is required by the **OnlinePayment** component.

The analyst may wish to show more detail about the interfaces that are required by or provided by the component. If this is the case then the analyst can use **«interface»** definitions, as described in Chapter 7, to show the attributes and operations that are defined by the interfaces used by the component. An example of this type of clarification is shown in Figure 8-4.

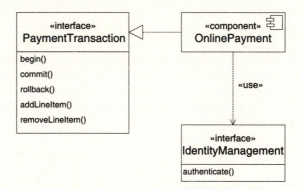

Figure 8-4: Definition of interfaces for a component

Given this knowledge, we can design the rest of our system (outside of the **OnlinePayment** component) to work with these interfaces. At this level of treatment, we don't need to know or need to care how the specific **OnlinePayment** component we are using will realize the provision of those attributes and operations. We could substitute in a different implementation of the **OnlinePayment** component with a totally different implementation. So long as that replacement component provides and requires the same interfaces, in line with our specification, then the internal mechanics of that component should not concern us.

Figures 8-5 and 8-6 illustrate this point. In Figure 8-5, the **OnlinePayment** component is shown along with some other components which interface with that component. In Figure 8-5, the **OnlinePayment** component is shown along with two other components. **MemberManagement** provides the **IdentityManagement** interface required by the **OnlinePayment** component. **InsuranceBrokerage** requires the **PaymentTransaction** interface that is provided by the **OnlinePayment** component.

Should CarMatch find that there is a cost-effective off-the-shelf solution that provides and requires the same interfaces as their own envisaged component then they would be able to substitute in that

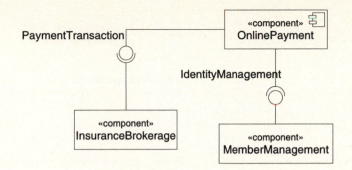

Figure 8-5: The OnlinePayment component in context

component without having to redesign the internal mechanics of either the **InsuranceBrokerage** or **MemberManagement** components. Figure 8-6 shows the replacement of the **OnlinePayment** component with the off-the-shelf **EPayToday** component.

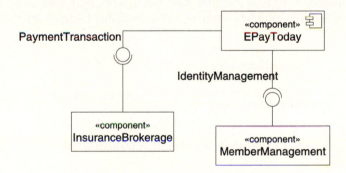

Figure 8-6: Replacement of the OnlinePayment component with an off-the-shelf component

Clearly, the kind of example used here is less likely to happen in this way in the real world. It is more likely that specific components will be selected early on in the development life-cycle and be woven into the overall architecture and design from the outset. However, bounding components of the application in terms of their required and provided interfaces does promote the flexibility and maintainability of that application as those interfaces set up fire breaks that insulate one component from substitution of, or changes to the internal mechanics of, another component.

Figures 8-5 and 8-6 show the *assembly* of components in a specific context.

8.3.3 Component Assemblies

These distinct components can be 'wired' together to form subsystems. The notion of assembling a system from well-bounded components was introduced at the start of this chapter. This wiring can use either the 'ball-and-socket' notation introduced in Section 7.5.6 and illustrated in Figures 8-5 and 8-6, or dependency-based wiring as shown in Figure 8-7.

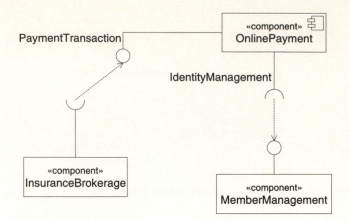

Figure 8-7: Using dependencies to 'wire' components together

8.3.4 Ports

As with classes, ports can be specified on components. In the context of a component diagram, the purpose of a port definition is to indicate that the component itself does not supply the required or provided interfaces. Instead, the interface requirement is delegated to an internal class of the component.

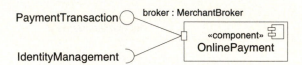

Figure 8-8: Ports on a component

The UML notation for a port is a small box placed at the side of the component whose port(s) are being defined. The required and provided interfaces that are delegated by the component are then connected to the port. Naming and typing the port further defines the specific services that are provided through that port. The value of adding a port definition name is that the port can itself be named (see **broker : MerchantBroker** in Figure 8-8), and thus addressed directly.

8.3.5 Component Realization

A component might implement (or realize) the provided interfaces for the component itself, or it may delegate that realization to other classes that make up the component. For example, the **OnlinePayment** component might be realized by **Payment**, **PaymentItem** and **PaymentController** classes. This realization dependency can be shown in three ways: by listing the realization classes, by the use of realization dependency relationships, or by graphical containment. These three approaches are shown in Figures 8-9, 8-10 and 8-11 respectively.

Using the listed representation can be combined with listing the required and provided interfaces as shown in Figure 8-3 rather than using the graphical representation as shown in Figure 8-9.

In Figure 8-10 the **«realizes»** dependency is shown in its dashed-line form rather than using an annotated solid-line dependency.

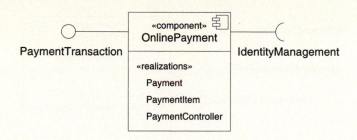

Figure 8-9: Component realization shown by listed classes

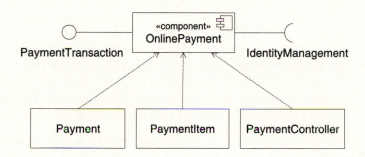

Figure 8-10: Component realization shown by realization dependency

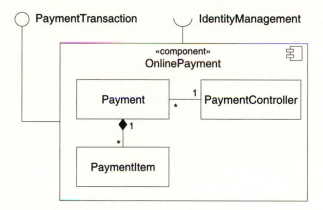

Figure 8-11: Component realization shown by graphical containment

Finally, Figure 8-11 shows the use of graphical containment to define the classes that realize the **OnlinePayment** component.

8.3.6   Port Forwarding and Filtering

Ports connect to the required and provided interfaces on the *outside* of the ported class. They can also connect to the classes that the ported class is composed of, and which will interact with the external system through those interfaces.

Figure 8-12 shows the notation for connecting ports with the elements of a ported component. In this case, the **broker** port (which has been defined as being of type **MerchantBroker**) is connected to the

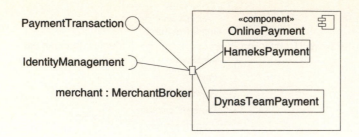

Figure 8-12: Ported component

HameksPayment and **DynasTeamPayment** classes. The **HameksPayment** and **DynasTeamPayment** classes are capable of fulfilling the **MerchantBroker** contract that is specified on the port.

This raises the question of how a message arriving at a port from one of its interfaces is passed on to the *internal* classes connected to that port. Possible options may include:

- filtering the incoming message to see whether it should be handled at all, and if so forwarding it;
- inspecting the content of the incoming message to determine which internal class should handle that message;
- multi-casting the incoming message to some or all of the internal classes, again depending upon the content of the incoming message;
- load-balancing incoming messages to the internal classes by forwarding, for example, on a round-robin basis.

Where the port has been typed, as in the example used in Figure 8-12, it is reasonably clear that the behaviour of the class type used for the port would define the behaviour of the port in the face of these incoming messages. The UML Specification describes this concept as 'semantic variation'. Where the port has not been typed, then the behaviour of the port is taken to be not explicitly specified.

8.3.7   Subcomponents

At the start of this chapter, it was suggested that component diagrams provide a means of either hiding the complexity of a component or deferring the specification of the complexities of a component. In the latter case, it may be that a component represents a collection of other components. This may be the situation where a complex but discrete subsystem is being used and that subsystem is itself made up of several components. Alternatively it may be that a component turns out to be more complex and have discrete internal components that were not envisaged when the modelling process was begun. These subcomponents can usefully be modelled as components in their own right as they may be reused in other applications.

In this situation, the main component can be 'wired' to its subcomponents using the «delegate» stereotype to connect the ports of the main component to the interfaces of its subcomponents. This notation is illustrated in the partially complete Figure 8-13.

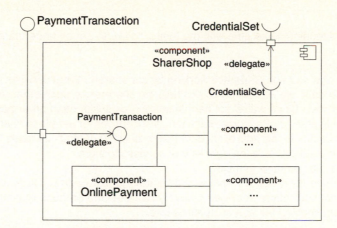

Figure 8-13: Using «delegate» connectors to wire into subcomponents

8.4   MODELLING GUIDANCE

Component diagrams provide an excellent means of documenting a system from the very first model produced to the very last. The very first model of a system may be a coarse-grained sketch of the components that can be envisaged when only a rudimentary understanding of the system has been gained. The very last view of a system may need to hide the implementation detail of the system yet still show the key functional components and the precise boundaries (the interfaces) between those components.

A practitioner or student capable of producing a component diagram at the start of the development process will have all the understanding and skills necessary to produce a component diagram for any stage of the development process. Thus, we will focus our attention here on the start of the development process.

In the modelling process, producing a component diagram will require the analyst to iterate over a series of activities. These activities will each contribute to the overall picture and specification being produced.

- Find components and dependencies.
- Identify and level subcomponents.
- Clarify and make explicit the interfaces between the components.

8.4.1   Find components and dependencies

Components and dependencies will be identified from the information gathered in the early stages of the development life-cycle. As use cases are crystallized and (or) activity diagrams are formulated, the technical analyst will be able to begin to pick out the key components that will make up the envisaged system. This process will be akin to identifying classes and associations, as described in Section 4.5.1, though it will be based upon a much coarser-grained view of the system.

EXAMPLE 8.1   Here is an excerpt from an early meeting between Janet Hoffner (one of the CarMatch directors) and Mick Perez (the systems analyst). Identify any components and dependencies mentioned in the transcript.

Mick Perez: Thanks for spending some time with me today. I'd like to get an understanding of how you see the big picture for CarMatch.

Janet Hoffner: Big picture?

Mick Perez: Yes, tell me how you see CarMatch working for car sharers. What services will you offer them?

Janet Hoffner: OK. Essentially, we want to be able to help car sharers find each other. At the moment they have no effective way of doing that. Once we've got people sharing cars with each other because they think it's the right thing to do, we'd like to start to offer some real financial incentives for people to share. Primarily, that means offering better insurance deals. In the future, we could offer all kinds of financial deals to our sharers; once we know who they are we can help promote the right kind of services to them.

MP: What sort of services did you have in mind?

JH: We're thinking insurance for a starter—that would be the biggest saving. Other ideas on the table are to introduce preferential credit card offers, roadside recovery services and perhaps real-time navigational services ("turn left in 100m" type services)...but at a competitive rate.

MP: ...

SOLUTION   Mick Perez went through this transcript, using his experience to pick out possible components and dependencies. He came up with the model shown in Figure 8-14. He picked out the following concepts as components:

- 'Help car sharers find each other' became the **SharerMatching** component.
- 'Offering better insurance deals' and 'all kinds of financial deals' suggested the need for both **Payment** and **SharerService** components. **Payment** is needed to enable sharers to make payments. **SharerService** represents generic financial services that CarMatch might offer.
- Finally, Mick felt that if all these components and services were to be offered then a **SharerManagement** component would be needed to provide administrative and related functionality around sharers. He included a component to provide this interface.

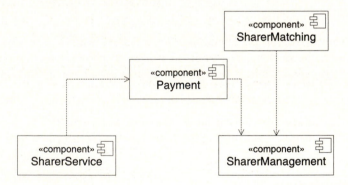

Figure 8-14: The basic CarMatch components

8.4.2   Identify and level subcomponents

The next activity is to establish if there are any significant subcomponents in the model that could be promoted from within one component to become one of the primary components being modelled. Alternatively, there may be components that will only interact with one other component. These components could be subsumed as a subcomponent of that other component.

EXAMPLE 8.2   Mick looked at the **Payment** component a little more closely. He had planned to provide a **PaymentLogger** subcomponent to the **Payment** component. However, he realized that the logging mechanism he was considering could be used by several other components of the solution—and perhaps even in other systems altogether.

SOLUTION   Mick reworked the PaymentLogger subcomponent to become a first-class component as shown in Figure 8-15.

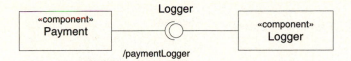

Figure 8-15: Promoted subcomponent

Now the more general Logger component provided a Loggerinterface to the Payment component and to other components in the system as well. The required dependency for the Payment component was mapped onto the provided interface. The Logger interface now fulfilled the role of the payment logger service for Payment. Mick showed this on his diagram using the role annotation /paymentLogger.

8.4.3   Clarify interfaces

Now that we have this preliminary model, we can begin to clarify the interfaces between the different components. Remember that components are bounded by the interfaces that they provide or require.

EXAMPLE 8.3   Taking his preliminary component diagram, with simple dependencies between each component, Mick Perez began to consider the specific nature of the interfaces between the components. The SharerService component was responsible for delivering financial services offerings to end-users and for capturing subsequent payments. The Payment component was responsible for processing these payments. Considering how these two components would interact with each other, Mick wanted to be able to encapsulate all issues relating to the mechanics of raising payments to the Payment component and simply have the SharerService component raise payment transactions.

SOLUTION   Mick introduced a PaymentTransaction interface that was provided by the Payment component and required by the SharerService component. This interface is shown in Figure 8-16.

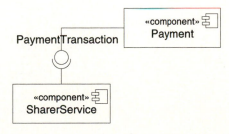

Figure 8-16: Adding interface definitions

Finally, Mick decided that the SharerMatching and Payment components both required services that authenticated the access credentials of a sharer or provided access to some of the personal details of a sharer. Thus he defined the interface between these components as being one of IdentityManagement.

Now his component diagram was as shown in Figure 8-17.

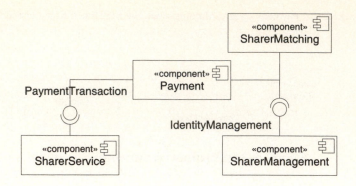

Figure 8-17: Clarified interfaces between components

8.5   RELATIONSHIP WITH OTHER DIAGRAMS

Component diagrams have a strong link with class diagrams both at the start and the end of the development process. We have already seen how component diagrams can be used to model an application in terms of coarse-grained components with well-defined interfaces. In Chapter 14 we will consider how component diagrams can be used to show the bundling of classes into components and how those components are deployed onto the hardware infrastructure for an application.

8.6   COMPONENT DIAGRAMS IN THE UNIFIED PROCESS

The treatment of component diagrams in the Unified Process reflects the origins of component diagrams in structuring the implementation of a system. Figure 8-18 shows the implementation workflow from the Unified Process.

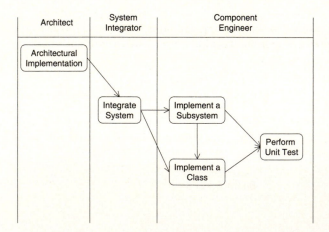

Figure 8-18: Implementation workflow as an activity diagram

Component diagrams are used in most of the activities in this workflow. In the activity *Architectural Implementation* they are used in the step *Identifying Architecturally Significant Components*, when important components are identified and a decision is made about the nodes on which they will reside. Deployment diagrams are also used to show the allocation of components to nodes.

In the activity *Integrate System*, components are used in planning a build of the system. The activity *Implement a Subsystem* uses component diagrams to model how components will be used to implement the design classes that have been allocated to each subsystem. Finally, components are the 'units' in the activity *Perform Unit Test*. Components are subjected to black-box testing to ensure that each component produces the correct outputs in response to different sets of input values, and to white-box testing to verify that the component works internally as it is designed to do. This can include coverage tests to ensure that all code is executed at least once under some circumstance.

UML now enables components to play a more general role in the modelling process than was previously the case. It would be reasonable to begin to sketch out the overall structure of an application using components as part of the analysis workflow. This usage would be akin to the use of classes in the analysis workflow (see Section 4.7). This usage might be especially appropriate for large and complex systems consisting of very many interacting subcomponents.

Review Questions

8.1 Define what is meant by a component.

8.2 What are the different notations for a component?

8.3 How are interfaces used in a component diagram?

8.4 What are the different notations for connecting two components together (via an interface)?

8.5 What is the purpose of ports in a component diagram?

8.6 How can ports be linked to the internal elements of a component?

Solved Problems

8.1 Mick was talking with Jan Cusack, a fellow member of his team. Mick was talking through the interviews he'd had with CarMatch staff.

Jan Cusack: How complex is the system then?
Mick Perez: Well, CarMatch need to be able to maintain sharer details as part of their system. One thing that struck me is that it is really important for them to be accurate and consistent about how they capture address information. We could make use of that Zip-O-Matic address look-up tool from P-Pat Industries.
JC: Could we also patch into the TigerLatte geolocating code my team have been working on?
MP: Remind me how that works.
JC: It provides a GeoLocation service. It simply needs a distinguishing address, like a house number and zip postal code. Then it can locate the house and provide a grid, or the route finder functionality can take two locations and plot a navigation route for you.
MP: Cool...

Mick could see that there were some components to be modelled here. The Zip-O-Matic tool was the first clear candidate. As a commercial tool, Mick wouldn't know the internal details of the commercial Zip-O-Matic component. There was also the GeoLocation utilities that Jan had mentioned. Mick knew that these were also available as a packaged component. Thus Mick began to sketch out a component diagram. His first attempt is shown in Figure 8-19. This model shows the components at a conceptual level. Mick has used a general dependency to show that in his first-cut model both **SharerManagement** and **SharerMatching** would be dependent upon the **GeoLocator** functionality.

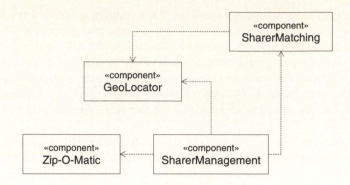

Figure 8-19: Component diagram with dependencies

8.2 Mick then reflected on his model. He had dependencies running from both **SharerManagement** and **SharerMatching** to **GeoLocator**. In all probability, the only component to use the **GeoLocator** component would be **SharerMatching**. Thus Mick decided to make **GeoLocator** a subcomponent of **SharerMatching**.

Mick's second model is shown in Figure 8-20. This shows **GeoLocator** as a subcomponent of **SharerMatching**. This meant that now the nature of the dependency between **SharerMatching** and **GeoLocator** had shifted. Instead of the dependency being a kind of interface between the two components, **SharerMatching** now made use of the **GeoLocator** as part of its implementation.

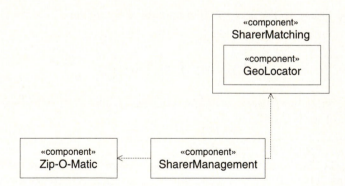

Figure 8-20: GeoLocator as a subcomponent of SharerMatching

8.3 Mick now wanted to clarify the nature of the interfaces between the different components. He considered the nature of the interface and investigated the application programming interface (API) for the Zip-O-Matic product.

Mick wanted to expose the **GeoLocator** functionality to the rest of the application through the **SharerMatch-ing** component. To do this, he provided two interfaces; one for routing (**Router**) and for determining location (**Locator**). Figure 8-21 shows the results of this analysis. It should be noted that the direction of the dependencies used earlier ran toward the component with the provided interface. The component with the required interface is dependent upon the component with the provided interface.

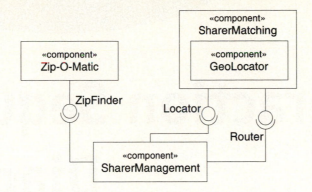

Figure 8-21: Interfaces added to component diagram

Supplementary Problems

8.4 Said Hussain has been sketching out some notes on the high-level structure of the VolBank system. These are shown below. From this list, sketch out an initial component diagram, using dependencies between components.

- Volunteer maintenance will need a matching component.
- Think we can use the geographical matching component that Mick Perez has been using on the CarMatch project as part of this. (Must double check the interface.)
- Need to capture audit log of approval to use personal information for matching purposes. Must provide logging component.
- Getting accurate address information would be helpful—can I reuse mechanism from Car-Match?

8.5 Refine the diagram you produced in Problem 8.4 by adding the provided and required interfaces for each dependency.

8.6 Consider the class and package structure shown in Figure 5-27. This diagram suggests that the packages **OSRef**, **LatLongRef** and **TigerRef** are imported. Assume that each of these three packages is implemented as a different component and that the **GeoLocation** component is implemented as another component. Draw three component diagrams showing how the required and provided interfaces of the **GeoLocation** component are provided or required by the three packages **OSRef**, **LatLongRef** and **TigerRef**.

CHAPTER 9

Interaction Sequence Diagrams

9.1 INTRODUCTION

In object-oriented systems, tasks are performed by objects interacting with each other by passing messages. Interaction diagrams are used to model these object interactions. An interaction is a specification of the way in which messages are sent between objects in order to perform a task. In UML there are variations of *interaction diagrams*: *sequence diagrams*, *interaction overview diagrams*, *timing diagrams* and *communication diagrams*. In this chapter we explain the notation and use of sequence diagrams; we cover the use of the other types of diagrams in Chapter 10. Sequence diagrams and communication diagrams were in UML 1.X, although communication diagrams were formerly known as *collaboration diagrams*; interaction overview diagrams and timing diagrams are new in UML 2.0.

Class diagrams model the static structure of the system; interaction diagrams model the dynamic aspects of the system: they show how objects interact with one another to achieve some high-level functionality that individual objects cannot achieve on their own. Sequence diagrams are used to show this interaction and emphasize the order of the messages over time. Communication diagrams show the same interaction in the context of the classes that participate in the interaction and show the structural relationships of the classes to one another.

9.2 WHAT IS A SEQUENCE DIAGRAM?

Thus far in the book, we have considered static, structural models. Use-case diagrams show the static relationship between actors and use cases; class diagrams show the static relationship between classes or instances. However, as we said above, the way in which object-oriented systems produce useful results for actors is by instances of those classes collaborating together by sending messages. We can produce a class diagram that shows the subset of classes that appear in a particular use case, and this is often done as a way of identifying classes, in conjunction with a technique like CRC cards (see Section 4.5.2). Figure 9-1 shows the objects involved in the use case **Record sharing agreement**, including instances of a boundary class and a control class. Diagrams similar to this that show the participants in a particular interaction are known as *collaborations* and are discussed in more detail in Chapter 17. The links shown in this diagram are based on associations in the class diagram and on identifying the links that are likely to be necessary for messages to be sent between participants.

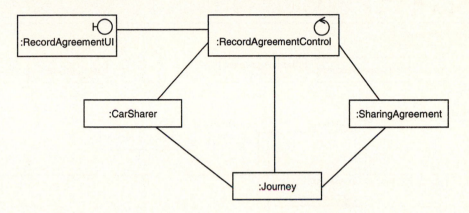

Figure 9-1: Object diagram for the use case Record sharing agreement

Messages can be added to a diagram like this to show the interaction, and this results in a communication diagram like the one in Figure 9-2. (See Chapter 10 for an explanation of communication diagrams.)

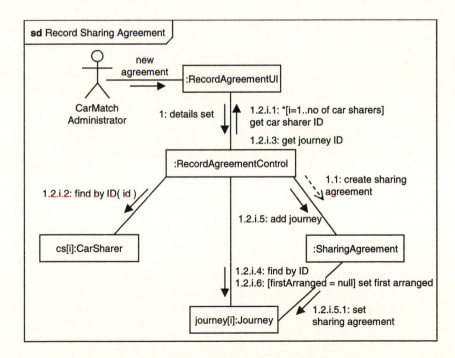

Figure 9-2: Interaction added to Figure 9-1

As a way of representing an interaction graphically, communication diagrams have two main characteristics: they show the structural relationships between the class roles or objects in terms of association roles or links—reflecting the structure of the class diagram—and they show the order of the interaction textually—using the sequence-numbers in the messages. Sequence diagrams represent some of the same information, but not all: they show *lifelines* that represent the objects or systems that participate in the interaction; they do not show the structural relationships between the lifelines and they show the order of the interaction visually by using the vertical axis of the diagram to represent time. Figure 9-3 shows a sequence diagram for the interaction in the use case **Record sharing agreement**. The lifelines in this diagram represent instances of the classes shown in the class diagram in Figure 9-1.

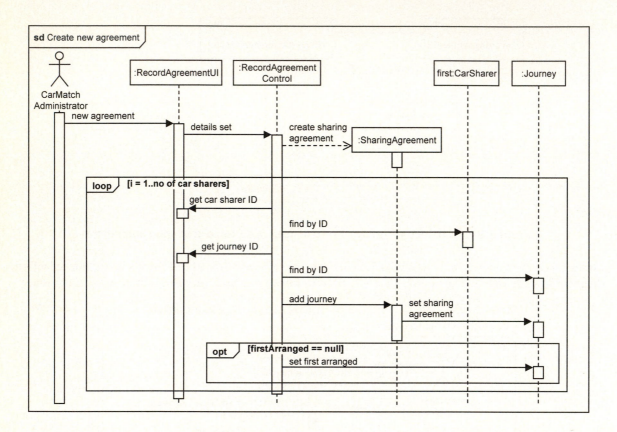

Figure 9-3: Sequence diagram for the use case Record sharing agreement

Figure 9-3 illustrates the way in which the order of the messages can be read from the diagram by looking at their sequence down the page.

The sequence diagram does highlight some aspects that are not so obvious in communication diagrams. The creation of an object instance is shown explicitly by drawing the arrow to the rectangle containing its name (as in the case of the **:SharingAgreement** object, and its *lifeline* (the vertical dashed line) begins at the point when it is created. The *focus of control*, represented by the long thin rectangles on the lifeline, shows when an object is active, either because it is performing some action or because it has sent a message to another object, which is carrying out an action on its behalf.

9.3 PURPOSE OF THE TECHNIQUE

Sequence diagrams are used to model the interaction between object instances by showing the sequence of messages that are exchanged by the objects.

Sequence diagrams can be used in the following ways.

- They are used to model the high-level interaction between active objects in a system.
- They are used to model the high-level interaction between subsystems.
- They are used to model the interaction between object instances that realize a use case.
- They are used to model the interaction between objects within an operation.
- They can be used to model reusable fragments of interactions that can be combined in other sequence diagrams or in interaction overview diagrams.

9.4 NOTATION OF SEQUENCE DIAGRAMS

9.4.1 Frames

Sequence diagrams are drawn in *frames*. Frames are new in UML 2.0. In UML 1.X, sequence diagrams were drawn without frames. Figure 9-4 shows a frame.

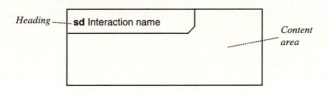

Figure 9-4: Sequence diagram frame

Frames are rectangles with a heading in a compartment in the top left-hand corner, in which the keyword **sd** for sequence diagrams and the name of the interaction are shown. Parameters of the interaction and a return value can also be included in the heading. (The syntax of parameters and return values is explained in Section 9.4.3 for messages.) The compartment for the heading is drawn as a rectangle with the lower right-hand corner cut off.

In sequence diagrams, lifelines (which usually represent object instances) are arranged inside the frame horizontally across the page, and time runs vertically down the page (Figure 9-5).

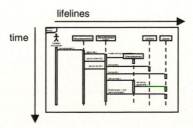

Figure 9-5: Vertical time axis

In timing diagrams, time runs from left to right across the page; timing diagrams are covered in Section 10.9.

The order of lifelines across the page is not significant, but by convention, external actors and lifelines representing interface objects are placed to the left and there is a general flow of messages across the page from left to right in societies that use a left-to-right, top-down way of writing (Figure 9-6).

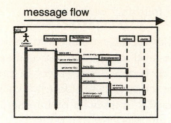

Figure 9-6: Direction of message flow

9.4.2   Lifelines

Participating instances are represented in a sequence diagram by a dashed vertical line with, usually, a rectangle representing an object at the top of the line. These are *lifelines*, as shown in Figure 9-7. The shape at the top of the lifeline represents the kind of classifier that is participating in the interaction.

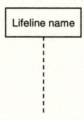

Figure 9-7: Lifeline notation

The lifeline represents participation of the object in the interaction. If a particular object exists before an interaction starts and continues to exist after the interaction ends, then the dashed line runs from top to bottom of the diagram.

Lifeline names are simpler than in UML 1.X and are no longer underlined. The syntax for the name of the lifeline is as follows:

```
[connectable-element-name]['['selector']'][:class-name][decomposition]
```

A *connectable element* is any kind of model element that can be linked by a connector. In this case, it is typically an object or a subsystem. Its use is optional here, as is the name of the class. The *selector* notation is used if the object is one of a set that can be selected by an index value, for example an array of objects. The selector itself can be an expression; typically it is the name of a counter or an integer value. The optional *decomposition* part of the name is used if the lifeline represents something like a subsystem that can be decomposed, and is used to reference another sequence diagram in which the behaviour of the components of the subsystem is shown, and that behaviour corresponds to the interaction of the subsystem in the current diagram. It uses the keyword **ref** followed by the name of the related sequence diagram.

Table 9-1 shows some examples of the various forms that lifeline names can take. Objects have been used here in the examples, but they could equally well be any other kind of connectable element.

Table 9-1: Examples of lifeline names

Syntax	Explanation
o	An object named o.
o : C	An object named o of class C.
:C	An anonymous object of class C.
o[i]	The object o that is selected by the index value i.
s ref sd3	A subsystem s whose internal interaction is shown in sequence diagram sd3 (decomposition).
self	The connectable element that owns the interaction shown in the sequence diagram.

9.4.3   Messages and Focus of Control

In a sequence diagram, a message is shown using an arrow going from the sender to the receiver (see Figure 9-8). The arrow is labelled with the message that is being sent.

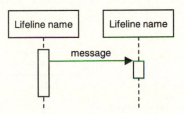

Figure 9-8: Message notation

The arrow is usually shown going from the *focus of control* region of the sending object to the focus of control region of the receiving object. The focus of control is shown as a narrow white or grey rectangle placed over the lifeline of the object. This is not always shown in sequence diagrams, and appears to be used less in UML 2.0 than in UML 1.X. The focus of control indicates which object is currently controlling the interaction because it is performing some task itself or because it has sent a message to another object requesting it to carry out a task. The idea of focus of control really applies only when the messages that are sent are procedural calls from one object to another; these calls are synchronous. In an asynchronous interaction, one object can send a message to another object, and the first object then carries on with its next task without waiting for a reply; in a synchronous interaction each object waits for a response. The return of control (*reply*) in procedural interactions can be shown with a dashed arrow returning to the calling object, as in Figure 9-9. Figure 9-11 shows the sequence diagram of Figure 9-3 with explicit replies.

The term focus of control comes from UML 1.X. In UML 2.0 the formal term that is used is *execution occurrence*. Each execution occurrence is associated with two *event occurrences*, representing the start event of the execution occurrence and the end event of the execution occurrence. Event occurrences also apply to messages: the start event and the end event of each message is an event occurrence. This is shown in Figure 9-10.

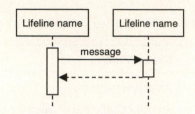

Figure 9-9: Reply notation

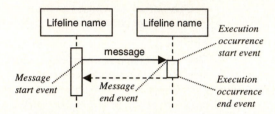

Figure 9-10: Event occurrences

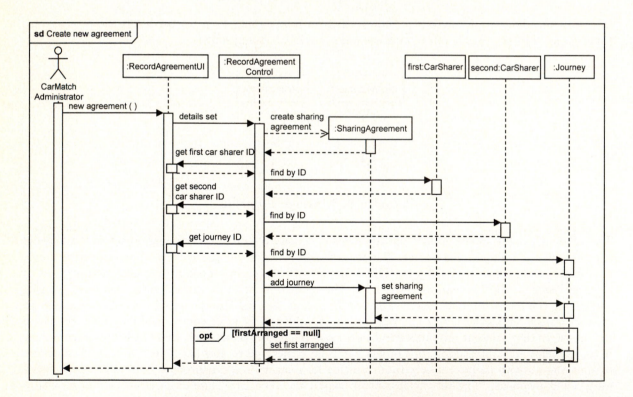

Figure 9-11: Sequence diagram with explicit replies

Returning to Figure 9-11, the focus of control rectangles in the objects to the right of the diagram are not continuous because they are active only for short periods of time; the user interface and control objects are active all the time and delegate responsibility for carrying out specific tasks to the other objects.

Sequence diagrams like this can give a clear picture of which objects are active when in an interaction. However, they can also become cluttered with lines and difficult to understand. In Section 10.10, we shall see how interaction overview diagrams can be used to show what is happening in a more manageable form.

Not all messages are synchronous, and different style arrows are used to represent different types of message (Figure 9-12):

- **Synchronous**—A message is sent by one object to another and the first object waits until the resulting action has completed. This may include waiting for the completion of actions invoked by the second object on other objects.

- **Asynchronous**—A message is sent by one object to another but the first object does not wait until the resulting action has completed, it carries on with the next step in its own sequence of actions.

- **Creation**—Represents a message that causes the creation of an object instance to which the message is sent. This use of a specific arrow style is new in UML 2.0. The **«create»** stereotype of UML 1.X is no longer used.

- **Reply**—Represents the explicit return of control from the object to which the message was sent. The UML 2.0 Specification is ambiguous about whether these arrows have a filled arrowhead or an open one. We have followed the style described in the text in the Specification. Replies are not normally shown on communication diagrams (see Chapter 10).

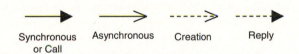

Synchronous   Asynchronous   Creation   Reply
or Call

Figure 9-12: Message type notation

UML 2.0 also introduces notation for messages that are *lost* and *found* (Figure 9-13). Lost messages have a send event but the receive event is unknown, normally because they do not reach their destination. Found messages have a receive event, but their origin is unknown, possibly because it is outside the scope of the description.

Lost message   Found message

Figure 9-13: Lost and found messages

The arrow represents the sending of a message or a signal. Where the message is synchronous, there is only one thread of execution, and activity passes from one object to another. Where the message is asynchronous, more than one object can be active at any one time. Figure 9-14 shows a sequence diagram with asynchronous messages. Note that an asynchronous message is sent between the objects, :WordProcessor and :PrintSpooler. The :Printer is also shown as an active object, and we have drawn it here with an asynchronous **ready** message to acknowledge that it has printed a block before it carries on with the next.

The objects participating in this interaction are shown as *active objects*. They are drawn with double lines at each end of the rectangle of the lifeline. Active objects are objects that can carry on their own

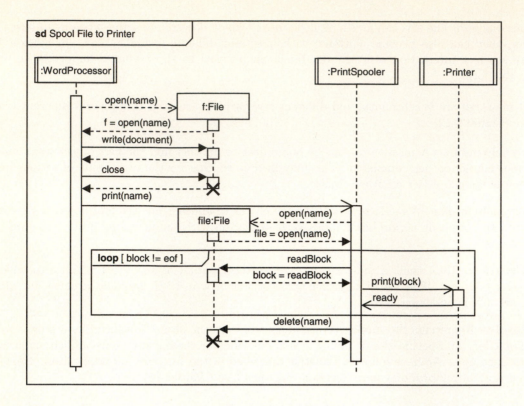

Figure 9-14: Sequence diagram with asynchronous messages and active objects

behaviour without the need for invocation of a method. In effect they run with their own thread of control.

This diagram also illustrates the destruction of an object using a large 'X' at the end of the lifeline of an object where it has received a message that represents a *stop*. In this figure, the **:File** object is both created and destroyed in the course of the interaction. In this example, the 'X' is shown at the end of a region of focus of control, as the **:File** has to carry out some actions to delete itself and free up system resources, but it can be shown on the lifeline if the stop simply results in the destruction of the object. Also in this case, we have drawn the deletion as synchronous, as the **:File** explicitly passes back control (and a result code) to the **:PrintSpooler**. Messages to create and destroy objects are shown in Figure 9-15. The names of the messages would be valid constructors and destructors.

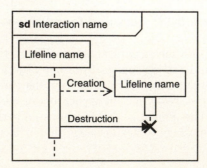

Figure 9-15: Notation for creation and destruction of an object

An object can send a message to itself or call one of its own operations. This can be explicitly shown in the focus of control region by placing a separate rectangle over the existing one and offsetting it slightly to the right (Figure 9-16).

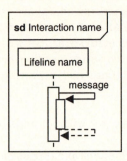

Figure 9-16: Notation for reflexive message

The syntax for messages has been simplified in UML 2.0, as some things that were in the message syntax have been removed and placed elsewhere, for example the conditions associated with **alt**, **opt** and **loop** combined fragments. The new syntax is summarized here.

The amount of detail about the message that is shown alongside the arrow can vary considerably. At its simplest, it is just the name of the message.

At its most complex, it can consist of all of the elements of the following syntax.

```
[attribute=] signal-or-operation-name [(arguments)] [:return-value]|'*'
```

Everything is optional apart from the *signal-or-operation-name*. The *attribute-assignment* and the *return-value* are only used on reply messages, as for example in the attribute assignment in Figure 9-14. The attribute assignment is a shorthand for the action to assign the result of the operation call represented by the message to an attribute of the object that sent the message. The return value can be used to show a literal return value. The asterisk is shorthand for a message of any type.

signal-or-operation-name—The signal or operation name is the event that is sent to the target object. An operation name will be the name of an operation in the class of the target object, for example, **readBlock**.

The term *signal* is used to refer to events that are sent from one object to another. A signal can have attributes, for example a **MouseDown** signal may have the attributes **button**, **xyCoordinate** and **timestamp**. These are shown as arguments.

arguments—Operations and signals are uniquely defined only if their full list of parameters is also specified. In sequence diagrams, actual arguments are used. The arguments are a comma-separated list of arguments, for example **setArranged (dateArranged)** or **MouseDown(button, xyCoordinate, timestamp)**. Note that according to the syntax above, in UML 2.0, unlike in UML 1.X, you do not show empty brackets after the operation or signal name if there are no arguments. The full syntax for each argument is as follows.

```
[parameter-name=] argument-value | attribute=out-parameter-name [:argument-value] | -
```

The distinction is made here between the names of the parameters and the argument values. For example, in the operation on a **File** of **open(name)**, **name** is the parameter; a value of **'sequenceDiagrams.doc'** is one of many possible argument values that could be assigned to that parameter. The formal syntax implies that open('sequenceDiagrams.doc') and open(name='sequenceDiagrams.doc') are both valid, but open(name) is not valid. However, the text also states, 'If parameter-names are used to identify the argument-value, then arguments may freely be omitted'. There are plenty of examples in the diagrams in the Specification that indicate that parameter names are valid. UML 2.0 sequence diagrams make far more use of argument values than in UML 1.X. The intention is to show 'actual' sequences of inter-actions, with specific values rather than general sequences with parameter names. Sequences specified with actual values can be compared with the actual results when a program is run, and some modelling environments are capable of running programs and capturing a trace of the interaction that can be compared with the design.

The dash can be used to represent a parameter with an undefined argument value.

return-value—Some messages are asynchronous and do not have return values. Synchronous messages may have a return-value that is sent back to the object that sent the message. This is typically used with assignment to an attribute, for example fileHandle = open('sequenceDiagrams.doc'):2. Return values are only shown on reply messages.

9.4.4   Combined Fragments

Where a sequence of messages takes place within an iteration, the messages can be shown grouped together in a *combined fragment* with the keyword loop and the *expression*, which controls how many times the loop is executed, in the heading area at the top left of the rectangle (Figure 9-17).

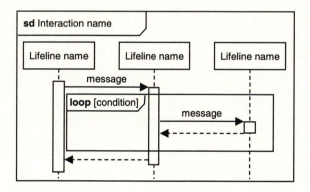

Figure 9-17: Notation for iteration (recurrence)

An example of this is shown in Figure 9-18, where the :PrintSpooler repeatedly reads a block from the :File and writes it to the :Printer until it reaches the end of the file.

Branching can be shown in a sequence diagram by a combined fragment with the keyword alt and two or more compartments. These compartments are known as the *operands* of the combined fragment. A *condition-clause* is added near the top of each operand compartment to show the condition that is used to make the decision about which branch to take (Figure 9-19). The keyword else can be used as the default condition.

UML 2.0 has added specific notation to show actions being carried out in parallel, using a combined fragment with the keyword par and the parallel actions in separate operand compartments (Figure 9-20). An alternative shorthand notation for parallel messages in a par combined fragment is the *coregion* notation shown in Figure 9-21.

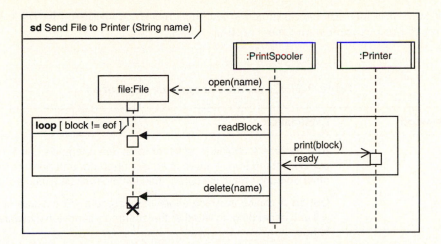

Figure 9-18: Sequence diagram with iteration shown using the *loop* notation

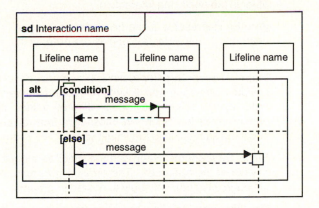

Figure 9-19: Notation for branching using an alternative (alt) combined fragment

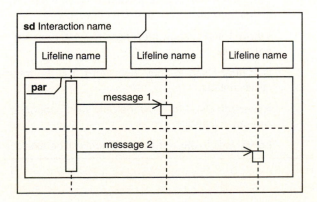

Figure 9-20: Notation for parallel actions

The full set of keywords for combined fragments and their meanings are listed in Table 9-2. We have concentrated on the most common and most useful.

Table 9-2: Combined fragment keywords

Keyword	Explanation
alt	**Alternatives** A choice in which at most one operand's condition will evaluate to true. If there is an else operand, and none of the other operands have executed, then the else will be executed.
opt	**Option** A choice in which either this fragment will execute or it will not, depending on whether the operand's condition evaluates to true.
break	**Break** A fragment with a condition which, if it is true, will be executed and will break out of the enclosing fragment. Shorthand for an alternative combined fragment with one operand, where the other is the enclosing interaction.
par	**Parallel** Represents a merge of the messages in the different operands in any order, as long as the order within each operand is preserved.
seq	**Weak Sequencing** Represents a weak sequencing of the behaviour of the operands. Events within each operand occur in the order shown. Where they affect different lifelines, they may happen in any order, but where messages from different operands affect the same lifeline they must occur in the order shown.
strict	**Strict Sequencing** Represents a strict sequencing of the behaviour of the operands. The order shown must be preserved, although this does not apply to nested fragments.
neg	**Negative** Used to show message traces that are not allowed to occur.
critical	**Critical Region** A region of messages that takes precedence over others in a parallel set of operands. If this region is invoked, it must execute before the other operands.
ignore	**Ignore** Used to show messages that the fragment must explicitly not handle.
consider	**Consider** Used to show messages that the fragment must explicitly handle.
assert	**Assertion** Used to show the only valid sequence of events in a sequence diagram.
loop	**Loop** Used to show that a fragment will be executed repeatedly.

Detail of interactions can be hidden in a sequence diagram. A message can be sent to a lifeline, resulting in messages being sent to further lifelines, but to show all the detail would make the diagram unwieldy or cluttered. The detail of how the lifeline carries out its response to the message can be shown in a separate diagram. The diagram in Figure 9-14 can have the detail of how the spooler subsystem operates removed to produce Figure 9-22. The detail of spooler operation is in Figure 9-23.

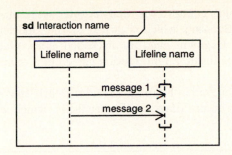

Figure 9-21: Notation for coregion

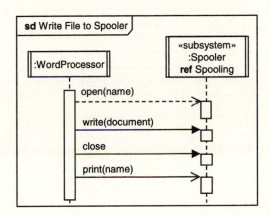

Figure 9-22: Sequence diagram with detail of interaction in :Spooler subsystem not shown

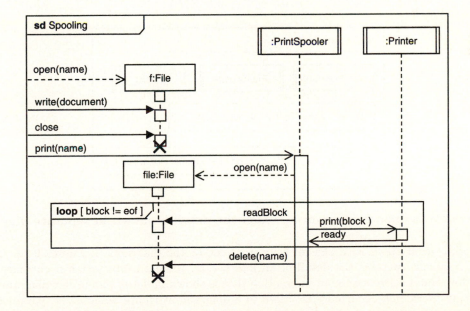

Figure 9-23: Sequence diagram with detail of interaction in Spooler subsystem

Note that the sequence of messages going to the :Spooler subsystem must be the same as in the decomposed sequence diagram called Spooling, which is owned by the :Spooler subsystem. The points where the messages enter the Spooling fragment diagram are called *gates*. Gates are the points that connect messages outside to the messages inside an interaction shown in a separate diagram.

The ownership of the sequence diagram in Figure 9-23 and the parts that make up the :Spooler subsystem can be shown in a composite structure diagram (Figure 9-24), which will be explained in more detail in Chapter 17.

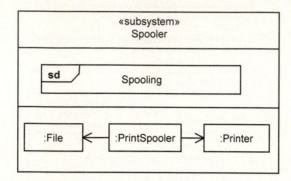

Figure 9-24: **The Spooler subsystem as a composite structure diagram**

9.4.5   Interaction Occurrences

Another way of hiding detail in sequence diagrams has been introduced in UML 2.0 with the use of *interaction occurrences*. Figure 9-25 shows this for the word processor and spooler example.

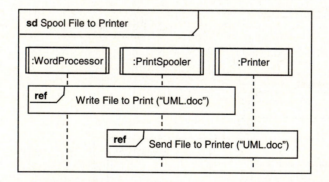

Figure 9-25: **Sequence diagram in which the detail is shown in separate diagrams**

The interaction occurrences with the **ref** keyword refer to the diagrams in Figure 9-26. Note that a combined fragment contains the detail of an interaction, while an interaction occurrence acts as a placeholder for, and a reference to, an interaction that is shown in detail in another diagram. Where a reference to an interaction occurrence is shown in a diagram, attribute assignment, parameters and a return value can be shown, as in the syntax for messages on page 165. Figure 9-26 shows the parameter **name** in the heading of the fragments, and Figure 9-25 shows the string value "**UML.doc**" being used as the argument in invoking these two fragments.

Gates are used for the points where messages enter and leave the fragments.

The way gates are drawn is shown in Figures 9-27 and 9-28. Gates are used for outgoing reply messages as well as incoming messages.

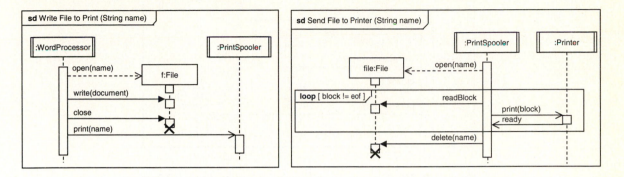

Figure 9-26: Sequence diagrams referred to in Figure 9-25

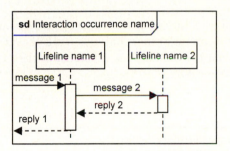

Figure 9-27: Gates in a sequence diagram

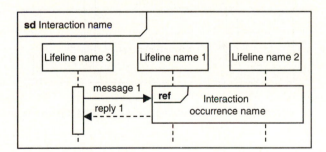

Figure 9-28: Gates connected to an interaction occurrence shown in a separate sequence diagram

9.4.6   States

States can be placed on a lifeline to indicate the state that an object must be in as a pre-condition of an action or that it makes a transition to as the post-condition of an action.   States are explained in more detail in Chapter 12. Figure 9-29 shows an example of a state on a lifeline. The spooler must be in the **idle** state when it receives the instruction to print the named file. If it were already printing, then it would not start printing the file until it had finished the other jobs in the print queue. This situation could be shown in another sequence diagram.

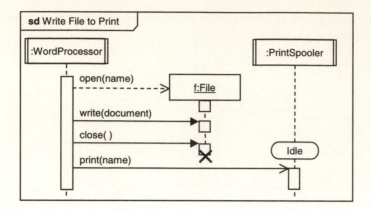

Figure 9-29: Sequence diagram with a state added

The sending of messages is usually assumed to be virtually instantaneous. However, in a situation where the message is sent over a communications link and a significant amount of time (in the context of the application) elapses between the sending and receiving of the message, the arrow can be shown slanting down the page, as in Figure 9-30.

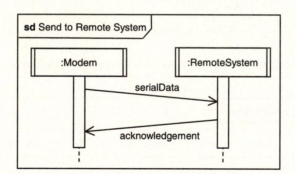

Figure 9-30: Sequence diagram with message that takes time to reach its destination

9.4.7   Continuations

A sequence diagram can contain a *continuation*, shown as a rectangle with semi-circular ends, as in Figure 9-31. This is the same symbol as for states, but it may cover more than one lifeline. This indicates that the interaction leaves off at the point of the continuation and carries on in another fragment at the continuation of the same name, and is used to show continuation in **alt** combined fragments. Figure 9-32 shows an example of this. The interaction **Share Journey** (on the right) includes the interaction occurrence **Get Journey Status** (on the left). The latter contains an **alt** combined fragment. One of the two operands will be selected, depending on the value of **status**, and the interaction will run until it reaches one or other of the continuations, **available** or **notAvailable**. After the interaction occurrence completes, the interaction in **Share Journey** will continue at the continuation of the same name in its **alt** combined fragment.

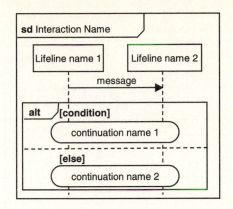

Figure 9-31: Notation for continuation

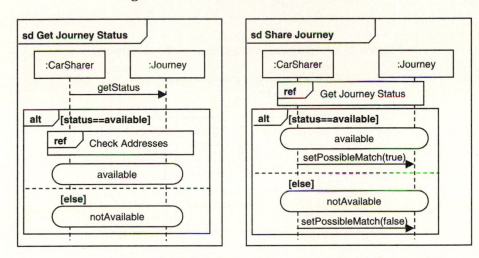

Figure 9-32: Example of the use of a continuation

9.4.8　Textual Annotation

Sequence diagrams can be annotated with textual information in three ways:

- comments
- time constraints
- duration constraints.

Comments—Comments can be added to a sequence diagram as to any UML diagram. Figure 9-33 shows an example of this.

Time constraints—Time constraints are usually used to show timing constraints on messages. They apply either to the time taken by one message or to time intervals between event occurrences on lifelines. Figure 9-34 shows examples for the time taken by a message (in the range 0 to 10 seconds) and the time between the event t and a subsequent event (which must take place no later than t+30 seconds). The second uses construction marks, as used in engineering blueprints.

Duration constraints—Constraints that are related to the duration of messages can be shown as in Figure 9-35. The example indicates that the time between the two points marked on the lifeline must be at least **d** seconds and no greater than **d*3** seconds.

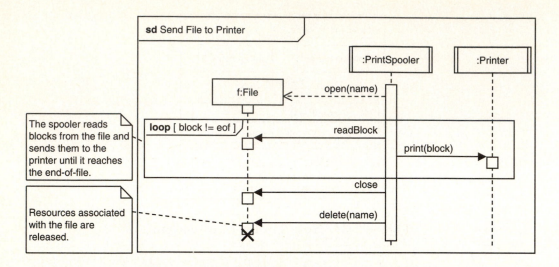

Figure 9-33: Sequence diagram with comments

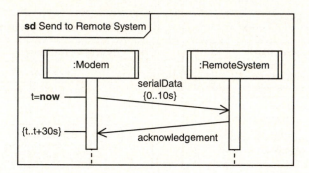

Figure 9-34: Sequence diagram with timing constraints

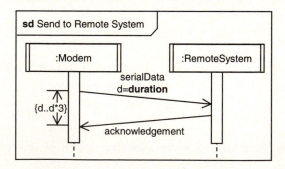

Figure 9-35: Sequence diagram with duration constraints

9.4.9   Tabular Notation

One final point to mention on the notation of sequence diagrams is that it is possible to represent a sequence diagram in a table instead of a diagram. This is covered in an appendix to the UML Specification (Object Management Group, 2004c), in which it states that the approach can also be used for other behavioural diagrams, although no examples are given. The tabular notation requires that every event occurrence is given a name, and for each message, the table shows the class and instance names of the lifelines that send and receive it; the event occurrence names; the message name; parameter names, types and values; the return value; constraints; and information about the ordering.

9.5 HOW TO PRODUCE SEQUENCE DIAGRAMS

Sequence diagrams can be drawn to model high-level interaction between users of the system and the system, between the system and other systems, or between subsystems (sometimes known as *system sequence diagrams*). In such sequence diagrams, the participants are drawn as active objects, as in Figure 9-36.

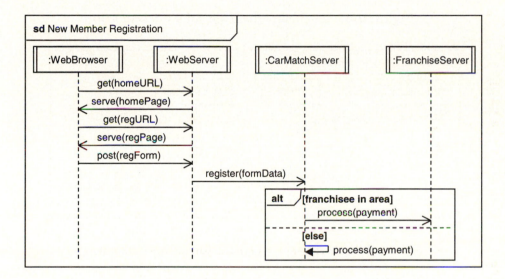

Figure 9-36: High-level system sequence diagram

Sequence diagrams can also be used to model the interaction that realizes either a use case or an operation. The examples that we have used so far in this chapter fall into this category.

UML 1.X made the distinction between *instance diagrams* and *generic diagrams*. An instance diagram showed one particular instance of an interaction, equivalent to a scenario in a use case. There could be several instance diagrams, with a slightly different path taken through the interaction in each. A generic diagram showed the combination of different possible paths through the interaction in a single diagram. In UML 2.0 this distinction is no longer made. The use of argument values rather than parameter names can be used to distinguish between the sequence of messages associated with a particular set of values.

Figures 9-37 and 9-38 show two different sequence diagrams for an application in which a **Connection-Control** object has to open up a connection to a modem. If the modem does not respond within a certain amount of time, this operation times out and an error dialogue box is displayed. The first instance shows the successful connection and the second instance shows the scenario where the timeout occurs first.

Figure 9-39 shows the two combined into a single sequence diagram with alternative conditional actions.

The same sequence diagram could be shown with actual argument values instead of the parameter names, as in Figure 9-40.

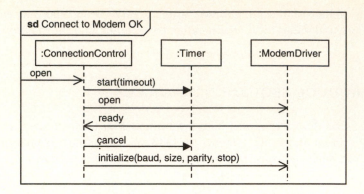

Figure 9-37: Sequence diagram for first scenario

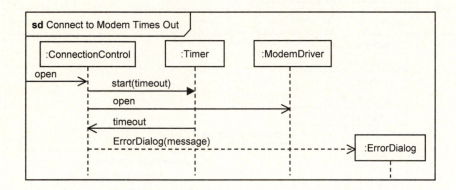

Figure 9-38: Sequence diagram for second scenario

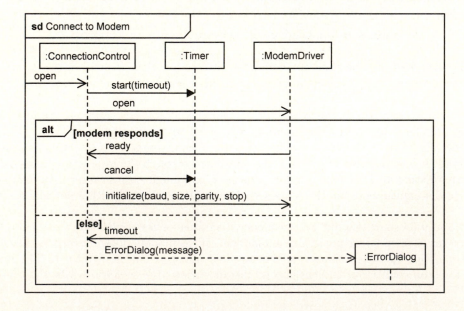

Figure 9-39: Sequence diagram for both scenarios

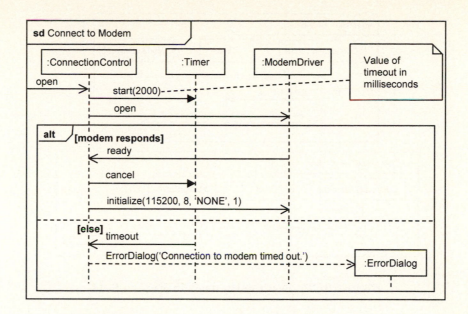

Figure 9-40: Sequence diagram for both scenarios with argument values

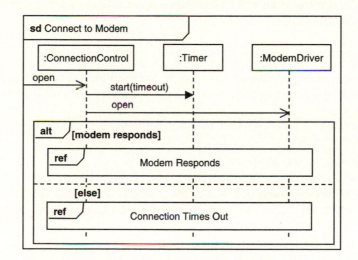

Figure 9-41: Sequence diagram for both scenarios using fragments

In UML 2.0 we can use the idea of fragments to produce the diagram of Figure 9-41. The fragments that are used in this diagram are shown in Figure 9-42.

It may seem like a contradiction, but UML 2.0 has made the construction of sequence diagrams both easier and more difficult. The use of combined fragments to represent iterations (**loop**), choices (**alt**), optional parts of interactions (**opt**) and so on makes the construction of sequence diagrams clearer than in UML 1.X. However, the introduction of interaction occurrences means that the person developing a sequence diagram has to consider whether there are existing interaction occurrences that can be used in a new sequence diagram, and consider whether to create new interaction occurrences in order to simplify the new diagram by factoring out potentially reusable fragments.

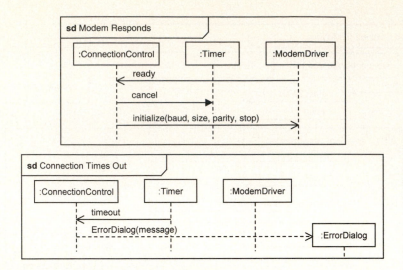

Figure 9-42: Fragments used in Figure 9-41

Rather than try to create a set of steps that cover all possibilities, we are presenting a set of standard steps here. In the examples that follow, we show how opportunities to use interaction occurrences and fragments might be identified.

The steps in drawing sequence diagrams are as follows:

- Decide on the context of the interaction: system, subsystem, use case or operation.
- Identify the structural elements (classes or objects) necessary to carry out the functionality of the use case or operation.
- Consider the alternative scenarios that may be required.
- Draw sequence diagrams.
    - Create a frame for the sequence diagram.
    - Lay out the lifelines from left to right.
    - Starting with the message that starts the interaction, lay out the messages down the page from top to bottom. Show the properties of the messages necessary to explain the semantics of the interaction.
    - Include combined fragments where necessary.
    - Add the focus of control if it is necessary to visualize nesting or the point in time where an execution occurrence is taking place.
    - Add constraints if necessary.
    - Attach annotations to the diagram as comments if required, for example pre- and post-conditions.
    - Add state invariants to the diagram if required.
- If required, combine alternative scenarios into a single diagram using the **alt** operator, or refactor diagrams to extract common fragments of the interaction into separate interaction occurrences.

9.5.1   Decide on Context

The sequence diagram can model interaction at the system, subsystem, use case or operation level. The stage in the development of the project and the task being undertaken will determine which is to be modelled.

EXAMPLE 9.1   In this case, we are going to model an operation: the constructor operation that creates a new instance of the class Journey in the CarMatch system.

9.5.2   Identify Structural Elements

Where the interaction is modelling an operation, the starting point is the classes that participate in that operation. If you have used an approach like CRC cards to analyse use cases (Section 4.5.2), you will have class diagrams that show the classes that participate in each use case. From these, you can identify the classes that are involved in a particular operation. If we examine the class diagram for the use case Register car sharer we can see what happens when a Journey is created.

EXAMPLE 9.2   When a Journey is created, it creates two instances of Address, one as the start address and one as the destination address. We are interested in the lower part of the diagram in Figure 9-43.

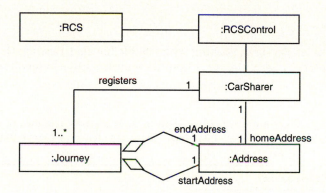

Figure 9-43: Classes involved in the use case **Register car sharer**

9.5.3   Consider Alternative Scenarios

We should check through the use cases to see if there are any other situations in which a Journey is created. In this case, there are none. We also consider the different possible paths through the operation in response to different inputs.

EXAMPLE 9.3   For the use case Register car sharer, there are two different possible scenarios. In the first, the addresses have already been geolocated on the web server, and do not need to be geolocated again. In the second, they have not been geolocated, and this must be done when the new Address objects are created. (Geolocation is the process by which an address is converted into a map reference, typically using the postal code or zip code for the address. Geolocation results in Address objects being linked to instances of Location.)

9.5.4   Draw Sequence Diagrams

We now step through the process of drawing the sequence diagrams for the two scenarios that have been developed. We shall explain the first in detail.

9.5.4.1 Create a Frame

Create a frame for the interaction and give it an appropriate name.

EXAMPLE 9.4   The operation is creating a Journey, so we draw a frame and give it the name **Create Journey** (Figure 9-44).

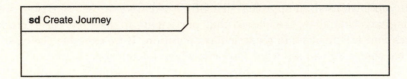

Figure 9-44: Frame for the sequence diagram to create a Journey

9.5.4.2 Lay out Lifelines

Lay the lifelines out from left to right, starting with the lifeline that receives the message that triggers the interaction. If modelling a use case, there may be interface objects involved, and these should be shown at the left.

EXAMPLE 9.5   In this case, there are no interface objects. It is the new instance of **Journey** that receives the triggering message. It creates two instances of **Address**. These are shown in Figure 9-45.

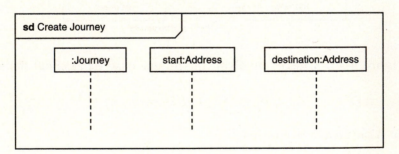

Figure 9-45: Lifelines involved in Create Journey

9.5.4.3 Lay out Messages

The messages are laid out down the page. We have a lot of discretion about how much detail to show in the messages. We should show enough that someone looking at the diagram can understand the diagram and how it works.

EXAMPLE 9.6   The new instance of **Journey** that is created receives the triggering message. It in turn creates two instances of **Address**. Each of these is created by its constructor.

The Journey is passed a number of parameters when it is created. If we look at the class definition, we can see which values are set when a **Journey** is created. This is shown in Figure 9-46 with the required attributes in bold. The values that hold references to associated instances have been implemented here as attributes.

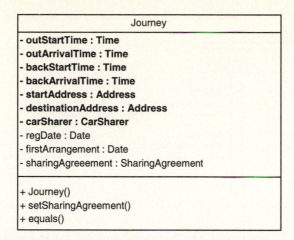

Figure 9-46: **Journey** class (with attributes passed in the constructor in bold)

The Address instances will have to be created. The data that is passed in is unlikely to be an existing instance of Address; it is more likely to be a list of values, which will be passed on to construct the new instances of Address. The geolocated location is an optional item in this list of values. Figure 9-47 shows the messages laid out with parameters. They are all creation messages. Note that the constructor message for Journey comes from a gate at the edge of the frame. Note that we do not show all the reflexive *set* operations or all the *get* operations on the instances of AddressList.

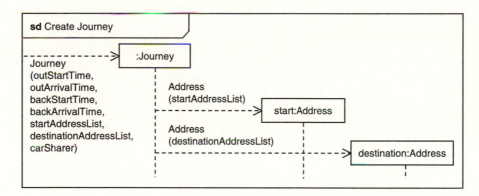

Figure 9-47: Messages for the operations

9.5.4.4   Add Focus of Control

The focus of control region can be added if required.

EXAMPLE 9.7   The focus of control regions add nothing to the readability of the sequence diagram for this scenario, but will be useful for the alternative scenario, so we add them in here, as in Figure 9-48.

9.5.4.5   Add Timing Constraints

Timing constraints can be added. There are none in this example. (See Solved Problem 9.8 later in the chapter for an example of this.)

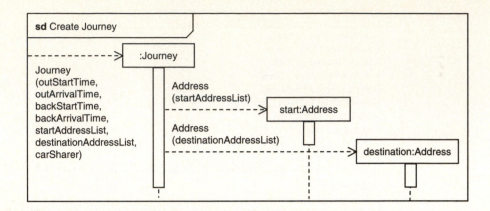

Figure 9-48: Focus of control added

9.5.4.6   Add Annotations

Any annotations that are necessary can be added to the diagram. There are none in this example. (See Solved Problem 9.8 later in the chapter for an example of this.)

9.5.4.7   Repeat for Each Scenario

The same steps can be repeated for all the other scenarios.

EXAMPLE 9.8   In this case, we have one alternative scenario, in which the addresses have not yet been geolocated. This results in the diagram in Figure 9-49.

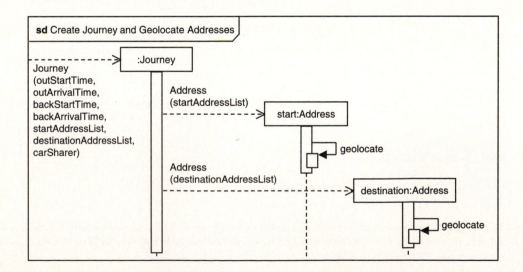

Figure 9-49: Alternative scenario

We have added a UML comment to explain where the location comes from.

9.5.5 Combine Alternatives

We can combine the alternative scenarios into a single diagram.

EXAMPLE 9.9   The alternative scenarios can be combined by making it clear that the geolocation is optional. This is done using the opt keyword and a frame around the optional operations. Note that there are two separate optional elements that are independent of one another (see Figure 9-50).

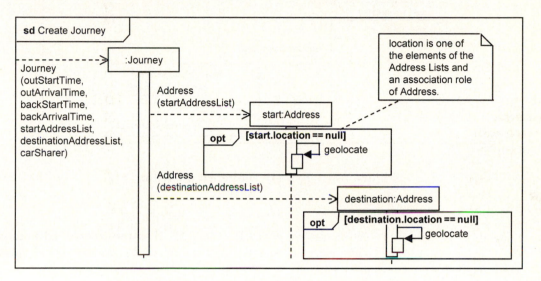

Figure 9-50: Combination of alternative scenarios

We could potentially create interaction occurrences for the creation of the **Address** instances and reference them in this diagram using the ref keyword. However, that would create interaction occurrences that have trivial content. Note that this interaction for **Create Journey** could be used in other diagrams and referenced using the ref keyword.

9.6 BUSINESS MODELLING WITH SEQUENCE DIAGRAMS

In the UML profile for business modelling, five class stereotypes are defined for business objects. These are: **Actor**, **Worker**, **Case Worker**, **Internal Worker** and **Entity**. These stereotyped icons could be used in sequence diagrams to model the interactions between workers and entities in use-case realizations.

System sequence diagrams can be produced to model the interaction within business use cases. Figure 9-51 shows an example of this.

This is the kind of diagram that would be produced at an early stage in the development of a system, as part of the business modelling and before detailed analysis is carried out.

9.7 RELATIONSHIP WITH OTHER DIAGRAMS

Sequence diagrams can be used to model the realization of either use cases or operations of classes. In the latter case, each operation being modelled must exist in a class diagram. The names of messages

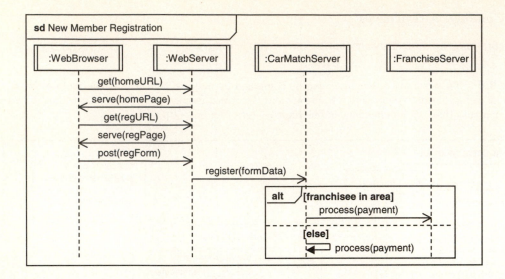

Figure 9-51: System sequence diagram

must be signals or be operations of the class receiving the message. If states are referred to in guard conditions or shown on a lifeline, they must be valid states of the relevant class and should appear in a state machine diagram (see Chapter 12).

Sequence diagrams and communication diagrams (see Chapter 10) model the same aspects of the system: the objects that collaborate and the messages that are exchanged among them to achieve some objective. Sequence diagrams and communication diagrams could be converted into one another in UML1.X. Some CASE tools can do this automatically. They were almost but not quite interchangeable; some information was lost in the conversion: sequence diagrams do not show the links between objects or the associations between class roles; communication diagrams do not show information about timing constraints. However, the introduction of interaction occurrences and fragments into sequence diagrams makes them more difficult to convert into communication diagrams.

9.8   SEQUENCE DIAGRAMS IN THE UNIFIED PROCESS

Sequence diagrams are used in the Unified Process first of all in the Design workflow. This is shown in Figure 9-52.

Communication diagrams (Chapter 10) are produced as part of the analysis model and are refined in design. In the Unified Process, it is suggested that sequence diagrams rather than communication diagrams should be used to model interactions in the design phase.

The activity *Design a Use Case* is similar to the analysis activity of the same name, except for the fact that design classes are used and there are more steps, as more detail is required when a project gets closer to implementation. The main steps are: *Identifying the Participating Design Classes*, *Describing Design Object Interactions*, *Identifying the Participating Subsystems and Interfaces* and *Describing Subsystem Interactions*. Design classes may be different from analysis classes. For example, collection classes may be added in design to handle interactions that involve a set of objects. The interactions in the communication and sequence diagrams will have to be modified to include instances of these classes

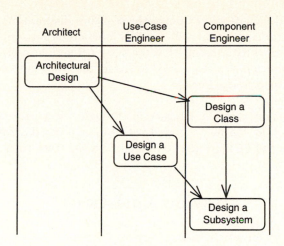

Figure 9-52: Design workflow as an activity diagram

and their interactions. It is also possible to consider a use case in terms of interactions among design subsystems rather than design objects. This provides a hierarchical decomposition of the interactions, as the detail of the interaction within a subsystem can be hidden in one diagram and shown in a separate lower-level diagram. In order to support this approach, the interfaces of subsystems must be identified, so that it is clear what operations or events each subsystem will handle. There is a fifth step, *Capturing Implementation Requirements*, in which requirements to be handled in implementation are documented.

Sequence diagrams are also used in the Test workflow. This is shown in Figure 9-53.

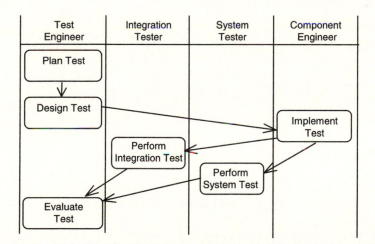

Figure 9-53: Test workflow as an activity diagram

Sequence diagrams are used in the activity *Design Test*. This consists of the steps *Designing Integration Test Cases*, *Designing System Test Cases*, *Designing Regression Test Cases* and *Identifying and Structuring Test Procedures*. Sequence diagrams are used particularly in the first of these. Integration testing is concerned with ensuring that the different components of the system work correctly together. Most test cases can be derived from the use-case realizations produced in design, as these describe how objects interact. The alternative paths through use cases documented by instance sequence diagrams provide the basis for test cases that handle (and test) the different possible routes that can be taken through the use case. Test designers will examine the sequence diagrams to find combinations of user input, output and system start state that will test the interaction between the participating objects. (System test cases are concerned with testing that the system functions correctly as a whole; regression test cases re-test test cases which have been passed to ensure that they have not been broken by changes made in subsequent iterations or to fix bugs.)

Some automated test tools can trace the interaction through a test case and produce output in the form of a sequence diagram that can be compared with the sequence diagrams produced in design. In such cases, argument values will be used and compared with the trace results.

Review Questions

9.1 Define what is meant by an interaction.

9.2 Explain how sequence diagrams represent time.

9.3 What are the main purposes of using sequence diagrams?

9.4 What is the notation for a frame?

9.5 What is the notation for the lifeline of an object?

9.6 What is the notation for the focus of control region?

9.7 What is the notation for a message in a sequence diagram?

9.8 How is return of control shown in a sequence diagram?

9.9 Which of the following are valid lifeline names?

  (a) returnJourney : Journey

  (b) returnJourney

  (c) Journey

  (d) j[i]

  (e) self

  (f) :Journey

  (g) j ref Create journey

  (h) returnJourney

9.10 What are the four types of messages that can be represented by different arrow styles in a sequence diagram?

9.11 What is meant by an arrow going to a small black circle and an arrow coming from a small black circle?

9.12 How is the creation of a lifeline shown in a sequence diagram?

9.13 How is the destruction of a lifeline shown in a sequence diagram?

9.14 What is an active object?

9.15 What is the notation for an active object?

9.16 In what way can iteration be represented in a sequence diagram?

9.17 In what way can choices between alternative interactions be represented in a sequence diagram?

9.18 In what way can optional interactions be represented in a sequence diagram?

9.19 What is an interaction occurrence?

9.20 What is the usual purpose of constraints in a sequence diagram?

9.21 What are the main steps in producing a sequence diagram?

9.22 Which two Unified Process workflows are sequence diagrams used in?

9.23 What are the five steps in the Unified Process activity Design a Use Case?

9.24 What are the four steps in the Unified Process activity Design Test?

Solved Problems

9.1 CarMatch refunds the membership fee to members if it is unable to match them up with another car sharer. The following is a description of the process.

> If it has not been possible to match a member's journeys with any other car sharer within three months, the member is entitled to a refund of the membership fee. The member's details are kept in the system. He or she is asked whether the records of the journeys requested can be kept for statistical purposes. If they are to be kept, they are flagged as defunct, otherwise the journeys are deleted. The accounting subsystem is requested to issue the refund (by cheque or by credit card, depending on how the member paid the fee in the first place).

The first task is to decide on the context of the sequence diagram.

This is a use case: **Refund membership fee**. The sequence diagram will be produced in the context of this use case.

9.2 What are the structural elements of this interaction?

This interaction involves objects from the classes **CarSharer** and **Journey**. It also involves the **Accounts** subsystem. We shall treat this as a subsystem in this sequence diagram and not attempt to model the detail of what happens within the subsystem. When a **Journey** is deleted, the objects embedded within it (**Addresses** and the **Locations** embedded within them) must also be destroyed, but we can model this as a sequence diagram for the destructor operation for **Journey** as a separate sequence diagram, in the same way as we modelled the constructor in Section 9.5.4. The interaction will also involve a user interface class and a control class.

9.3 What are the possible alternative scenarios for this sequence diagram?

There are two, which depend on input from the user.

In the first, the member allows their journey details to be kept, and the journeys are flagged as defunct.

In the second, the journey details are deleted.

There may be other alternative scenarios that depend on how the member originally paid the membership fee, but these are hidden inside the **Accounts** subsystem for the purpose of this example.

9.4 We now work through the steps of drawing sequence diagrams for each of the scenarios. We shall first consider the scenario in which the journeys are kept. The first step is to draw a frame.

Figure 9-54 shows the frame.

The next step is to lay out the lifelines involved.

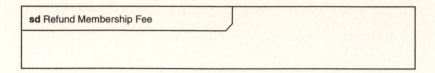

Figure 9-54: Frame for the sequence diagram Refund Membership Fee

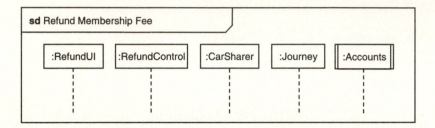

Figure 9-55: Lifelines involved in the sequence diagram Refund Membership Fee

Figure 9-55 shows the lifelines that are involved in this sequence diagram. Note that the user interface and control class have been drawn to the left of the diagram, then the **CarSharer** and **Journey** objects and finally the **Accounts** subsystem. Note that the **Accounts** subsystem has been drawn as an active object.

The third step is to lay out the messages down the page. The focus of control can be added at the same time.

Note that in some CASE tools, you may not have any choice about whether to add a focus of control region or not. If you are drawing the diagrams in a general-purpose drawing package (not recommended), draw the focus of control regions from the start if you plan to include them.

The interaction is triggered by an event from the actor **CarMatch Administrator**. This could be a click on a **Refund** button on the screen. We shall assume that the **CarSharer** has been selected from a list and a checkbox has been clicked to indicate whether the user wants his or her journey details kept or deleted. The interface could look something like the one in Figure 9-56.

Figure 9-56: User interface for the use case Refund membership fee

When the user clicks on the **Refund** button, an event will be sent to the control object. This will get the data from the interface object: first the id of the **CarSharer**, which must then be found in the database or activated in some way; second the boolean value that tells the control object whether or not to delete the journeys. The **CarSharer** in this design contains a collection of **Journey** objects. There must be at least one, so we get the first one and set it to be defunct, then iterate through the collection, getting each **Journey** in turn, until we reach the end of the collection. Each **CarSharer** has a link to an **Account** object in the **Accounts** package, and a message is now sent to the **Accounts** subsystem, requesting it to pay the refund for the relevant **Account**. Figure 9-57 shows the first part of this sequence diagram up to the point where the iteration through the **Journey** objects starts.

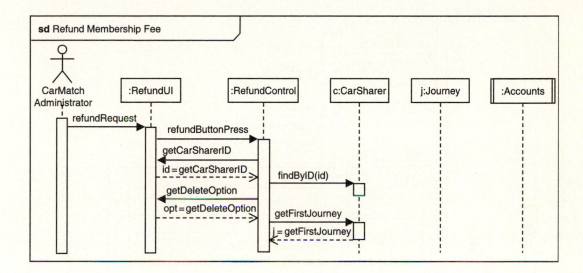

Figure 9-57: First part of sequence diagram for Refund Membership Fee

Within the iteration through the **Journey** objects, there are two alternative paths. We can show the different interactions as interaction occurrences, as in Figure 9-58.

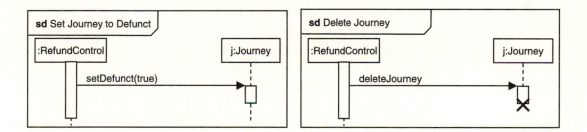

Figure 9-58: Alternative interaction occurrences

These interaction occurrences can be referenced within the loop, as in Figure 9-59.

Next, we add timing constraints and comments. In this case, there are none to add.

We could also add state invariants. For example, before setting a **Journey** to the **defunct** state, it must not already be defunct. A state invariant can be added as in Figure 9-60.

We have already combined the alternative paths into a single diagram through the use of the interaction occurrences in Figure 9-58. We would examine the sequence diagram in the context of other sequence diagrams to find interactions that could be extracted into interaction occurrences and referenced in the diagram in Figure 9-59 in order to simplify it.

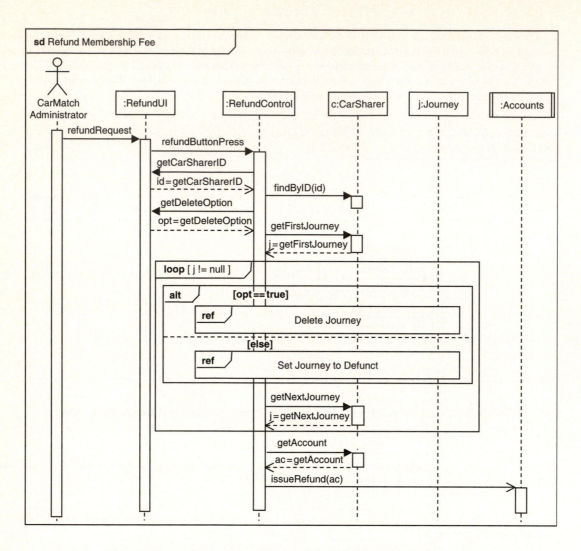

Figure 9-59: Sequence diagram for **Refund Membership Fee**

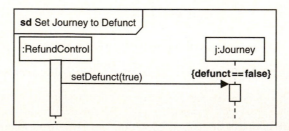

Figure 9-60: State invariant added to the **Set Journey to Defunct** interaction occurrence

9.5 Draw a sequence diagram to model the interaction that takes place when a CarMatch member drives past a road-charging beacon at the roadside, using a proposed in-vehicle radio transponder system to communicate with the beacon. The interaction is described as follows.

The beacon at the roadside is constantly transmitting a signal to any transponder that passes. Whenever a transponder responds, the beacon and the transponder must exchange data within 0.25 s. The transponder transmits its identification to the beacon. The beacon transmits the charge information for that stretch of road to the transponder, which displays the information on an LCD screen for the driver. It also communicates with a central database to verify the identification. A response must come from the database within 1 s. If the identification is not valid, the beacon sends a request to a roadside camera to photograph the vehicle as it goes past.

The first task is to decide on the context of the sequence diagram.

This is a use case: **Vehicle passes beacon**. The sequence diagram we produce here will be a high-level diagram to model this use case rather than a detailed one with all the objects involved. It will be modelled in terms of subsystems.

9.6 What are the structural elements of this interaction?

This interaction involves four subsystems: **Transponder**, **Beacon**, **Database** and **Camera**. We could also include the **LCDScreen** associated with the transponder.

9.7 What are the possible alternative scenarios for this sequence diagram?

There are two, which depend on the result that comes back from the central database.

In the first, the identification is valid; in the second, the identification is not valid and a message is sent to the camera.

9.8 We now work through the steps of drawing sequence diagrams for each of the scenarios. First, we shall consider the scenario in which the identification is valid. The first step is to lay out the lifelines involved. In this case, the lifelines are instances of the subsystems, and are active objects each operating independently on its own thread of control.

Figure 9-61 shows the lifelines that are involved in this sequence diagram. We have drawn them straight into the frame and skipped drawing the frame as a separate task.

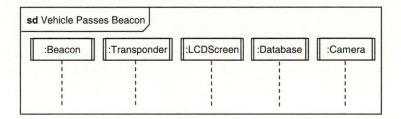

Figure 9-61: Lifelines involved in the use case Vehicle passes beacon

The second step is to lay out the messages down the page. The communication here is asynchronous. We will not include the focus of control regions. Figure 9-62 shows the resulting sequence diagram.

We may feel intuitively that the start of the interaction should involve a loop. Figure 9-63 shows a loop round the message **requestResponse** until a response is received. However, this is wrong, as the **response** message is not inside the loop, so it can never break out of the loop.

Figure 9-64 shows an alternative solution, with the **response** inside the loop. However, in this case, it will only execute the loop once, as there is a response, so the loop is redundant.

Potentially this is a case to use the notation for a lost message. Figure 9-65 shows a lost message being sent before the message is received by the transponder, which sends a response. However, the lost message has not been put in a loop, as it is still not clear what the correct condition is that would allow it to break out of the loop when a message is received.

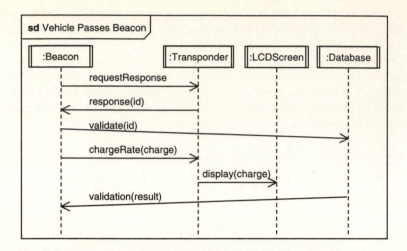

Figure 9-62: Sequence diagram for **Vehicle passes beacon**, first scenario

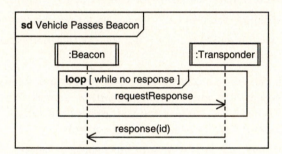

Figure 9-63: Possible loop for **requestResponse**

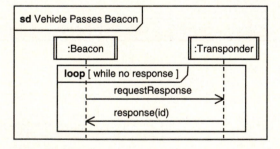

Figure 9-64: Alternative loop for **requestResponse**

In order to represent this correctly, we need to use the break combined fragment notation, where the response message is in the **break**, as it is what breaks out of the loop. We could combine this with the notation for a continuation, and show the loop in an interaction occurrence, which we add as a fragment to the main diagram. This is shown in Figures 9-66 and 9-67.

For the subsequent diagrams, we have concentrated on the situation where a transponder responds to the beacon, avoiding the additional complexity of the **break**.

We have assumed that the sending of signals and messages locally is more or less instantaneous, whereas there is a significant delay in communicating with the remote database.

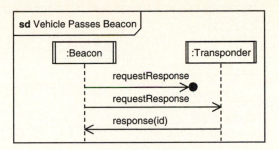

Figure 9-65: **requestResponse** as a lost message

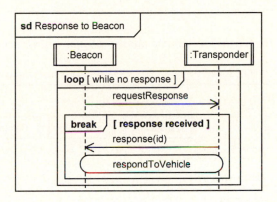

Figure 9-66: **break** combined fragment in the interaction occurrence **Response to Beacon**

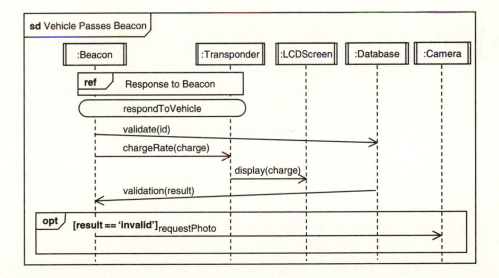

Figure 9-67: Interaction occurrence **Response to Beacon** referred to in **Vehicle Passes Beacon**

There are timing constraints on this interaction, and we may want to add these, as in Figure 9-68.

In the second scenario, the only difference is that when the identification is not valid a request is sent to the camera. This can simply be added as a combined fragment using the **opt** keyword to produce the diagram of Figure 9-69.

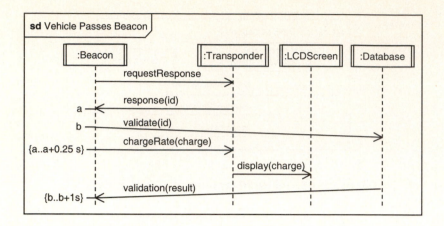

Figure 9-68: Sequence diagram for **Vehicle passes beacon**, first scenario, with timing constraints

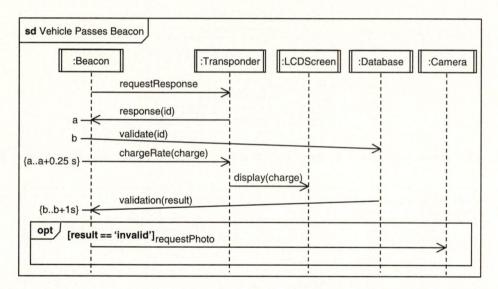

Figure 9-69: Sequence diagram for **Vehicle passes beacon**, including the second scenario

This diagram is also the combined sequence diagram: by default it covers the case in which [result = valid] and no message is sent to the camera.

Note that we could use the notation for a lost message to model the situation where the beacon is sending out **requestResponse** messages, but no vehicle is within range. However, the diagram would be trivial and hardly worth drawing.

9.9 The diagram in Figure 9-69 could be extended to show the states of the **Beacon**. At the simplest level, there could be two states: **Waiting** and **Communicating**. Add these to the sequence diagram.

The **Beacon** is **Waiting** until it receives a response from a passing **Transponder**. It then switches into the **Communicating** state. After completion of the interaction it switches back to **Waiting**. This can be shown on the sequence diagram as in Figure 9-70. We could add states for the other lifelines if their behaviour is dependent on their state.

9.10 The relative order of the two sets of messages to validate the id and display the charge rate is not significant. In fact, they could happen in parallel. How could this be shown?

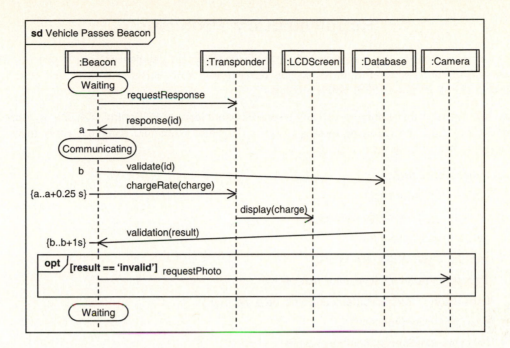

Figure 9-70: Sequence diagram with states added for Transponder

There is a keyword par that can be used to show messages that are sent and received in parallel. The structure of the combined fragment is like the alt fragment that we used earlier, but the events are not mutually exclusive, but happening in parallel. This is shown in Figure 9-71.

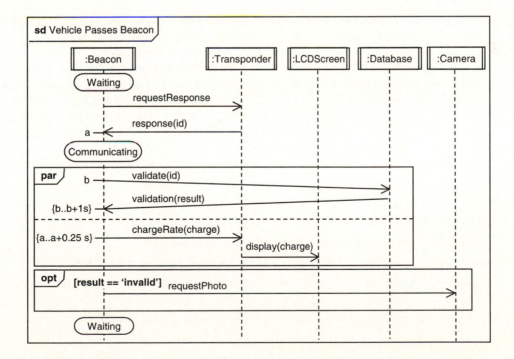

Figure 9-71: Sequence diagram with parallel combined fragment

Supplementary Problems

9.11 Lay out the lifelines for a sequence diagram called **Process payment** in which objects from the classes **CarSharer**, **Account** and **Transaction** participate. Add suitable control and user interface classes. (Look at page 188 if you are stuck.)

9.12 Lay out lifelines for instances of the classes **PPUserInterface**, **PPControl**, **CarSharer**, **Account** and **Transaction**. Add the following messages to the diagram. Note that some are reply messages and one is a creation message.

1. transactionReady( )
2. getTransactionDetails( )
3. itemList = getTransactionDetails( )
4. getCarSharerAccount( )
5. account = getCarSharerAccount( )
6. Transaction(amount, type, date, account)
7. transaction = Transaction(amount, type, date, account)
8. postTransaction(transaction)
9. balance = postTransaction(transaction)
10. displayBalance(balance)

The variable **itemList** contains the following items: **carSharerID, amount, type, date.**

9.13 One of the use cases that you found in Chapter 3 should have had a name such as **Record an individual's request for help**. In case you did not have a use case like this, here is a short summary description.

> Individuals can request help from VolBank. This includes volunteers requesting help themselves. The Volbank administrator first enters the details of the individual. If this is an existing volunteer, then the name is entered and the details are displayed. If there is more than one person with the same name, then a list is displayed with the first part of the address, and the administrator selects the right one. If this is not an existing volunteer, then the name, address and telephone number are entered. It is important that the zip or postal code is entered, as it is required to match this request with volunteers in the same area. Details of the help required are then entered: a text summary of the help and a code that describes the type of help wanted, for example DEC for decorating, GAR for garden work or PET for pet care. A start and a finish date for when the help is required are also entered.

Work through the following steps.

1. What are the domain classes that are involved in this use case?
2. What other subsystems (if any) are involved in this use case?
3. What are the additional classes that will be required for this interaction?
4. Draw a class diagram showing the associations among the classes, including associations if required.
5. What are the association roles that these classes take in this interaction?

9.14 What are the alternative scenarios that may occur?

9.15 Draw a sequence diagram for each of these scenarios. For each diagram work through the following steps:

1. Lay out the lifelines.

2. Lay out the messages down the page.

3. Add constraints and comments.

9.16 Draw a sequence diagram combining the alternative scenarios.

9.17 When a volunteer registers with VolBank on the VolBank web-server, he or she goes through the following interaction.

Go to the VolBank home page. Request the VolBank registration page. Complete the form and submit it. The server validates the data. If there is any error, the form is redisplayed with the contents as entered by the volunteer and with the incorrect field highlighted. If there is no error, the data is submitted to a database.

Draw a sequence diagram for this interaction.

CHAPTER 10

More on Interaction Diagrams

10.1 INTRODUCTION

In UML 1.X, there were two kinds of interaction diagrams—sequence diagrams and collaboration diagrams—and these two kinds of diagrams were semantically more or less equivalent although graphically different. In UML 2.0 other variations on interaction diagrams have been introduced, and collaboration diagrams have been renamed *communication diagrams* and reduced in significance. In this chapter, we explain communication diagrams and the other variations on interaction diagrams: *interaction overview diagrams* and *timing diagrams*.

10.2 COMMUNICATION DIAGRAMS

In object-oriented systems, the functionality that users require of the system is produced by objects working together. Each individual object provides only a small element of the functionality—its particular responsibilities—but when they work together, objects are able to produce high-level functionality that people can use. In order to work together in this way, objects need to communicate with one another, and they do this by passing messages. This 'working together' to produce some useful result is modelled by interaction diagrams of various types. Chapter 9 has introduced sequence diagrams; *communication diagrams* are another type of interaction diagram.

UML 1.X collaboration diagrams were frequently used to specify the interaction that occurs within use cases. Rosenberg & Scott (1999) uses them as the basis of the *robustness diagram* notation. In this introduction, we shall give an example of this approach.

We want to specify the participants in the use case **Record sharing agreement**. When an agreement to share a journey is reached between two or more members of CarMatch, a new **SharingAgreement** object is created. The **SharingAgreement** has an association with the **Journeys** rather than the **CarSharers**, as

198

each **CarSharer** can have several **Journeys** that he or she wants to share, and each journey may be shared with a different car sharer through a sharing agreement. As a minimum, this use case will involve five objects, from the classes shown in Figure 10-1: two instances of **CarSharer**, two instances of **Journey** and one of **SharingAgreement**.

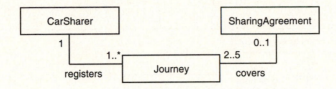

Figure 10-1: Classes involved in the use case Record sharing agreement

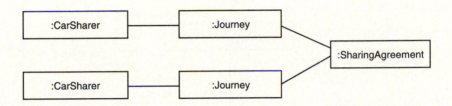

Figure 10-2: Objects in the collaboration Record sharing agreement

The links between the objects in Figure 10-2 map onto the association between the classes **CarSharer** and **SharingAgreement** in the excerpt from the class diagram in Figure 10-1. This use case will also involve some additional classes, and these are shown in the collaboration in Figure 10-3. At this stage, we have tried to keep this collaboration simple: in a project that uses UML, we may want to get an idea of the domain classes that are involved in a collaboration, without worrying too much about the detail of how it will be implemented. For example, we have not included collection classes or classes to manage persistence. Because there is not a distinction between the roles played by different instances of **CarSharer**, we can show them as a single object as in Figure 10-3.

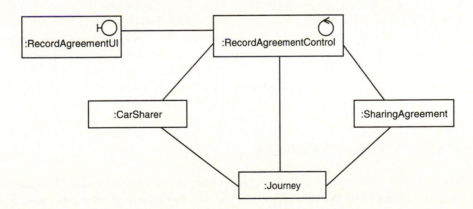

Figure 10-3: Objects involved in the communication diagram, including boundary and control objects with likely communication links

The additional objects shown here are a user interface object **RecordAgreementUI** and a control object **RecordAgreementControl**. Association roles and multiplicities can be added to this diagram if required, although we have not shown them here. It is also possible to add the details of an interaction to this diagram to create a communication diagram. An interaction specifies the communication between lifelines performing a specific task in terms of a trace of the messages that are sent between the lifelines. In the early stages of a project, the messages that make up the communication of the interaction may be informally defined. Later they will be *signals* or *operations* sent between object instances. Figure 10-4 shows some informally defined messages on the diagram of Figure 10-3 and the inclusion of an actor to trigger the interaction.

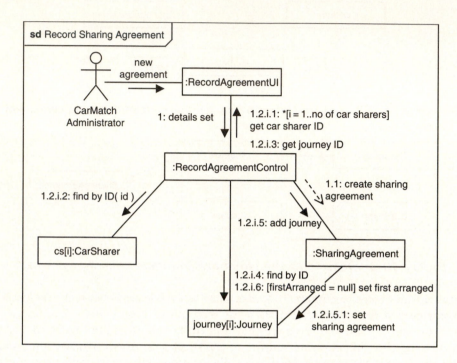

Figure 10-4: Interaction added to Figure 10-3

This diagram shows which objects will participate in the realization of the use case **Record sharing agreement** and the relationships between them that are meaningful for the purpose of creating a new car sharing agreement. The relationships with the control class **RecordAgreementControl**, which will be used only in this use case, will not be meaningful in the context of another use case, such as **Register car sharer**, but equally the relationship between the classes **CarSharer** and **SharingAgreement** will not be relevant in many other use cases. It is in this sense that a collaboration is described as something that 'defines a set of participants and relationships that are meaningful for a given set of purposes'.

10.3   PURPOSE OF THE TECHNIQUE

Communication diagrams can be used while the class diagrams are being elaborated to help the analyst understand the groupings of objects that participate in the realization of each use case. They can be used when the class diagrams are more complete in order to understand and document the interactions among objects. They can also be used to specify the objects that take part in operations. Bear in mind that in many object-oriented projects, the process of developing the system is an iterative one. Modelling interactions using communication diagrams or sequence diagrams may result in the recognition of the need for new classes, attributes or operations. These must be added to the class diagrams. The addition of these new elements may result in the need for changes to existing sequence diagrams or the addition of new ones to model the new operations. Ultimately, a line must be drawn somewhere on this process of iteration or no system would ever be finished. Where and how the line is drawn is an issue determined by project management and the development process. (Note that there are some people who claim that no system is ever finished. In his book on *Extreme Programming* (Beck, 2000), Kent Beck argues that systems should be put into production (that is into productive use) as soon as possible, even when partially developed.)

The main purposes of producing communication diagrams are as follows:

- They are used to model interactions between objects that deliver the functionality of a use case by showing the messages that are passed between lifelines.
- They are used to model interactions between objects that deliver the functionality of an operation by showing the messages that are passed between lifelines.
- They are used to model mechanisms within the architectural design of the system.
- They are used to model alternative scenarios within a use case or operation that involve the collaboration of different objects and different interactions.
- They are used in the early stages of a project to identify the objects (and hence classes) that participate in each use case. The objects in each communication diagram represent a partial view of a class diagram, and these partial models can be combined into a model of the whole system.
- They are used to show the participants in a design pattern (see Chapter 17).

10.4   NOTATION OF COMMUNICATION DIAGRAMS

The importance of communication diagrams appears to have been downgraded in UML 2.0. However, it is likely that software developers will continue to use them in the same ways as collaboration diagrams were used in UML 1.X to model the interaction involved in the realization of a use case. However, for complex interactions, it is likely that the new aspects of sequence diagram notation will encourage people to use sequence diagrams and interaction overview diagrams with interaction occurrences to manage complexity. The UML Specification (Object Management Group, 2004c) specifically states that communication diagrams are equivalent to simple sequence diagrams with none of the structuring that interaction occurrences and combined fragments make possible.

10.4.1   Collaborations as the Context of an Interaction

Collaborations can be drawn with no interaction in order to show the context of an interaction, effectively the subset of the class or object model that will be involved in the interaction. This is explained in more detail in Chapter 17.

Such diagrams show the *structural* aspects of the collaboration—the objects or classes involved and the associations among them. However, the main value of communication diagrams lies in using them to model the *behavioural* aspects of the system by showing the interaction between those objects and classes in order to achieve the objectives of the system.

10.4.2   Frames

Rectangular frames around communication diagrams have been introduced in UML 2.0, as for sequence diagrams. The notation is explained in Section 9.4.1.

10.4.3   Lifelines

Communication diagrams show how instances of classifiers collaborate to achieve some objective—the implementation of an operation or the realization of a use case. The classifier instances that are most common are objects and these (and any other classifiers) are shown as lifelines, as in sequence diagrams but without the dashed line.

Lifeline names are simpler than in UML 1.X and are no longer underlined. The syntax for the name of the lifeline is as follows.

```
[connectable-element-name] ['['selector']'][:class-name][decomposition]
```

This is explained in Section 9.4.2, and typical examples are shown in Figure 10-5. Compare this with the lifeline notation in sequence diagrams in Figure 9-7.

Figure 10-5: Lifeline notation, as used in communication diagrams

Table 10-1 shows the various alternative forms that lifeline names can take.

Table 10-1: Examples of lifeline names

Syntax	Explanation
o	An object named o.
o : C	An object named o of class C.
:C	An anonymous object of class C.
o[i]	The object o that is selected by the index value i.
s ref sd3	A subsystem s whose internal interaction is shown in sequence diagram or communication diagram sd3.
self	The connectable element that owns the interaction shown in the communication diagram.

In UML 1.X, rather than using object instances, class roles could be drawn in a collaboration diagram (communication diagram in UML 2.0). Role names were prefixed by a forward slash '/'.

10.4.4   Links

Links between lifelines are added to the communication diagram. Links may be instances of associations that are shown in class diagrams, or they may be temporary links between lifelines that enable them to send messages to one another. For example, a control object may need to create an instance of a particular class as part of a collaboration, but the link between them is only temporary—it will not be shown on the class diagram—and it may represent the fact that a reference to the object instance is held in a local variable of the control object. (See Figure 10-6.) Links are only drawn on communication diagrams to support the passing of messages between the participants in the interaction.

Figure 10-6: Links

10.4.5 Messages

The links on a communication diagram are included to show the paths along which messages can be sent from one lifeline to another. The links can be labelled with the names of messages. In early versions of UML, message was the only term used; however, in Version 1.3 a distinction was made between *messages* in specification-level diagrams and *stimuli*. In UML 2.0 this distinction has become obsolete and we only refer to messages.

A *message* is defined as 'a specification of the conveyance of information from one instance to another, with the expectation that activity will ensue. A message may specify the raising of a signal or the call of an operation' (Object Management Group, 2004*c*). A message can be one of the following:

- a signal sent from one object to another—for example, a button press in a user interface object being sent to a control object;
- an operation being invoked on another object—for example, a control object invoking the **getName()** operation of a **CarSharer** object in order to pass the name to the user interface to be displayed;
- the creation or destruction of an object instance—for example, a control object creating a new instance of **SharingAgreement**.

Messages are shown by an arrow pointing in the direction that the message is sent and a label that specifies the message (Figure 10-7).

Figure 10-7: Message notation

The arrow can take one of four forms in core UML, although the notation can be extended by the use of stereotypes, for example to show time-outs (Figure 10-8).

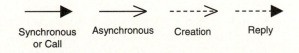

Figure 10-8: Message flow notation

- **Synchronous**—A message is sent by one object to another and the first object waits until the resulting action has completed. This may include waiting for the completion of actions invoked by the second object on other objects.

- **Asynchronous**—A message is sent by one object to another but the first object does not wait until the resulting action has completed, it carries on with the next step in its own sequence of actions.

- **Creation**—Represents a message that causes the creation of an object instance to which the message is sent. This use of a specific arrow style is new in UML 2.0. The «create» stereotype of UML 1.X is no longer used.

- **Reply**—Represents the explicit return of control from the object to which the message was sent. The UML 2.0 Specification is ambiguous about whether these arrows have a filled arrowhead or an open one. We have followed the style described in the text in the Specification. Replies are not normally shown on communication diagrams.

The arrow represents the flow of control. Where the flow of control is procedural or synchronous, there is only one thread of execution, and activity passes from one lifeline to another. Where the flow of control is asynchronous, more than one lifeline can be active at any one time.

The amount of detail about the message that is shown alongside the arrow can vary considerably. At its simplest, it is just the name of the message and a sequence number, as in Figure 10-9.

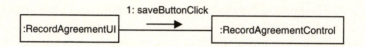

Figure 10-9: Message on a communication diagram

The syntax for messages in communication diagrams is almost the same as that for sequence diagrams, which is explained in Section 9.4.3:

```
sequence-expression [attribute=] signal-or-operation-name [(arguments)] [:return-value]|'*'
```

However, the notation for communication diagrams includes the *sequence-expression* at the start.

Sequence-expression—The sequence-expression defines the order in which the interactions take place. It is a dot-separated list of *sequence-terms* followed by a colon. Each term represents a level of nesting within the interaction. If an object receives an operation call numbered **1:** and as a result sends an operation call to another two objects, then those operation calls will have sequence-expressions **1.1:** and **1.2:**.

The syntax given in the UML 2.0 Specification is incorrect and inconsistent with the examples given.

Each sequence-term can consist of an integer or an integer and a name with an optional *recurrence*. The UML Specification does not explain this clearly, as it states that each term is either an integer or a name, but it does not define a name in this context, and it is not clear whether it means a *name*, as discussed in Section C.1.7. Examples given for message sequence-expressions incorporating names include **3.1a** and **1b.1.1**. In Booch et al. (1999), names of objects are used to prefix the sequence-numbers in messages originating from them.

Gomaa (2000) suggests using initial names to represent the use case that is being realized by a collaboration, for example **Use1.1.2**, as in Figure 10-10, despite the fact that this is implicit in the metamodel. He also suggests the use of letters as suffixes to indicate both concurrent messages and alternative messages where there is a choice.

A name can be used with an integer to show concurrent nested operations; that is, the operations take place at the same time. So **3.1.1a** and **3.1.1b** are concurrent within the activation resulting from

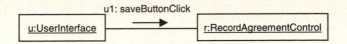

Figure 10-10: Prefixing a sequence-term with an object name

message **3.1**. Names can also be used to distinguish alternative messages that result from a guard condition on the message, for example **3.1.2a[x <= 0]** and **3.1.2b[x > 0]**.

Recurrence—The *recurrence* is used to denote messages that are sent iteratively or are sent depending on some guard condition. An iteration is denoted by an asterisk * and optionally an *iteration-clause* in square brackets, for example ***[i:0..journeys.length]** or ***[while not end-of-file]**. Where a name is used for an index in an iteration (like **i** in the first example), this can be used in subsequent sequence-terms, for example **2.i.1:**, but the iteration-clause is not shown again at the nested level. An iteration in a communication diagram is equivalent to a **loop** combined fragment in a sequence diagram. If the operations within an iteration will be performed in parallel (in a device that provides parallel processing), then the asterisk is followed by two vertical lines, ***||**. Figure 10-11 shows an example of a message with a recurrence in the sequence-expression.

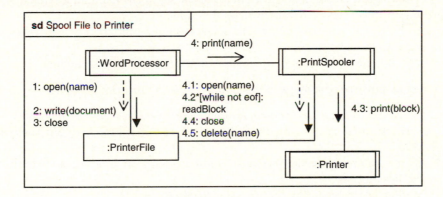

Figure 10-11: Using a recurrence in a sequence-expression

A *guard* uses the square brackets syntax without the asterisk, for example **[dateArranged = null]**, and represents a point in the interaction where there is a choice. It is equivalent to an **opt** or **alt** combined fragment in a sequence diagram.

The guard is a condition that must evaluate to true for the message to be sent. A guard condition is a Boolean expression, typically written in *Object Constraint Language*, pseudocode or a programming language. The expression can be written in terms of parameters of the message, attributes of the current object, concurrent states of the current object or states of other objects that are reachable via links from the current object, for example **[percentageComplete = 100]** or **[self.carSharer.homeAddress.location != null]**. The use of a guard can also have the effect of synchronizing threads of control. Figure 10-12 shows an example, in which **Failed** would be a state of **:ConnectionControl**.

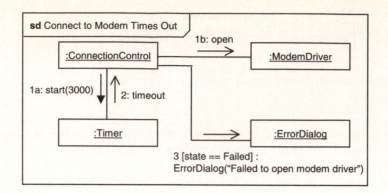

Figure 10-12: Message with condition in sequence-expression

10.5 HOW TO PRODUCE COMMUNICATION DIAGRAMS

Communication diagrams may be produced at a number of stages in the development of a system:

- Early in the development of a system, as part of the process of developing class diagrams. In this case, the objects participating in each use case can be modelled in a communication diagram, the objects can be assigned to possible classes and the classes in the communication diagrams merged to produce a first draft class diagram or class diagrams.
- Once the classes in a system are known, to specify the interaction that will take place between objects in order to realize use cases.
- In order to specify the realization of operations that have complex behaviour.

Whatever the stage or purpose, the steps in developing a communication diagram are as follows:

- Decide on the context of the interaction: system, subsystem, use case or operation.
- Identify the structural elements (objects, subsystems) necessary to carry out the functionality of this interaction.
- Model the structural relationships between those elements to produce a diagram showing the context of the interaction.
- Consider the alternative scenarios that may be required.
- Draw communication diagrams. (Alternatively, sequence diagrams can be drawn if the timing of messages is an important aspect of the interaction—see Chapter 9.)

10.5.1 Decide on Context

The communication diagram can model interaction at the system, subsystem, use case or operation level. The stage in the development of the project and the task being undertaken will determine which is to be modelled.

EXAMPLE 10.1   In this case, we are going to model a use case: the use case **Register car sharer** in the CarMatch system.

10.5.2 Identify Structural Elements

The first step is to identify the structural elements that will participate in the interaction. These will include user interface elements, control elements and classes or objects that represent the business entities that the system deals with.

EXAMPLE 10.2 The use case Manually add car sharer was described in Chapter 3. This is a specialization of the use case Register car sharer (described on page 26), which is also specialized by the use case Add car sharer web service. The use case Register car sharer has to handle the common functionality of creating a new CarSharer, creating as many new Journeys as required, and for each new Journey validating the Addresses. For the purpose of this example, we shall assume that all this takes place in one go. The aim is to create an interaction that is capable of handling the creation of a car sharer via a user interface, in a web application or from data sent to a web service.

The classes involved here are CarSharer, Journey and Address. These are shown in Figure 10-13. There will also be an instance of some kind of control class that manages the interaction and a boundary class, either a user interface class, a value object or a web service document to provide the data, as in Figure 10-14. (A value object is a lightweight object—one with no operations that implement business logic—used to pass data between layers in a layered architecture.)

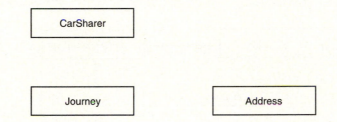

Figure 10-13: Classes participating in the collaboration

Figure 10-14: Boundary and control classes added

Booch et al. (1999) suggests laying the objects out with the most important in the centre and the less important round the outside. Depending on the structure of the collaboration, this is not always appropriate. A top-down or left–right structure of message-passing may be easier to lay out. In this example, boundary classes are to the left, the control class in the centre and entity classes to the right.

10.5.3   Model Structural Relationships

The associations between classes are added to the diagram. In some cases, the same class will participate in different associations. In such cases, it is best to distinguish between these by using different lifeline names.

EXAMPLE 10.3 There are associations between CarSharer and both Journey and Address, and two aggregation relationships between Journey and Address. These are shown in Figure 10-15. A control class and a source for the data are also required. Without modelling the interaction in detail, it is not always obvious what the links will be between such objects and the domain objects, so some possible links have been added in Figure 10-16.

Drawing these structural relationships highlights the need for the class **Address** to appear in the diagram in different lifelines. These have been added in Figure 10-17.

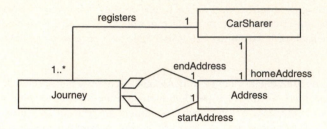

Figure 10-15: Domain class associations

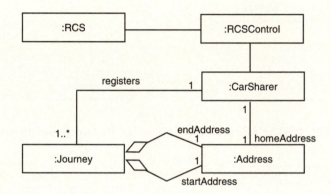

Figure 10-16: Possible links with the boundary and control classes

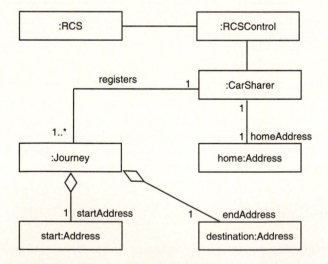

Figure 10-17: Additional lifelines for Address

All the interaction associated with the user via the user interface or with the transfer of data via the web transaction is outside the scope of this use-case realization. The use case provides the functionality that is inherited by the others. In order for this to work, the classes **RCSTransaction**, **RCSValueObject** and **RCSUserInterface** must support the operations **getCarSharerDetails()** and **getJourneyDetails()**. One way to do this is to define an interface which they all implement, as in Figure 10-18. This interface (**RCS**) has been used in the diagrams.

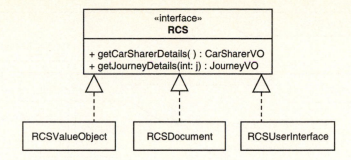

Figure 10-18: Classes implementing the interface RCS

10.5.4   Consider Alternative Scenarios

There may be a number of different ways in which the interaction may develop, depending on inputs into the system or the state of existing objects in the system. These may already have been documented in behaviour specifications in the use case model, or the system developer may have to work through these alternatives as part of the process of producing communication diagrams. These alternatives may involve points in the interaction where one of two or more paths must be chosen, or they may involve iterations that execute a specific number of times. Communication diagrams can be drawn for the significant alternatives.

EXAMPLE 10.4   The two main alternatives for the realization of the use case Register car sharer depend on whether this use case's functionality is invoked from the use case Manually add car sharer, the use case Add car sharer web service or the use case Transfer car sharer from web-server. In the first case, the control object will be interacting with a user interface object, and the address data will already have been validated against the geographical information system and a location allocated to it. In the second case, the control object will be interacting with a representation of an XML document, and in the third case, the control object will be interacting with a web transaction object, and the addresses will have to be geolocated (allocated a location). In each case, the number of iterations will depend on the number of journeys that have been entered.

10.5.5   Draw Communication Diagrams

The diagrams show object instances participating in the collaboration. If communication diagrams are being used to develop the class diagram, the classes of objects may not be known at this stage. In the example below, we know the class roles that are being played.

Starting with the message that triggers the interaction, add each message to the appropriate link and add a sequence-term to each message.

EXAMPLE 10.5   Figure 10-19 shows the situation where the interaction involves addresses that have already been geolocated, and Figure 10-20 shows the situation where the interaction involves addresses that need to be geolocated.

Some assumptions have been made here. Firstly, objects have been created using constructors that have the same name as the class. This is a convention in some languages, such as Java and C++. Secondly, to keep the diagram simple, return-values and parameters have been left out in most cases. The exception to this is where a new instance of Journey is created by the control object and then added to the CarSharer. Thirdly, it is assumed that the CarSharer is responsible for creating its own Address object, but that Journeys are created

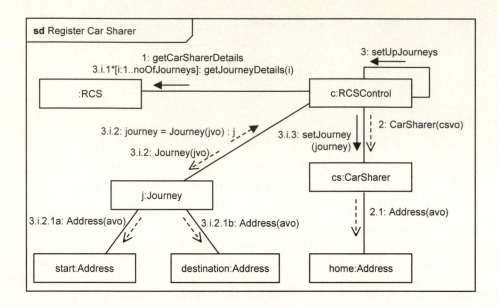

Figure 10-19: Collaboration for Register Car Sharer—first version

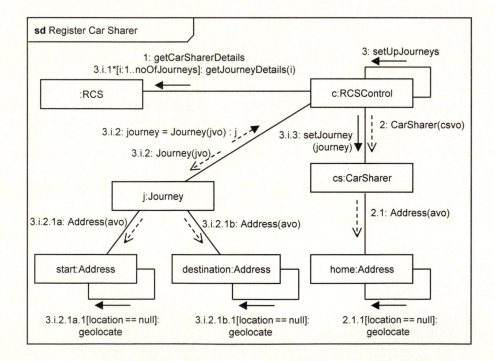

Figure 10-20: Collaboration for Register Car Sharer—second version

by the control object. This is to avoid having to pass all the data associated with creating Journeys via the CarSharer.

Note also that there are many alternative paths that could be taken as a result of incorrect input or invalid data, but it is not the role of the communication diagram to model all the possible error paths.

10.6 BUSINESS MODELLING WITH COMMUNICATION DIAGRAMS

In the UML profile for business modelling, five class stereotypes are defined for business objects. These are: Actor, Worker, Case Worker, Internal Worker and Entity. Actors are defined in the UML. The meanings of the other stereotypes are as follows.

- **Worker**—an abstraction of a human who acts within a system to interact with other workers and manipulate entities in a use-case realization.
- **Case worker**—a worker who interacts directly with actors outside the system.
- **Internal worker**—a worker who interacts with other workers and entities inside the system.
- **Entity**—a passive class that is manipulated by workers, participates in different interactions and usually outlives any single interaction. Entities are business classes, such as Address, Journey, Invoice and Product.

Entity classes have already been used, and are part of the UML software development process profile, together with boundary and control class stereotypes.

There are icons that can be used to represent these class stereotypes, and these are shown in Figure 10-21.

Worker or   Case worker   Entity
Internal worker

Figure 10-21: Icons for business class stereotypes

These stereotyped icons can be used in communication diagrams to model the interactions between workers and entities in use-case realizations. Figure 10-22 shows their use in a communication diagram to model the use case Manually add car sharer.

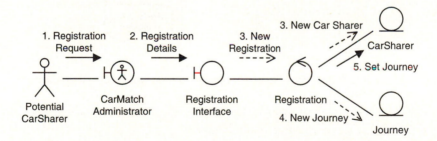

Figure 10-22: Business communication diagram

This is the kind of diagram that would be produced at an early stage in the development of a system, as part of the business modelling and before detailed analysis is carried out.

10.7 RELATIONSHIP WITH OTHER DIAGRAMS

Communication diagrams can be used to model the realization of either use cases or operations of classes. In the latter case, each operation being modelled must exist in a class diagram. The names of messages must be events or be operations of the class receiving the message. If states are referred to in guard conditions, they must be valid states of the relevant class and should appear in a state machine diagram (see Chapter 12).

Communication diagrams and sequence diagrams (see Chapter 9) model the same aspects of the system: the objects that collaborate together and the messages that are exchanged among them to achieve some objective. Communication diagrams and sequence diagrams can be converted into one another. Some CASE tools could do this automatically for UML 1.X. It is not clear whether this will continue to be the case with UML 2.0 as communication diagrams do not have the combined fragments which are now part of the sequence diagram notation.

10.8   COMMUNICATION DIAGRAMS IN THE UNIFIED PROCESS

Communication diagrams are used in the Unified Process first of all in the Analysis workflow. This is shown in Figure 10-23.

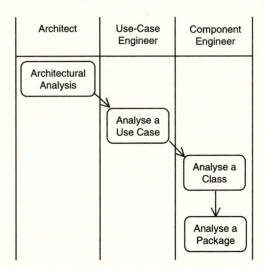

Figure 10-23: Analysis workflow as an activity diagram

The Analysis Model in the Unified Process consists of a set of use case realizations and a set of classifiers (classes) that participate in those use-case realizations.

In the activity *Analyse a Use Case*, each use case is analysed to produce a use-case realization. This is carried out in two main steps: *Identifying Analysis Classes* and *Describing Analysis Object Interactions*. First, the participating classes are identified and class diagrams produced to show just the classes involved in each use case, then the collaborations are analysed to produce communication diagrams. In the Analysis Model, these communication diagrams will use informal names for messages to show the intent of each message. These will be replaced later with event names or the names of specific operations of the design classes. Use cases are classifiers in UML terms, and can also be described by activity diagrams, statechart diagrams and sequence diagrams. Sequence diagrams can be used to represent the interaction if there are important timing issues that are apparent during analysis. The collaborations can also be documented using *Flow of Events Analysis*. This uses text to describe the interaction taking place within a use case realization. These textual descriptions are different from those produced to specify the behaviour of use cases in the requirements workflow, as they describe the interaction between classes that are internal to the system, whereas use case descriptions describe the external behaviour of the use case (see Section 3.3.2). There is a third step, *Capturing Special Requirements*, in which all requirements relating to the use case are documented, including non-functional requirements, even if they are to be addressed in design rather than analysis.

The communication diagrams produced as part of the analysis model are refined in design. Figure 10-24 shows the Unified Process design workflow.

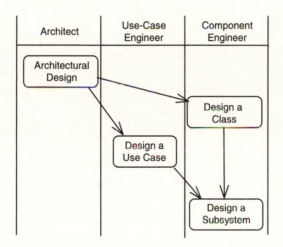

Figure 10-24: Design workflow as an activity diagram

In the *Architectural Design* activity, the architects look for and design generic collaborations that will be specialized by specific collaborations within the system. To do this, they look for common patterns of interaction in different collaborations. These involve similar actor roles and the same structure of participating class roles. Design patterns (see Chapter 17) can be used to model this kind of generic collaboration.

The activity *Design a Use Case* is similar to the analysis activity of the same name, except for the fact that design classes are used and there are more steps, as more detail is required when a project gets closer to implementation. The main steps are: *Identifying the Participating Design Classes*, *Describing Design Object Interactions*, *Identifying the Participating Subsystems and Interfaces* and *Describing Subsystem Interactions*. Design classes may be different from analysis classes. For example, collection classes may be added in design to handle interactions that involve a set of objects. The interactions on the communication and sequence diagrams will have to be modified to include instances of these classes and their interactions. In the Unified Process, it is suggested that sequence diagrams rather than communication diagrams should be used to model the interactions in design. It is also possible to consider a use case in terms of interactions among design subsystems rather than design objects. This provides a hierarchical decomposition of the interactions, as the detail of the interaction within a subsystem can be hidden in one diagram and shown in a separate lower-level diagram (see Chapter 9). In order to support this approach, the interfaces of subsystems must be identified, so that it is clear what operations or events each subsystem will handle. As in analysis, there is a fifth step, *Capturing Implementation Requirements*, in which requirements to be handled in implementation are documented.

10.9   TIMING DIAGRAMS

10.9.1   Introduction to Timing Diagrams

Timing diagrams are new in UML 2.0. They are like sequence diagrams, in that they show lifelines; however, they are specifically intended to depict the changes that take place on lifelines over time. Douglass (1998) included them in his book on real-time systems development using UML. However, they are not the only possible kind of diagram to model timing issues for real-time systems, and Gomaa (2000) presents two other kinds of diagrams, one of which is a variation on sequence diagrams.

10.9.2   Purpose of Timing Diagrams

Timing diagrams are of particular use in the development of real-time systems: systems in which the timely execution of operations is essential to the correct running of the system. Timing diagrams are preferred to sequence diagrams where strict timing is required. Their purpose can be summarized as follows:

- They are used to help the analyst to reason about the time-related behaviour of objects, subsystems and systems.
- They are used to specify the time-related behaviour of objects, subsystems and systems.
- They are used to model the relationships between lifelines whose interaction depends on adherence to timing considerations.

10.9.3   Notation of Timing Diagrams

Timing diagrams are a type of interaction diagram and are drawn in a frame with the keyword **sd** and the name of the interaction in the heading area at the top left-hand corner. The names of lifelines are written at the left of the frame and may be written running left to right or bottom to top. It is possible to draw a meaningful timing diagram with only one lifeline in it, as the purpose of these diagrams is to reason about the effect of interactions on lifelines over time rather than to show the passing of messages between lifelines. Where more than one lifeline is shown in a diagram, they are separated by horizontal lines.

Time runs from left to right in a timing diagram rather than from top to bottom, and where message arrows are shown, they run vertically (or near vertically) rather than horizontally. The time axis should be linear.

There are two styles of timing diagram. In the type shown in Figure 10-25, the states of the lifeline are shown to the left and transitions between states are shown as changes in the line running from left to right. In this type, the line is called the *state or condition timeline*. The state changes need not be discrete step changes, but could be continuous values such as temperatures.

In the type shown in Figure 10-26, the states of the lifeline are shown with the states written from left to right as they change. The lifeline in this type is called a *general value lifeline*.

Timing and duration constraints can be added to timing diagrams, as in Figure 10-27. This diagram also shows the use of the *timing ruler* at the bottom of the frame to show *tick marks* with time values or timing observations.

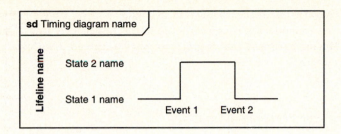

Figure 10-25: Timing diagram notation showing state timeline

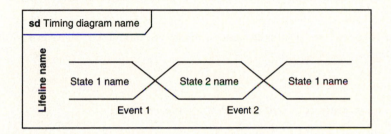

Figure 10-26: Timing diagram notation showing changes in state using general value lifeline

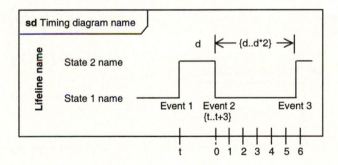

Figure 10-27: Timing diagram notation showing constraints

10.9.4   How to Produce Timing Diagrams

The steps in producing a timing diagram are as follows:

- Decide on the lifelines to model.
- Decide on the type of timing diagram: whether to produce a state timeline diagram or a general value lifeline diagram.
- Determine the states or conditions that should be shown.
- Identify the events that result in changes of state.
- Add timing and duration constraints with the necessary timing ruler and tick mark values.
- Review and elaborate the diagram.

10.9.4.1   Decide on the lifelines to model

The first step is to decide which lifelines to include. It may be a good idea to start with single lifelines and then combine them.

EXAMPLE 10.6 If we consider the sequence diagram in Figure 9-70 on page 195 for the interaction **Vehicle Passes Beacon**, we may want to model the changes in state in the :Beacon over time. This lifeline has behaviour that is linked to states. Having produced this diagram, we want to extend it with the :Transponder as well, in order to see how the two interact.

10.9.4.2   Decide on the type of timing diagram

The type of diagram chosen will depend on its purpose and the number of states. Where more than one lifeline and the interaction between lifelines is to be modelled, a timeline diagram is better. For single lifelines or where the number of states is large, the general value lifeline is better.

EXAMPLE 10.7 In this case, we eventually want to model the interaction between two lifelines, so we shall use a timeline diagram.

10.9.4.3   Determine the states or conditions that should be shown

The states and conditions should be identified from the sequence diagrams that show the same interaction, and checked against the state machine diagrams for the object or system represented by the lifeline (see Chapter 12).

EXAMPLE 10.8 The sequence diagram shows just two states, **Waiting** and **Communicating**. We can show these states in a timing diagram, as in Figure 10-28.

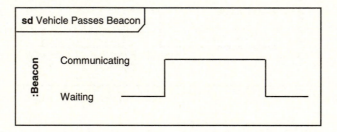

Figure 10-28: Timing diagram for Vehicle Passes Beacon

10.9.4.4   Identify the events

From the sequence and state machine diagrams identify the events that trigger the changes of state.

EXAMPLE 10.9 In the sequence diagram, it appears to be the **response** from the transponder that triggers the first state change and the **validation** from the database that triggers the second. These have been added in Figure 10-29.

10.9.4.5   Add constraints and timing values

Add timing and duration constraints from the sequence diagrams as well as any others that are necessary to support the purpose of the diagram: to reason about the behaviour of the lifeline over time. Add timing ruler and tick mark values that are required by the constraints.

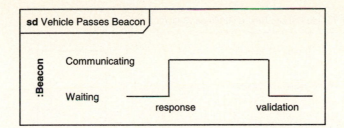

Figure 10-29: Timing diagram for Vehicle Passes Beacon

EXAMPLE 10.10   The constraints on the sequence diagram all occur within the **Communicating** state. It appears that we need to add some additional states before adding the constraints. It is not clear which is really the event that triggers the change back to the **Waiting** state. Is it the **validation** receive event for the response from the database, or the send event for the optional **request** to the camera? If it is the latter, then what happens if the result of the validation is **valid** rather than **invalid** and no request is sent to the camera? We can add two more states to clarify the behaviour of the beacon: **Charge Calculated** and **Validated**. When the charge has been calculated the beacon changes to the **Charge Calculated** state, and when the validation response is received from the database, it changes to the **Validated** state before changing to the **Waiting** state again. Figure 10-30 shows these additional states and the timing constraints associated with them. (States are covered in more detail in Chapter 12 on State Machines.)

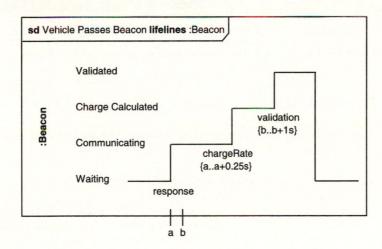

Figure 10-30: Timing diagram for Vehicle Passes Beacon with additional states and constraints

10.9.4.6   Review and elaborate the diagram

Review the diagram that you have produced. Check that it makes sense and that the timings and states shown make sense. Consider alternative scenarios. If you require a diagram for multiple lifelines, add the other lifelines and cross-check the events and timings.

EXAMPLE 10.11   The diagram for the situation where the request for a photo is sent to the camera would be similar to Figure 10-31, with a **requestPhoto** event. Conditions can be shown instead of states on the diagram. The beacon would change state to [result == 'Invalid'] as soon as it received the result of the validation and detected that the result was equal to **Invalid**. To distinguish between the two conditions of the **Validated** state, we have

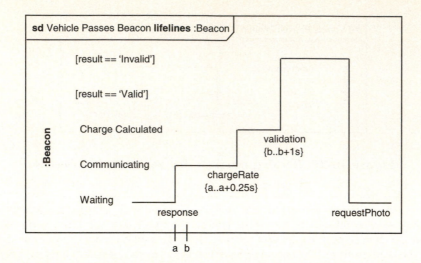

Figure 10-31: Timing diagram for Vehicle Passes Beacon with conditions

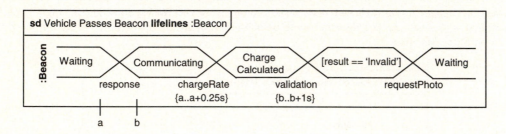

Figure 10-32: Timing diagram for Vehicle Passes Beacon using general value lifeline

replaced Validated in Figure 10-30 with the condition [result == 'Valid']. The Specification gives no guidance on, or examples of, how conditions should be represented in timing diagrams.

The same diagram can be shown using the general value lifeline approach, as in Figure 10-32.

The lower line of the frame can be used as a timing ruler with tick marks to show the passing of units of time or to note points that are used in timing constraints. Tick marks could be used to show that the beacon stays in the [result == 'Invalid'] state longer than in the [result == 'Valid'] state, as it has work to do in sending the requestPhoto message to the camera.

Timing diagrams can be used to show timing in relation to multiple lifelines. In Figure 10-33, we have added the :Transponder in the vehicle, and can show how the two lifelines interact over time.

In the figure, we have added tick marks at 0.1 second intervals. We have also added a duration constraint: the transponder will stay in the Displaying state for ten to fifteen seconds, during which time the charge rate will be displayed on the LCD screen in the vehicle, then switch off the display and return to the Idle state. Clearly, it doesn't work very well to try to combine lifelines of objects that operate on timescales that differ by orders of magnitude, unless you are prepared to accept that the timelines are not drawn to scale.

10.9.5   Relationship with Other Diagrams

Timing diagrams are clearly related to sequence diagrams as they are both types of interaction diagrams, and timing and duration constraints can be shown in both.

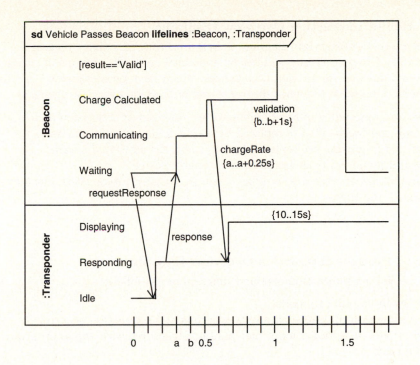

Figure 10-33: Timing diagram for **:Beacon** and **:Transponder** lifelines

10.9.6   Timing Diagrams in the Unified Process

Timing diagrams did not exist when the Unified Process was developed by Jacobson et al. (1999). However, they are likely to be used in the same workflows as sequence diagrams (see Section 9.8). In a project that involves real-time components, the Unified Process workflows for Analysis and Design could be extended to include additional roles and activities relating to performance analysis and timing analysis of the components of the system.

10.10   INTERACTION OVERVIEW DIAGRAMS

10.10.1   Introduction to Interaction Overview Diagrams

Interaction overview diagrams are new in UML 2.0. They combine activity diagrams (see Chapter 11) with interaction diagrams, particularly sequence diagrams, to provide an overview of the flow of control through an interaction. Activity diagrams show workflow, and the main notational elements that they use are *actions* (units of work), *object nodes* (objects that are affected by actions), *activity edges* (links between actions or between actions and objects), *decision and merge nodes* (where flows split and merge based on choices), and *fork and join nodes* (where parallel flows split and join). In an interaction overview diagram, the nodes can be replaced with interactions or interaction occurrences. The lifelines and messages do not appear in the overview diagram, although the diagram can be labelled with the names of the lifelines that it covers.

10.10.2   Purpose of Interaction Overview Diagrams

Interaction overview diagrams are used to give a high-level overview of the flow of control within an interaction without showing all the detail of the lifelines and messages.

10.10.3   Notation of Interaction Overview Diagrams

The notation of interaction overview diagrams is based on that of activity diagrams. This notation is explained in detail in Chapter 11 and will not be explained here. The actions in activity diagrams are replaced by interactions and interaction occurrences, which have been explained in Chapter 9. There are certain differences between sequence diagrams and interaction overview diagrams:

- Alternative and optional combined fragments are replaced by a decision node and a merge node.
- Parallel combined fragments are replaced by a split node and a join node.
- Loop combined fragments are replaced by a cycle in the activity diagram.
- Branching and joining of branches must be properly nested.
- Lifelines are not shown except where they occur in included interactions, but may be listed in the heading text of the frame.

10.10.4   How to Produce Interaction Overview Diagrams

The steps in producing an interaction overview diagram are as follows:

- Decide on the interaction to model.
- Break the interaction up into separate interactions and interaction occurrences.
- Replace alternatives, options, loops and parallel structures with the appropriate notation from activity diagrams.

10.10.4.1   Decide on the interaction to model

The interaction is likely to be one where there are a number of paths through a use case and where the alternatives can be visualized better using the interaction overview diagram notation than with a standard sequence diagram.

EXAMPLE 10.12   The sequence diagram in Figure 9-59 for the use case Refund membership fee will be the subject of the interaction overview diagram. This sequence diagram has a loop and alternative branches in it. We shall focus on the lifeline of the control class RefundControl.

10.10.4.2   Break up the interaction

For it to be meaningful to produce an interaction overview diagram, the interaction needs to be broken down into separate parts that can be linked together by the activity diagram notation. Referenced interaction occurrences do not need breaking down further, but the rest of the diagram will need splitting into either separate interactions that are included inline in the overview diagram or turned into interaction occurrences that can be referenced.

EXAMPLE 10.13   In the sequence diagram, we already have two referenced interaction occurrences: Delete Journey and Set Journey to Defunct. The messages before the loop can be considered as one interaction occurrence or used as an inline interaction. Within the loop, there is the message getNextJourney to the CarSharer. Finally there are the messages concerned with communicating with the Accounts system.

10.10.4.3   Replace structures with activity diagram notation

You can either work top-down through the sequence diagram or start with obvious structures like loops and alternatives. If the diagram is complex, it is probably best to work top-down.

EXAMPLE 10.14   We first draw a frame for the diagram, then an initial node. All activity diagrams and interaction overview diagrams begin with an initial node. Then we can include the first set of messages as an inline interaction within its own frame. This is shown in Figure 10-34.

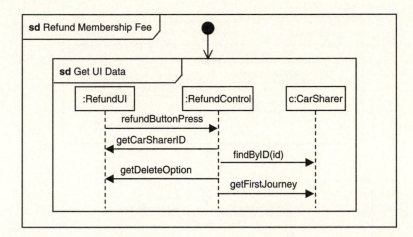

Figure 10-34: First part of interaction overview diagram for Refund Membership Fee

The next step is to include the branch into the two alternative paths: the one to delete journeys and the other to set them to the defunct state. We add the interaction occurrences and decision and merge nodes with the appropriate conditions, as in Figure 10-35.

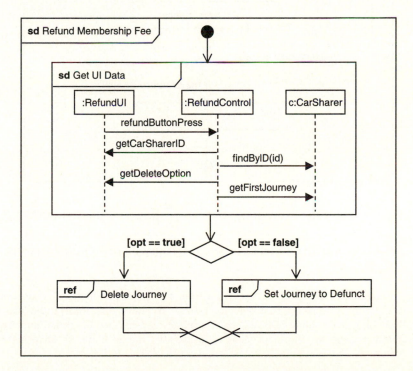

Figure 10-35: Interaction overview diagram for Refund Membership Fee with branching

We then need to add in the message to get the next journey. We have added this as an interaction occurrence. There is then a loop decision point: if there are no more journeys—[nextJourney == null]—then carry on, otherwise loop back and deal with the next journey. Finally, there is an interaction occurrence to deal with notifying the

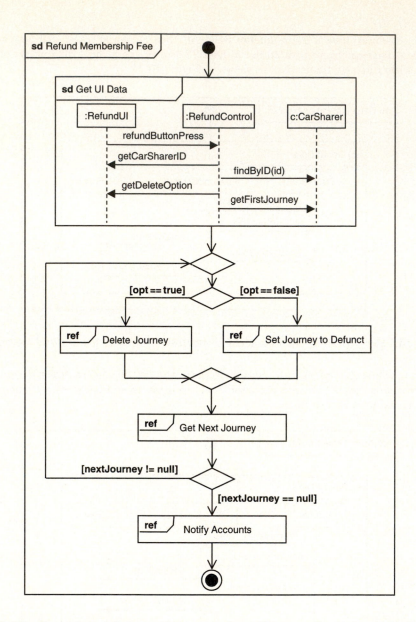

Figure 10-36: Completed interaction overview diagram for Refund Membership Fee

accounts system, followed by an activity final node, which is required in the same way as the initial node (see Figure 10-36).

Note that we have changed the name of the variable j from the sequence diagram to **nextJourney**, as j is not meaningful without the return message that sets its value. We have also interpreted the comment in the Specification that branching and joining of branches in interaction overview diagrams must be properly nested to mean that the decision node for the loop needs an associated merge node, so have inserted it above the branch.

It is important to recognize that the new interaction occurrences that have been created here must be backed up by the creation of associated sequence diagrams that show the lifelines and messages within them.

It is not clear from the UML Specification when inline interactions should be used and when interaction occurrences should be used. It makes sense to reuse interaction occurrences that have been defined already in the process of constructing sequence diagrams. It is not obvious in what circumstances new interaction occurrences should be created.

10.10.5   Relationship with Other Diagrams

Clearly interaction overview diagrams draw from the notation of both sequence diagrams and activity diagrams. In the situation where an activity diagram covers the same interaction as an interaction overview diagram, they should have the same structure.

10.10.6   Interaction Overview Diagrams in the Unified Process

Interaction overview diagrams did not exist when the Unified Process was developed by Jacobson et al. (1999). However, they are likely to be used in the same workflows as sequence diagrams (see Section 9.8).

Review Questions

10.1 What is the difference between how sequence diagrams model an interaction and how communication diagrams model an interaction?

10.2 What is meant by a collaboration?

10.3 What is meant by an interaction?

10.4 What effect does iterative development have on the way that communication diagrams are developed?

10.5 What are the main purposes of using communication diagrams?

10.6 Which of the following are valid lifeline names in a communication diagram?

   (a) returnJourney : Journey

   (b) returnJourney : Journey

   (c) returnJourney

   (d) :Journey

10.7 What two kinds of message can be used in a communication diagram?

10.8 What are the four types of messages that can be represented by different arrow styles in a communication diagram?

10.9 What is meant by a return-value?

10.10 What is a sequence-term in a message?

10.11 How can names be used in sequence-expressions?

10.12 What is meant by a guard?

10.13 What are the steps in producing a communication diagram?

10.14 What are the five class stereotypes defined in the UML Business Modelling profile?

10.15 In which two Unified Process workflows are communication diagrams used?

10.16 What are the three steps in the Unified Process activity Analyse a Use Case?

10.17 How does a Flow of Events Analysis differ from a Use-Case Description?

10.18 What are the five steps in the Unified Process activity Design a Use Case?

10.19 What are the names for the two types of lifeline shown in timing diagrams?

10.20 In a timing diagram, in which direction does time normally flow?

10.21 What are the main purposes of timing diagrams?

10.22 What do tick marks represent in a timing diagram?

10.23 What is the notation for tick marks in a timing diagram?

10.24 What can be shown instead of states in a timing diagram?

10.25 What is the notation for a general value lifeline in a timing diagram?

10.26 What are the steps in the construction of a timing diagram?

10.27 What kind of diagram notation is combined with sequence diagram notation in interaction overview diagrams?

10.28 What is the purpose of drawing interaction overview diagrams?

10.29 In an interaction overview diagram, what elements of activity diagram notation replace alternative and optional combined fragments in a sequence diagram?

10.30 What shape represents a decision in an interaction overview diagram?

10.31 What are the steps in the construction of interaction overview diagrams?

Solved Problems

10.1 One of the use cases in the CarMatch system is called Match car sharers. Here is a summary use case description.

> When a new member joins CarMatch as a car sharer, the member's journeys are matched against the unmatched journeys of other members to try to find suitable people with whom he or she could share travel. The automated part of the matching is carried out by passing the locations of the start and finish addresses of two journeys to a geographical information system (GIS). The GIS returns a percentage value, which is a measure of how close together the two journeys are. If this percentage is greater than or equal to 80%, the journeys are looked at by a member of staff, who also looks at the members' requirements notes to decide whether they are compatible. If it looks like the journeys are similar and the people are compatible, a letter is sent out.

Within this use case, we want to model the operation matchJourney. This is an operation of the class Journey; it takes another Journey as an argument and returns a percentage value as a Float, which indicates how close a match there is between the two journeys.

It is clear that the context of this collaboration is an operation. What are the domain classes that are involved in the operation matchJourney? (You may want to look at the class diagrams in Chapter 5.)

There are two classes from the class diagram involved in this use case: Journey and Address.

10.2 What other subsystems are involved in this use case?

The geographical information system is a separate subsystem. We are not concerned here with how it works, only with the service it provides (matching journeys) and the interface that must be used to obtain that service.

10.3 What are the additional classes that will be required for this collaboration?

None. We are not modelling the full use case, so have no need of control or boundary classes.

10.4 Draw a class diagram showing the associations between the classes, including stereotyped associations if required.

Figure 10-37 shows a possible solution. Note that there is no association in the class diagram between Journey and GIS.

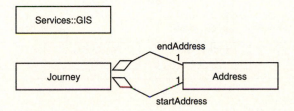

Figure 10-37: Classes participating in the collaboration

The GIS is another subsystem that provides a service. It could be a web service or it could be accessed via an object that encapsulates the service. It may be a design objective to make it possible to change how the service is implemented in the future. The **Service Locator** pattern could be used to help make this possible. (Patterns are explained in Chapter 17.) However, for this example, we shall just assume that there is a GIS class in the **Services** package with a class-scope operation (see Section 7.4) that provides the service.

10.5 What are the roles that the classes in Figure 10-37 take in this collaboration?

For each **Journey** there are two address roles: **startAddress** and **endAddress**. The lifelines are shown in Figure 10-38.

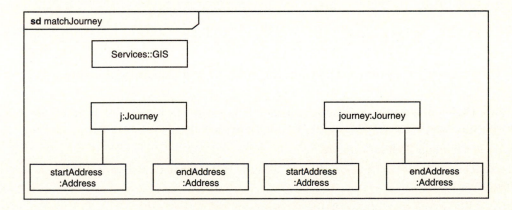

Figure 10-38: Lifelines for matchJourney

10.6 What are the alternative scenarios that may occur?

There are no significant alternatives in this operation.

10.7 Draw a communication diagram for each scenario.

Figure 10-39 shows the communication diagram.

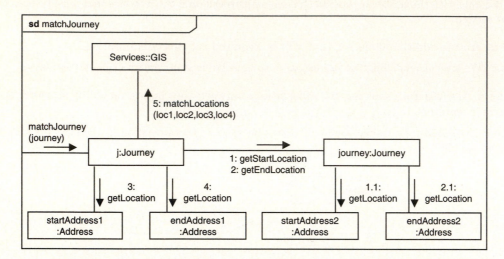

Figure 10-39: Communication diagram for matchJourney

The message sent to the GIS, matchLocations(loc1,loc2,loc3,loc4), passes the locations that have been retrieved from the start and end addresses of each journey. The map locations could be shown using return values and attribute assignment, as in the partial diagram in Figure 10-40. However, this makes a communication diagram very cluttered, so we have left the return values out of Figure 10-39.

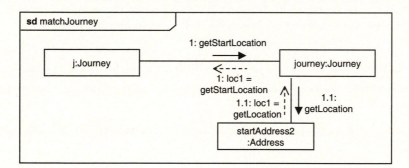

Figure 10-40: Part of a communication diagram for matchJourney showing a return value

10.8 Draw a timing diagram based on the sequence diagram for the interaction from Figure 9-37, which has been redrawn here as Figure 10-41 with states and timing constraints.

What is the main lifeline to model?

The lifeline for :ConnectionControl is the main lifeline. It is the one that controls the interaction with the other objects.

10.9 What type of timing diagram should be drawn?

There are only four states, so this is suitable for a timeline style of diagram.

10.10 Which states or conditions should be shown?

The states shown on the sequence diagram need to be shown. There may be others that become apparent as we develop the diagram, but we start with the ones that are already documented. With this information

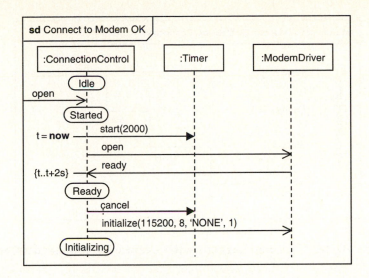

Figure 10-41: Sequence diagram for first scenario of connecting to modem

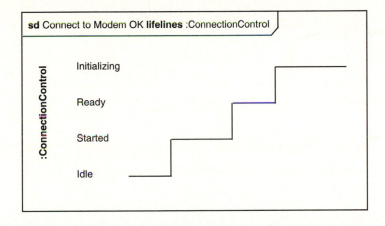

Figure 10-42: Timing diagram with states and timeline for :ConnectionControl

we can draw the first part of the timing diagram, with a timeline for the states. This is shown in Figure 10-42.

10.11 What are the events that result in the changes of state?

The receipt of the **open** message changes the state from Idle to Started. After the :ConnectionControl has received the **ready** message from the :ModemDriver it changes state to Ready. After it has sent the **initialize** message, it changes to the Initializing state. After that, we don't know what states it changes to. Presumably, the ModemDriver responds to state that it is initialized, and the :ConnectionControl changes to a Communicating state, but that is out of the scope here. This is shown in Figure 10-43.

10.12 Add the necessary timing and duration constraints.

The only timing constraint is that the :ModemDriver must respond within 2 seconds with the **ready** message, otherwise the :Timer will time out. This is shown by the addition of t on the timing ruler and the constraint on the **ready** message in Figure 10-44.

10.13 Add the lifeline for :Timer to the diagram.

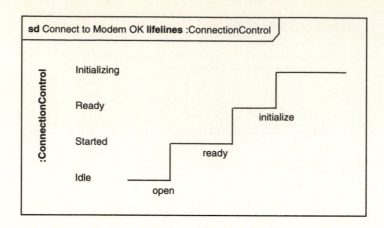

Figure 10-43: Timing diagram with events for :ConnectionControl

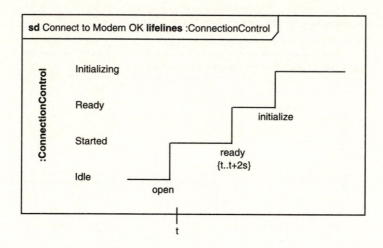

Figure 10-44: Timing diagram with timing constraint for :ConnectionControl

The sequence diagram does not show any states for :Timer. There must be at least two with names such as Running and Stopped. The :Timer will change to the Running state when it receives the start message, and back to the Stopped state when it receives the cancel message. These are shown in Figure 10-45.

10.14 Draw an interaction overview diagram for the interaction in Figure 9-71, which has been redrawn here in a slightly different form as Figure 10-46. Break the interaction up into separate interactions and interaction occurrences.

We first need to create an inline interaction or an interaction occurrence for each of the following sets of messages:

- requestResponse and response
- validate and validation
- chargeRate and display
- requestPhoto

10.15 Replace the structures in the sequence diagram with activity diagram structures.

We start by drawing a frame and adding an initial node. The first set of messages can be included as an inline interaction. We then have a parallel structure. The activity diagram notation for split and join nodes is a horizontal bar. The two parallel sets of messages can be shown as interaction occurrences.

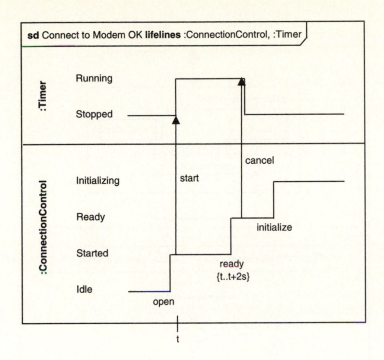

Figure 10-45: Timing diagram for :ConnectionControl and :Timer

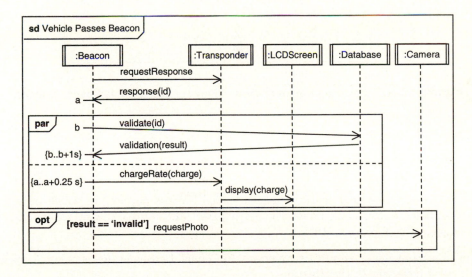

Figure 10-46: Sequence diagram for Vehicle Passes Beacon

Finally, there is a decision node and the optional request to the camera. The paths that split at the decision node must be merged again before the final node. Figure 10-47 shows the finished diagram.

The inline interaction **Receive Response** could be drawn as an interaction occurrence like the others, but we have included it as an interaction as an example. To complete the set of diagrams, separate sequence diagrams would need to be drawn for each of the referenced interaction occurrences.

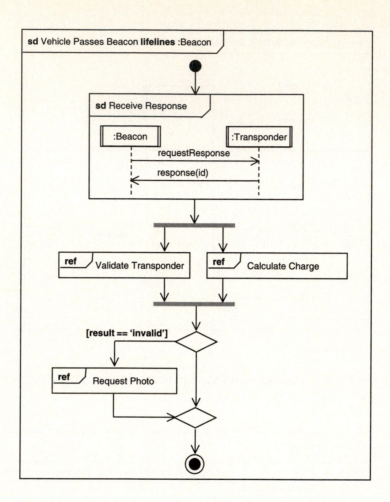

Figure 10-47: Interaction overview diagram for Vehicle Passes Beacon

Supplementary Problems

10.16 Draw lifelines for a communication diagram called **Process payment** in which objects from the classes **CarSharer**, **Account** and **Transaction** participate. Add suitable control and boundary objects. (Look at page 208 if you are stuck.)

10.17 Lay out objects of the classes **PPUserInterface**, **PPControl**, **CarSharer**, **Account** and **Transaction**. Add the following messages to the diagram:

1. transactionReady
2. getTransactionDetails
3. getCarSharerAccount(carSharerID)
4. Transaction(amount, type, date, account)
5. postTransaction(transaction)
6. displayBalance(balance)

The variable **itemList** contains the following items: carSharerID, amount, type, date.

10.18 One of the use cases that you found in the exercises for Chapter 3 should have had a name such as **Record an individual's request for help**. In case you did not have a use case like this, here is a short summary description.

> Individuals can request help from VolBank. This includes volunteers requesting help themselves. The Volbank administrator first enters the details of the individual. If this is an existing volunteer, then the name is entered and the details are displayed. If there is more than one person with the same name, then a list is displayed with the first part of the address, and the administrator selects the right one. If this is not an existing volunteer, then the name, address and telephone number are entered. It is important that the zip or postal code is entered, as it is required to match this request with volunteers in the same area. Details of the help required are then entered: a text summary of the help and a code that describes the type of help wanted, for example DEC for decorating, GAR for garden work or PET for pet care. A start and finish date for when the help is required are also entered.

Again, the context of the collaboration is a use case. What are the domain classes that are involved in this use case?

10.19 What other subsystems (if any) are involved in this use case?

10.20 What are the additional classes that will be required for this collaboration?

10.21 Draw a class diagram showing the associations between the classes.

10.22 What are the lifelines involved in this communication diagram?

10.23 What are the alternative scenarios that may occur?

10.24 Draw a communication diagram for each of these scenarios. For each diagram work through the following steps:

1. Lay out the lifelines.
2. Add links between the lifelines.
3. Lay out the messages starting with the triggering message.

10.25 Either from a book on Java 2 Platform Enterprise Edition (J2EE) patterns or from a web search, find out about the **Service Locator** pattern. This is the pattern that we would recommend in order to separate the implementation of the GIS service from its clients, as we discussed in Solved Problem 10.4.

10.26 Draw a timing diagram for the interaction in Figure 9-38, which has been redrawn in Figure 10-48 with states. What lifeline will you draw?

10.27 What type of timing diagram is best?

10.28 What states or conditions should be shown?

10.29 What events result in changes of state?

10.30 Add timing and duration constraints.

10.31 Add a lifeline for the :**Timer** with the messages that are sent between the two lifelines.

10.32 Consider the scenario where the :**ConnectionControl** has changed to the **Ready** state (see Figure 10-41), and then receives the **timeout** message (as in Figure 10-48) before it has had time to send the **cancel** message. Draw a timing diagram to show this situation. What do you think should happen?

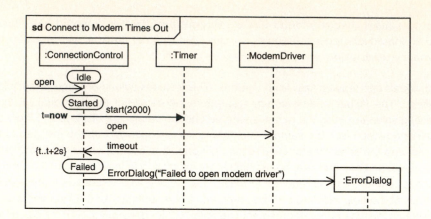

Figure 10-48: Sequence diagram for second scenario of connecting to modem

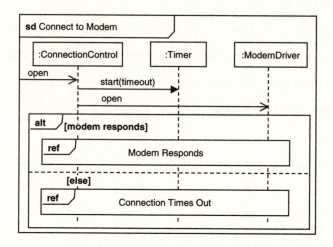

Figure 10-49: Sequence diagram **Connect to Modem**

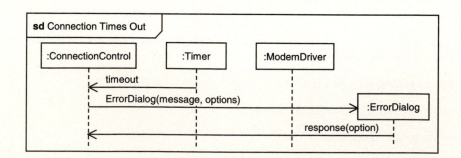

Figure 10-50: Sequence diagram for interaction occurrence **Connection Times Out**

10.33 Figure 10-49 shows a sequence diagram for the interaction **Connect to Modem**. Draw an interaction overview diagram based on this sequence diagram.

10.34 Figure 10-50 shows a variation of the sequence diagram for the interaction occurrence referenced in Figure 10-49. The object :ErrorDialog is created with an argument called **options**. In this case, the options are **Retry** and **Cancel** and mean that the dialogue is created with buttons with these as their labels. When the user clicks a button, the value of that button is returned to the object that created the dialogue. Extend the interaction sequence diagram from your answer to Problem 10.33 to include a loop back to retry the connection if the user clicks the **Retry** button.

CHAPTER 11

Activities

11.1 INTRODUCTION

Activities (sometimes referred to as *activity diagrams*) are a means of describing workflows that can be used in a variety of ways. As an analysis tool they can describe business flows in varying levels of detail. They can also be used to describe complex flows within or between use cases. At the design level, they can be used to describe in detail the flow within an operation. In this sense, they are very flexible. They can be used before the identification of use cases in the determination of high-level business requirements, as a means of describing complex use cases, and as a means of describing complex behaviour within an object. Activity diagrams complement communication diagrams and sequence diagrams, which are alternative ways of describing workflows.

11.2 WHAT IS AN ACTIVITY?

Activities consist of *action nodes*, *object nodes* and *control nodes* linked by *activity edges*. Let us look at a simple example. We have a business use case defined that allows a client to register for CarMatch. This is drawn as in Figure 11-1.

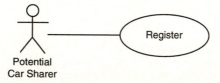

Figure 11-1: Business use case for a potential car sharer registering with CarMatch

Before we define the system use cases, we may wish to understand the business process where the use cases fit. One way is to develop an activity for a business process or business workflow as in Figure 11-2.

This activity describes the main process (or primary path) for a member registration for CarMatch. You can see that this is a simple flow chart describing business actions in the order that they need

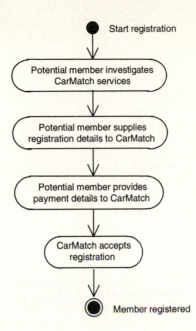

Figure 11-2: Activity diagram to describe business workflow of registration

to be followed. In this chapter we shall investigate how activities can be used to describe business workflows in detail. We shall be considering how conditions can be added, how parallel workflows can be described, how conditions can be applied to workflows, and how actions can be fully described.

At the other extreme, we may want to describe complicated flows within an operation. The **CarSharer** object has an operation **addRequirement()** as shown in Figure 11-3. We may realize during design that it is a complicated operation. We can then use an activity to describe the flows through this operation. The first attempt might just look at the primary flow, as in Figure 11-4.

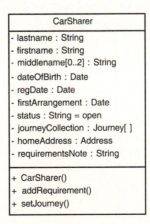

Figure 11-3: Class definition for CarSharer object

In practice it would be unusual to describe any but the most complicated operations in this way, and the complexity would probably be well in excess of the above simple example. The actions in such a workflow will map to one or a few simple instructions in a programming language, and it is acceptable to put program instructions in the text within the actions.

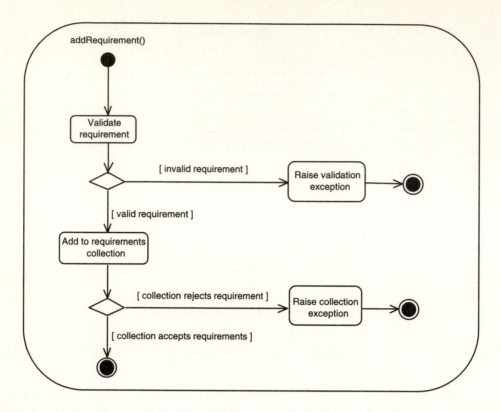

Figure 11-4: Activity diagram to describe primary flow of addRequirement operation

11.3   PURPOSE OF THE TECHNIQUE

Activities can be used throughout a project, from business analysis through to program design. They can be attached to many types of object, such as business use cases, system use cases, use case diagrams and operations. They are generic flow diagrams with the uses listed below:

- They are used to model business workflows.
- They are used to identify candidate use cases, through the examination of business workflows.
- They are used to identify pre- and post-conditions for use cases.
- They are used to model workflow between use cases.
- They are used to model workflow within use cases.
- They are used to model complicated workflows in operations on objects.
- They are used to model complex activities in a high-level activity diagram in more detail.

11.4   NOTATION

The following notation is very rich. All aspects of the notation need not be used at any one time, and some aspects of the notation, such as control icons, are there to add visual impact rather than provide additional expressiveness. In the early stages of analysis, business workflows may not need the full notation for activity description and a simple subset will suffice. Activity partitions make sense only when there are significant organizational or technological boundaries that are crossed by a workflow.

11.4.1 Activities

An activity is a workflow, and can be drawn with a diagram as in Figure 11-5. The activity is surrounded by a round-cornered rectangle, though this is often omitted in practice. Parameters, where used, are indicated by rectangular inserts in the perimeter of the activity. The activity name can be written in the top left-hand corner. Inside the activity, a number of actions are linked by activity edges to describe a workflow. In the top right, optional pre-conditions and post-conditions can be recorded. Activities should have only one start point, but may have a number of end-points.

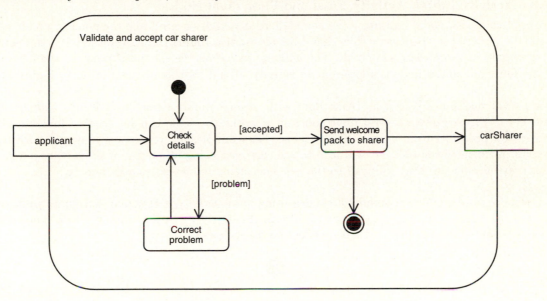

Figure 11-5: A simple activity

Often activities are drawn as simple flows without the bounding box.

11.4.2 Actions

An *action* is a unit of work that needs to be carried out. In practice, this can be large or small, taking place over a long or short period of time. A business action, such as debt recovery, might take many weeks. A computer action, such as changing an attribute of a customer, can be almost instantaneous. We draw actions as rectangles with rounded corners, with a descriptive name for the action inside as in Figure 11-6. The name needs to be descriptive of the action. For design-level actions, it can even be a program instruction.

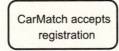

Figure 11-6: An action with a descriptive name

Actions normally carry out work, but occasionally may be a stop-point waiting for an event. If the action is complex, it can be documented by another activity, effectively nesting an activity in an action. The action could also be documented by a textual description stored in a text file.

Actions may have multiple flows in, and multiple flows out. When there are multiple flows in, the action does not fire until all the inward flows arrive (an implicit join—see join nodes in Section 11.4.7).

When there are multiple flows out, parallel flows are initiated (an implicit fork—see fork nodes in Section 11.4.7). There are exceptions to this rule which are managed by parameter sets (see Section 11.4.9). (Note that this is very different from earlier versions of UML, where an implicit 'or' is applied on entry and exit.)

11.4.3   Activity Initial, Activity Final and Flow Final Nodes

There are two special nodes indicating the point where an activity begins, and the point or points where an activity terminates. Because a flow may take alternative routes through an activity, the activity may terminate at more than one point. The *activity initial node* is the entry point to the flow in an activity. Only one initial node is allowed in an activity. It is drawn as a black dot, as in Figure 11-7.

Activity final nodes are drawn as black dots with a surrounding circle (a bulls-eye shape), as in Figure 11-8. There can be several final nodes in a workflow. This can be used to indicate different follow-on processes from a particular process. For example, bill processing may end with either successful payment of the bill that will lead to the customer being allowed to make further purchases, or unsuccessful payment that will lead to the customer being registered as a bad debtor.

Because there can be multiple parallel flows executing in an activity, a flow may terminate while other flows continue. This is indicated by a *flow final node* (Figure 11-9). A flow final node does not trigger the termination of the activity, and has no effect on other flows.

Figure 11-7: An activity initial node

Figure 11-8: An activity final node

Figure 11-9: A flow final node

11.4.4   Activity Edges

An *activity edge* indicates the movement between actions or between actions and objects. Activity edges are drawn as arrowed lines between pairs of actions or between actions and objects, as in Figure 11-10. In this example, when a payment request has been made, waiting for payment begins. Between actions these are known as control edges, and indicate that control flows from one action to another; there is another type of activity edge known as an object flow (see later).

An activity edge may have a name, as indicated by Figure 11-11, but not necessarily so. An activity edge can be split, to simplify the drawing of an activity by terminating at a label and resuming at a label, where the label is placed in a circle, as in Figure 11-12.

Conditions can be set on activity edges, and these are recorded in rectangular brackets and known as *guards*. Flow along the edge will then only take place if the condition is true. For example, suppose that

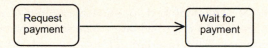

Figure 11-10: An activity edge (control edge) between actions

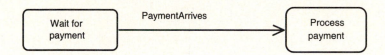

Figure 11-11: An activity edge with a name

Figure 11-12: An activity edge split for diagrammatic ease using labels

in processing payments, there is an option to pay by cash, and that requires an extra step in modifying the cash balance before clearing the debt. The flow of work would then be as in Figure 11-13.

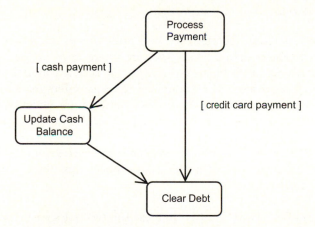

Figure 11-13: Multiple exits from an action, using guards

11.4.5   Decision Nodes and Merge Nodes

A *decision node* is a point in a workflow where the flow on exit from an action may go in alternative directions, depending on a condition. This can be signified by a diamond shape that can have one or more entry and two or more exit edges. The exit edges must be indicated by non-overlapping guards. In Figure 11-14 we see three alternatives from the exit of a Process Payment activity, depending on whether the payment was by cheque, cash or credit card. Note that UML does not specify the syntax of the conditions. This might be structured text, or the logic syntax of a programming language, or the Object Constraint Language (OCL) described later. The same diamond shape is used as a *merge mode* to bring a number of alternate flows together. This should only be used to bring together flows which are alternatives, not parallel flows—parallel flows need to be brought together with a join (see below).

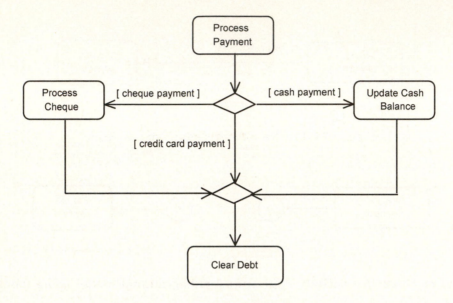

Figure 11-14: Alternative paths described using a decision node

11.4.6   Activity Partitions

Activity partitions are a very useful notation for indicating where an action takes place. This may be where in a business a business action takes place, or where in a complex system a system action takes place. Activity partitions are columns or rows on an activity, and the actions in the diagram are grouped in the activity partitions. For example, CarMatch offers insurance policies on behalf of insurance agents to its members. To take out a policy, actions are undertaken by the customer, by CarMatch and by the insurer. The process can be mapped out in two dimensions as in Figure 11-15.

Note that a number of actions in the business workflow are carried out by the customer. For the construction of an information system by CarMatch to support this, there would need to be use cases to support the results of these actions.

Activity partitions can also be used to identify areas at the technology level where actions are carried out. A common use is in determining where actions can be carried out in an Internet environment. CarMatch has web-servers in each country. Members and interested parties can access these web-servers. These link in to CarMatch's central server, which takes the initial registration and then, where there is a local franchise, passes on the final aspects of the registration. This is illustrated in Figure 11-16. Note the use of hierarchical partitioning to break the servers in the CarMatch area down into further subdivisions. (On rare occasions, horizontal and vertical partitions may be useful to indicate actions in overlapping business or technology areas.)

There are similarities with the use of interaction sequence diagrams in the elaboration of business use cases. It is possible that the above flow could be modelled by a sequence diagram, though more complicated flows with more branching would be better described by activities and activity partitions.

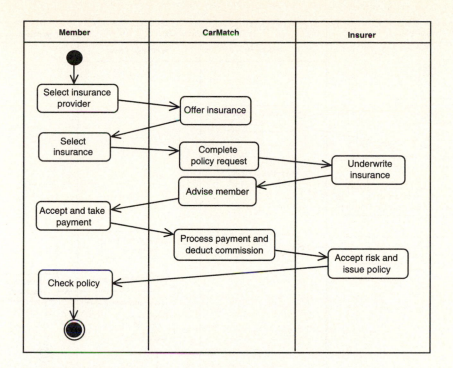

Figure 11-15: Business workflow for describing the sale of insurance policies through CarMatch, highlighting organizational units with activity partitions

11.4.7   Fork Nodes and Join Nodes

Sometimes it makes sense to allow a number of actions to run in parallel. An activity edge can be split into multiple paths and multiple paths combined into a single activity edge by using a *fork node* and a *join node*. Let us look at the matching of sharers by CarMatch. To elaborate the business process for the matching use case, once the journeys have been matched, we may realize that it is sensible to notify potential sharers in parallel. However, members will have to negotiate at the same time, and draw up an agreement together with the help of CarMatch. We would draw an activity as in Figure 11-17.

A fork node may have one entry activity edge and two or more exit activity edges. A join node must have multiple entry activity edges and one exit activity edge. It is permissible to merge a join and a fork together so that multiple parallel flows synchronize and then split into another set of parallel flows as in Figure 11-18. It is important when workflow is split into parallel flows that these flows are re-combined on the same diagram.

Note that multiple exits and multiple entries to an action have implicit fork and join semantics. (This is a departure from earlier versions of UML.)

11.4.8   Objects in Activities

So far, activities feel a little removed from objects. However, in an implementation all actions need to be carried out by objects in an object-oriented system. Sometimes it is useful to indicate on an activity where an action impacts an object. This is done by placing an object on the diagram and linking it to an action by a dependency relationship. Such dependencies are known as 'object flows' because they indicate how an object is used in a flow of control.

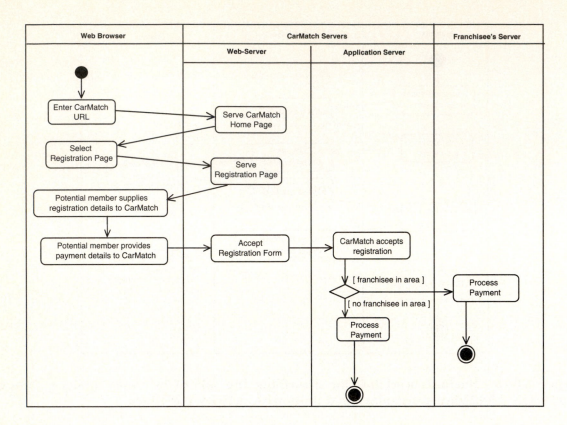

Figure 11-16: Workflow describing registration of a CarMatch member through the web, highlighting technology areas with activity partitions

The workflow will change the state of objects. Therefore, an object can have a state associated with it. We shall be examining state modelling of objects in the chapter on state machines. Let us look at the example of matching potential sharers. We might want to see the impact the workflow has on the journeys in a matching process. We can place an instance of a **Journey**, called **j1**, with a state **available** on the diagram to indicate the state of the object, as in Figure 11-19.

We can then tie the objects to actions that transform them. Thus in the activity we can show that there are two journeys that start in an **available** state. The members offering those journeys are then notified of a possibility of each sharing and the journeys enter a **notified** state so that the matching process does not try matching them again until this process completes. Then finally the journeys either end up in either a **sharing** state if the members agree to share, or an **available** state if agreement is not reached. We show this in Figure 11-20.

11.4.9 Pins and Parameter Sets

A pin is an object connected to an action, which is used as either input to or output from that action. Pins are drawn as small rectangles on the side of an action as in Figure 11-21. There may be a number of pins on an action (or activity), indicating multiple data input to or output from the action. The name of the object is written by the pin, and the same notation for state can be used. In Figure 11-22 the diagram in Figure 11-21 is redrawn using pins instead of object flows; the meaning is the same (here we have used the full activity notation, linking parameters in, and the implicit fork and join from the **Matching** action to the **Members negotiate** action).

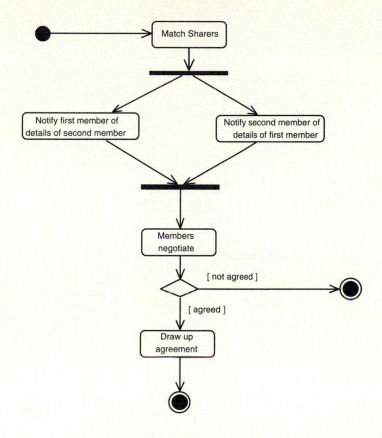

Figure 11-17: Parallel activities indicated using fork and join nodes

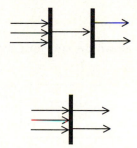

Figure 11-18: Alternative ways of showing combined fork and join, with the second example merging the symbols for fork and join

Figure 11-19: An object in an activity with an associated state

An action may have a number of inputs and/or outputs, and these can be grouped together as parameter sets. This is done by surrounding the pins representing the inputs (or outputs) by a further rectangle. Figure 11-23 shows the output pins on the match sharers action from Figure 11-22.

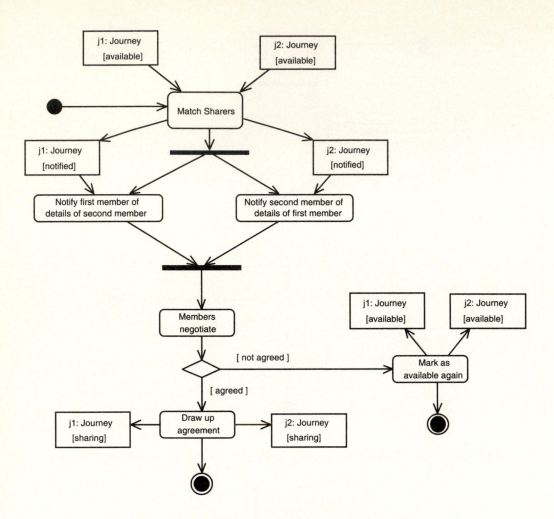

Figure 11-20: Object flows on the journey matching use case

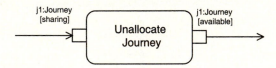

Figure 11-21: Pin notation

Actions may have multiple input parameter sets and multiple output parameter sets. The effect of using parameter sets is that the action fires as soon as one of the input parameter sets is satisfied, and completes as soon as one of the output parameter sets is ready. (With multiple parameters sets, there is an implicit 'or' on firing the action, whereas there is an implicit 'and' without.)

11.4.10   Interruptible Regions and Interrupting Edges

A set of actions on an activity may be interrupted by some event. This can be shown by surrounding the actions by a round-cornered dashed-line rectangle. A zig-zag activity edge, known as an interrupting edge, is used to show a move from the interruptible region to some action that is used to deal with the

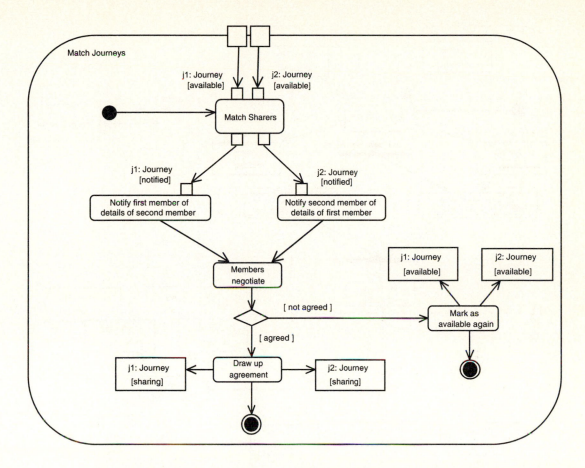

Figure 11-22: The journey-matching use case flow using pins

Figure 11-23: An output parameter set on the Match Sharers action

interrupt. Figure 11-24 shows an interruptible region in the **Match Journeys** activity, showing that the process may be interrupted at any time up to the point of agreement.

An individual action may be interrupted, and this is shown by using an interrupting edge exiting the action. Figure 11-25 shows the match sharers action interrupted because of problems on a sharer's record.

11.4.11   Nesting Activities

As you can see, activities can grow quite complicated. Actions within an activity can be complicated too. To manage the complexity, an action can be modelled by an activity. Thus, the **Match Sharers** action above may have an activity to describe how the matching is done. In Figure 11-26 we see that

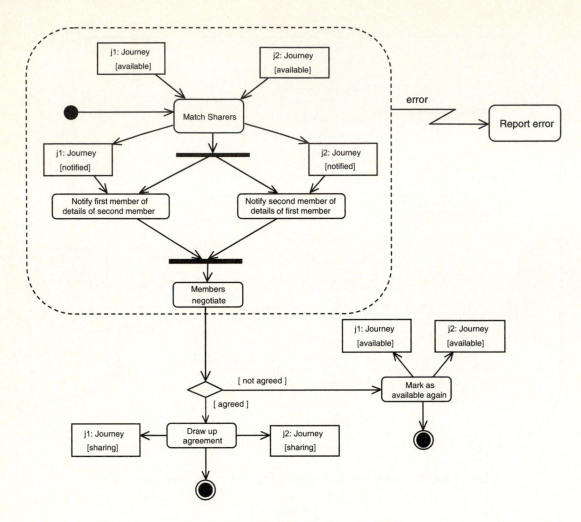

Figure 11-24: An interruptible region

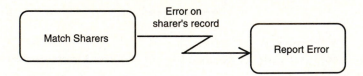

Figure 11-25: An interruptible action, and an exception handler to deal with the interrupt

to find a match, first an available journey is found, then a candidate journey for sharing is found. If no candidate journey to share is found, then the first journey would be skipped, and another sought, and so on until a pair is found.

11.4.12   Signal Objects

Signals are special types of object that are used to handle events. During the execution of an activity, it may be necessary to respond to an event that happens outside of the activity, or conversely for the activity to raise an event for another activity to respond to. Figure 11-27 shows the special action

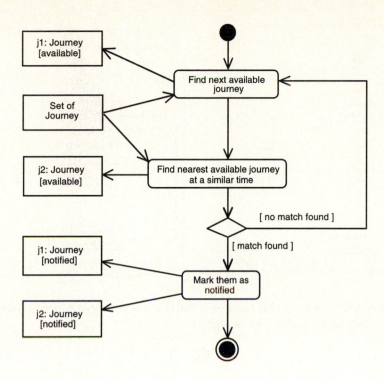

Figure 11-26: A subactivity to elaborate an action in an activity

notation for sending a signal, the object notation for a signal, and the action notation for receiving a signal.

Figure 11-27: Actions to send and receive a signal object to deal with a car passing a beacon

We might have a process in a beacon to manage the capture of passing cars, and a process in a separate congestion-monitoring system that takes the signal from the beacon and updates volumes of cars in a particular district, as in Figure 11-28. These processes would take place in separate computer systems, and be linked via some communication system along which the signal would be carried. Note that in this example, multiple beacons may be sending the same type of signal to impact the same region.

It is also allowed to put onto the diagram dependencies with the objects that need to process the signal. For example, in the beacon there may be an object to manage the car that needs to respond to the signal that a car has passed the beacon, say to update the number of times the owner needs to be charged for. This would be indicated by putting an object flow on the diagram, as in Figure 11-29.

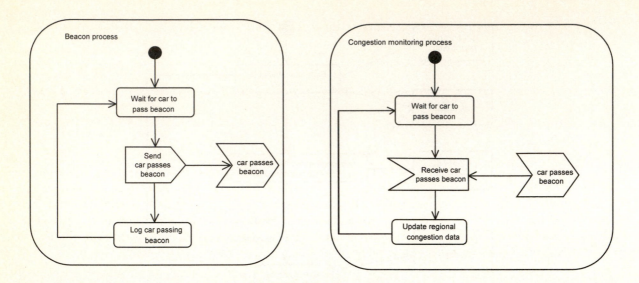

Figure 11-28: The activities in the beacon and the congestion monitoring system to deal with cars passing beacons, linked by a signal

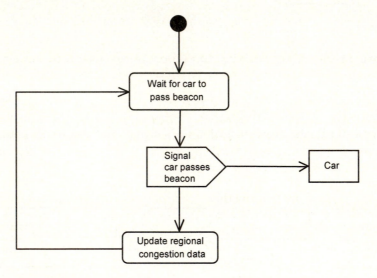

Figure 11-29: An object flow showing that a car object needs to respond to the signal when a car passes a beacon

11.5 HOW TO PRODUCE ACTIVITIES

11.5.1 Activities for Business Modelling

Activities are a means of describing workflows in the development of a business model. Business models consist largely of processes that can be described very comprehensively by activities. The development of business models consists of:

- finding business actors and business use cases;
- identifying key scenarios of business use cases, using primary and alternative paths;
- combining the scenarios to produce comprehensive workflows described using activities;
- where significant object behaviour is triggered by a workflow, adding object flows to the diagram;

- where appropriate, mapping activities to business areas and recording this using activity partitions;
- refining complicated high-level activities in a similar fashion.

Once the business model has been described in this way, the definition of system use cases can begin.

11.5.1.1   Identifying Business Use Cases

The first major stage of a substantial IT project is modelling the business. Jacobson, Ericsson & Jacobson (1995) view a business as a system, and model a business in terms of business use cases. This has been incorporated into the Unified Process. The reason for making this the starting point for analysis is that it is important to gain a common understanding among all stakeholders in a project, including funders, customers, users, managers and of course members of the development team. Further, the context of a system very much determines how that system behaves.

By viewing the business as a system in itself, where the computer systems are embedded subsystems, we can model the behaviour of the environment in which a computer system operates. The first stage to this process is identifying the business actors that utilize the business, and this will include customers, investors, banks, suppliers and maybe regulators. Each of these will invoke a set of business use cases. (These would be thought of as business processes in other approaches.)

11.5.1.2   Identifying Key Scenarios in Business Use Cases

A business use case typically consists of a complex workflow with many possible paths through it. When a business use case has been identified, the next stage is to analyse the key scenarios that are executed by the business use case. A scenario is best viewed as a simple sequence of business activities or actions. For the simplest business, the number of scenarios through a business use case can be very large.

The business analyst needs a structured method of acquiring a representative sample of scenarios from which a comprehensive description of the flows through the business use case can be determined. A recommended approach is to begin by looking for the *primary path*. This is the instance of the use case (i.e. scenario) that is most commonly used. The reason for doing this is twofold. Firstly, the majority of executions of the use case will involve this primary path, at least in part, and the use case will be ineffective if it cannot at least cope with this. Based on the rule of thumb that 80% of activities uses 20% of the capability of any system, implementing the primary path can provide a quick route to a usable system. Secondly, by identifying the primary path, a framework is established to identify representative alternative scenarios.

EXAMPLE 11.1   CarMatch wish to sell consultancy. This is recorded at a high level as a business use case, as in Figure 11-30.

After discussions with the head of the new consultancy division, the following is the ideal process for the sale of consultancy.

1. Contact with potential consultancy customer, either direct from CarMatch, or by referral from an associate organization, or by direct contact from the customer.
2. Preliminary investigation of the customer's needs.
3. Construction of a project proposal.
4. Proposal accepted.
5. Contracts agreed.

Figure 11-30: Sell consultancy business use case

6. Project executed.
7. Customer is billed, and project closed.

Now we have a primary path, we can look for alternatives by examining each stage of the primary path and looking for alternatives. Let us look at the area of accepting a proposal in step 4. Clearly the ideal is that the customer has no objections, but in practice there may be minor or major changes required, or even withdrawal from the process altogether. After discussing this with the head of consultancy, there are three alternatives identified:

4.1 The client wants changes to the proposal but is agreeable to the proposal as a concept, so revision of the proposal is required.
4.2 The client feels that this proposal does not meet his or her needs, but is prepared to consider alternative proposals.
4.3 The client no longer wishes to discuss a project with CarMatch, at least for the time being.

11.5.1.3   Merge Scenarios to Provide a Comprehensive Workflow

The workflow for each scenario can now be drawn, starting with the primary path and adding in the alternative paths one by one.

EXAMPLE 11.2   From the primary path of the Sell consultancy business use case, we can draw an initial straight line flow as in Figure 11-31. Then, looking at the alternative paths we can start adding alternative flows. Figure 11-32 shows how we have used an event to take us out of the Accept proposal action, and we make a decision as to whether to quit the proposal process, modify the current proposal, or seek another proposal idea; these decisions are recorded as guards. We can proceed with our analysis in this way, questioning each stage of the process as it is defined to look for alternative paths through.

The outcome of this cycle will be a set of comprehensively defined business use cases with supporting business workflows. Clearly, it only makes sense to elaborate in detail those business use cases that are the focus of the project.

11.5.1.4   Assign Object Flows to Model Key Business Entity Behaviour

Objects are added to the workflow for key areas, where it is useful to model the changes of state that result from activities in the activity diagram.

EXAMPLE 11.3   In the CarMatch example of matching car sharers, we saw that the journeys that were matched went through significant state changes (see Figure 11-20). For example, it is not sensible to offer a journey to another potential sharer while it is being considered for sharing. Only for key areas like this is it appropriate to add objects to the workflow, indicating key state transitions. In this example it is not appropriate to consider object flows, as the workflow is very high level.

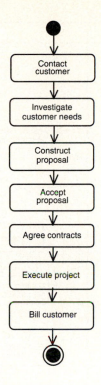

Figure 11-31: The workflow for the primary path of the **Sell consultancy** business use case

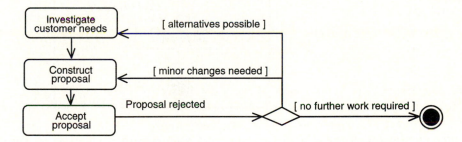

Figure 11-32: An alternative path on the workflow of the **Sell consultancy** business use case

11.5.1.5   Assign Actions to Business Areas Using Activity Partitions

Where a particular business organization is prescribed, and a workflow passes through a number of business areas, it is sometimes useful to draw workflows using activity partitions to indicate the business areas that carry out the activities (see Figure 11-15).

EXAMPLE 11.4   In this example, activity partitions would not be appropriate as the negotiation takes place in arbitrary and overlapping business areas.

11.5.1.6   Further Refine Actions

The top-level actions identified in this way will often require further detail. The same process of refinement can be applied, looking for primary and alternative paths through the action, then combining them to produce a comprehensive workflow described as an activity. This can continue until sufficient

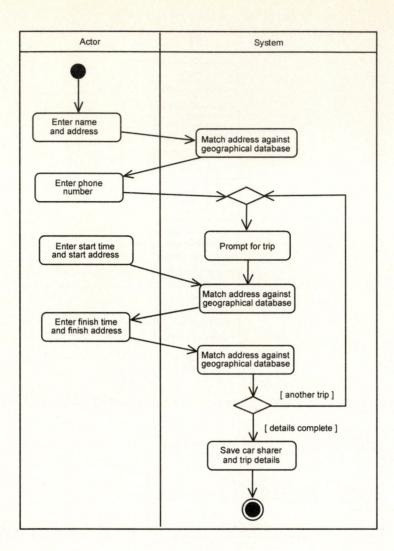

Figure 11-33: Workflow for the primary path of the system use case to register a car sharer

detail has been gathered to comprehensively describe the business model for the purposes of the project. In practice, no greater than three levels of decomposition are usually necessary and sometimes one is enough, though for complex processes more will be required.

11.5.2 How to Produce Activities to Describe Use Cases

The production of activities for system use case models is similar to that of preparing them for business workflows:

- identifying key scenarios of system use cases, using primary and alternative paths;
- combining the scenarios to produce comprehensive workflows described using activities;
- where significant object behaviour is triggered by a workflow, adding object flows to the activity;
- where workflows cross technology boundaries, using activity partitions to map the actions to technology areas;
- refining complicated high-level activities in a similar fashion.

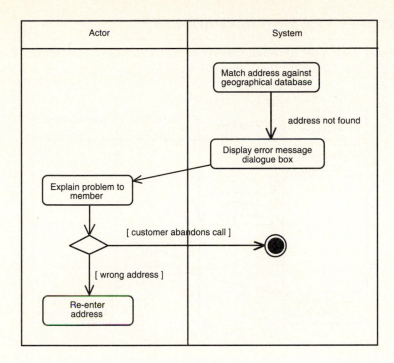

Figure 11-34: Part of an alternative path on the system use case to register a car sharer

Remember that activities are just one way of recording workflows in a system. Sequence diagrams and communication diagrams give alternatives that link workflows more comprehensively to the underlying object models. Typically you would use activities earlier on to describe those use cases where complex flows need a full description before an object model has been elaborated.

The use case elaboration in Figure 3-10 illustrates a primary path for registering a car sharer. We can draw an activity to illustrate the flow through the use case as in Figure 11-33.

Now we could consider from this primary path the alternatives, such as what might happen if the address is not found on the geographical database. For each of the points where the address is matched we might paste in the fragment as in Figure 11-34.

However, as it is repeated three times, it would be sensible to relegate this flow as a subflow of the activity that matches the address against the geographical database by attaching an activity to the **Match address against geographical database** action.

11.6 RELATIONSHIP WITH OTHER DIAGRAMS

Activities describe workflows, focusing on sequences of actions. They allow for sequential and parallel flows. Alongside communication diagrams and sequence diagrams, they provide a means of describing the dynamic behaviour of a system. Within a modelling tool, they would be linked as subdiagrams of business use cases, use cases, classes and operations.

11.7 ACTIVITIES IN THE UNIFIED PROCESS

The Unified Process is itself a set of recommended workflows for the construction of software-intensive systems. An example workflow from the Unified Process for the development of requirements is given in Figure 11-35.

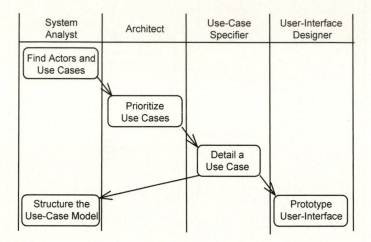

Figure 11-35: A workflow describing development of requirements in the Unified Process

You can see that this is a very high-level workflow, and quite simplistic. Most of the actions here are very long in execution, and within them there may be many parallel strands. The Unified Process defines nine core workflows, spanning business modelling, requirements, analysis and design, implementation, test, deployment, project management, configuration management, and environment. This is an example of workflow modelling to describe at a very high level a very complex business activity.

The Unified Process is a use-case-driven approach, and use cases themselves are groupings of workflows. In business modelling, the definition of business use cases can be supported by activities to fully model the complex workflows that a business use case represents. Likewise, system use cases can be elaborated using activities to fully describe the complex workflows that need to be implemented in a computer system; in this case the analyst may also decide to use sequence diagrams and communication diagrams to further describe workflows and link them to the underlying object model.

In the Unified Process, activities are specifically used in the activity *Detail a Use Case*. In this activity, there is a step *Formalizing the Use Case Descriptions*, and activities can be used to document the behaviour of the use case if a textual description is too informal.

Review Questions

11.1 What types of flow can be described by an activity?

11.2 When would you first consider using an activity?

11.3 Why do you draw activities?

11.4 What is an action?

11.5 How can you describe a complex action?

11.6 How long can it take for an action to complete?

11.7 What is a pin?

11.8 What is an activity edge?

11.9 What is the name of an activity edge between two actions?

11.10 When two activity edges leave an action, which direction does the flow take?

11.11 When multiple control edges arrive at an action, when does the action start?

11.12 What is a merge node?

11.13 What is a decision node?

11.14 What is a guard?

11.15 How many activity edges can go into a merge node?

11.16 How many activity edges can leave a decision node?

11.17 What is an activity partition?

11.18 Why would you use an activity partition?

11.19 What is a fork node?

11.20 What is a join node?

11.21 What is an object flow?

11.22 What information can you keep about an object on an object flow?

11.23 What is an interruptible region?

11.24 To what UML elements can activities be attached?

11.25 What are signals, and why would you use them?

Solved Problems

11.1 Here is a description of a business process in CarMatch.

> CarMatch intend that members could obtain a discount for road-pricing schemes. CarMatch negotiates with each authority independently. Each pricing scheme has its own computer system. CarMatch would prefer to take over the billing of their own members and attempt to negotiate this first, but sometimes that is not possible. They will then negotiate discounts for members. Finally, they will agree on the mechanism for exchanging information. If negotiations are successful, then contracts will be drawn up and agreed. Sometimes the contract stage will cause some renegotiation. At any time, either party can suspend or cancel negotiations.

Draw a workflow for this process.

We identify the business use case as **Obtain road-price discounts for members**. This involves the CarMatch central office and the road pricing agency. We show this business use case in Figure 11-36. We then produce a primary path analysis, and alternative paths that result in the following steps:

Figure 11-36: The business use case for Obtain road-price discounts for members

1. Propose to road pricing agency that CarMatch bill the members for road pricing.
2. Negotiate discounts with the agency.
3. Agree mechanism for data exchange.
4. Draw up contracts.

Further information from CarMatch leads to the recognition that there are some alternative paths.

3.1 There may be a suspension of the negotiation process while working on data exchange, which can lead to resumption at a later stage, or a cancellation.
4.1 There may be minor amendments to the contract, so return to step 4.
4.2 There may be issues with the data exchange when it comes to contract, so return to step 3.
4.3 There may be issues with the discounts, so return to step 2.

We are making the simplifying assumption here that after suspension of negotiations, resumption would always start at the discount negotiation. Another simplifying assumption is that on contract changes, the process would backtrack to the point of negotiations where the area of dispute has arisen. In practice this is not a problem, because the other activities would, unless something changes earlier in the process, run through with no action necessary. Too many decision points cloud the diagram. You should be able to identify lots more alternatives than this, but the above are representative. We then merge these scenarios to provide a combined workflow as in Figure 11-37.

This is a high-level business process, so there is no point at this stage in identifying objects and placing them on the object flow. Later, there may be an appropriate linkage of a contract object to the flow. Following this analysis we may wish to break down any of the above activities into subactivities, and provide activities to elaborate those workflows. Also, at this level, the activities are collaborative and it would not be appropriate to use activity partitions as the activities could not be assigned to particular business areas.

11.2 Assume that CarMatch has negotiated a deal with the pricing authority. Whenever a member passes a toll point, the toll beacon records the event and then passes it on to the pricing authority. The pricing authority then calculates the fee and passes it on to the Car Match system. To understand the linkages between the different computer systems involved, an activity is needed.

After interviewing all parties, the following sequence of events is determined. This is the primary path scenario.

1. The member passes a road toll point. His car is detected by a beacon and its details are recorded on the beacon and transmitted to the charging authority's computer.
2. The charging authority determines that this is a CarMatch client, and calculates the discounted fee.
3. The charging authority increments the charge to CarMatch.
4. The charging authority computer notifies the CarMatch server that a charge is to be made.
5. CarMatch adds the charge to the member's account.
6. CarMatch adds to the total outstanding for the Authority.

There are three technology areas, first the pricing beacon itself, which can keep records and pass information to the second area, the pricing authority computer; thirdly there is the CarMatch server. We use activity partitions to indicate the three technology areas, and produce a workflow as described in Figure 11-38. Note that this is a process that could take place over a length of time. The transfer from

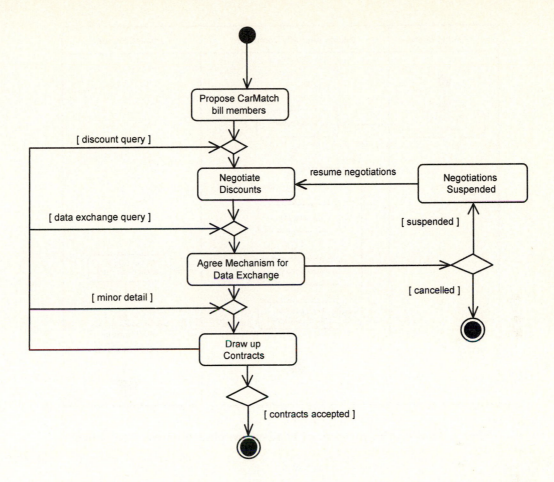

Figure 11-37: The CarMatch negotiation process with road pricing agencies

the beacon to the pricing authority computer could be real time, or done on some regular batch basis. The transfer to CarMatch's server would almost certainly be done on a batch basis.

The next stage would be to identify system use cases from this business workflow, and these use cases may have activities or sequence diagrams to describe their internal flows.

Supplementary Problems

11.3 Look at the VolBank case study in Chapter 1, and draw up the process for matching a volunteer with voluntary organizations in his or her area and producing a volunteering agreement. Assume that a volunteer cannot be matched with more than one voluntary organization at a time, but that a voluntary organization will use many volunteers, up to a set limit.

11.4 After analysing the above business process, it is decided that there will be a daily batch process to match volunteers with organizations. It is decided that an organization can have a maximum of three candidates in interview at any one time. The batch process is drawn up as a use case, which includes two other use cases to notify volunteers and organizations, see Figure 11-39.

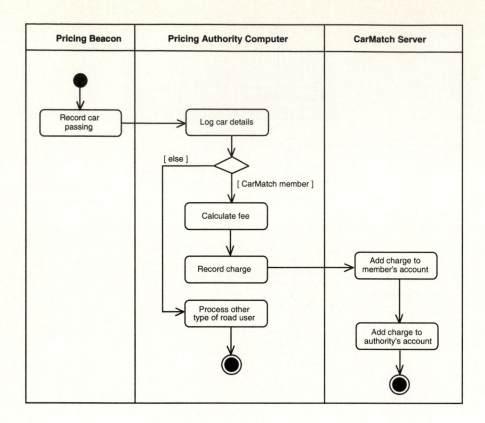

Figure 11-38: The process of road-price charging via CarMatch

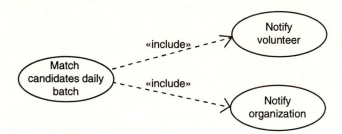

Figure 11-39: System use case for Match volunteers with organizations

The primary flow through the use case is as follows:

1. Get next volunteer who is available.
2. Get first matching organization seeking a volunteer who has not got three interviews active.
3. Mark the volunteer as notified.
4. Increment the number of interviews scheduled for the organization.
5. Notify the volunteer.
6. Notify the organization.
7. If there are volunteers left to consider, return to step 1.

There are three alternatives identified.

2.1 The candidate has already been interviewed by the organization.
2.2 The candidate has expressly asked not to be considered by the organization.
2.3 There are no matching organizations for the volunteer.

Produce an activity to document these flows through the use case.

11.5 For the VolBank case study, produce a workflow to cover the registration of a volunteer over the web and transfer to the VolBank server.

11.6 For the VolBank case study, consider the use case Notify member discussed above. Produce an activity to describe the production of the letter, with date, volunteer's address, organization details and description of the activity sought by the organization.

CHAPTER 12

State Machines

12.1 INTRODUCTION

State machines are another means of describing the behaviour of dynamic model elements, and they are closely related to activities. Whereas activities describe flow between areas of work, state machines describe flow between states. For example, a telephone is either hung up, dialling, engaged in a call or disconnected. These are states of the telephone, and we can use a state machine to link the states together and determine the legal flows through the system. While an item is in a state, work may or may not be going on—when a phone is hung up, there is no activity in the phone, but when it is engaged in a call, there is lots of activity in the phone. States are useful logical views of an entity.

State machines are used mostly to describe the behaviour of classes, but they can be used to describe the behaviour of other elements of a model, such as use cases, actors, subsystems and operations. They can be used during analysis to describe complex behaviour of elements in the system environment, such as the behaviour of a customer. They can be used at the design level to describe the behaviour of control objects, boundary objects (such as screens) or complex entity objects (such as accounts). They are one of a number of diagrams in UML that can be used to model workflow, namely activities, communication diagrams and sequence diagrams. The choice of a workflow diagram very much depends on the nature of the workflow that is being described, and sometimes a number of different views are useful. As well as behavioural state machines, protocol state machines can be used to express legal transitions of classifiers, without dictating the internal behaviour—the keyword {protocol} is postfixed to the name in the frame of a protocol state machine..

Figure 12-1 illustrates a simple state machine for the journey class in the CarMatch system. The state machine is drawn as a rectangle with a name label in the top left-hand side, though the frame may be omitted if the context is clear. Once the journey is created, it enters the Available state. Once a sharer has been found and agreement on sharing reached, the journey becomes Active as far as the CarMatch system is concerned. Later the sharing agreement may terminate, say because one of the sharers drops out of the agreement, and the journey goes back to being Available. At any time, the journey may be terminated.

In this chapter we shall introduce the notion of *state*, *transition* and *event*, and relate them to other UML elements.

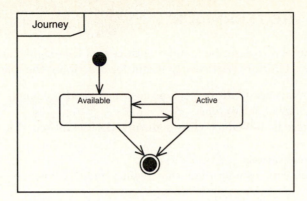

Figure 12-1: A simple state machine describing the Journey class in the CarMatch system

12.1.1   States

Systems and entities within a system, such as objects, can be viewed as moving from state to state. External events trigger some activity that changes the state of the system and some of its parts. In a banking system, money may be withdrawn from a chequing account, and that account may move from a state of credit to an overdrawn state. An item can be in several states at once. For example, a customer may be waiting for a delivery, in debit, in dispute of a bill, all at the same time. States may also be nested. For example, the credit state of an interest-bearing chequing account may move between high and low interest states dependent on the balance.

Viewing a system as a set of states and transitions between states is a very useful way of describing complex behaviour. It is a way of describing the legal paths through a system, and understanding the legitimate transitions from one state to another is a key part of analysis and design. It is a common practice in the business world to think of entities as passing through a number of states.

12.1.2   Events

Systems are driven by *events*, both external and internal. Systems are there to respond to events, and they in turn trigger other events. An external event will usually cause a series of internal events to occur, and sometimes these may trigger external events too. For example, a customer depositing a cheque into her savings account will trigger an internal event to place an uncleared credit against her account, and trigger an external event to request transfer of the monies by the banking system from the issuer of the cheque. Time is also a major source of events, such as the arrival of a billing date, which in turn may generate an event to print invoices.

Events pass information, expressed in UML as arguments. This information will flow around a system as events trigger other events. These arguments can be used as part of the decision-making, say to determine which state is the next appropriate state when an event occurs. Ultimately events have to be realized by objects, in the form of operations (some programming languages include events, and operations can be implemented as event handlers), and the design process will involve examining all the events in a state machine and considering how those events will be supported by the objects in the system.

12.2 PURPOSE OF THE TECHNIQUE

The key role of state machines is to describe complex entities that have significant states and complicated transitions between states. They are particularly useful for describing the following purposes:

- To describe complex business entities, such as customers and accounts.
- To model the behaviour of subsystems.
- To model interactions in boundary classes during the definition of system interfaces such as screens.
- To model use case realizations.
- To model complex objects, usually those that realize complex business or design entities.

12.3 NOTATION

12.3.1 States and Pseudostates

A *state* in a state machine is a point in the life-cycle of a model element that satisfies some condition, where some particular action is being performed, or where some event is awaited. A state is drawn as a rectangle with rounded corners with the name of the state written inside, as in Figure 12-2, which describes a **Debit** state for an **Account class**. Optionally, a state may be drawn with a name tab as in Figure 12-3. A state is considered to last for a period of time, though in practice this may be very brief for some states.

Figure 12-2: The Debit state of an Account

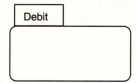

Figure 12-3: A state with a name tab

States may be *simple* or *composite*. A *simple* state is not broken down further, and for an object it is likely to be represented by a simple set of values of attributes. A *composite* state is broken down further, usually by a nested state machine or sometimes by embedding states within a state on a single diagram (see Section 12.3.4).

There are two special pseudostates. The initial pseudostate is the start of a flow. The start state may be labelled by the trigger that starts the state machine, and in this case multiple initial states are valid. If the start state is not labelled, then it is the default start point for the state machine. It is drawn as a black dot, and it can be labelled with a trigger as in Figure 12-4. End pseudostates are drawn as black dots with a surrounding circle (a bulls-eye shape), as in Figure 12-5. There can be several end states in a state machine. An end state represents a normal completion of the state machine.

A state or state machine may also have an *entry point pseudostate* drawn as a circle, with an associated name. This may be embedded on the border of the state machine diagram, outside the state machine diagram, or inside the state machine diagram. The use of an entry point is optional.

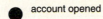

account opened

Figure 12-4: An initial state

account closed

Figure 12-5: An end state

A state or state machine may also have an *exit point pseudostate*, drawn as a circle with a cross, as in Figure 12-6. This may be labelled with a name, indicating the reason the exit has taken place. This is used to represent abnormal exits from a state, and may be thought of as equivalent to exceptions.

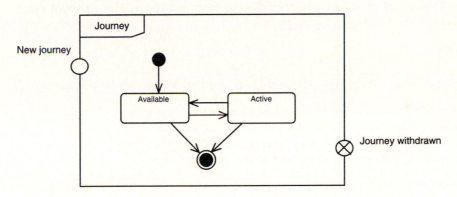

Figure 12-6: Entry and exit points on a state machine

12.3.2 Transitions

A *transition* is the movement between states. Transitions are drawn as arrowed lines between pairs of states, as in Figure 12-7. This illustrates that an **Account** can move between the **Credit** and **Debit** states. In a state machine, the transition is always in response to some event. (In activities transitions out of activities can be when the work of the activity is complete, and this is known as a triggerless transition.) The event that triggers the transition is written adjacent to the line.

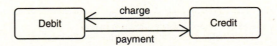

Figure 12-7: Transitions between the Credit and Debit states of the Account class

More than one transition can leave a single state. This occurs either when different events result in a state terminating, or when there are *guard conditions* on the transitions. In Figure 12-8 we see an extra state introduced into the **Account** class to cover the possibility that the account has a zero balance. There are three events triggering exit from the **Zero balance** state, namely **charge**, **payment** and **close**. Conditions can be set on transitions, and these are recorded in rectangular brackets and known as guards. The transition will then only take place if the condition is true. In Figure 12-8, the transition to **Zero balance** or **Credit** on a payment depends on the value of the payment and the balance of the account.

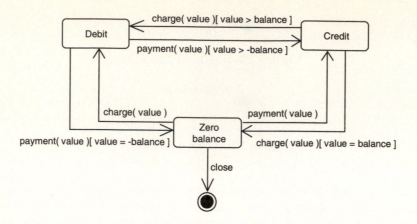

Figure 12-8: Multiple transitions from states of the Account class

12.3.3 Actions

A state can have *actions* triggered. There are four ways an action can be triggered:

- On Entry: these actions are triggered as soon as the state is entered.
- Do: these actions take place during the lifetime of the state.
- On Event: these actions take place in response to an event.
- On Exit: these actions take place just before the state exits.

We indicate this as in Figure 12-9. The name of the state is placed at the top and separated from the list of actions below by a horizontal line. The syntax of the actions is:

```
action-label / action
```

where *action-label* is one of **entry**, **do**, **exit** or the name of a trigger. In the special case of a trigger, the syntax for actions is:

```
trigger-name(arguments)[constraint]/action
```

where *arguments* is a comma-separated list of arguments supplied by the trigger, and *constraint* is a condition that must be true for the action to be triggered.

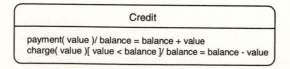

Figure 12-9: Actions within the Credit state for the Account class

The action can be described in a simple English statement, or for more detailed design, using a programming language statement. An alternative form of action is the firing of a trigger and this is written as

```
^target.trigger(arguments)
```

where *target* is some object that needs to respond to the trigger, *trigger* is the name of the trigger, and *arguments* are the information that is conveyed with the event expressed as a comma-separated list.

Transitions can also trigger actions. The syntax is the same as for an event action inside a state, and written adjacent to the transition. If there is a single transition out of a state, the action is probably best expressed as an exit action on the state, but if there are multiple exits out of a state that have different actions, then these actions need to be attached to the appropriate transitions.

In Figure 12-10 we see a full description of the states of the **Account** class. When an account is opened the exit action of the start state sets the balance to zero and puts the instance in the **Zero balance** state. A payment will take the account to the **Credit** state, and a charge will take it to the **Debit** state. Credit balances remain in credit, until a charge is made that either zeroes the account (taking the instance back to the **Zero balance** state) or takes it to the **Debit** state. Likewise debit balances remain in debit until a payment takes them to the **Zero balance** state or the **Credit** state. The same event can be handled within a state or trigger a state change depending on the guards (for example, the **payment** event on the **Debit** state).

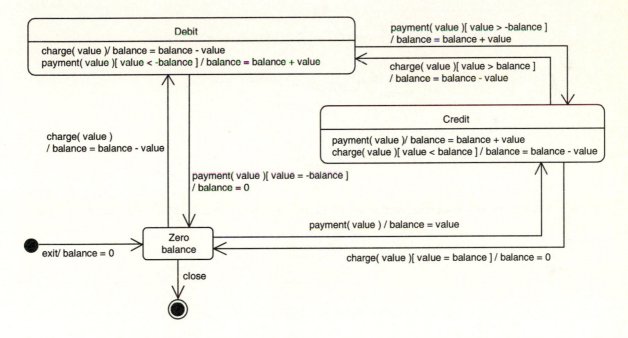

Figure 12-10: The full description of the states of the **Account** class

12.3.4   Composite States

A *composite state* can be further broken down into *substates*. The substates can be drawn either within the state or in a separate diagram. Consider the statechart for the **Journey** class in Figure 12-9.

Once a journey is created, because someone has stated they want to share that particular journey, it goes into an **Available** state. Eventually someone agrees to share on the journey, and the journey enters an **Active** state. One of the sharers may drop out, and the journey may return to an **Available** state because there is only one person registered on the journey. Whilst the journey is **Active**, additional drivers may join. The **Active** state can have two substates, **Vacant** representing that someone else could join the sharing, and **Full** indicating that the journey cannot take more sharers. We can therefore draw a state machine to indicate this behaviour as in Figure 12-12. We now have two choices to modify the top diagram, Figure 12-11, either by updating the **Active** state icon as in Figure 12-13, or by adding the substates to the diagram as in Figure 12-14.

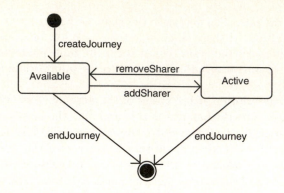

Figure 12-11: State machine for the **Journey** class

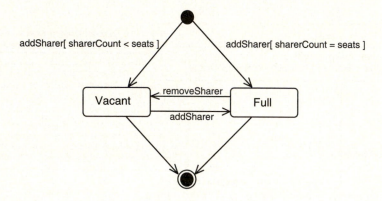

Figure 12-12: Subflow of the **Active** state of the **Journey** class in the CarMatch system

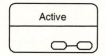

Figure 12-13: Notation to indicate that there is a subflow on a state

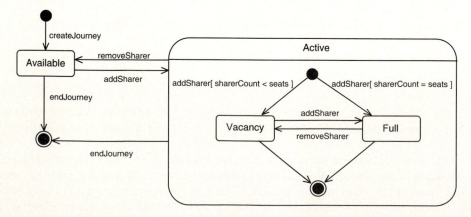

Figure 12-14: Subflows drawn within a composite state in the state machine for the **Journey** class

12.3.5   Concurrent Substates and Regions

It is possible for a composite state to consist of multiple, *concurrent substates*. A state can be split into regions separated by a dotted line. Consider Figure 12-15. When a car sharer applies for membership, he or she initially is considered to be an applicant, and unable to participate in car sharing agreements. The application process may involve payment processing and legal checks to make sure that the applicant is not breaking the law, or that the person applying is not barred from such activity. These may take time, and therefore the Applicant state of a car sharer must continue until these two substates have exited. These substates in the regions are independent, and can complete at different times. This is shown on a diagram by separating the concurrent flows by a dotted horizontal line within the containing state.

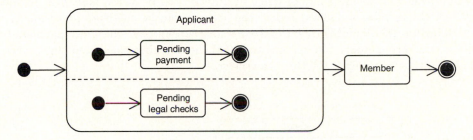

Figure 12-15: Concurrent substates of the Applicant state for the CarSharer class

Note that in contrast to the previous example, an instance of the CarSharer class will be in both the Pending payment state and the Pending legal checks state.

12.3.6   Forks and Joins

Sometimes concurrent states occur and it is possible to show them on a diagram. A transition can be split into multiple paths by using a *fork* and multiple paths combined into a single transition by using a *join*. Forks and joins are represented by thick lines. Let us reconsider the application process for membership. Instead of creating concurrent substates of the Applicant state, we might do away with the Applicant state and promote the subactivities up as in Figure 12-16. Now we show on one diagram that the Member state only occurs once the Pending legal checks and Pending payment states have completed.

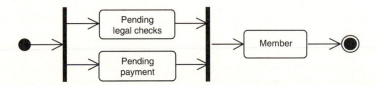

Figure 12-16: Parallel states on a state machine, using a fork and a join

A fork may have one entry transition and two or more exit transitions; a join may have multiple entry transitions and one exit transition. It is important when workflow is split into parallel flows that these flows are recombined on the same diagram.

12.3.7   Transitions to and from Composite States

A transition drawn to the boundary of a composite state starts the subflow at the initial state of the composite state. If the composite state is concurrent, then the transition is to each of the initial states.

The entry actions of the composite state are fired on entry, and then the actions of the start state (or states) are applied appropriately.

A transition drawn from the boundary of a composite state is immediate and effective on any of the substates; that is, the current substate (or substates if this is a concurrent composite state) exits and executes any exit actions.

Transitions may be drawn directly into substates of a composite state, or from a substate in a composite state out to other states. Consider Figure 12-17. We have reintroduced the idea of a state of membership prior to the full activation of membership, and called it **Dormant**. As in Figure 12-15, once a member joins for the first time, a legal check and payment clearance must be forced before the membership can be active. When the member's renewal is due, the account can be switched to dormant, and this is indicated by taking a transition directly into the substate, **Pending payment**. Once payment has arrived, it is possible to reinstate membership without the legal check taking place, and this is indicated by a guarded transition that can only fire if this is a renewal.

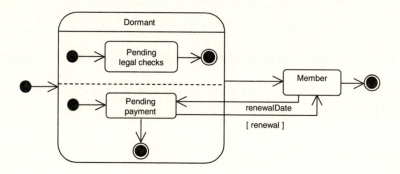

Figure 12-17: Transitions into and out of substates in a composite state

12.3.8 Choice Pseudostates and Junction Pseudostates

A *choice pseudostate* allows for a transition to be split along a number of transitions based on a condition, or for a number of transitions to converge at a single point, or both of these. Consider Figure 12-18. This models the behaviour of a journey before it becomes active. This would be the elaboration of the composite state **Available** in Figure 12-11. The diamond shape represents the choice at which the transition can take a number of alternative paths depending on some condition. On start, there is a decision to be made whether there is a driver in the sharing agreement or not. If there is not, then the state **No driver** is entered. When another sharer is added, it makes sense to go back to the earlier decision point. If the new sharer is a driver, then the available state can complete, otherwise it goes back to **No driver**. If the first sharer is a driver, then it is only necessary to wait for another sharer, irrespective of their driving ability, to progress out of the **Available** state into the **Active** state.

An alternative notation is the *junction pseudostate*, which is drawn (confusingly) using the same black circle as a start state. This is shown in Figure 12-19. There is also a slight notational variant where a choice has multiple exit conditions based on a single value where the value is written in the choice diamond and the conditions on the exit transitions as in Figure 12-20, where the exit route is based on the value of a variable v being less than, equal to or greater than zero. Note that choice and junction pseudostates may have more than one entry transition, and must have at least two exit transitions.

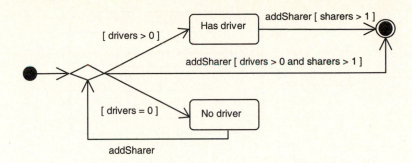

Figure 12-18: A choice pseudostate on a state machine

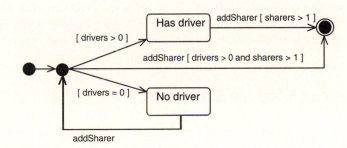

Figure 12-19: A junction pseudostate on a state machine

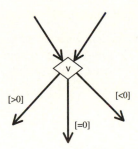

Figure 12-20: Alternative notation for a choice pseudostate

12.3.9   History States

Ordinarily, when a composite state is entered, it begins at the initial state (or the indicated substate if the transition is directly into that substate). Sometimes, however, it is useful to re-enter a composite state at the point at which it was last left. This is done by adding a history state, indicated by a circle with an **H** inside it. Consider the membership state in Figure 12-21. A member can be either **Sharing** or **Not sharing**. On entry for the first time, the member is **Not sharing**. If the member goes into the **Dormant** state, because the member is late paying a renewal fee, then it would be sensible to bar the member from entering new sharing agreements, but the existing sharing agreements would not normally be suspended, because of inconvenience to other members. When the membership is re-activated, the state of **Sharing** would be resumed as it was when the membership was suspended. This is indicated by the history state.

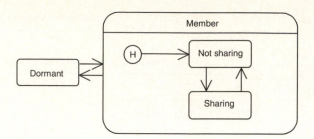

Figure 12-21: A history state in a composite state

If the states within a composite state are themselves composite states, it may be necessary on some rare occasions to resume those nested states at the point they were suspended. If the history state indicator contains an H*, instead of an H, this is known as a deep history state, and the substates are restarted at the point where they left off; the restart continues all the way down the nested states.

12.4   HOW TO PRODUCE STATE MACHINES

State machines model the behaviour of entities (e.g. classes, use cases, subsystems), and are closely related to activities. While activities are good at describing processes, state machines are better suited to describing the life history of classes in terms of the discrete stages that an object instance can pass through. The state machine depicts the generic set of states and transitions between them for the class. Individual instances can take different paths through these states, depending on the sequence of events that affect each instance.

The classes that state machines model can be classes in the analysis domain, such as actors, or representations of parts of the system, or classes that need to be implemented. State machines are not essential for all of the entities, just those that have reasonably complex behaviour that can be represented as sets of states.

State machines are developed as follows:

- Identify entities that have complex behaviour.
- Determine the initial and final states of the entity.
- Identify the events that affect the entity.
- Working from the initial state, trace the impact of events and identify intermediate states.
- Identify any entry and exit actions on the states.
- Expand states using substates where necessary.
- If the entity is a class, check that the actions in the state are supported by the operations and relationships of the class, and if not extend the class.

12.4.1   Identifying Entities that have Complex Behaviour

At the analysis level, the objects to model are business actors with which the system interacts, and any real-world classes such as accounts, policies and agreements that have changeable states and complicated relationships between states. At the design level, a number of complex classes are typically introduced, such as boundary classes to represent screens, and control classes to manage transactions. These are also candidates for state machine modelling.

Having identified a complex entity, it is necessary to determine the appropriate workflow notation. State machines are most appropriate for workflows where the entities have a clear set of states that they pass through. If the entity has complex processing to be described, an activity diagram may be more appropriate, and if there is a complex interaction of objects involved then a sequence diagram or communication diagram may be more appropriate. In some cases, more than one workflow description is useful, and this is particularly true of complex use cases.

12.4.2　Determine Initial and Final States of the Entity

The first question to ask is "How is an entity created?" In the CarMatch system, car sharers are registered before they can begin to enter into sharing agreements. The next question is "How is an object destroyed?" (That is, how does it reach the point where it no longer needs to be processed by the system?) A car sharer may let his or her membership lapse, or may be disqualified from membership for reasons of misbehaviour, or withdraw membership for reasons of moving away from the area, or withdraw because of illness or disaffection with the service.

12.4.3　Identify Those Events that Affect the Entity

The events that affect a car sharer would be registration, entering a journey, the matching of a journey with another car sharer, the entering of an agreement, the cancellation of an agreement, payment date arriving, and so on. The primary source of events for objects is the set of use cases. Use cases are groupings of events that provide meaningful functionality for a system, and a use case is realized by a group of collaborating objects.

12.4.4　Trace the Impact of Events and Identify Intermediate States

Start at the initial state, and ask what events may impact the initial state. A car sharer may have to pay membership and have a legal check carried out. As in Figure 12-17, we may decide to show this by creating a **Dormant** state that the **CarSharer** enters, and place two substates in it that operate in parallel, namely **Pending legal checks** and **Pending payment**. Thus we would continue, examining what events took the **CarSharer** out of the **Dormant** state into the **Member** state, and then on out of the **Member** state either back into the **Dormant** state or to the end state.

12.4.5　Identify Entry and Exit Actions on States

When an instance of **CarSharer** enters the **Pending payment** state in Figure 12-17, entry actions would be to request payment from the member, create an instance of the **Account** class, and debit that account with the membership fee. An exit action, responding to an event that signals payment received, would be to credit the account of the car sharer with the payment made.

12.4.6　Expand States using Substates

A car sharer can be in the **Dormant** state for lots of reasons. Two of these would be payment being due, or legal checks necessary. Alternatively, a customer may suspend membership while working away from home for an extended period. Each of these could be modelled as substates of dormant account as in Figure 12-17.

12.4.7   Check that Operations Exist to Support the Actions

All actions have to be implemented via operations on classes. For the **CarSharer** class there would need to be operations to support requesting payment, receiving payment, recording results of legal checks, and so on. These operations can be either directly on the class itself or on related classes (payment, for example, would normally be implemented on the **Account** class, not on the **CarSharer** class itself).

12.5   RELATIONSHIP WITH OTHER DIAGRAMS

State machines describe workflow, focusing on states and transitions between states. They allow for sequential and parallel flows. Alongside activities, communication diagrams and sequence diagrams, they provide a means of describing the dynamic behaviour of a system. They are closely related to activities, and the event flow notation in an activity describes the states of objects in relation to workflow. Within a software modelling tool, they would be linked as subdiagrams of business use cases, use cases, classes and (occasionally) operations.

12.6   STATE MACHINES IN THE UNIFIED PROCESS

The Unified Process is a use case driven approach, and use cases themselves can have state dependent behaviour, which is best modelled using state machines. (In business modeling, the definition of business use cases can also be supported by activities to model fully the complex workflows that a business use case represents.) State machines are used in the Requirements Workflow (see Figure 12-22) in the *Detail a Use Case* activity. They can be used to define formally the behaviour of a use case as a set of states and transitions between those states that are dependent on events initiated by the user or from within the system.

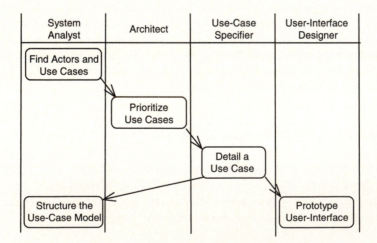

Figure 12-22: Requirements Workflow

State machines can be used to describe the behaviour of the classes that collaborate to realize a use case. These are typically classes with significant, complex behaviour. The work to create these state machines is carried out in the Design Workflow (see Figure 12-23) in the *Design a Class* activity. At the same time as the attributes, operations, associations and other features of each class are designed, state machines can be used to design and document state dependent behaviour.

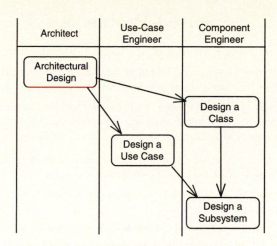

Figure 12-23: Design Workflow

Review Questions

12.1 State machines describe workflows. What other diagrams do?

12.2 What do state machines model?

12.3 What is a state?

12.4 How long can a state last?

12.5 How do events affect states?

12.6 What types of entity can a state machine model?

12.7 Can you have a triggerless transition out of a state?

12.8 What are the four types of actions on a state?

12.9 What is the syntax for an action?

12.10 What is the syntax for the action-label for an event?

12.11 How are actions shown on a state?

12.12 How many actions can be triggered by a transition?

12.13 What is a composite state?

12.14 How do you depict composite states?

12.15 What are concurrent substates?

12.16 What are forks and joins?

12.17 When a transition is direct to the boundary of a composite state, what happens?

12.18 When an event triggers a transition from the boundary of a composite state, what happens?

12.19 When a transition is to a substate of a composite state, what happens?

12.20 What are choice and junction pseudostates?

12.21 What is the difference between history states containing H and H*?

Solved Problems

12.1 Consider Problem 11.1 in which the CarMatch procedure for members to obtain a discount for road-pricing schemes is described. The **Contract** would be one candidate business entity that we might consider modelling. Draw a state machine for the **Contract** class.

The first stage is to identify entities that need modelling with state machines. In the negotiation on road pricing, the key entity will be the **Contract** that will be drawn up, agreed and signed by all parties. We then consider the key events that impact the contract. These would be:

- Drawing up the contract: this would be a detailed piece of work by lawyers, and once the contract is drawn up, it will be a draft for consideration by all parties.
- Revise contract: this will be an event that will occur a number of times throughout the life of the contract until it is signed.
- Agree contract: this will be when all parties accept the contract prior to signing.
- Sign contract: this will be the point in time when all parties formally accept the contract.
- Abort negotiations: prior to signing, all parties will be able to withdraw from negotiations, and the contract will terminate.
- Dispute: during the lifetime of the contract, once in force, there may be disputes under the contract.
- End contract: there are lots of ways a contract may end. It may expire, agreement may be reached between parties to terminate the contract, one of the parties may disappear and the contract would ultimately terminate.

The start state will be when the contract is drawn up. The end state will either be when negotiations are aborted, or when the contract terminates for whatever reason. We can now work from the start state, to the end state, looking for the changes. The first attempt might be a diagram as in Figure 12-24.

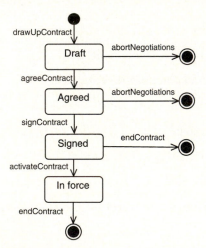

Figure 12-24: First draft state machine for Contract

If we consider the **Draft** state, then we can see that this has to respond to the event to revise the contract. This does not involve a state change, and we enter this as an action in the state. It may also be allowed, though not commonly accepted, that even after agreement, before signing, there might be requested revisions that take it back to the **Draft** state. Once the contract is signed, then during the lifetime of the contract there may be disputes that need to be handled. Thus the diagram is extended as in Figure 12-25.

If we were now moving on to implement a system to maintain an electronic version of the contract, then we would consider the events and actions identified above. Operations to create a contract, create, update and delete clauses, record that the contract is agreed and signed, and to record disputes would support the above. They would all have to be added to the **Contract** class.

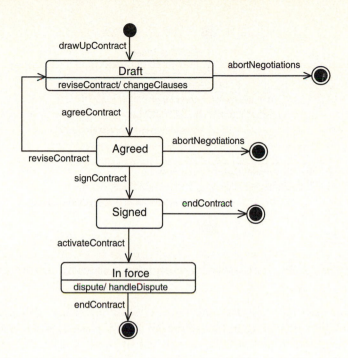

Figure 12-25: State machine for Contract with actions

12.2 In the CarMatch system, an agreement is drawn up to protect sharers against problems with insurance and taxation, and to formalize the relationship between sharers. This agreement can be drawn up when two or more sharers have been matched for a journey. Note that each sharer will have entered a journey on the system, and the matching takes place against journeys. Matching may take place against journeys where there is already an agreement, as there might be space in a car for an additional sharer. We have seen above how the journey registered for a sharer may go from **Available** to **Active** when a sharing agreement has been reached, and that active journeys may be full or have vacancies. Draw a state machine for the **SharingAgreement** class.

The start state for a sharing agreement is brought about when two or more sharers have been identified for a journey. The end state is when a sharer withdraws and there is only one sharer left. The agreement first enters a state of preparation, during which sharers are added to the agreement, and clauses of the agreement may be modified. Once the agreement has been accepted by all sharers, they sign copies and return them to CarMatch, which duly files them and records the state of the agreement on the system. During the life of an agreement, when it is in force, sharers may join the agreement or withdraw, and CarMatch keeps records on the system of these changes. The resulting state machine is shown in Figure 12-26.

Supplementary Problems

12.3 In the VolBank system, volunteering opportunities are registered, and matches are sought for people with time and skills that suit the opportunity. Opportunities can be open, partly filled or filled. Volunteers may have to withdraw from an opportunity, or the opportunity may require additional help from time to time. While the opportunity is open, or partly filled, an interviewing process can go on. This involves identifying potential volunteers, inviting them for interview, considering candidates, and selecting them. For sensitive areas, there may also have to be some vetting of candidates, by checking police files or seeking references. Draw a state machine with composite states to model the class **Opportunity**.

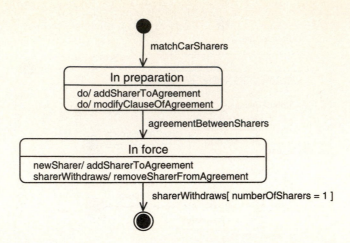

Figure 12-26: The state machine for a sharing agreement

12.4 In VolBank, volunteers may register, and enter into volunteering agreements. Before VolBank allows volunteering, it checks that the volunteer is not prevented for some reason (say by a previous disqualification from VolBank, or because of some queries on the application such as claimed qualifications that need to be validated). Certain voluntary activities involving care provision require additional checking before a volunteer can be matched against an opportunity. Volunteers may suspend membership for work reasons, or if they are moving temporarily out of VolBank's operational area. Volunteers may also withdraw or have their membership expire. Volunteers can also be expelled for reasons of misconduct. Draw a state machine to model the class **Volunteer**.

CHAPTER 13

Object Constraint Language (OCL)

13.1 INTRODUCTION

A *constraint* is a rule that allows you to specify some limits on model elements. Warmer & Kleppe (1999) describe it as 'a restriction on one or more values of (part of) an object-oriented model or system'. Constraints exist in the real world, such as a car should not be driven beyond the speed limit, or voters in government elections need to be above a certain age. They are an important addition to a model, more precisely defining behaviour, notably in terms of limits of the system.

For example, it might be that in the CarMatch system an individual may not have more than 10 agreements for car sharing. In a car sharing agreement, there needs to be at least one sharer who can drive and owns a car. In the VolBank system, a member may not be able to offer more than five types of service.

As the analysis of a problem progresses, the details of constraints emerge. At first these can be imprecise, such as 'a customer must not have a large outstanding debt'. As the analysis progresses the constraints become more concrete, such as 'before making an order, a standard customer should not have more than the standard limit of outstanding debt and have no invoice outstanding beyond the standard payment period'.

Ultimately, the constraints need to be expressed in some language that can be translated into computer statements. UML itself does not specify the particular language in which constraints can be expressed, and English (for example) is perfectly acceptable, or even the syntax of the implementation language. However, natural language statements are prone to ambiguity, and the implementation language may not be suitably expressive. UML therefore includes as an option the Object Constraint Language for a more rigorous expression of constraints. (OCL is now specified in a separate document managed by the OMG (Object Management Group, 2003a).) Various formal languages, such as Z, have been used for specification of constraints, but these can be onerous and difficult for non-mathematicians. OCL has been designed as a formal language that is straightforward to read, and provides rigour in specification without great difficulty in either its construction or interpretation.

In a diagram, a constraint is shown as a text string enclosed in braces {...}, and placed near the associated element or connected to that element by a dependency relationship. You may also put constraints in notes (comments). Let us look at a simple example. In the CarMatch system, a journey has two addresses, for the start and end of the journey. It may be decided that CarMatch will only register journeys of greater than two miles. There is then a dependency between the **startAddress** and the **destinationAddress**, which is drawn as a dashed-line arrow, and a constraint on that dependency is written in braces, as in Figure 13-1.

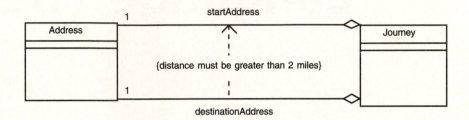

Figure 13-1: A constraint attached to a dependency in a UML diagram

Another simple example would be if we wished to constrain the age of a car sharer to be over 21 for legislative or insurance reasons—this is known as an invariant as it is a property of the model that must not change. This could be shown by attaching a note to the **CarSharer** class and placing the constraint in the note, as in Figure 13-2. This constraint applies to all instances of this class.

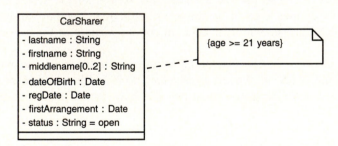

Figure 13-2: A constraint on an object attached using a note in a UML diagram

An alternative notation is to keep the constraints in a separate text file. The constraint in Figure 13-2 could also be written as follows:

    context CarSharer **inv:**
        age>21

The keyword **context** introduces a model element to which the invariant applies, and **inv** introduces the constraint as an invariant (this syntax will be explained fully later). This is much more concise, though it is often useful to indicate constraints on diagrams as illustrated in Figures 13-1 and 13-2.

This chapter will introduce the notions of invariant, post-condition and pre-condition, and explain how these can be expressed as constraints in the Object Constraint Language.

13.1.1　Invariants

An *invariant* is a property that must remain true throughout the life of a model element, such as an object. For example: a car sharer must be aged 21 years or over; a car sharer must have a valid driving licence to offer to drive in part of a sharing agreement; journeys must be two miles or over.

The reason for introducing invariants is to specify the constraints under which the system can operate. A system might be able to operate if the invariants are violated (ideally it should not), but the designer does not guarantee the results. Just as it is viable to use a hammer to force screws into wood, a computer system can be used for purposes for which it is not intended, but the results of such actions cannot be predicted.

Whenever the system carries out a task, the invariants should be true at the start of the task, and remain true at the end of the task. It is the responsibility of the designers and the implementers to make sure that the invariants remain true for legal execution of the system. A designer or implementer cannot be held responsible for uses of the system that fall outside its official use.

13.1.2　Pre-conditions

A *pre-condition* is something that must be true before a particular part of the system is executed. This can be applied to operations during design and implementation, and to use cases during analysis. (Use cases are implemented using operations, so that pre-conditions are translated through the design process from use cases to operations.) For example, to register as a car sharer, it must be true that the candidate is aged 21 or over. On registering a journey, the distance of the journey must be two miles or more. Pre-conditions can therefore be used to make sure that invariants are never violated.

The designer and implementer can use pre-conditions to perform checks before an operation is executed. This is a way of preventing the system from entering illegal states. If a pre-condition is violated, then the sensible action is to raise an exception and refuse to execute the operation. A simple example would be if someone entered an illegal ZIP or post code in the car sharer registration screen. Instead of registering the candidate, it makes sense to put up an error message on the screen and ask the user to re-enter the information. Another example would be making sure that enough money is in a savings account before making a withdrawal, and that would be written in OCL as follows:

```
context Account::withdraw(amount:Integer)
pre: balance >= amount
```

13.1.3　Post-conditions

A *post-condition* is something that must be true after a particular part of the system is executed, if that execution was legal (that is, all pre-conditions were met), and the system has successfully carried out its action. For example, after registering a car sharer, the car sharer's details must be recorded, a request for payment must be sent to the car sharer or to his or her credit card or bank account, and the **CarSharer** instance should be enabled for submitting journeys. As with pre-conditions, post-conditions can be applied to operations or to use cases, and as use cases are translated into operations through the analysis and design process, so they ultimately become translated into post-conditions on operations. To note that on an account the balance must be reduced by the amount withdrawn after a withdrawal, we can write as follows:

```
context Account::withdraw(amount:Integer)
post: balance = balance@pre - amount
```

Post-conditions are part of the definition of what an operation does. The designer and implementer must devise code to ensure that the post-conditions are met. In a formal development (for example for safety-critical systems) this might involve a rigorous proof that the code results in the post-conditions being true if the pre-conditions are true. It is possible to incorporate checks as operations complete to make sure that the post-conditions are true.

13.1.4   Design by Contract

Design of the operational elements of a system can proceed by a definition of pre-conditions and post-conditions. This is known as *design by contract*. This is not all that design is about—much of the design that is facilitated by UML is structural. Pre-conditions and post-conditions are used to define how parts of the model fit together and what their purpose is. The early phases of design focus on identifying the overall structure and the components. The later stages involve detailing the behaviour of those components and how they interact.

The value of the Object Constraint Language is in providing a precise notation for the definition of the behaviour of parts of the system. Ultimately any system must be implemented in a computer language that is unambiguous in its execution. OCL provides a stepping stone to that implementation that removes ambiguity.

13.2   PURPOSE OF THE TECHNIQUE

OCL is designed to provide a clear and unambiguous way to describe rules about the behaviour of elements in a set of UML models. Constraints will be captured throughout the requirements and analysis phases, and translated in the design implementation to checks and balances on the system that is being constructed. The primary purposes of a constraint are as follows:

- They are used to specify pre-conditions and post-conditions on use cases and operations.
- They are used to describe invariants in operations.
- They are used to describe guards on transitions.
- They are used to describe invariants for classes and types in the class model.

The purposes of OCL are as follows:

- It is used to provide a clear and unambiguous language for the description of constraints.
- It is used to accurately specify the behaviour of elements of the model.

13.3   NOTATION

The Object Constraint Language is an expression language that is guaranteed to be without side-effect. That means that the expressions do not change the value of any element of a model. Expressions simply return values. It is the developer's job to interpret OCL expressions and convert them into meaningful actions in a programming language. Consequently, OCL does not provide any notion of control. One can think of OCL in programming language terms, as the expressions that are used in conditions to determine action, such as the condition on a while loop or an if statement, rather than instructions that carry out an action.

OCL is a typed language. OCL statements must therefore conform to type rules, such as not comparing integers with strings. The results of OCL statements are of a particular type, according to the rules of OCL in combining the elements of an expression.

13.3.1   Convention

All OCL statements must take place within a *context*. This might be a class, association class or a use case. The statements themselves can be invariants, pre-conditions or post-conditions. The UML convention is that the keyword **context** is written in bold type, and the stereotype of the constraint is written in bold type as **inv** for «invariant», **pre** for «precondition», and **post** for «postcondition». Thus we could write the invariant that a sharing agreement must be for a number of days by the following statement:

> **context** SharingAgreement **inv:**
>   startDate < finishDate

13.3.2   Context

The context of an OCL expression must be a class (or type) for invariants, or an operation for pre-conditions and post-conditions. (Pre-conditions and post-conditions on use cases are not normally written in OCL, and are included in the use case description as natural language statements.) For invariants this can be simply the name of the class if that is unambiguous, or the package name can be used to define the context of the class. For pre-conditions and post-conditions, the name of the class is extended by the name of the operation and its full signature. (Because of overloading, the name of an operation is insufficient to fully determine the operation.) The syntax for an invariant context is as follows:

> **context** TypeName **inv:**

where **TypeName** is the name of the type or class for which the invariant constraint applies. Package names are introduced using the following syntax:

> **context** PackageName::TypeName **inv:**

Packages can be nested, so if package 2 is nested in package 1, the syntax would be:

> **context** PackageName1::PackageName2::TypeName **inv:**

For pre-conditions and post-conditions on an operation the full syntax is:

> **context** TypeName::operationName(param1 : Type1, ...): ReturnType
>   **pre:** constraint
>   **post:** constraint

During a post-condition it is sometimes necessary to refer to the initial value of a property that is changed by an operation. This is done by using **@pre** as a postfix on the property. So, for example, to note that an account balance is changed accordingly by an operation it might be done by the following:

> **context** Account::deposit(amount: Integer)
>   **post:** balance = amount + balance@pre

13.3.3   Navigation

Within a context, the navigation to an element of a model is by the left-to-right traversal of a path separated by full-stops. For example, to refer to a car sharer's account balance, with an association as in Figure 13-3, and placing an invariant on the car sharer that the balance should be no more than $100 overdrawn, we could write the following:

> **context** CarSharer **inv:**
>   Account.balance >= -100

Note that, strictly, the role name on the association is used to navigate to the class; where there is a missing role name, as is often the case, then the name of the type (i.e. **Account** in the above example) at the end of an association is the default role name, provided there is no ambiguity. We could indicate this on the model using a note as in Figure 13-4.

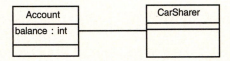

Figure 13-3: Relationship between the classes Account and CarSharer

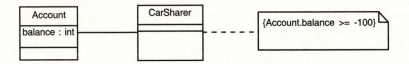

Figure 13-4:   Relationship between the classes Account and CarSharer with constraint attached as a note

There are three ways of referring to item within a context. If the item is unambiguous, then the reference in the previous example is sufficient. If the expression is complex, however, then the word **self** can be used to refer to the instance of the class that is named as the **context**. So the following expression is equivalent to the previous one:

> **context** CarSharer **inv:**
>   self.Account.balance >= -100

This would be used in cases where another instance of the same class is involved in a different role, and it is necessary to distinguish between the two. Alternatively it is possible to refer to a named instance of the class and use the following syntax:

> **context** c:CarSharer **inv:**
>   c.Account.balance >= -100

Ordinarily we will not complicate expressions in this way, though the use of **self** is common to aid readability.

For associations, the role name can be part of the path. Suppose that CarMatch introduce separate accounts for members for their insurance. Then there may be two associations between **CarSharer** and **Account**, as in Figure 13-5, with a role name used to discriminate between the two types of association.

To indicate that the insurance account must not be overdrawn by more than $500 we would write the following:

> **context** CarSharer **inv:**
>   insurance.balance >= -500

Note that it is unnecessary to indicate the type name at the end of the association (i.e. **Account**) as this is unambiguous (only one type is defined by the role). The role name that is used in navigation is the one at the far end of the association, that is at the **Account** end for paths running from **CarSharer**.

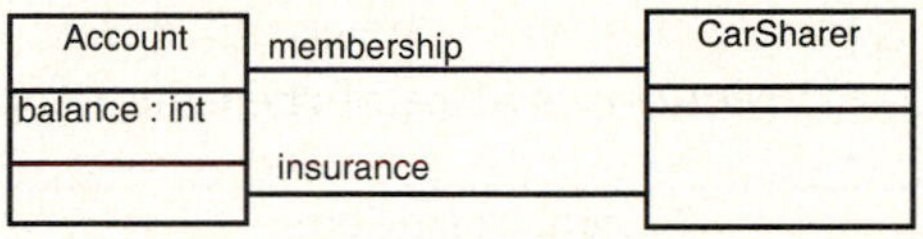

Figure 13-5: Two relationships between the classes Account and CarSharer delineated by roles

It is possible to navigate across a number of associations. So, for example, if it is made a condition that the driver in a journey has paid his or her insurance, using the associations in Figure 13-6 we can express this as follows:

> **context** Journey **inv:**
>   driver.insurance.balance >= 0

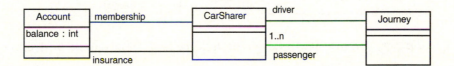

Figure 13-6: Relationships between the classes Journey, CarSharer and Account

13.3.4   Types and Expressions

Elements of an OCL expression are made up of *types*. There are four basic types provided by OCL, namely Boolean, Integer, Real and String. Other types are obtained from the model. Typical values of basic types are provided in Table 13-1.

Table 13-1: Typical values of basic types in OCL

Type	Typical values
Boolean	true, false
Integer	0, 1, -1, 123, -256
Real	12.7, -3.6
String	'Fifth Avenue'

The basic types may be combined using operations, as indicated in Table 13-2. In addition it is possible to use operations defined in the model, and where the values are model types then model operations are necessary.

The result of an OCL expression using basic types is a basic type. The result of an expression involving model types may be a model type or a basic type.

Consider the model in Figure 13-7. We may want to express that the distance of any journey is two miles or more. To do this we construct an operation on an address that allows us to calculate the distance to any other address. We could express this using the following expression:

context Journey **inv:**
    startAddress.distanceTo(self.destinationAddress) >= 2.0

Table 13-2: Typical operations on basic types in OCL

Type	Typical operations
Boolean	and, or, xor, not, implies, if-then-else
Integer	multiply, add, subtract, divide, compare
Real	multiply, add, subtract, divide, compare
String	toUpper, concat

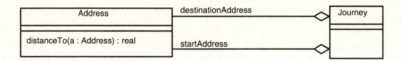

Figure 13-7: Relationship between Journey and constituent addresses

This invokes a model operation **distanceTo** on the start address of the journey, indicated by the role name **startAddress** on the association with an **Address**. The argument is the destination address, indicated by **self.destinationAddress**, from the role name on the association with **Address**. The result is a real, which is then compared with 2.0.

All types in an expression are considered to be subtypes of the type **OclType** whether they are basic types, collections or model types. OCL has a full set of operations on types, but these are not normally necessary to manipulate types for ordinary modelling purposes, and these are not all included in this chapter. The ability to check the type of an object or whether it is a subtype is, however, often useful and is therefore included.

A comprehensive set of operations for basic types is given in Table 13-3. Some sample expressions and their results are given in Table 13-4.

13.3.5   Sets, Bags and Sequences

Because associations are rarely one-to-one, it is often necessary to deal with collections. OCL provides three types of *collection*. A *set* consists of distinct instances; that is, there are no repetitions in the set. Sets have no ordering. A *bag* is an unordered collection that allows repetitions. A *sequence* is an ordered collection that allows repetition—the order is the order written or collected rather than the

Table 13-3: Operations on basic types in OCL

a	b	Operation	Result type	Meaning
Integer or Real	Integer or Real	a = b	Boolean	equality
Integer or Real	Integer or Real	a <> b	Boolean	inequality
Integer or Real	Integer or Real	a < b	Boolean	less than
Integer or Real	Integer or Real	a > b	Boolean	greater than
Integer or Real	Integer or Real	a <= b	Boolean	less than or equal
Integer or Real	Integer or Real	a >= b	Boolean	greater than or equal
Integer or Real	Integer or Real	a + b	Integer or Real	addition
Integer or Real	Integer or Real	a - b	Integer or Real	subtraction
Integer or Real	Integer or Real	a * b	Integer or Real	multiplication
Integer or Real	Integer or Real	a / b	Real	division
Integer	Integer	a.mod(b)	Integer	modulus
Integer	Integer	a.div(b)	Integer	integer division
Integer or Real		a.abs	Integer or Real	absolute value
Integer or Real	Integer or Real	a.max(b)	Integer or Real	maximum
Integer or Real	Integer or Real	a.min(b)	Integer or Real	minimum
Integer or Real		a.round	Integer	round to nearest integer
Integer or Real		a.floor	Integer	round down (truncate)
Boolean	Boolean	a or b	Boolean	or
Boolean	Boolean	a and b	Boolean	and
Boolean	Boolean	a xor b	Boolean	exclusive or
Boolean	Boolean	not a	Boolean	negation
Boolean	Boolean	a <> b	Boolean	inequality
Boolean	Boolean	a implies b	Boolean	implies
Boolean	Anything	if a then b else b'	type of b or b'	if then else
String	String	a.concat(b)	String	concatenate two strings
String		a.size	Integer	size of string
String		a.toLower	String	convert to lower case
String		a.toUpper	String	convert to upper case
String	String	a = b	Boolean	equality
String	String	a <> b	Boolean	inequality

order of the values. Collections are written in braces, with the type of collection before it. Examples are as follows:

```
Set{4, 7, 2, 9}
Sequence{2, 3, 8, 9, 3, 5, 7, 7, 9}
Bag{3, 5, 4, 6, 8, 3, 5, 2, 5}
Set{'orange', 'apple', 'banana'}
```

Because of the usefulness of sequences of consecutive integers, these can be shown by using n..m to denote the sequence in the range from n to m. For example Sequence{2..6} is the same as Sequence{2,3,4,5,6}.

Consider the association in Figure 13-8. A car sharer has the possibility of a number of agreements. An agreement can involve two to five car sharers. The expression self.agreement in the context CarSharer will return a set of agreements for that car sharer. The expression self.agreement.sharer will return a bag of all the people that a sharer shares with, including the CarSharer instance for him or herself repeated in the bag for each of the agreements. (Note that it is a bag and not a set because the same instance of CarSharer can occur more than once.)

Table 13-4: Sample expressions on basic types in OCL

Expression	Result
1 + 2	3
3 + 4.5	7.5
(3 + 4) = 7	true
3 < 4	true
(7.8).floor	7
(7.8).round	8
7.mod(3)	1
7.div(3)	2
true or true	true
true or false	true
false or false	false
(1 > 2) or (7 > 6)	true
if (7 > 6) then 2 else 3	2
if (7 < 6) then 2 else 3	3
'Washington'.concat(' State')	'Washington State'
'Washington'.toLower	'washington'
'New York' = 'new york'	false
'New York'.toLower = 'new york'	true
'Ohio'.size	4

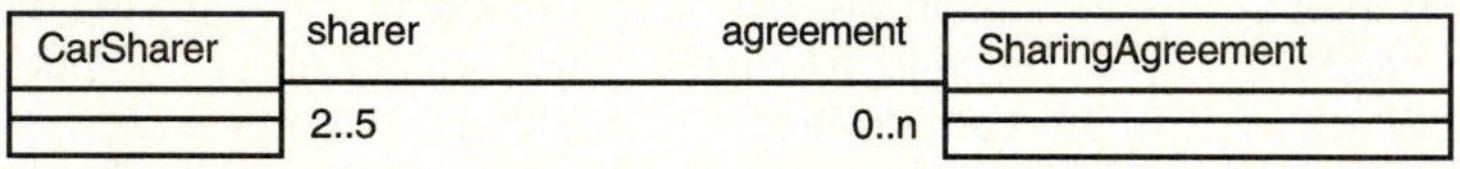

CarSharer	sharer		agreement	SharingAgreement
	2..5		0..n	

Figure 13-8: Relationship between the classes CarSharer and SharingAgreement

A list of some of the operations you can apply to collections is given in Table 13-5. A set of examples is given in Table 13-6. The majority of the operations are straightforward. However, some of the collection operations need explanation.

13.3.5.1   *The Select Operation*

The select operation picks out a subset of elements from a collection that meet a particular condition. The syntax for the select operation is:

    collection->select(v | boolean-expression-with-v).

The action to implement the operation is to assign **v** to each of the values in the collection, evaluate the expression, and if the result is true add that to the resultant collection. The type of the resultant collection is the same as the source collection, with repetitions preserved for bags, and sequence preserved for sequences. For example, we may wish to select from a set the elements greater than a particular value. Thus

    a->select(x | x > 100)

would select all items in the collection **a** that are greater than 100 and provide a new collection. Thus, if we apply this to the collection

Bag {12,86,342,3,12,567,432},

the result would be

Bag {342,567,432}

The vertical bar can be read 'such that', for example '**x** such that **x** is greater than 100'.

13.3.5.2 The Reject Operation

The *reject* operation picks out a subset of elements from a collection that fail a particular condition. The syntax for the reject operation is:

collection->reject(v | boolean-expression-with-v)

The action to implement the operation is to assign **v** to each of the values in the collection, evaluate the expression, and if the result is *false* add that to the resultant collection. The type of the resultant collection is the same as the source collection, with repetitions preserved for bags, and sequence preserved for sequences. For example, we may wish to select from a set the elements not greater than a particular value. Thus

a->reject(x | x > 100)

would select all items in the collection **a** that are not greater than 100 and provide a new collection. Thus, applied to the collection

Bag{12,86,342,3,12,567,432}

the result would be

Bag{12,86,3,12}

13.3.5.3 The Collect Operation

The *collect* operation creates a new collection by applying an expression to each element of a collection. The syntax for the collect operation is:

collection->select(v | expression-with-v)

The action to implement the operation is to assign **v** to each of the values in the collection, evaluate the expression, and put the result in the returned collection. The type of the resultant collection is the same as the source collection, with repetitions preserved for bags, and sequence preserved for sequences.

For example, to create a collection of squares of all numbers in a given collection we could use the expression:

a->collect(x | x * x)

Table 13-5: Operations on collections in OCL

a	b	Operation	Result type	Meaning
Set	Set	a->union(b)	Set	All elements in either a or b, without repetition
Set	Bag	a->union(b)	Bag	All elements in a or b, repeated as often as in a and b together
Set	Set or Bag	a->intersection(b)	Set	All elements in both a and b, without repetition
Set	Any	a->including(b)	Set	All elements of a with b added in if it was not in the set a
Set	Any	a->excluding(b)	Set	All elements of a with b removed if it was in the set a
Set	Set	a - b	Set	All elements of a not in b
Set	Set	a = b	Boolean	True if a and b have identical elements, else false
Set	Set	a.symetricDifference(b)	Set	All elements in a not in b or in b not in a
Set		a->asBag	Bag	The elements of a in a bag
Set		a->asSequence	Sequence	The elements of a as a sequence of undefined order
Bag	Bag	a->union(b)	Bag	All elements in either a or b, with repetition as many times as in both bags
Bag	Set	a->union(b)	Bag	All elements in a or b, repeated as often as in a and b together
Bag	Set or Bag	a->intersection(b)	Set	All elements in both a and b, without repetition
Bag	Any	a->including(b)	Bag	All elements of a with b added in
Bag	Any	a->excluding(b)	Bag	All elements of a with all occurrences b removed
Bag	Bag	a = b	Boolean	True if a and b have identical elements with the same repetition, else false
Bag		a->asSet	Set	The elements of a with repetitions removed
Bag		a->asSequence	Sequence	The elements of a as a sequence of undefined order
Sequence	Sequence	a->union(b)	Sequence	All elements in a followed by all elements of b, in order
Sequence	Any	a->including(b)	Set	All elements of a with b added at the end
Sequence	Any	a->excluding(b)	Set	All elements of a with all occurrences of b removed, in the order they appear in a
Sequence		a->first	The type of the first element of a	The first element of a
Sequence		a->last	The type of the last element of a	The last element of a
Sequence	Integer	a->at(b)	The type of the element at position b	The element of a at position b
Sequence	Any	a->append(b)	Sequence	Appends b to the end of the sequence a

Table 13-5: Continued

a	b	Operation	Result type	Meaning
Sequence	any	a->prepend(b)	Sequence	Places b at the beginning of the sequence a
Sequence		a->asSet	Set	The elements of a with repetitions removed and order no longer considered
Sequence		a->asBag	Bag	The elements of a with order no longer considered
Collection	expression	a->select(b)	Collection	The subcollection of a for which the expression b is true
Collection	expression	a->reject(b)	Collection	The subcollection of a for which b is false
Collection	expression	a->collect(b)	Collection	The collection of results of the expression b applied to the elements of a
Collection	expression	a->forall(b)	Boolean	True if b evaluates as true for every element of a, otherwise false
Collection	i;acc=init I e	a->iterate(b)	Collection	Assigns the result of the expression init to acc, then iterates over a, assigning each element of a to i and evaluating the expression e with the values of i and acc and assigning the result to acc
Collection	expression	a->exists(b)	Boolean	True if b evaluates as true for at least one element of a, otherwise false
Collection		a->size	Integer	The number of elements in a
Collection	any	a->count(b)	Integer	The number of occurrences of b in a
Collection	any	a->includes(b)	Boolean	True if a includes b
Collection	Collection	a->includesAll(b)	Boolean	True if a includes all the elements of b
Collection		a->isEmpty	Boolean	True if a is empty (i.e. has no elements)
Collection		a->notEmpty	Boolean	True if a is not empty
Collection		a->sum	Integer or Real	The sum of the elements in a, all of which must be integer or real
any		a.oclType	OclType	The type of a
any	OclType	a.isTypeOf(b)	Boolean	True if a is of type b
any	OclType	a.isKindOf(b)	Boolean	True if a is of type b or any subtype of b

13.3.6   Messages

It is sometimes useful to check if a message has been received by an operation, or to query the *collection of messages* received by an operation. OCL provides a means of querying the messages received during an operation, so that post-conditions can be set that ensure correct receipt of messages. The messages can arrive either as method calls or signals. The ^ operator is used to determine if a message has been received. For example, suppose we have a **Car** class with a method to charge for congestion, then we may need a post-condition that shows that a signal has been received that a car has passed a beacon with the registration number of the car to be charged. This can be done by writing the post-condition as:

Table 13-6: Examples of operations on collections

a	b	Operation	Result
Set{1,2,3}	Set{3,4,5}	a->union(b)	Set{1,2,3,4,5}
Set{1,2,3}	bag{2,3,3,4,5}	a->union(b)	Bag{1,2,2,3,3,3,4,5}
Set{1,2,3}	Set{3,4,5}	a->intersection(b)	Set{3}
Set{1,2,3}	Bag{3,3,4,5}	a->intersection(b)	Set{3}
Set{1,2,3}	5	a->including(b)	Set{1,2,3,5}
Set{1,2,3}	1	a->excluding(b)	Set{2,3}
Set{1,2,3}	Set{3,4,5}	a - b	Set{1,2}
Set{1,2,3}	Set{3,4,5}	a = b	false
Set{1,2,3}	Set{3,4,5}	a.symetricDifference(b)	Set{1,2,4,5}
Bag{1,2,2,3}	Bag{3,4,5,5}	a->union(b)	Bag{1,2,2,3,3,4,5,5}
Bag{1,2,2,3}	Set{3,4,5}	a->union(b)	Bag{1,2,2,3,3,4,5}
Bag{1,2,2,3,3}	Bag{3,3,4,4,5}	a->intersection(b)	Set{3}
Bag{3,3,4,5}	Set{1,2,3}	a->intersection(b)	Set{3}
Bag{1,1,2,3}	5	a->including(b)	Bag{1,1,2,3,5}
Bag{1,1,2,2,3}	1	a->excluding(b)	Bag{2,2,3}
Bag{1,1,2,2,3}		a->asSet	Set{1,2,3}
Bag{1,2,3}	Bag{3,2,1}	a = b	true
Sequence{1,2,3,2,1}	Sequence{3,4,5,4,3}	a->union(b)	Sequence{1,2,3,2,1,3,4,5,4,3}
Sequence{1,2,3,2,1}	3	a->including(b)	Sequence{1,2,3,2,1,3}
Sequence{1,2,3,2,1}	3	a->excluding(b)	Sequence{1,2,2,1}
Sequence{4,5,6}		a->first	4
Sequence{4,5,6}		a->last	6
Sequence{4,5,6}	Integer	a->at(2)	5
Sequence{7,2,3}	Sequence{5,3,9}	a->append(b)	Sequence{7,2,3,5,3,9}
Sequence{7,2,3}	Sequence{5,3,9}	a->prepend(b)	Sequence{5,3,9,7,2,3}
Set{2,4,5,7,9}	x | x > 5	a->select(b)	Set{7,9}
Set{2,4,5,7,9}	x | x > 5	a->reject(b)	Set{2,4,5}
Set{2,4,5,7,9}	x | x + 1	a->collect(b)	Set{3,5,6,8,10}
Set{2,4,5,7,9}	x | x > 1	a->forall(b)	true
Set{2,4,5,7,9}	x | x > 3	a->forall(b)	false
Set{2,4,5,7,9}	x | x > 1	a->exists(b)	true
Set{2,4,5,7,9}	x | x > 9	a->exists(b)	false
Set{2,4,5,7,9}		a->size	5
Set{2,4,5,7,9}		a->includes(7)	true
Set{2,4,5,7,9}		a->includesAll(set {2,3})	false
Set{2,4,5,7,9}		a->isEmpty	false
Set{2,4,5,7,9}		a->notEmpty	true
Set{2,4,5,7,9}		a->sum	27
Bag{2,2,4,5,7,7,9}	x | x > 5	a->select(b)	Bag{7,7.9}
Bag{2,2,4,5,7,7,9}	x | x > 5	a->reject(b)	Bag{2,2,4,5}
Bag{2,2,4,5,7,7,9}	x | x + 1	a->collect(b)	Bag{3,3,5,6,8,8,10}
Bag{2,2,4,5,7,7,9}	x | x > 1	a->forall(b)	true
Bag{2,2,4,5,7,7,9}	x | x > 3	a->forall(b)	false
Bag{2,2,4,5,7,7,9}	x | x > 1	a->exists(b)	true
Bag{2,2,4,5,7,7,9}	x | x > 9	a->exists(b)	false
Bag{2,2,4,5,7,7,9}		a->size	7
Bag{2,2,4,5,7,7,9}		a->includes(7)	true
Bag{2,2,4,5,7,7,9}		a->includesAll(Bag {2,3})	false
Bag{2,2,4,5,7,7,9}		a->isEmpty	false
Bag{2,2,4,5,7,7,9}		a->notEmpty	true
Bag{2,2,4,5,7,7,9}		a->sum	36
Sequence{2,3,2,4,5,9,6}	x | x > 5	a->select(b)	Sequence{9}
Sequence{2,3,2,4,5,9,6}	x | x > 5	a->reject(b)	Sequence{2,3,2,4,5}
Sequence{2,3,2,4,5,9,6}	x | x + 1	a->collect(b)	Sequence{3,4,3,5,6,10,7}

context Car::charge(regNo)
post: Beacon^carPassed(regNo)

This can be read as: 'the charge method on car has completed legally if the method has received a signal from the beacon with the registration number of the car'. There is another operator ^^ that returns the collection of messages received by an operation. To count the number of cars passing in a period we might have

> **context** Car::count(from, to): Integer
> **post:** count = Beacon^^carPassed(?) -> size

which can be read as 'the count of the number of cars that passed a beacon is the number of **carPassed** messages received by the count operation that was active in the period between from and to'; the ? is a wildcard.

13.3.7   Tuples

A *tuple* is a composition of a number of values. The parts are named. So, for example

> Tuple{ name="James Bond", Address = "12 Regent Street" }

pairs up a name with an address. The order of elements is not important, so that

> Tuple{ Address = "12 Regent Street", name="James Bond" }

is the same tuple. To access the value of one of the elements, the element name is postfixed to the property that is a tuple. So, if **personDetail** is a tuple with the structure and content above, then

> personDetail.name = "James Bond"

is **true**.

13.4   HOW TO PRODUCE CONSTRAINTS

The acquisition of constraints will take place throughout the analysis and design process. To begin with these will inevitably have to be recorded as natural language statements. Continual refinement will be necessary until it is possible to express these more formally in an expression language such as OCL. Ultimately, the constraints will be used by developers to enable them to write clear and reliable code that conforms to the system specification. Constraints are identified by:

- determining pre-conditions and post-conditions on use cases;
- determining invariants on objects in the analysis;
- translating use-case constraints to constraints on operations;
- translating pre-conditions, post-conditions and invariants to code in the implementation.

The refinement will be continuous and iterative throughout analysis and design. The ambiguity of natural language will mean that it is often necessary to ask further questions to clarify issues. Until the structural design is complete, it will not be possible to express all constraints fully in OCL because, for example, the complete set of objects and operations will not be available.

13.4.1   Determining Constraints on Use Cases

Use cases are legitimately invoked only under particular conditions. As part of the definition of use cases, it is important to capture these conditions. One way of doing this is to supply a document template for the description of use cases. This template will include the scenario descriptions as illustrated in Figure 3-10, and any additional requirements for the use case, including pre-conditions and post-conditions.

Consider the use case for registering car sharers, illustrated in Figure 13-9. The elaboration of the registration use case could be provided in a format as indicated in Figure 13-10. It would be infeasible at this stage to express these pre-conditions and post-conditions in OCL, as the underlying object structure is unlikely to be complete.

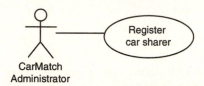

Figure 13-9: The use case **Register car sharer**

Use Case: Register car sharer
Pre-conditions:
1. Car sharer must be older than 21 years.
2. If the car sharer offers to drive, he or she must have a current driving licence and valid insurance
3. Car sharer must not be already registered
4. Car sharer must not have been disqualified from membership in the past
Post-conditions:
1. Car sharer details registered
2. Car sharer has paid for membership
3. Welcome pack has been issued to car sharer
4. Registration of journeys for car sharer enabled
Description
etc.

Figure 13-10: The use case description **Register car sharer**

13.4.2   Determining Constraints on Objects

The realization of use cases is through workflows that result in a network of communicating objects. These objects are configured to provide the use case functionality. Therefore, the pre-conditions and post-conditions for use cases must ultimately be translated into constraints on the objects. As part of realizing the **Register car sharer** use case, we have an object **CarSharer** with a date of birth attribute **dateOfBirth**. It does not make sense to store age as an attribute, so it is necessary to implement an operation on **CarSharer** to return the age. Translating the constraint from the use case for registration we arrive at an invariant for **CarSharer** expressed as follows:

```
context CarSharer inv:
    self.age() >= 21.
```

13.4.3   Translating Use Case Constraints to Operation Constraints

The CarSharer class is an entity class, instances of which are likely to have their operations called from a control object of the class RCSControl, which provides the implementation of the Register car sharer use case and contains two collections, of CarSharer and of DisqualifiedCarSharer. To enforce the invariant on CarSharer, it makes sense to implement a pre-condition on the operation on RCSControl that creates the new CarSharer

The constraint that car sharers must not have been disqualified from membership in the past implies that we need to keep a register of car sharers who have been disqualified. The class diagram in Figure 13-11 indicates the object relationships to support the Register car sharer use case. Now we can write a set of pre-conditions on the register operation on RCSControl as follows:

> **context** RCSControl::register(fName, lName, address)
> **pre:** self.CarSharer –> forall(c | c.firstName <> fName and
> c.lastName <> lName and c.homeAddress <> address) and
> self.DisqualifiedCarSharer –> forall(d | d.firstName <> fName and
> d.lastName <> lName and d.homeAddress <> address) .

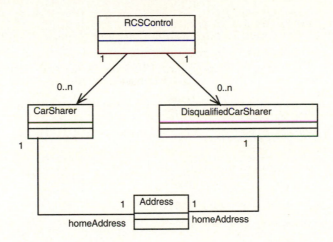

Figure 13-11: The object model to implement the **Register car sharer** use case

13.4.4   Translating Constraints into Code

Pre-conditions and invariants are not, in themselves, executable. However, as they define the legal conditions under which a system operates it makes good sense to provide checks in code to ensure that as far as possible they are not violated. If the constraints are violated, then it would be normal to raise some exception so that the system or the user of the system can take corrective action. Pre-conditions on operations can be translated into simple checks at the beginning of the code that implements the operations. Invariants can be checked by introducing code before and after a change to the attributes indicated by the invariant.

Post-conditions are part of the contractual requirement of an operation. The code should have left the post-conditions as true for legal execution of the operation. The post-conditions are used by the programmer as part of the specification. It is possible, though not routine, to check that the post-conditions are true on exit from a procedure; this would be sensible if there is some complexity in the code or some safety-critical issue that means that the operation must be double-checked.

13.5 RELATIONSHIP WITH UML DIAGRAMS

OCL expressions can be held separately or tagged on to diagrams in some way. Invariants can be placed in a note and attached to the object they relate to. Guards can be expressed in OCL, and are drawn on transitions in activities and state machine diagrams. There is no natural place to record pre-conditions and post-conditions on operations; placing them in notes is cumbersome, so that the only effective means is to record them separately. Software modelling tools support different means of associating text with elements in a UML model and these may be used to record OCL expressions.

13.6 OCL IN THE UNIFIED PROCESS

OCL is not specifically referenced in the Unified Process. Its primary role is to provide rigour to the recording of constraints. Because OCL expressions are constructed out of model elements, the model itself needs to be very well elaborated before constraints can be expressed in this way. OCL can be used to describe constraints in the business model once the business objects have been defined. Requirements are likely to be recorded in natural language, to be translated once object models have been defined through analysis and design. Unit testing can make use of pre-conditions and post-conditions to develop test plans.

In the *Implementation Workflow* activities *Implement a Class* and *Perform Unit Test*, constraints would be used firstly to determine conditions in the program code for each class, and secondly to provide tests that can be applied to instances of each class. Figure 13-12 shows the workflow.

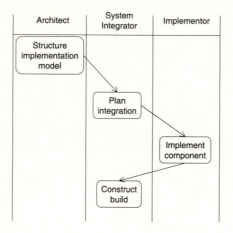

Figure 13-12: Implementation Workflow as an activity diagram

Review Questions

13.1 What is a constraint?

13.2 Why do you add constraints to a model?

13.3 What is OCL?

13.4 What is the problem with using natural language to define constraints?

13.5 What is a pre-condition?

13.6 What is a post-condition?

13.7 What is an invariant?

13.8 What is 'design by contract'?

13.9 What is the context for a constraint?

13.10 What are the basic types in an OCL expression?

13.11 What types, other than basic ones, can be used in OCL expressions?

13.12 Evaluate the OCL expression: if ((3 + 4) > 7) then 1 else 2

13.13 What are the different types of collection?

13.14 How do you find the first element of a sequence?

13.15 Evaluate the OCL expression: Bag{2,5,2,3,8,3,4,6} -> select(x | x < 5)

13.16 Evaluate the OCL expression: Bag{2,8,4,6,0,4,8,2} -> forall(x | x.mod(2) = 0)

13.17 Would you express pre-conditions and post-conditions on use cases in OCL?

13.18 What is the difference between the ^ and the ^^ message operators.

13.19 What is a tuple?

Solved Problems

13.1 Consider the use case to sell insurance policies, indicated in Figure 13-13. As part of the discussions with the insurance companies, requirements are agreed as follows:

- Members must be fully paid up before taking out insurance.
- The first payment of the payment schedule must be made before cover is granted.
- Two policies must not be in force at the same time for a given car sharer.

Write OCL constraints to handle these requirements.

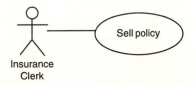

Figure 13-13: The use case for selling an insurance policy

These are added to the use case as pre-conditions and recorded as indicated in Figure 13-10 above. Then, as part of the design process an object model is devised as in Figure 13-14. Here a control object, **SPControl** has been introduced to manage the use case transactions, and it has three operations (among others) to gather insurance details, to create a new policy and to create a new payment schedule. The first pre-condition should sensibly be checked before insurance details are gathered—it is not appropriate to gather information when there is something that is easily checked that could block the transaction. We would therefore put this as a pre-condition on the gatherInsuranceDetails operation, thus:

```
context SPControl::gatherInsuranceDetails()
pre: CarSharer.membership.balance >= 0
```

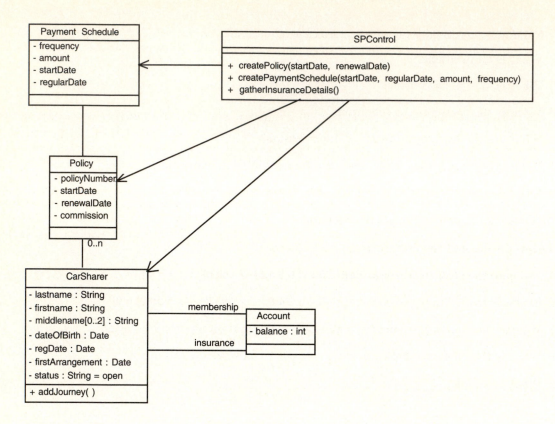

Figure 13-14: Partial class diagram to implement the Sell policy use case

Thus we have used the **CarSharer** that is linked to **SPControl**, and traced through the membership role to the account that holds the outstanding balance on membership fees, and checked that the balance is greater than zero.

The second requirement is sensibly mapped onto the **createPaymentSchedule** operation. Because dates are not basic types, an operation will have to be available on the date type to check that it is before another date, using the other date as the argument (this operation must return a boolean value). The constraint becomes:

> **context** SPControl::createPaymentSchedule(startDate, regularDate, amount, frequency)
> **pre** : startDate.before(Policy.startDate)

The third requirement is an invariant on **CarSharer** that can be expressed as 'the renewal date of a policy must fall before the start date of any later policy', and this becomes in OCL a set operation:

> **context** CarSharer
> **inv** : Policy -> forall(p1,p2 | p1 <> p2 and p1.startDate.before(p2.startDate)
>   implies p1.renewalDate.before(p2.startDate))

In considering this, then we need to place a constraint on **Policy** that makes sure that renewal dates fall after start dates, thus:

> **context** Policy
> **inv:** startDate.before(renewalDate)

On further consideration of the design of the system, the invariant on **CarSharer** is best ensured by placing a pre-condition on the **createPolicy** operation that can be expressed as

> **context** SPControl::createPolicy(startDate, renewalDate)
> **pre** : CarSharer.Policy->forall(p | p.startDate.before(self.startDate)
>   implies p.renewalDate.before(self.StartDate)

The translation of the pre-conditions into code would depend very much on the programming language chosen. However, in each case the operation would inevitably begin with some simple tests to check that the pre-conditions were true. If a pre-condition is false, then the operation would either exit with some return value set, or raise an exception.

13.2 Consider the use case **Match car sharers**. The requirements for sharing include the condition that, to create a sharing agreement, there must be at least one driver, and at least two people in the agreement. Write OCL constraints to handle these requirements.

This would be a post-condition of the use case **Match car sharers**. We might then design a control class **MCSControl** with an operation to choose sharers for a particular journey and then create a sharing agreement. The object model is indicated in Figure 13-15. The requirement would mean that the **chooseSharers** operation must return a list of car sharers among whom is a driver. We clearly need a means of checking if a car sharer can drive, and we might elect to put a **canDrive** attribute in the object. The requirement can be expressed as a post-condition:

> **context** MCSControl::chooseSharers(journey): CarSharerList
> > **post:** chooseSharers -> exists(x | x.canDrive) and (chooseSharers->size) >= 2.

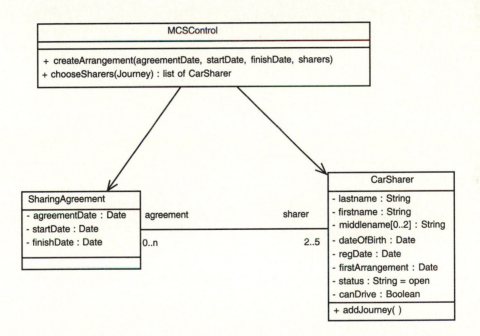

Figure 13-15: Partial class diagram to implement the Match car sharers use case

This would then become a pre-condition on the **createArrangement** operation, expressed thus:

> **context** MCSControl::createArrangement(agreementDate, startDate, finishDate, sharers)
> > **pre:** sharers->exists(x | x.canDrive) and (sharers->size) >= 2.

Meeting these pre-conditions and post-conditions would be instrumental in implementing the invariant on a sharing agreement as follows:

> **context** SharingAgreement
> > **inv:** sharer->exists(x | x.canDrive) and (sharer->size) >= 2.

Supplementary Problems

13.3 In VolBank, a requirement is made to prevent anyone depositing more than 200 hours, and no one overdrawing more than 100 hours. Express this as a constraint in OCL.

13.4 In VolBank, a requirement is made to ensure that no volunteer works for more than three organizations at any one time. For the use case that matches a volunteer with an organization, express this as a pre-condition on the use case. Devise a set of classes to implement the use case, and express this constraint in OCL both as an invariant and as a pre-condition on an operation that implements the matching.

CHAPTER 14

Deployment Diagrams

14.1 INTRODUCTION

Deployment diagrams are used to model the hardware that will be used to implement the system, the links between different items of hardware and the deployment of software onto that hardware. Figure 14-1 shows an example of a deployment diagram that models the hardware of a system and the way that the different processors will be linked together.

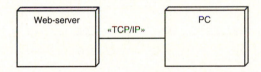

Figure 14-1: A deployment diagram showing the communication path between a PC and a web-server

14.2 PURPOSE OF THE TECHNIQUES

Deployment diagrams model aspects of the physical implementation of a system. Deployment diagrams are used to model the configuration of the hardware elements (or *nodes*) that make up the system. These include computers (clients and servers), embedded processors and devices such as sensors and peripherals. They are also used to show the nodes where software artefacts reside in the run-time system. They are used for the following purposes:

- to model physical hardware elements and the communication paths between them;

- to plan the architecture of a system;

- to document the deployment of software artefacts on hardware nodes.

14.3　NOTATION

14.3.1　Node

In their most basic form, deployment diagrams show *nodes* connected by *communication paths*. The notation for a node is a cuboid, as in Figure 14-2.

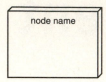

Figure 14-2: The notation for a node

Nodes represent the processing resources in a system, typically computers with processing power and memory, but can also be used to represent sensors, peripherals or embedded systems.

14.3.2　Communication Path

Nodes are connected by communication paths, which can be stereotyped to show the nature of the communication between the connected pair of nodes. Figure 14-3 shows a client and a server connected using the TCP/IP network protocol.

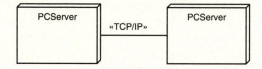

Figure 14-3: The stereotyped communication path between a client and a server

Deployment diagrams can be used to show node types, as in Figure 14-3, or instances of nodes, as in Figure 14-4, which depicts the specific clients and servers that will be in an implemented system.

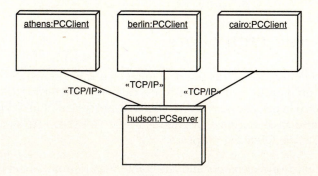

Figure 14-4: Instances in a deployment diagram

Finally, nodes can be stereotyped as either a «device» or as a particular type of «execution environment».

Using the «device» stereotype allows the analyst to show how specific processing devices are used in the implemented system. A node may consist of one or more devices, as shown in Figure 14-5.

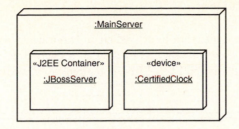

Figure 14-5: A «device» and a «J2EE Container» execution environment

Different execution environments can also be shown. Execution environments are distinct areas within a node that can again be used to show specific aspects of the implementation environment. Execution environments will normally be shown as a particular type of environment, for example «container», «sandbox» or «J2EE Container» as shown in Figure 14-5.

14.3.3   Artefacts

We said earlier that deployment diagrams can be used to show the deployment of software onto the hardware of the system. We have looked at modelling the hardware of the system. Now let us turn our attention to the modules of code that are to be deployed.

The UML notation for an artefact is shown in Figure 14-6. This is the same convention as other stereotyped classes we have seen earlier in the book. The «artefact» stereotype is used, along with an optional icon in the top right corner of the class symbol. The icon is shown in Figure 14-6.

Figure 14-6: Notation for an «artefact»

Artefacts are bundled collections of source code that can be deployed onto a node as a coherent set of functionality. An artefact may represent a deployment bundle for a component. This can be shown using the notation in Figure 14-7.

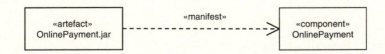

Figure 14-7: An «artefact» that manifests a component

This notation shows that the application code that is part of the **OnlinePayment** component is manifested in the **OnlinePayment.jar** artefact for deployment purposes. An «artefact» can manifest classes and packages as well as components.

14.3.4   Deployment of Artefacts

The deployment of artefacts to nodes can be modelled in three ways within UML. The first way is to use graphical containment, as shown in Figure 14-8. The second is to use a text list of the artefacts deployed to a node, as shown in Figure 14-9. Finally, a **«deploy»** stereotyped dependency can be used, as shown in Figure 14-10.

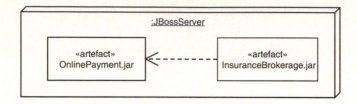

Figure 14-8: Artefact deployment using graphical containment

Figure 14-9: Artefact deployment using a text list

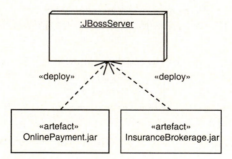

Figure 14-10: Artefact deployment using «deploy» stereotypes

Mapping artefacts to nodes in this way makes it clear how the analyst or architect envisages the functional capability of the application being deployed across the available hardware. Artefacts can be deployed to devices or execution environments to show a more specific deployment configuration.

14.3.5   Deployment Specifications

Using an implementation technology such as the Java 2 Enterprise Edition (J2EE), it is necessary to instantiate and bind the functionality contained in an artefact to the application server upon which it is deployed. The mechanism used to achieve this is known as a deployment descriptor. By separating out the instantiation and binding information, the portability of the software artefact itself is enhanced. However, it is necessary to identify clearly the particular deployment descriptor that must be used to deploy a specific artefact onto a specific node.

UML supports this requirement with the deployment specification, or «deployment spec». The notation for a «deployment spec» is shown in Figure 14-11.

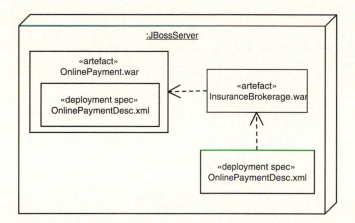

Figure 14-11: Deployment specifications for deployed artefacts

As Figure 14-11 shows, deployment specifications can be associated with their artefacts either using a dependency or by graphical containment.

A deployment specification can incorporate a number of properties to describe the nature of the deployment. The specific properties to be used are not determined by UML and should reflect the practical requirements of the particular technology infrastructure being used. These properties can be shown as either attributes or tagged values of the deployment specification. If attributes are used, then a deployment specification instance can be shown with instantiated values for those attributes.

14.4   MODELLING GUIDANCE

Deployment diagrams can be used for a number of purposes, either as a type diagram or as an instance diagram and either with or without artefacts and deployment specifications. The general approach can be set out as follows.

1. Decide on the purpose of the diagram.
2. Add nodes to the diagram.
3. Add communication paths to the diagram.
4. Map artefacts and deployment specifications to the nodes, if required.

14.4.1   Decide on Purpose

The first step is to decide on the purpose of the diagram. Is it being used to model only nodes or the deployment of artefacts and deployment specifications on nodes? (In the Solved Problems for this chapter, we model both types.)

EXAMPLE 14.1   In this example, we are going to model the deployment of components involved in the registration of new car sharers. The purpose of the diagram is to show where the components will reside. This will be an instance diagram.

14.4.2   Add Nodes

The first step in producing the diagram itself is to decide on the nodes involved. These are the processors on which the executables will run.

EXAMPLE 14.2   There are two types of nodes in this system: PC clients and servers. A typical office will have three clients and one server. We do not know what names will be assigned to these machines, so they will be anonymous instances. This is shown in Figure 14-12.

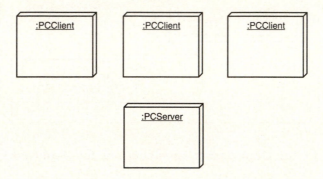

Figure 14-12: Nodes in the deployment diagram

14.4.3   Add Communication Paths

The channels for communication between pairs of nodes must be added. Stereotypes are used to show the protocol for the communication.

EXAMPLE 14.3   The clients communicate with the servers using TCP/IP. We could show a network as a node in the diagram, to illustrate the fact that each client can also communicate with the other clients. However, for this diagram, we are interested only in the communication between clients and the server. The result is shown in Figure 14-13.

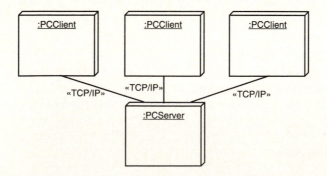

Figure 14-13: Communication paths in the deployment diagram

14.4.4   Add Other Elements

Artefacts and deployment specifications can be added to the diagram if the purpose of the diagram is to show where they reside in the system.

EXAMPLE 14.4   In this system, the RegisterCarSharer.jar artefact will reside on each of the clients, but the components that implement the entity classes will reside only on the server. The help file is held on the server, as is the deployment specification for CarSharing.jar. The result is shown in Figure 14-14.

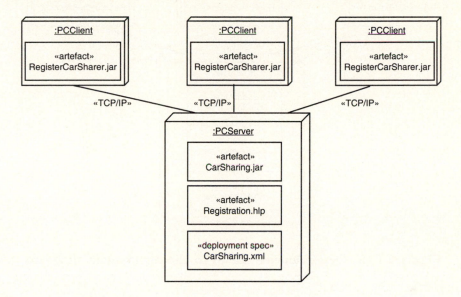

Figure 14-14: Components added to the deployment diagram

14.4.5   Add Dependencies

It may help to show dependencies between artefacts in the deployment diagram. However, the diagram can become very cluttered with lines. It may be better to produce a set of deployment diagrams, each of which illustrates a different facet of the implementation architecture.

EXAMPLE 14.5   In this case, we have chosen to show the «RMI» dependencies between each of the RegisterCar-Sharer.jar artefacts and the CarSharing.jar artefact, as Java Remote Method Invocation is used to call operations of the CarSharing classes. This is shown in Figure 14-15.

14.5   RELATIONSHIP WITH OTHER DIAGRAMS

Deployment diagrams are relatively standalone from other UML notations. The artefacts that are deployed to nodes are themselves manifestations of components.

The choice of which nodes to deploy artefacts to and which components to map to which artefacts will be steered by the application structure (class structure) and the use-case descriptions.

14.6   DEPLOYMENT DIAGRAMS IN THE UNIFIED PROCESS

Deployment diagrams are used in the Design Workflow (see Figure 14-16) in the *Architectural Design* activity. One of the products of this activity is an **Outline Deployment Model**. The first step in the

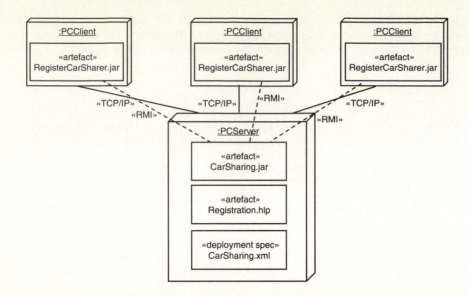

Figure 14-15: Dependencies added to the deployment diagram

activity is *Identifying Nodes and Network Configurations*, during which the architect produces a high-level architectural model of the nodes in the system and the channels of communication that they will use. Factors such as performance requirements, capacity, network protocols and data security are considered and any decisions are recorded in supporting text documents.

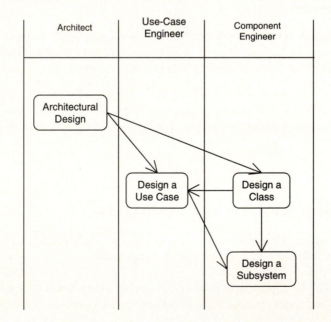

Figure 14-16: Design workflow as an activity diagram

Deployment diagrams are also used in the Implementation Workflow, which is shown in Figure 14-17.

Deployment diagrams are also used to show the allocation of artefacts to nodes.

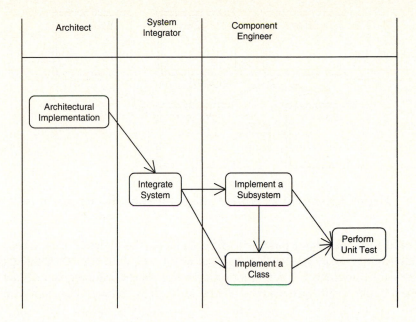

Figure 14-17: Implementation workflow as an activity diagram

Review Questions

14.1 What are the main purposes of using deployment diagrams?

14.2 Define what is meant by a node and describe its notation.

14.3 Define what is meant by a device.

14.4 Define what is meant by an execution environment and give some illustrative examples of execution environments.

14.5 Define what is meant by a communication path.

14.6 Describe two ways in which artefacts can be mapped to nodes.

14.7 Give two examples of stereotyped elements on deployment diagrams.

14.8 By what mechanism are software components mapped to nodes in the deployment model?

Solved Problems

14.1 Matching car sharers will take place on any of three client PCs, connected to a server using TCP/IP, but the **CarSharing** objects will reside on the server, so the server needs to be included in the deployment diagram. A parallel printer is attached to the server to print out details of car sharers who have been matched up. Draw the deployment diagram.

The purpose of this deployment diagram is to show the nodes that will be required in this system. The nodes are the three client PCs, the server and the printer. The communication paths between the clients and the server use TCP/IP; that between the server and the printer uses the standard parallel printer protocol. In this case, there are no additional elements or dependencies between nodes to show (Figure 14-18).

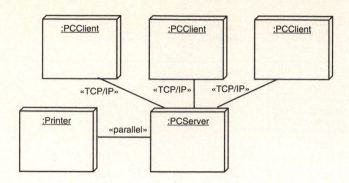

Figure 14-18: Deployment diagram showing nodes only

14.2 Next, we need to model the deployment of artefacts on the nodes in the system. The **MatchCar-Sharer.jar** artefact is to be deployed onto each client PC. The core **CarSharing.jar** artefact is to be deployed onto the main PC server along with the **MatchCarSharer.hlp** artefact and the **Match-CarSharer.xml** deployment specification. Draw a diagram showing the deployment as described here.

The purpose of this diagram is to show the deployment of specific artefacts. (Note that there are many other run-time artefacts that have to be deployed for this system to work: the Java run-time environment, printer drivers, maybe a database, even the operating system for the PCs. However, we limit this diagram to the things that we are interested in for this particular purpose.)

The user interface and control objects will run on the clients, so the **MatchCarSharer.jar** artefact needs to be on each client. The other artefacts need to be on the server (Figure 14-19).

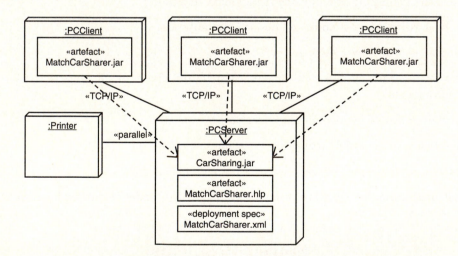

Figure 14-19: Deployment diagram with artefacts

Supplementary Problems

14.3 The **Process payments** use case runs only on a single PC Client. It is connected to a server via TCP/IP. A modem is connected to an RS232 port on the server for transferring data to the banking system. Draw a deployment diagram.

If you are unsure how to do this, you should work through the following steps.

1. Decide on the purpose of the diagram.

2. Add nodes to the diagram.

3. Add communication paths to the diagram.

4. Add other elements to the diagram, such as artefacts, if required.

5. Add dependencies between artefacts if required.

14.4 The user interface and control classes (in their .jar file) reside on the client PC; all the other component artefacts reside on the server. Draw a deployment diagram that shows the artefacts on the appropriate nodes.

14.5 The VolBank system can be described as follows.

> We use the Tomcat application server on three application servers. On each Tomcat instance, we will deploy the main VolBank application component and the ServSecure security module. On each application server, the VolBank application component will be configured by a single, reused deployment descriptor. The application servers will used a jdbc connection to the Oracle database running on the main database server.

Draw a deployment diagram to show the elements deployed on the servers. Include a communication path that uses the hypertext transfer protocol (HTTP).

CHAPTER 15

Extending UML

15.1   INTRODUCTION

In this chapter we explain the extension mechanisms that exist within UML that make it possible to extend it or to specialize it for particular kinds of systems. This is done through the use of *Profiles*, and a number of profiles are maintained by the OMG, the organization that manages the UML standard. We have explained some of these standard profiles in this chapter. There are also profiles that have been produced by individuals and organizations. We have included an example of one of these from the work of Jim Conallen on the use of UML to model web applications, originally described in an article (Conallen, 1999), and later developed in Conallen (2002).

15.2   EXTENSION MECHANISMS IN UML

UML has been designed to be extensible. The aim is to make it possible to create specialized versions of UML for modelling specific kinds of system. It should be possible to do this without having to invent new or conflicting elements of notation. Three mechanisms were introduced in UML 1.X to support the process of extending it: *stereotypes*, *tagged values* and *constraints*. However, in UML 2.0, the extension mechanisms have been specified more formally in the Infrastructure Specification (Object Management Group, 2004*b*), which defines the metamodel. We begin by explaining the way that *profiles* have been defined more formally in UML 2.0, and then explain the way that stereotypes, tagged definitions and constraints work with examples. Some of the examples that are used here come from the work of Jim Conallen on the use of UML to model web applications (Conallen, 2002).

15.2.1   Profiles

As we explained in Chapter 2, UML is based on a metamodel, and the Infrastructure Specification (Object Management Group, 2004*b*) both describes the core concepts of UML, on which the Super-structure Specification (Object Management Group, 2004*c*) is based, and forms the basis of the Meta Object Facility (MOF), the metamodel that is used to define UML. Fundamental changes to UML are defined in terms of the MOF, and any changes to UML 2.0 (for example to produce UML 2.1 in

310

the future) will be defined in terms of the MOF. The MOF can also be used to define new modelling languages. It is the basis of the Common Warehouse Metamodel (CWM), a modelling language like UML that is designed to be used to model data warehouse requirements and applications.

However, one of the aims of UML is to provide a standard that makes the development of new modelling languages unnecessary. It does this by providing extensibility mechanisms that make it possible to extend UML in order to model particular kinds of system. As an example, UML itself is not especially suitable for modelling aspects of real-time systems. Although UML 2.0 has introduced the new timing diagrams (see Section 10.9), which make it easier to model the temporal aspects of interactions, there are still some specialized features of real-time systems that are not covered by UML notation. In typical business information systems, interactions are triggered by events from human actors or other systems, and for many such interactions precise timing is not critical. Even where events are triggered by the passage of time, time is typically measured to the nearest minute or second. For example, it usually will not make much of a difference if a process that runs overnight to update some system starts at 1.00 am, 1.01 am or even 1.05 am. In real-time systems, however, events are triggered at intervals measured in milliseconds or even microseconds. The UML Profile for Schedulability, Performance, and Time Specification (Object Management Group, 2003*b*) introduces new extensions such as *Clock* and *ClockInterrupt* to define clocks whose resolution and accuracy can be defined and event triggers that are sent by such clocks.

The OMG maintains the UML Profile for Schedulability, Performance, and Time Specification as well as some other profiles. The UML specifications have also contained small example profiles. However, some profiles have been developed by individuals and other organizations. Table 15-1 lists a number of these profiles.

At the time of writing, of the formal OMG profiles, only the UML Testing Profile is based on the mechanisms introduced in UML 2.0. The others are still based on UML 1.4. the example profiles in the 2.0 specification are not complete and are intended only as illustrations of how the approach can be applied.

Profiles are extensions of packages. A profile contains the stereotypes (see next section) that extend existing metaclasses in the metamodel. Each profile must refer to an existing *reference metamodel*, such as UML. This is what distinguishes profiles from metamodels based on the MOF. As an example, if you wanted to create a modelling language for modelling quantum computing systems, you would probably create a new metamodel, based on the MOF, because the concepts could well be fundamentally different from those in conventional information systems. On the other hand, if you wanted to create a modelling language to model geographical information systems (GIS), you could create a UML profile based on the existing UML metamodel and add stereotypes that would be particularly useful in modelling geographical concepts. Figure 15-1 shows a **GIS** profile.

Figure 15-1: Example of a profile for GIS

Profiles are *applied* to packages in a model, and elements of that model are stereotyped with the stereotypes in the profile. Figure 15-2 shows the **GIS** profile applied to the **CarSharer** package in the CarMatch system.

Table 15-1: UML Profiles

Profile	Purpose	Maintainer
UML Profile for Schedulability, Performance, and Time Specification	Modelling real-time systems	OMG
UML Profile for Enterprise Application Integration (EAI)	Modelling EAI (Enterprise Application Integration)—software that integrate applications running on heterogeneous platforms	OMG
UML Profile for Enterprise Distributed Object Computing (EDOC)	Modelling business processes and collaborations of loosely coupled distributed components	OMG
UML Testing Profile	Modelling the artefacts of test systems.	OMG
Web Application Extension Profile	Modelling web applications	Jim Conallen
UML Profile for Database Design	Modelling database systems	Eric J Naiburg and Robert A Maksimchuk
UML Profile for Software Development Process	Software development—includes the widely used Boundary, Control and Entity stereotypes	OMG in UML 1.4
UML Profile for Business Modelling	Modelling relationships between business organizational units	OMG in UML 1.4
UML J2EE/EJB Component Profile Example	Example profile for modelling Enterprise Java Bean components	OMG in UML 2.0
UML .NET Component Profile Example	Example profile for modelling .Net components	OMG in UML 2.0

Figure 15-2: **GIS** profile applied to **CarSharer** package

15.2.2   Stereotypes

A stereotype is an extension to a metamodel class that is introduced in order to model a special kind of model element in a system. Stereotypes are used in UML itself, for example the «include» and «extend» stereotypes that are used to distinguish dependencies in use case diagrams.

Stereotypes are most often used to extend classes and associations but can be used to extend any metaclass. Figure 15-3 shows three stereotypes in the **GIS** profile, two of which extend the metaclass **Class** and one of which extends the metaclass **Association**.

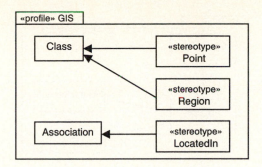

Figure 15-3: GIS profile showing the stereotypes that extend metaclasses

We can apply this profile to some of the classes in the **CarSharer** package in order to model the aspects of those classes that relate to geographical concepts. For example, a car sharer's address is a point in a geographical model, and is located in a city, which is a region. Figure 15-4 shows this approach used on some of the classes in the **CarSharer** package.

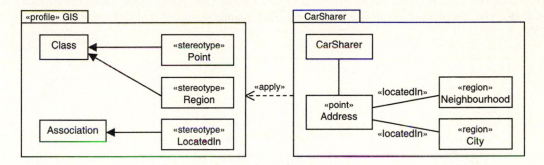

Figure 15-4: CarSharer package with stereotypes from GIS profile

More than one profile can be applied to a package, so it is possible to apply the **EJB** profile to the **CarSharer** package as well. Classes that have multiple stereotypes show the stereotype names as a comma-separated list in guillemets, as shown in Figure 15-5.

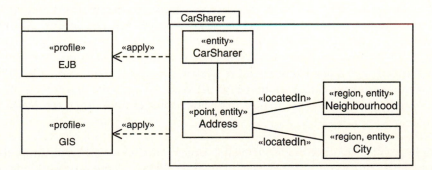

Figure 15-5: CarSharer package with stereotypes from GIS EJB profiles

If we unapply the profiles from a package, the stereotypes cease to apply to the elements of that package, any tagged values and constraints (see next two sections) will be lost, but other features of the elements in the package will be unaffected, as in Figure 15-6.

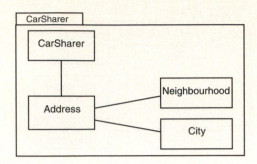

Figure 15-6: **CarSharer** package with profiles unapplied

The name of the stereotype can be displayed above the name of the class or other element or adjacent to the association in guillemets. Alternatively, the stereotype can be represented as an icon. Either this icon can be placed in the top compartment of the class symbol, at the top right, or the class symbol can be 'collapsed' and represented by the icon alone. Figure 15-7 shows these three options for classes using one of the stereotypes from Jim Conallen's Web Application Extension Profile.

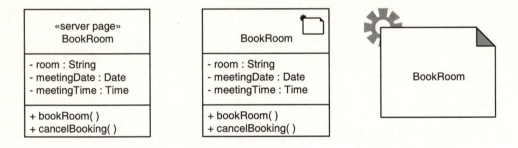

Figure 15-7: **Example of different notations for stereotypes**

Conallen's extensions to UML provide the following class stereotypes: **Server Page**, **Client Page**, **Form**, **Frameset** and **Target** among others. These stereotyped classes represent the building blocks of web applications. For example, a class stereotyped as «form» is an HTML (HyperText Markup Language) form, and a class stereotyped as «server page» is an HTML page that contains scripts that are executed on the web-server. The icons for **Form** and **Client Page** contain elements that look like HTML forms and web pages respectively; other icons are more abstract in their design. Conallen also stereotypes associations that represent the typical relationships between the elements of a web application, such as «link», «submit», «targeted link» and «build». Figure 15-8 shows some of these for a web-based room booking system.

Stereotypes can be applied to other model elements. Bruce Powel Douglass' real-time extensions to the UML notation include stereotypes for messages (Douglass, 1998). There are two kinds of stereotypes: those that relate to the arrival of the messages and those that relate to their synchronization. The two can be combined into single icons, as shown in Figure 15-9.

The ECG (Electro-Cardiogram) example indicates that a value is obtained at regular intervals by calling an operation of the target object. Note that this real-time profile is not the same as the UML Profile for Schedulability, Performance, and Time Specification, but an earlier precursor.

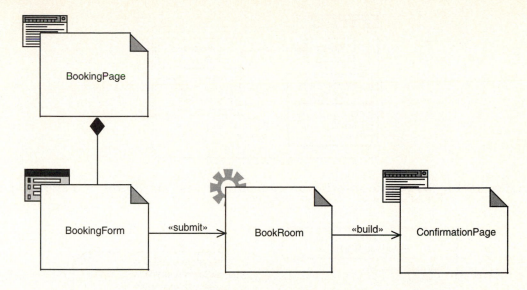

Figure 15-8: Example of stereotyped associations

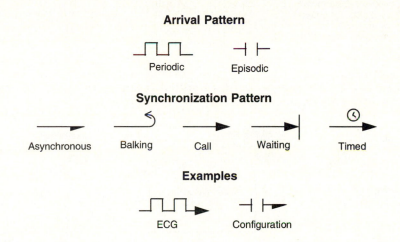

Figure 15-9: Example of stereotyped messages

15.2.3   Tagged values

Many stereotyped model elements have properties that cannot be represented graphically. These can be defined in the profile as *tagged definitions* and are shown in the model as *tagged values*. Tagged values consist of a *tag* or name and the associated value. Tagged values can be represented by strings in braces. Tagged definitions are the attributes of the stereotypes in the profile, and are typically shown in comments attached to the stereotyped model elements in the model. Figure 15-10 shows attributes of the stereotype Point, and Figure 15-11 shows how they are represented in the model.

Figure 15-12 shows the use of a tagged value to show the name and value of one of the parameters passed in from the web forms to the server program in a web application, using Conallen's extensions to UML.

If a tagged value has a Boolean value (true or false), then if the default value is true the word 'true' can be omitted, for example {abstract}. Boolean properties often have the form {isPropertyName} where

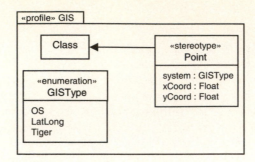

Figure 15-10: GIS profile showing an enumeration and attributes of a stereotype

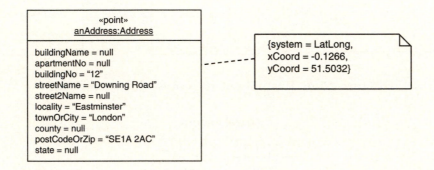

Figure 15-11: GIS tagged values applied to an instance of Address

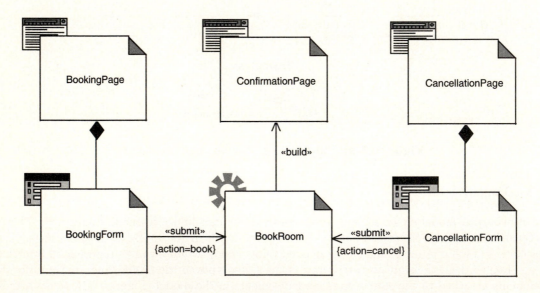

Figure 15-12: Example of tagged values

PropertyName is the name of the value that may be true or false. The property {abstract} is equivalent to {isAbstract=true}. Tagged values can also be used to provide information about the status of a model, for example {author="Simon Bennett", date=4-June-2004, status=draft}. Multiple values are separated by commas.

15.2.4   Constraints

Constraints are a standard feature of UML. They are used in combination with tagged definitions to define the characteristics of stereotypes in profiles. A constraint defines a relationship between model elements that must be true, otherwise the system described by the model ceases to be valid. Constraints are displayed in curly braces, for example {subset}. Some constraints are predefined in UML as keywords or standard elements (see Section C.1.9). For example, the {xor} constraint can be used in class diagrams to show that instances of a class participate in one of two optional associations but not both. (Simply making the multiplicity of the relationships 0..1 does not provide this piece of information.) This is a constraint on the associations and this is shown by joining them together with a dashed line that is labelled with the constraint. Figure 15-13 shows an example of this.

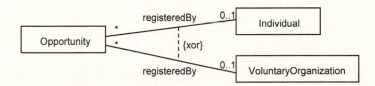

Figure 15-13: Example of {xor} constraint on associations

Constraints on classes are usually shown beneath the class symbol. Constraints on attributes or operations are shown as text strings in the appropriate compartment of the class to which they belong. Constraints that apply to a group of attributes or operations can be shown as an entry in the compartment and apply to all succeeding items until either another constraint is included or the end of the list. This implies that unconstrained attributes or operations should appear at the start of the list. When constraints apply to two symbols in a diagram the symbols are joined by a dashed line or an arrow (if the constraint has a direction), labelled with the constraint. When three or more elements in a model are constrained by a constraint, it is usually displayed in a comment, which is attached to each affected element by a dashed line. Constraints are usually written in Object Constraint Language, which is covered in detail in Chapter 13.

Constraints can be applied to derived attributes to enforce data integrity. For example, Figure 15-14 shows that the number of hours work done by a **Volunteer** must equal the total of the hours that person spent on each **VoluntaryActivity**. This also shows the use of a comment to display a constraint in a diagram.

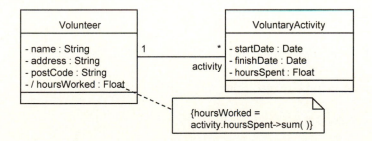

Figure 15-14: Example of a constraint on a derived attribute

Constraints are the last of the mechanisms that can be used to extend the UML notation. Many constraints are implicit in stereotyped classes. For example, the stereotyped classes of the Unified Software Development Process shown in Figure C-5 have implicit constraints: boundary classes are constrained to handle the interface between the system and the user, while entity classes are constrained not to participate in the user interface.

In a profile for GIS, it would be necessary to introduce a constraint that if the **GISType** of a class stereotyped as «point» is **LatLong** then the values for x-coordinates must be between −180 and +180, and for y-coordinates between −90 and +90. This constraint is shown in the OCL below, which could be attached to the **Point** stereotype definition in a comment.

```
context Point
    inv:self.system = LatLong implies
        xCoord >=  −180 and
        xCoord <= 180 and
        yCoord >=  −90 and
        yCoord <= 90
```

Constraints can be applied to models other than class diagrams. For example, constraints are used in sequence diagrams to show timing constraints between events (see Chapter 9).

Review Questions

15.1 Define what is meant by a profile.

15.2 How are profiles applied to models?

15.3 Define what is meant by a stereotype.

15.4 How are stereotypes used to extend UML?

15.5 How are stereotypes shown in a profile?

15.6 Describe the three ways in which stereotyped classes can be represented in a diagram.

15.7 Give an example of a stereotyped class.

15.8 Give an example of a stereotype of another kind of model element.

15.9 Define what is meant by a tagged definition.

15.10 How are tagged definitions shown in a profile?

15.11 Define what is meant by a tagged value.

15.12 How are tagged values displayed in a diagram?

15.13 Define what is meant by a constraint.

15.14 How are constraints displayed in a diagram?

15.15 Give an example of a constraint.

15.16 What is the name of the language often used to represent constraints?

Solved Problems

15.1 We want to extend UML to cover applications developed to use Wireless Access Protocol (WAP) and Wireless Markup Language (WML). These two standards are used to deliver Internet content to wireless devices such as mobile telephones and personal digital assistants (PDAs). Here is a summary of how WML works.

WML uses the metaphor of decks of cards. An application is typically made up of a single deck. Each deck consists of a number of cards; each card displays a screen-full of information on the screen of the mobile device. The whole deck is transferred onto the mobile device, and the user then moves between cards. This saves the delay associated with loading pages. The content of decks is transferred to the mobile device using a binary format to minimize the bandwidth required (GSM telephones transfer data at 9600 baud).

What stereotyped classes and associations might be created to extend UML to cover these elements of WAP?

The Application is probably the first class. This seems to involve server-side and client-side pages, but we know only about the client-side. An Application «delivers» a Deck to the mobile device and the Deck consists of Cards. The user can move to the «next» Card or to the «previous» Card.

Using stereotype strings displayed with the class name, we might develop something like Figure 15-15 for a hypothetical deck of cards containing static content about CarMatch. (You might like to try to devise suitable icons.)

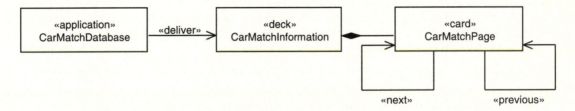

Figure 15-15: Possible solution for WAP/WML extensions to UML

15.2 How would these stereotypes be defined in a profile?

Application, Deck and Card are all extensions to the metaclass Class, while Delivers, Next and Previous are all extensions to the metaclass Association. These are shown in Figure 15-16.

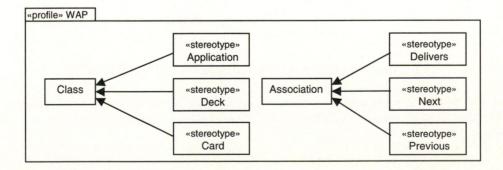

Figure 15-16: WAP profile showing the stereotypes that extend metaclasses

15.3 Different mobile devices, telephones and PDAs have different sized screens and navigational techniques. The browser on a mobile device is known as the user-agent and transfers information about the device it is running on to the server, so that appropriately formatted cards are sent to the mobile device.

We have not included the user-agent or device as classes in Figure 15-15, but what values might be sent from the client to the server to ensure that correctly formatted WML pages are delivered? How could these be represented as tagged definitions of the **Device** and **UserAgent** stereotypes?

We might want two values, one for the name of the user-agent and one for name of the device. This assumes that the server keeps some database of devices and their characteristics. Alternatively, it might be better to transmit the relevant characteristics of the device, for example: {useragent = "MobileBrowser 1.21", width = 640, height = 240, colour = false, greyscale = true, shades = 16, navigation = Touchscreen}. These characteristics could be attributes of the **Device** stereotype, as in Figure 15-17.

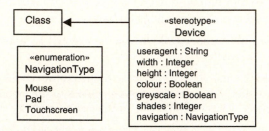

Figure 15-17: Stereotype for Device

15.4 The user moves through a set of cards in a deck from start to finish. It is possible to move forwards through the deck unless the card displayed is the last in the deck? Similarly, it is possible to move backwards through the deck until the first card is reached?

What constraints might be applied to the «next» and «previous» associations defined above?

The obvious constraint is that the user can only move forwards to the end or move back to the beginning of the deck. Moving to the end does not result in looping back to the beginning. This could be represented by two constraints, one each on the next and previous associations. These are shown in Figure 15-18.

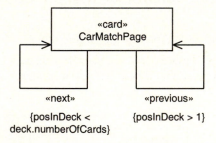

Figure 15-18: Possible constraints on associations

Note that posInDeck would need to be added as an attribute of the stereotype Card and numberOfCards would have to be added as an attribute to the stereotype Deck so that these could be used as tagged values and in constraints.

Supplementary Problems

15.5 Draw the stereotypes **Deck** and **Card** with the attributes **numberOfCards** and **posInDeck**.

15.6 Design your own icon to represent the stereotyped class **Device**.

15.7 Extend the WAP Profile to show a stereotyped association, **Runs**, which will connect the classes **Device** and **Application**.

15.8 Draw a class diagram showing the classes **CellPhone** and **PDA** stereotyped as «device».

15.9 Enterprise Information Portals (EIPs) are becoming widespread as a way of delivering a range of different types of information to employees of an organization.

Typically a portal application runs on a server. It delivers web pages to the client. The user must log in to the portal, sending their username and password to the application. Having logged in they are presented with a number of pages. They can move to any page by clicking on its number in a list of pages. Each page is made up of panes. Panes are small windows within the page presenting different kinds of information (for example, a calendar, a notice board, a search engine, a table of stock prices). If the user does not interact with the portal for a specified period of time, they are logged out, and the next time they attempt to change anything on the portal it will take them to the login page.

Suggest some stereotyped classes and associations that you could use to create a Portal profile.

15.10 What tagged definitions might be needed in this particular extension of UML?

15.11 What constraints might apply to a «moveTo» association between pages?

15.12 Choose some class of applications for which you think it would be useful to define a UML profile. Define stereotypes, tagged definitions and constraints.

CHAPTER 16

Software Tools for UML

16.1 INTRODUCTION

The production of software models for any substantial system is a time-consuming task, and almost universally requires the use of computer-based tools (sometimes known as CASE tools. CASE stands for Computer Assisted Software Engineering or sometimes Computer Aided Software Engineering). Software tools aim to automate as far as possible the software engineering process. Pressman (2004) characterizes a good workshop for the production of any artefact, be it a car, a piece of furniture or a computer program, as having three parts: there is a set of tools to aid the building of the product; there is an organized layout to enable the tools to be applied effectively; finally there is a skilled team of craftspeople who know how to apply the tools. This chapter will look at some of the key characteristics of UML-based software modelling tools, and how these relate to other tools used in the development of substantial software systems.

The modelling of a system is part of the much broader aspects of the construction of a system. Computer system development is a people-intensive activity. All but the smallest projects require co-operation among a wide number of stakeholders, including the sponsors and customers of the proposed system, the potential users, project managers, analysts, developers, testers, technical deployment teams, and finally the actual users themselves. An essential factor in effective development is good communication. Comprehensive and consistent use of an integrated suite of software tools to support the various work products of a software engineering process can be an important facilitator of good communication.

UML is a key enabler of the communication within a project, providing integration between software development tools through technical interchange of software models, and supplying a standard presentation of models to the many people involved in a project. In the process of development, there may be a number of software tools involved, from project inception through to project delivery, covering business analysis, requirements analysis, project management, through software modelling to implementation, testing and deployment. Software modelling tools can integrate with each other and with a variety of other tools, such as planning and testing tools. For the purposes of this chapter we shall concentrate on software tools that specifically incorporate UML, and that are focused on the generation and management of software models.

An appropriate software modelling tool can assist you in drawing the various UML diagrams, and usually much more. Different tools have different focuses and different ways of achieving results, and often incorporate additional or alternative non-UML notations; increasingly though, because of the development of the UML standard, there is growing commonality in the presentation and content of the software modelling aspects of many tools. Switching between modelling tools is more straightforward if they each comply with the UML standard; one of the key goals of UML has been to reduce the amount of wasted time and effort necessary to switch between notations when developers move between projects, or when projects need to change tools.

Software modelling tools contribute to model development in a variety of ways. Firstly, they aid in the construction of accurate UML diagrams, and provide checks to make sure that the diagrams are complete and consistent with each other. A good modelling tool will organize UML elements in a repository that keeps objects, activities, states, relationships, diagrams and so on grouped together. The various diagrams represent different views of the underlying repository that supplies the storage of the model elements and their linkages. The development process often produces many documents other than UML diagrams, such as use case descriptions, and a modelling tool should be able to integrate these into the repository. As all but the most trivial projects involve a number of people co-operating, the repository needs to be able to cope with people sharing different elements, and either allow shared access to the repository with some means of protecting against conflict, or some means of merging and reconciling repositories. The end result of any development project is a system, and software modelling tools offer a variety of means of generating program code, or importing program code, and even the generation of test plans.

It would be very foolish today to embark on a substantial IT development without incorporating a comprehensive set of computer-based tools, including a software modelling tool, to facilitate the project. Of course, use of IT tools does not ensure an effective development. Management and maturity of the organization are critical too. Jacobson et al. (1992) discuss organizations at different levels of maturity. At the initial level, no documented method is in place, and developers are working in their own, often quite diverse, ways. At the second level, an informal method is widely adopted. At the third level a formal method is in place. At the fourth level, there is close management tracking of the application of the method and the productivity of the development process. At the highest level, systematic changes are made to the method to optimize it for the organization. A modelling tool may be used at any of these levels of organization, but is likely to be most effective at the third level and above. As with any craft, good tools do not ensure success, but they are very important in helping the craftspeople achieve a good product efficiently and effectively.

16.2 UML AND MODELLING TOOLS

UML has a number of primary goals that relate to the use of modelling tools. It is a notation that allows for the specification of systems independently of the chosen programming language. It is designed to be extensible, so that other modelling features can be integrated into UML models. It is intended to encourage the growth of the object tools market, and to support higher-level development concepts such as frameworks and patterns.

Programming-language independence is essential, partly because languages are textual and there is a great need for a visual representation of a system, partly because systems are commonly built from a number of components implemented in different languages. However, there is a strong correspondence between object-oriented languages and UML. A language-independent description of the system is important for many stakeholders in a project, while linkage between UML and the programming language is extremely valuable during the construction phase. Modelling tools can support this linkage through automatic generation of program code and reverse engineering of program code to construct UML models.

Extensibility is a core aspect of UML, through tagged values and stereotypes (see Chapter 15). This is important because UML cannot possibly cover all possible aspects of software modelling and remain concise enough to be manageable. Modelling tools need to support extensibility and also depend on this for implementing many aspects of the software development process such as the embedding of documentation, integrating programming code into the models, and linkage to other tools.

The UML has enhanced the object tools market by shifting the area of competition away from notation. Modelling tools add value to the software development process over and above providing a modelling notation, by enforcing methods and by integrating with other tools and with programming languages; it is in these areas that UML-based software modelling tools compete rather than on the notation itself. The use of UML makes it easier for developers to move between projects using different tools, and between different tools in the same project.

16.3   FEATURES OF UML MODELLING TOOLS

16.3.1   UML Diagrams

A good modelling tool will provide a means of drawing the majority of the UML diagrams, and certainly the core diagrams such as use case, sequence, state machines, activities and class diagrams. A modelling tool will generally only allow legal diagrams, and can do some elementary checking of consistency, say by preventing cycles of inheritance, or highlighting potential name conflicts. This is particularly important when a number of people are working on a system and consistency between parallel development of the models is essential.

The construction of diagrams is usually a drawing activity, supplemented by entry of detailed information on UML elements through forms. For example, a typical tool will allow the drawing of a class by clicking on a class icon and placing the icon on a background. Completion of details such as attributes will involve typing into a form the name of the attribute and choosing the type from a list. Pre-built elements can be incorporated on diagrams by dragging and dropping from the repository or choosing from pick-lists. Diagrams and the repository are complementary views of UML elements such as classes and use cases, and modelling tools can provide different ways of managing these elements.

The UML has emerged from a number of earlier notations, and many modelling tools have evolved from these notations. At the time of writing, many tools still incorporate elements of an earlier notation (such as Booch or OMT), either as an alternative or alongside the UML notation. This is partly to support projects that started before the UML was defined or became widely adopted, and partly because the construction of modelling tools is a large-scale undertaking itself and the vendors of these packages may still be in the process of catching up. There are also other notations, such as business process modelling and architectural modelling, which the UML does not fully cover, and these may be incorporated alongside the UML in a modelling tool.

16.3.2   Compliance to UML Standards

The UML is a standard, and modelling tools should state to what extent they comply with the standard. The UML 2.0 Specification provides a number of compliance points, including the diagrams (use case, class, state machine, activity, sequence, collaboration, component, and deployment), UML profiles (software development process, and business modelling), and OCL. Each of these can be rated as 'no', 'partial', 'complete' or 'interchange', the latter implying full compliance and ability to exchange through XMI. There are other elements of compliance with the UML metamodel that we shall not consider here—these ensure that the semantics of the model elements used to compose the diagrams are standard. Compliance with a diagram implies being able to support all the associated adornments (stereotypes, tagged values, constraints).

To accurately declare that a modelling tool is compliant to the UML Specification, the vendor should refer to the language elements and the compliance points, rather than simply state that they are 'UML compliant', and the version of UML that they are complying with. Modelling tools may not comply with the whole of the UML Specification, but partial compliance will significantly impact the interchangeability of models. Care is advised in the selection of modelling tools, and due consideration is needed to make sure where possible that vendor-independence is maintained in the application of tools to prevent projects from becoming subject to the whims or problems of suppliers.

16.3.3   The Repository

The repository in a modelling tool holds all the UML elements, such as objects, attributes, operations, activities, states, relationships, as well as the diagrams themselves. UML diagrams are in fact only views of the repository. It is common to produce many different views of the repository with an element or set of elements repeated in different diagrams. For example, it is often useful to construct a class diagram for a use case to describe object collaborations in the use case; as a class usually supports more than one use case, the class may appear in multiple diagrams.

The repository is usually organized in a hierarchical way, much as the file store in an operating system is organized, and browsers are supplied to view the hierarchy. Figure 16-1 illustrates a possible organization of a repository. The repository is split into requirements, analysis, design and implementation models. Each high-level model is then broken down into packages, and under the packages are the UML elements and diagrams that constitute that model. The repository will be substantial, typically holding hundreds or thousands of elements even for a small project, and the view of the repository will allow opening and closing of parts of the hierarchy to zoom in and out of aspects of the project. The package concept of UML is particularly important for structuring the view of the repository.

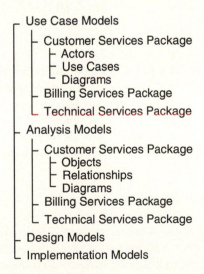

Figure 16-1: A typical repository structure in a modelling tool

The repository in some modelling tools can also incorporate non-UML elements. Commonly, other documents, such as word processing documents, can be linked into the repository and accessed through the repository. Linkage may be made out to other software development tools, such as those supporting requirements analysis. Some modelling tools also incorporate links from the repository to programming language source code.

16.3.4   Shared Access to the Repository

For any but the most trivial project, the development of UML models will require a number of people to develop models simultaneously. There are two basic approaches to this. The first is to allow people to have separate copies of the repository, and to merge those repositories periodically, checking for mutual consistency. The second and much better approach is to provide a single shared repository, with analysts and developers checking out parts of the repository they are working on. Variants of these are commonly used.

If a single repository is used, then team members are allowed, subject to privileges, to check out elements of the repository. While these are checked out, other team members may not update them, but usually are allowed to read a write-locked version that has been checked out. Once a person has checked out a set of elements, he or she is allowed to merge them back into the repository, overwriting the version that was checked out, and release them for others to view and update. A middle-ground option that can be used is to break a large repository into subrepositories. These subrepositories are then checked out, modified, merged back and checked in.

16.3.5   Integrity of the Repository

A key role of the repository is to validate entries and maintain integrity. Changes to a model element may have impact across a number of other model elements. For example, removing an operation on a class may affect the collaborations represented by (for example) a sequence diagram. A modelling tool will adopt a variety of tactics to ensure that consistency and integrity are maintained, from preventing illegal changes, through warnings, to consistency checks initiated by the user.

16.3.6   Version Control

At critical milestones in the lifetime of a project, there will be versions of the software models that need to be stored as baseline versions that represent the current state of the project. This may be for a release of the products, or some interim snapshot so that the project can be rolled back if there are problems with the development for some reason. UML modelling tools either need to support version control directly, or integrate with some version control package to manage this. Version control will continue throughout the lifetime of a software product as new releases are issued.

16.3.7   Traceability and Change Management

During the life cycle of any project, changes are made to the requirements. This may take place before the initial delivery of a software product, and frequently through the life of the product as improvements or adjustments are necessary to support a business. Changes to product specifications have implications for models.

As changes are requested, it is necessary to trace through all aspects of the system that are affected by the change, and protect those that are not affected. A large part of the requirements will be held outside a UML compliant modelling tool, for example, in text documents. The notion of use case is the key linkage between the analysis models and user requirements. The grouping of objects through collaborations to support a use case makes it possible to trace through from a requirement to the use case that supports the requirement. From the use case it is possible to trace the classes that support the design to realize the use case, and ultimately the classes used to implement the design.

Modelling tools assist in this by integrating with requirements capture and programming tools, and by structuring the repository in ways that support traceability (say by grouping communication diagrams with the use cases they support). The issue of traceability is project-wide, not just related to models, and requires careful application of a method, such as the Unified Process. Modelling tools and UML are facilitators in this process.

16.3.8   Tagged Values

The UML supports *tagged values* that may be attached to any model element (see Chapter 15). This is a simple mechanism for attaching information needed beyond the basic semantics of the UML. It is a pair usually represented as {tag = value} where **tag** is a name that indicates the property and **value** is an arbitrary value expressible as a string. Modelling tools use this for a variety of purposes. Commonly there is a tag for documentation of the model element, allowing the storage of a textual description of (for example) classes and use cases. Some modelling tools support tags for recording the primary and alternative paths in use cases, thereby embedding the use case descriptions in the repository. Tagged values are sometimes used to structure model elements such as use cases and operations, by allowing pre-conditions and post-conditions to be attached. Linkages to code can be embedded to provide tighter integration between the modelling tool and the programming environment.

16.3.9   Icons

We have seen the standard icons defined by UML, such as for an actor. UML allows the attachment of an icon to a stereotype. All objects with that stereotype may then, optionally, be displayed with the icon. Figure 16-2 shows a **worker** stereotype from the UML profile for business modelling displayed both as an icon and as a standard class notation with the stereotype name in guillemets. Modelling tools are free to add extensions of this type to provide improved visual descriptions of models.

Figure 16-2: A worker stereotype from the UML business modelling profile in standard and iconic notation

16.3.10   Code Generation

To improve the speed and accuracy of programming, many modelling tools offer code generation of programs and database schemas. At the simplest level, this involves the generation of classes in the programming language syntax, for the programmer to complete, and database table definitions. Some modelling tools also provide generation of the logic code from models such as sequence diagrams. Currently the degree of integration between modelling tools and programming environments varies considerably. At one end, the modelling tool can be treated as a programming environment itself. At the other, the modelling tool is only a way of bootstrapping the development of the code.

Modelling tools can also import programs and database schemas and construct a UML repository from them. The amount of information that can be imported is again very variable, and dependent on the modelling tool and the programming language. At the very least, a set of classes can usually be generated, with operations and attributes defined.

Most modelling tools offer some notion of *round trip engineering*. This means that some of the program code can be generated from the modelling tool and modified in the programming environment. Then the modified program imported and any changes made in the programming environment are reflected in the modelling tool repository. This is a very valuable facility, as it provides a means of keeping the implementation, the analysis and the design models in step, and thereby maintaining traceability. Some modelling tools now integrate much more tightly with code, and the modelling tool can be seen as very much an Interactive Development Environment (IDE) with the code and models tightly coupled; changes to models are instantly reflected in changes to code.

16.3.11   Model Interchange between CASE Tools and Other Tools

UML models can be described in a standard textual language, known as XMI (Chapter 2), which is an acronym for XML Metadata Interchange. XML stands for eXtensible Markup Language, which is an international standard for the description of documents. Modelling tools commonly have the facility to produce an XMI version of the models they contain, and to import XMI models.

This means that software tools supporting XMI can exchange models. There are many good reasons for this. Some modelling tools are tightly integrated with a particular development environment, and XMI allows for the import of UML models developed elsewhere. Increasingly, large systems are built by integrating subsystems that may be developed in different languages by different suppliers, and access to the various models used to develop the subsystems is essential. XMI permits the choice of the best tool for a particular task, with minimal cost in translation.

16.3.12   Relationship between Modelling Tools and Other Tools

Modelling tools support only certain parts of a project, and UML is designed to cover specifically the modelling aspects of the system development. Modelling tools usually link to other tools. At the simplest level, word processor documents can be linked in to the models to support requirements capture and documentation of aspects of modelling not supported by UML, such as textual descriptions of use cases. Requirements analysis tools exist that can be linked in to modelling tools to provide traceability between model elements and requirements statements. Modelling tools are commonly linked to development tools such as Interactive Development Environments that support the development of executable code. They may also link to testing tools for the generation, tracking and (sometimes) execution of test plans, and to version control packages to support versioning of systems. The UML and the XMI interchange formats are a key element in facilitating these linkages.

16.3.13   Method Support and Enforcement

The UML is a notation, not a method. Most tools aim at supporting a particular software development method. This may be based on the Unified Process, perhaps with a proprietary slant, or some other method. Method support is provided in a number of ways. At the elementary level, the tool will incorporate guidance in the form of help text and supporting documentation. Repositories can be structured according to the rules of the method—some tools permit you to rearrange the structure of the repository to adapt it to different methods. In some cases the modelling tool may enforce the rules of a particular methodology. Tools increasingly incorporate some critiquing facilities, including measures of design quality as well as checking accuracy and consistency of models.

16.3.14   Frameworks and Patterns

A *framework* is a reusable design that can be adapted to support and enhance the development of systems and to supply a generic structure to systems developed by an organization. *Design patterns* are solutions to common software development problems. Together they aid in the standardization and optimization of approaches to software development. A variety of types of framework exist. There are technical frameworks, such as the classes in the Java Development Kit, that provide pre-defined classes and components for a variety of programming tasks. There are application frameworks, such as that developed by the IBM San Francisco project, that focus on the development of generic classes and components for business systems (accounting systems, etc). There are development-oriented frameworks that structure the repository according to some development method such as the Unified Process. Some modelling tools permit the incorporation and definition of frameworks, represented as a set of pre-defined models available at the start of a project, and have a catalogue for storing and retrieving patterns. Depending on the approach to software development adopted, these may be of significant value. Patterns and frameworks are explained in more detail in Chapter 17.

16.3.15   OCL

At the time of writing, the OCL is often partially integrated into modelling tools for the definition of constraints. Full integration with generation of code to check pre-conditions is not yet achieved. Modelling tools usually allow constraints to be expressed in any textual form, as intended by the UML Specification, which may incorporate programming language constructs.

16.3.16   Profiles

UML supplies a set of profiles to ease certain types of modelling. These profiles typically consist of a set of stereotypes that focus the UML classes on types of software component. The current profiles include those listed in Table 16-1.

Table 16-1: UML profiles

Subject	Purpose
CORBA	For expressing the semantics of CORBA IDL using UML.
Enterprise Application Integration	For information about exchanging application interfaces.
Enterprise Distributed Computing	For the development of component-based distributed systems.
Schedulability, Performance and Time	For the development of real-time systems.
Testing	For designing artefacts of a testing system.

If a project covers some aspect of these, then tool support would be very valuable. Profiles are covered in more detail in Chapter 15.

16.3.17   Document Generation

UML models are of value to a wide number of stakeholders in a project. For example, end-users may wish to see use case models in the requirements capture phase. Modelling tools support the production of paper-based documentation, merging UML diagrams with text and tabular descriptions of model elements. Some tools permit generation of web-based views of their repositories, so that access to the models can be made widely available over an intranet to people without access to the modelling tool.

Review Questions

16.1 Are software tools just for UML?

16.2 In what way does UML support modelling tools?

16.3 What is XMI?

16.4 What is a repository in a modelling tool?

16.5 What is a tagged value?

16.6 Why are tagged values important?

16.7 What is *round trip engineering*?

Solved Problem

16.1 The project manager for the CarMatch system development wishes to choose a suite of software tools, including a modelling tool that supports UML. He has two months in which to select the suite of tools. Knowing that the market is unlikely to provide the perfect tool he commissions a consultant to run a tendering process for the supply of modelling tools. What might be the key questions that the consultant incorporates in the tender document regarding the software modelling tools?

The consultant provides a general section requesting information on prices, technical platforms and requirements, the supplier's track record, market penetration, turnover and profitability, plus a request for reference sites. She then adds the following specific questions relating to the software modelling tools:

1. Please state the compliance of the tool to the UML standard, specifically rating the compliance of the tool to the diagrams: use case, class, statechart, activity, sequence, communication, component, and deployment.
2. How is shared access to the repository managed?
3. How are repositories merged?
4. How is integrity of the repository managed?
5. How is version control of the repository managed?
6. What other modelling tools does this tool integrate with?
7. How is traceability from requirements through to implementation supported?
8. What notations over and above UML are supported by the tool?
9. For which programming languages does the tool support code generation, reverse engineering or both?
10. Is XMI supported?
11. What methods are supported by the tool?
12. What support is there for document generation, including web-based documentation?

Supplementary Problem

16.2 The VolBank project manager has not supplied an adequate budget for modelling tools to support the development of the system. Supply a one-page memo that argues for the use of a tool for software modelling. Highlight the benefits of using a software modelling tool that supports UML, and the risks involved in not using a modelling tool.

CHAPTER 17

Design Patterns

17.1 INTRODUCTION

Patterns are not a part of core UML but are widely used in object-oriented system design, and UML provides mechanisms that can be used to represent patterns in graphical form. For these two reasons, we have included this chapter about design patterns.

A *design pattern* is a solution to a common problem in the design of computer systems. It is a solution that has been recognized as worth documenting so that other developers can apply it to solve the same problem when they come up against it. In the same way as object-oriented analysis and design claims to promote reuse of class libraries and components, the use of patterns is claimed to promote the reuse of standard solutions to frequently occurring design problems.

Patterns are discovered, not invented: they are techniques that people have used for some time to solve particular problems, and which have been recognized as good solutions; they are not clever tricks that someone has just invented to solve a problem and then decided to promote to other developers.

UML includes some concepts that can be used to document patterns. The *collaboration* is the one that is most often used. However, to document a pattern fully, a class diagram and some kind of interaction diagram are typically also used.

Before giving examples and explaining how they can be represented in UML, we shall first explain their origin.

17.2 ORIGIN OF DESIGN PATTERNS

The idea of using patterns comes from architecture. Alexander, Ishikawa, Silverstein, Jacobson, Fiksdahl-King & Angel (1977) first proposed the idea of using standard patterns in the design of buildings and communities. They identified and documented related patterns that could be used to solve recurring problems in the design of buildings. These patterns are ways of designing buildings that have evolved over hundreds of years as solutions to the problems faced by people constructing buildings of all sorts. The best solutions have come through to the present day by a process of natural selection. These patterns have authority—as good solutions—without being the work of any one individual. Although software development does not have the same history as architecture, patterns have been found that represent good solutions to the problems of constructing software systems.

Evitts (2000) provides a summary history of the way that patterns infiltrated the world of software development. (His book is about patterns that can be used in UML rather than UML representations of more general patterns.) He credits Kent Beck and Ward Cunningham with the development of the first patterns in their work with Smalltalk reported at the OOPSLA'87 conference. These were five patterns found by Beck and Cunningham in conjunction with the users of a system that they were designing. These five patterns applied to the design of user interfaces in a windowing environment.

During the early 1990s patterns were discussed at conference workshops, and many attempts were made to draw up lists of patterns and to document them. The participants were driven by the need to provide some kind of structure at a higher conceptual level than objects and classes that could be used to organize classes. This was the result of a recognition that the use of object-oriented techniques alone was not delivering the claimed improvements in quality and effectiveness of software development. Patterns were seen as a way of organizing object-oriented development and encapsulating experience and good practice.

In 1994 the first Pattern Languages of Program Design (PLoP) conference was held. Also that year, *Design Patterns: Elements of Reusable Object-Oriented Software* (Gamma, Johnson, Helm & Vlissides, 1995) (sic) was published in time for OOPSLA'94. This was the seminal text in the emergence of patterns for software development; its contribution was to structure patterns into a *catalogue* with a standard format that was used to document each pattern. It is known as the *Gang of Four* book, and its patterns are often referred to as the Gang of Four patterns. Other books on patterns appeared in the following couple of years, and other 'standard' formats were proposed.

The first patterns were exclusively design patterns, intended to solve problems facing designers. Since then other kinds of pattern have emerged, notably analysis patterns, which represent concepts that are used in domain modelling, and organization patterns, which propose solutions to the common problems of managing business processes, including software development.

Frameworks and *idioms* are related to patterns, but should be distinguished from them. A framework is more comprehensive than a pattern and is essentially a partially completed application that can be applied to a specific domain. For example, a financial framework would contain a set of financial classes in relationships determined by patterns, and could be developed to produce a financial application. (In UML, *framework* has a specific meaning and is defined as either a stereotyped package that contains mainly patterns or an architectural pattern that provides an extensible template for applications in a specific domain.) An idiom is a set of guidelines for how to implement aspects of a software system in a particular language. Coplien (1992) first published a set of idioms for use in C++. These idioms captured the experience of expert C++ programmers in a way that could be used by inexpert programmers facing common problems in writing C++ programs.

17.3 DOCUMENTING PATTERNS

Patterns are grouped together in *pattern catalogues* and *pattern languages*. A pattern catalogue is a group of related patterns that can be used either together or separately. A pattern language documents patterns that work together and can be applied to solving problems in a particular domain. An example of a pattern language is the Java 2 Platform Enterprise Edition (J2EE) patterns (Crupi, Malks &

Alur, 2003), which provide a wide range of patterns that can be applied to the design of enterprise Java systems.

Patterns are documented using templates, which provide headings under which to enter details of the pattern and how it works that will enable users to decide whether it is an appropriate solution to their problem and, if it is, to apply it to that problem. There are different templates available; two of the most widely used are Coplien's (Coplien & Schmidt, 1995) and Gamma's (Gamma et al., 1995). The headings listed below are from Coplien's template.

- *Name*—The name of the pattern, ideally describing the solution in some way.

- *Problem*—The question that the pattern helps to resolve.

- *Context*—The context of the application of the pattern: architectural or business context and the critical success factors for the pattern that will make it work in a particular situation.

- *Forces*—The constraints or issues that must be resolved by the pattern. The forces create an imbalance, which the pattern helps to balance.

- *Solution*—The solution that balances the conflicting forces and fits the context.

- *Sketch*—Symbolic sketch of the forces and how they are resolved.

- *Resulting context*—The context as it is after being changed by the solution.

- *Rationale*—The reason and motivation for the pattern.

Documentation of patterns can include sample code and diagrams. UML diagrams can be used to illustrate the way that each pattern works. The choice of diagram type depends on the nature of the pattern. Design patterns have been classified as *creational*, *structural* and *behavioural*.

- *Creational*—Concerned with the creation of object instances, separating the way in which this is done from the application.

- *Structural*—Concerned with the structural relationships between instances, particularly using generalization, aggregation and composition.

- *Behavioural*—Concerned with the assignment of the responsibility for providing functionality among the objects in the system.

For structural patterns, class diagrams are more likely to provide the necessary information about the pattern; for behavioural patterns, interaction diagrams or statechart diagrams will illustrate the way that the functionality will be delivered; for creational patterns, the choice of diagram will depend on the nature of the pattern (whether it is more about behaviour or structure).

However, the UML Specification (Object Management Group, 2004a) specifically proposes collaborations as the way to model patterns, and these are explained in the next section.

17.4   HOW PATTERNS ARE REPRESENTED IN UML

One of the goals of UML 1.3 was 'to support higher-level development concepts such as components, collaborations, frameworks and patterns' (Object Management Group, 1999, p.1–5) although this statement is no longer in the UML 2.0 Specification (Object Management Group, 2004a). The intention is to support these concepts by providing a mechanism for clearly defining their semantics, so that it is easier to use them to gain the benefits of reuse that are claimed for object-oriented methods. The structural aspects of patterns are presented in UML using collaborations (see Section 17.4.1). A collaboration is defined in the UML Specification (Object Management Group, 2004c) as follows: 'A collaboration describes a structure of collaborating elements (roles), each performing a specialized function, which collectively accomplish some desired functionality.' It goes on to say that a collaboration 'defines a set of cooperating entities to be played by its instances (its roles), as well as a set of connectors that define the communication paths between the participating instances'. Collaborations describe the participants in the kinds of interactions explained in Chapters 9 and 10 that enable object-oriented systems to deliver functionality of value to the users of those systems.

17.4.1 Notation of Collaborations

Before discussing patterns in more detail, it is worth describing the notation of collaborations.

Collaborations can be represented as a dashed oval with the name of the collaboration inside the oval or beneath it (see Figure 17-1).

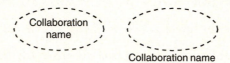

Figure 17-1: Collaboration notation

This notation can be used to show the relationship between collaborations and the use cases that they realize, as in Figure 17-2.

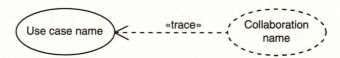

Figure 17-2: Collaboration «trace» relationship

A similar notation can also be used to show the relationship between a collaboration and some behaviour of the class that it realizes, as shown in Figure 17-3.

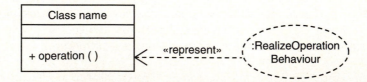

Figure 17-3: Collaboration «represent» relationship

However, these relationships are not usually represented explicitly in diagrams but by links between diagrams in a CASE tool. The UML Specification (Object Management Group, 2004a) describes the «trace» relationship as linking model elements that represent the same concept in different models.

The dashed oval notation can also be used to show a collaboration in terms of the objects that participate in it. In this case, the collaboration is linked to the classes of those objects by lines labelled with the names of the roles of the participants, as in Figure 17-4.

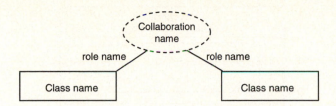

Figure 17-4: Collaboration roles

This notation can be used with stereotyped classes and the «trace» dependency to show the classes involved in the realization of a use case, as in Figure 17-5.

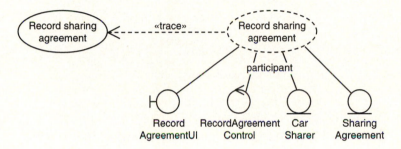

Figure 17-5: Classes involved in the collaboration that realizes the use case Record Sharing Agreement

There is an alternative notation that shows the collaboration as a large oval containing the roles that participate in the collaboration, as in Figure 17-6.

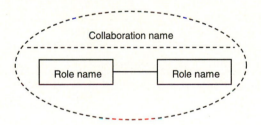

Figure 17-6: Collaboration as a large oval containing participants

Collaborations can also be shown as a composite structure diagram, as in Figure 17-7. In this figure, the sequence diagram frame refers to the sequence diagram that documents the behaviour of the collaboration.

Composite structure diagrams are used to show the internal structures of classifiers (as in Section 5.3.2 for composition by containment), the way that ports are used to show how classifiers interact with their environment (as in Section 7.6.2) and the structure of collaborations.

17.4.2   Notation of Patterns

It is possible to represent a design pattern using collaboration notation. The names of the types involved can be shown using the template or parameterized notation (described in Chapter 7), as in Figure 17-8.

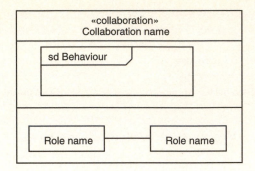

Figure 17-7: Collaboration as a composite structure diagram

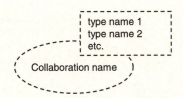

Figure 17-8: Template (parameterized) collaboration

A template collaboration is represented by a dashed ellipse with a dashed rectangle overlaying its top right-hand quadrant.

The types of the roles played by participating classes are written in the dashed rectangle as in Figure 17-9.

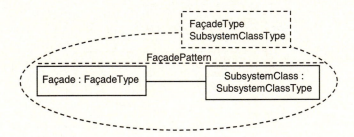

Figure 17-9: The roles and types involved in the Façade pattern

The Façade pattern is widely used in systems where the developers want to hide the complexity of a subsystem behind a single class, which provides an interface to its functionality. This is a common problem in system design. If a subsystem contains a lot of classes that collaborate together to provide the services of that subsystem, there is a risk of creating a complex interface to that subsystem. Every class might have several operations, and other subsystems will need to be capable of sending messages to instances of each class. This creates a high degree of *coupling* between the subsystems: changes to the classes in the subsystem providing the services will result in a lot of work tracking down all the places in other subsystems where the operations of all these classes are called.

One way of simplifying this situation is to create a façade class, which provides a single interface into the subsystem and co-ordinates the actions of the instances in the subsystem. In this way, changes to the implementation of classes in the subsystem will have a limited impact on other subsystems: it may be possible to limit the changes to the subsystem itself, as the messages to changed classes (within the subsystem) will come from the façade class; otherwise, tracking down the effect of changes is made easier, as it is necessary only to find the points in other subsystems where messages are sent to instances of the façade class—one class instead of many.

This notation can also be used to show the actual classes that are bound to the roles, as in Figure 17-10.

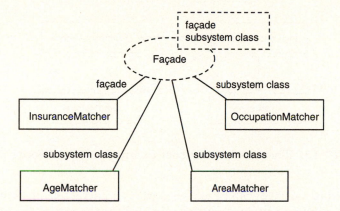

Figure 17-10: Example of a collaboration to document the use of the Façade pattern

The template collaboration shows only the participating roles and classes that fill those roles. In order to show the structure of the collaboration, we need to draw a class diagram for the participating classes. This can be included in a composite structure diagram, as in Figure 17-11. Note the navigability of the association.

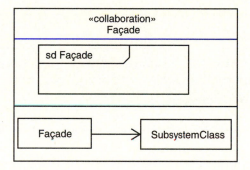

Figure 17-11: Composite structure diagram for the Façade pattern

This can also be shown using the notation in Figure 17-12.

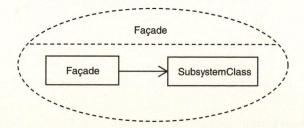

Figure 17-12: Collaboration for the Façade pattern

When a pattern is applied to a particular problem in the design of a system, the structural relationships among the classes that participate in the collaboration can be shown in a class diagram. In the CarMatch system, there is a requirement to match insurance policies to members based on three sets of characteristics of the members: age, home address and occupation. One way of hiding the complexity of the different classes that implement these three kinds of matching process is to create a façade class, in this case InsuranceMatcher, to provide a single interface to client objects, as in Figure 17-13.

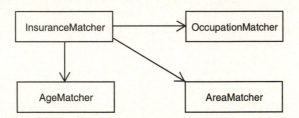

Figure 17-13: The **InsuranceMatcher** example of the **Façade** pattern

The interaction involved in a pattern can be modelled with an interaction diagram. Figure 17-14 shows three typical patterns of interaction that can be provided by the use of the **Façade** design pattern. In the first case (operationA), the façade class invokes operations of the subsystem classes to obtain some results and then organizes the results before passing them back to the client. In the second case (operationB), the façade class simply hides the operation that is invoked from the client. In the third case (operationC), the façade class again hides the operation that is invoked, but the operation involves interaction between roles in the subsystem, with the first SubsystemClass delegating some of the work to the second SubsystemClass.

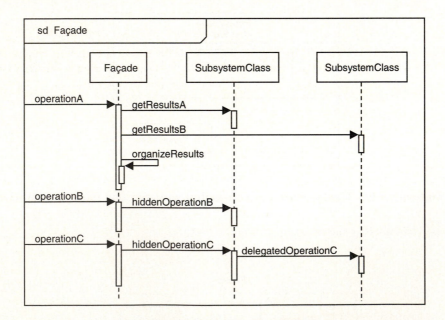

Figure 17-14: Typical interactions using the **Façade** pattern

In the case of the InsuranceMatcher example, the interaction is likely to be of the first type: the InsuranceMatcher receives a request from another object, despatches requests to each of the subsystem classes in turn, processes the results and returns a single result to the client, as in Figure 17-15.

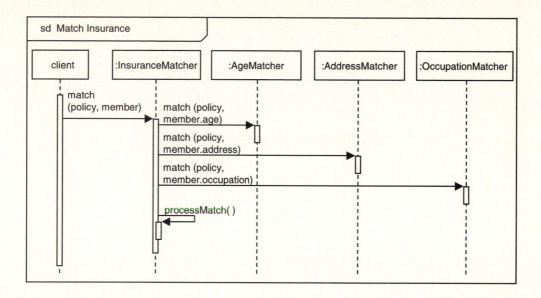

Figure 17-15: Sequence diagram for the Façade pattern applied to insurance matching

Other non-structural aspects of patterns are recorded in text or in tables using a template like the Coplien template described in Section 17.3.

17.5 APPLICATION OF PATTERNS

Patterns are applied at different stages in the development of systems. Organizational patterns can be used in planning a project; analysis patterns can be used in structuring the domain model; architectural patterns can be applied in determining the overall architecture of the system; design patterns can be used to design the relationships and interactions among design classes. Our focus here is on design patterns.

Patterns are intended to allow novice developers to make use of the accumulated experience of experts who have developed systems in the past and from whose work examples of good practice and effective solutions have been collected as patterns. However, in order to use these patterns, the novice developer needs to have at least some knowledge of what they are and the kinds of problems that they solve. Faced with a problem in the development of a system, it is not easy to find a pattern from scratch. In this section, we shall examine one design problem in the CarMatch system and propose a solution to this problem based on patterns.

EXAMPLE 17.1   In each CarMatch franchise office there will be a computer system that is used to run the business of that franchise. There is a need to hold local information about the franchise, such as the address and perhaps a company registration number. So the class diagram should include a **CarMatchOffice** class as in Figure 17-16. Unless the intention is to build a distributed system connecting all the franchise offices (which it is not), there should only ever be one instance of this class in any one system. How can we ensure that only one instance is ever created?

One approach to this problem is not to create any instances but to use the class itself and to make all the attributes and operations into class-scope attributes and operations, as in Figure 17-17. This approach was illustrated in Section 7.4.

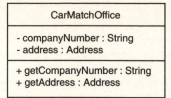

Figure 17-16: CarMatchOffice class

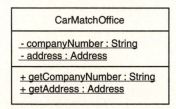

Figure 17-17: CarMatchOffice class with class-scope attributes and operations

This approach has shortcomings, as we may later want to subclass the class, and class operations cannot be redefined by subclasses in some languages. So, we may decide to create an object instance, but ensure that only one is ever created. The Singleton pattern is a way of doing this. The Singleton can be applied as a solution to the problem *How can a class be constructed that should have only one instance and that can be accessed globally within the application?* This is a creational pattern.

In the Singleton pattern, a class-scope operation getInstance() is added to the class definition. This operation returns a reference to a single instance of the class or creates that single instance if it does not already exist. The reference to the instance is held as a class-scope attribute within the class. To prevent other objects calling the constructor of the singleton class directly, the constructor is made private. The private constructor simply creates an instance of the singleton class, which is held in the class-scope instance attribute.

The Singleton pattern is very simple, involving only one class, so it is hardly worth drawing the template collaboration of Figure 17-18.

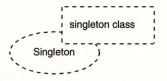

Figure 17-18: Template collaboration for the Singleton pattern

A singleton class will look something like the example in Figure 17-19.

This pattern can be applied to the CarMatchOffice class, and the result is shown in Figure 17-20.

We can model the getInstance() operation using a sequence diagram. There are two possible scenarios: in the first, the unique instance does not yet exist and must be created in order for a reference to it to be returned; in the second, it already exists, and a reference can be returned straight away. The client object can then invoke an operation on the instance. This is shown in Figure 17-21. Note the distinction between the class CarMatchOffice and the instance :CarMatchOffice.

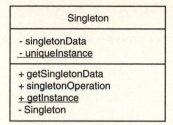

Figure 17-19: **Singleton** class pattern

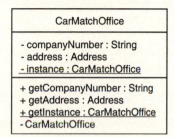

Figure 17-20: **CarMatchOffice** as a singleton class

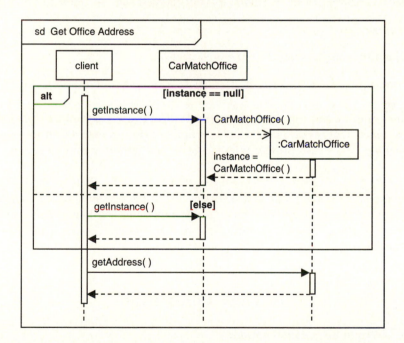

Figure 17-21: The **getInstance** operation of **CarMatchOffice**

17.6 HOW TO USE PATTERNS

Patterns are not always the answer to every problem in the design of a system. However, they can provide significant benefits by shortcutting the process of finding solutions to design problems in complex systems. If you plan to use patterns in a project, it is important that members of the team receive appropriate training before you even begin to consider individual patterns as design solutions.

When you face a problem in the design of a system, the following points should be considered:

- Does a pattern exist that addresses this or a similar problem?

- Does the documentation for this pattern suggest any other solutions that may be more acceptable?

- Is there a simpler solution? (Do not use patterns just for the sake of it.)

- Is the context of the pattern consistent with the context of the problem?

- Are the results of using the pattern acceptable?

- Are there constraints imposed by the software being used that would conflict with the use of the pattern?

Gamma et al. (1995) suggest seven steps in the application of a pattern in order to ensure that it is used successfully:

1. Read the pattern to get a complete overview.

2. Study the structure, participants and collaborations of the pattern in detail.

3. Examine the sample code to see an example of the pattern in use.

4. Choose names for the pattern's participants (i.e. classes) that are meaningful to the application.

5. Define the classes.

6. Choose application-specific names for the operations.

7. Implement operations that perform the responsibilities and collaborations in the pattern.

Patterns can be very helpful, but should not be applied without careful thought. They bring the benefit of reusing the experience of other developers and examples of good practice that have shown themselves to be widely applicable. They also provide a language for discussing architectural and design issues at an abstract level.

However, the use of patterns can result in over-design of simple systems, making them more complex than they need to be. Some patterns may have performance implications for the system, and should not be used without weighing up their advantages and disadvantages in the same way as is done with any other design decision.

Review Questions

17.1 What is the notation for a collaboration?

17.2 What dependencies can exist between collaborations and operations, and collaborations and use cases?

17.3 How can the template notation be used to represent a design pattern using a collaboration?

17.4 Define what is meant by a design pattern.

17.5 Define what is meant by a framework.

17.6 Define what is meant by an idiom.

17.7 How are patterns documented?

17.8 List and explain each of the headings in Coplien's pattern template.

17.9 What three different types of design pattern are there?

17.10 Explain what is meant by each of the types of pattern that you have listed in answer to the previous question.

17.11 Define what is meant by a collaboration.

17.12 How is a composite structure used to model a collaboration?

17.13 What is the notation for a template collaboration?

17.14 What four UML diagram types could you use to model a pattern?

17.15 List the steps that Gamma et al. (1995) suggest should be carried out to check that a pattern is appropriate.

Solved Problems

17.1 In Section 12.3.4 in the chapter on state charts, the example of the Journey class and the multiple states that it can be in is illustrated. This is described here.

> A journey can be in one of three states: Available, Vacant or Full. When it is first created, or when no one is sharing it, it is Available. When at least one person is sharing it, but the vehicle is not fully occupied, it is Vacant. When the vehicle is fully occupied, it is Full. The way in which instances of the Journey class respond to the two operations removeSharer and addSharer depends on the current state. For example, if it is Available the operation addSharer changes it to the Vacant state if there is more than one seat available or to the Full state if there is only one seat. If it is in the Vacant state, it will change to the Full state if adding another car sharer means that all the seats are occupied, but will stay in the Vacant state if there are still spaces. On the other hand, if it is already in the Full state, it is not possible to apply the operation addSharer.

What pattern is applicable to this situation?

The *State* pattern can be used here.

17.2 What are the characteristics of the State pattern?

Where a class has complex state-dependent behaviour, this may result in operations with complex if or **case** statements that check the current state before deciding what action to carry out. An alternative approach is to delegate the responsibility for each such operation to an instance of a class representing the current state of the object. If there are no attributes associated with the states, these state objects can be singletons.

17.3 Draw a composite structure representing the State pattern as a collaboration.

Figure 17-22 shows a composite structure. The Context is the role of the class that has complex state dependent behaviour. The State is the role for an abstract class that has the same set of state-dependent operations as the Context. There will be multiple classes in the ConcreteState role, representing the possible states of the Context.

17.4 Draw a class diagram for the classes involved in the example using Journey and its states.

Figure 17-23 shows the classes involved. JourneyState is an abstract class with three concrete subclasses: Available, Vacant and Full. These subclasses all implement the operations removeSharer and addSharer in their own way.

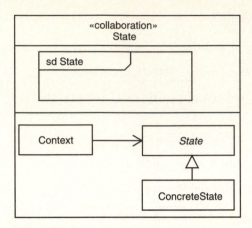

Figure 17-22: Composite structure for the **State** pattern

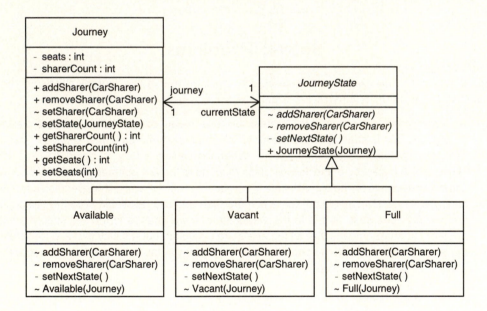

Figure 17-23: Class diagram for the **State** pattern applied to **Journey** states

17.5 Draw a sequence diagram to illustrate what happens when the message **addSharer** is sent to a **Journey** that is in the **Available** state.

When the **Journey** is in the **Available** state, adding a new car sharer will change it to the **Full** state if sharerCount == seats otherwise to the **Vacant** state. We are assuming here that the attribute sharerCount in **Journey** is set by the operation setSharer, but we haven't shown the reflexive operation here. This is shown in Figure 17-24.

Supplementary Problems

17.6 Find out about other design patterns (by reading a book or researching on the Internet). Consider which patterns could be applied to the CarMatch and VolBank case studies.

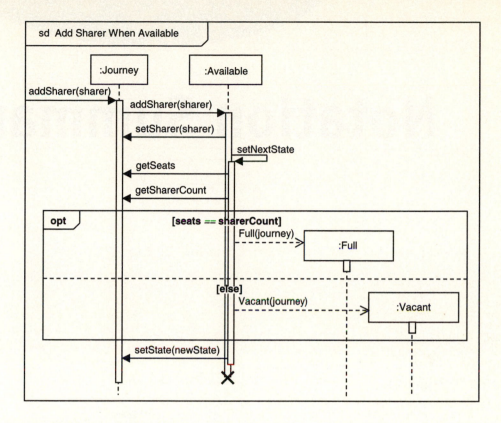

Figure 17-24: Sequence diagram for the State pattern applied to Journey states

17.7 Choose a design pattern from those about which you have read. Draw UML diagrams to model the structure and behaviour of this pattern.

APPENDIX A

Notation Summary

USE CASE DIAGRAM

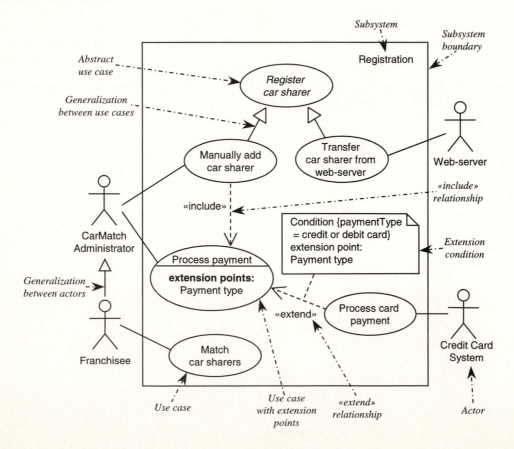

CLASS DIAGRAM

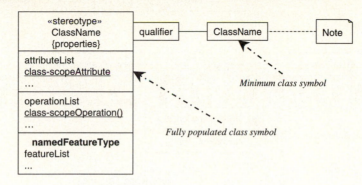

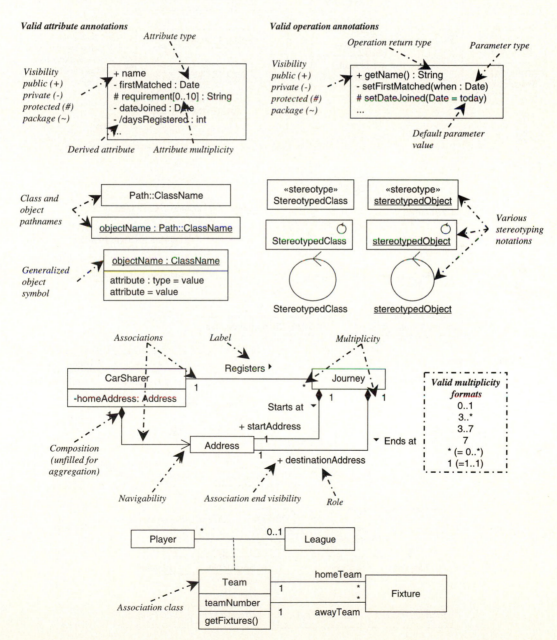

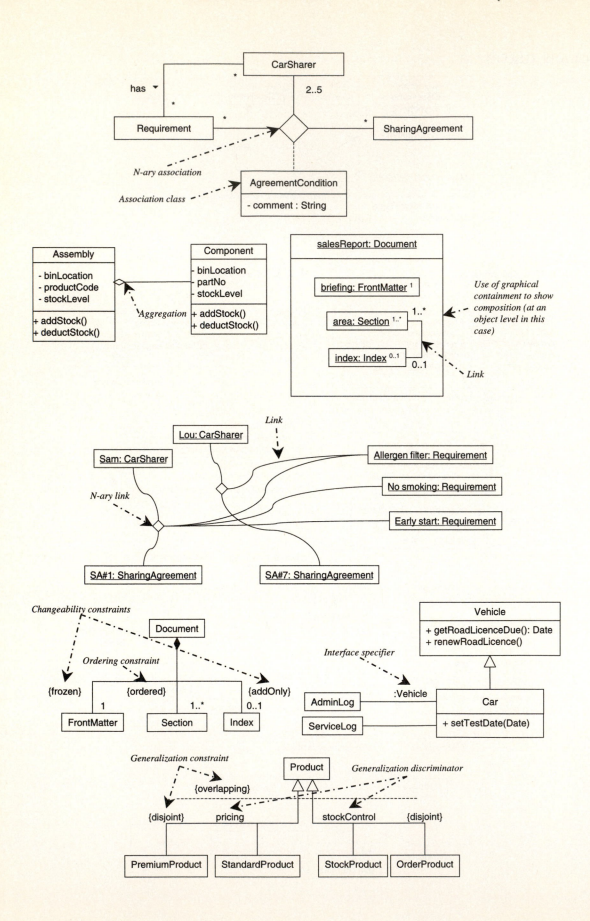

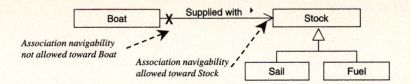

Association navigability not allowed toward Boat

Association navigability allowed toward Stock

Interface class name.

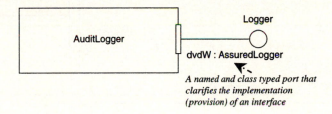

Relationship and node for a class which provides the List interface

Relationship and node for a class which requires the List interface

AuditLogger

Logger

dvdW : AssuredLogger

A named and class typed port that clarifies the implementation (provision) of an interface

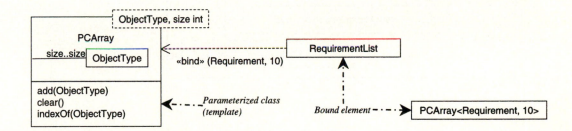

Parameterized class (template)

Bound element

SEQUENCE DIAGRAM

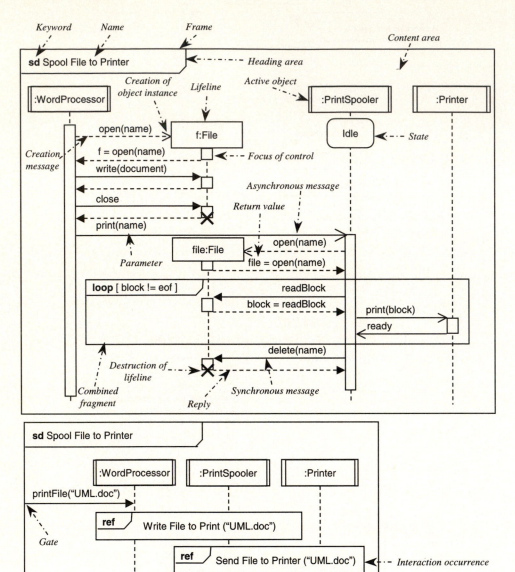

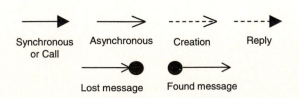

COLLABORATION DIAGRAM

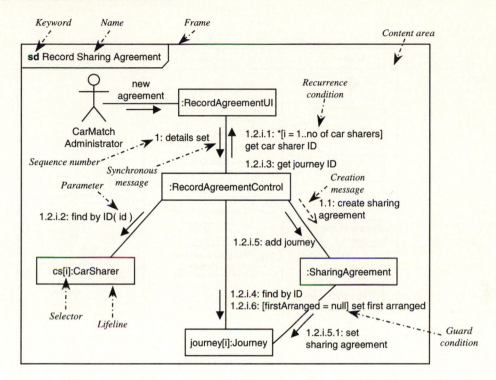

ACTIVITY DIAGRAM

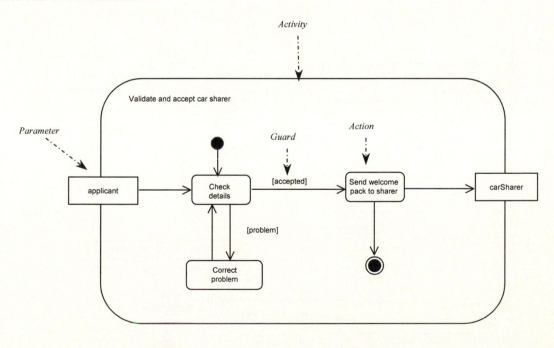

Activity partitions

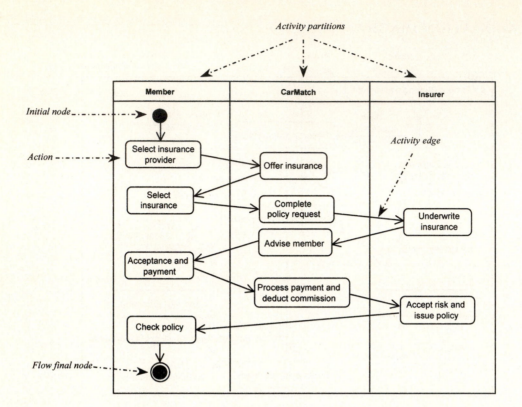

Object

Object state

Fork node

errpr

Report error

Interrupting edge

Interruptable region

Join node

Decision node

[not agreed]

[agreed]

Guard

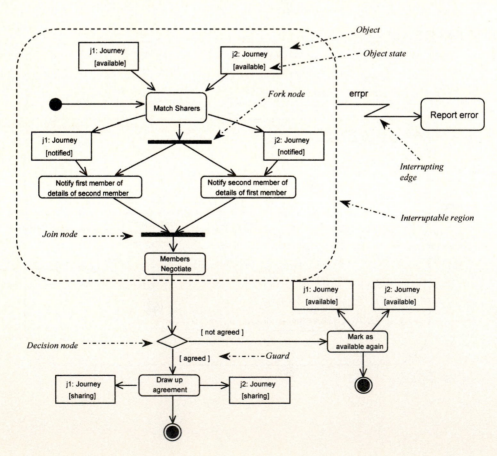

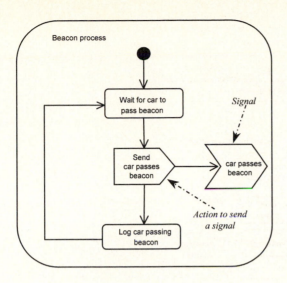

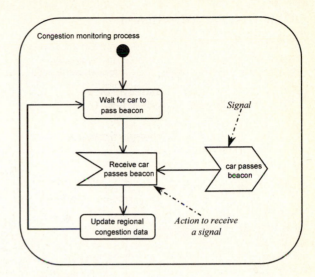

STATECHART DIAGRAM

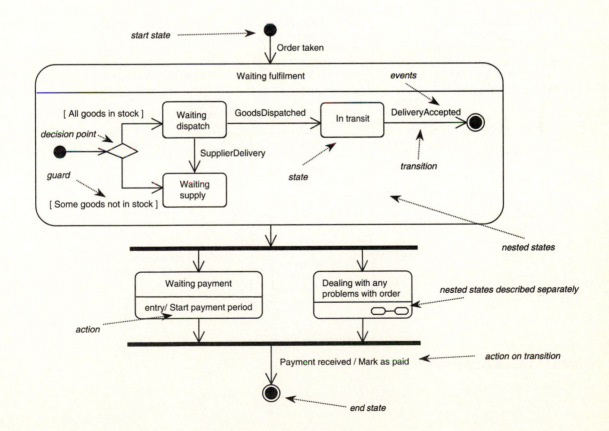

COMPONENT DIAGRAM

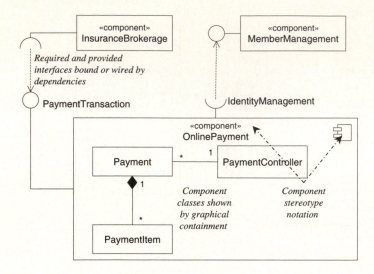

DEPLOYMENT DIAGRAM

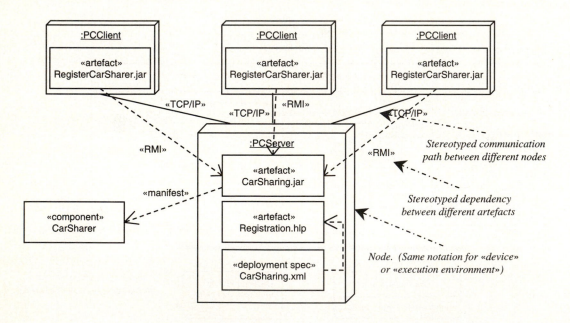

MODEL MANAGEMENT

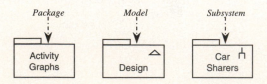

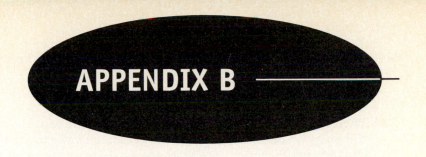

APPENDIX B

Review Questions: Answer Pointers

CHAPTER 2 BACKGROUND TO UML

2.1 James Rumbaugh, Grady Booch and Ivar Jacobson.

2.2 The Object Management Group (OMG).

2.3 It provides a specification of how UML models can be exchanged between applications.

2.4 Abstract syntax, well-formedness rules, semantics, notation and the XMI Schema.

2.5 User objects, model, metamodel and meta-metamodel.

2.6 They are specified in Object Constraint Language (OCL).

2.7 To group together diagrams that make up the UML based on the degree of cohesion that they have with one another.

2.8 The Revision Task Force (RTF).

2.9 They are used to provide sets of extensions to UML that can be applied to specific domains, such as business modelling or real-time systems development.

2.10 They are all abstractions apart from (c). (Unless of course, you believe that because it is just the name 'London, England' printed on a piece of paper, it must be an abstraction!)

2.11 They are all models apart from (d).

2.12 Choose three reasons from the following.

- It has become the *de facto* industry standard.
- It unifies the approaches of different authors in a single notation.
- It can be extended to apply to specific domains.
- It is supported by the Unified Software Development Process, which provides a process model for how it can be applied.

2.13 Inception, Elaboration, Construction and Transition.

2.14 Workflows specify the activities in a project that are carried out and the roles of the workers who will carry out the activities. Workflows group activities together into major project tasks, such as requirements elicitation. Activities specify the work that must be done, and are defined in terms of a sequence of steps that describe the detail of the work to be done.

CHAPTER 3 USE CASES

3.1 A sequence of activities carried out by the system that produce a meaningful outcome for an external user or system.

3.2 An oval with the name of the use case written in or below it.

3.3 An external user or another system that communicates with the system or subsystem that is being modelled.

3.4 A stick figure with the name of the actor written beneath it.

3.5 One of a number of possible different paths that can be taken through a use case, depending on different circumstances, the state of the system or the responses of actors.

3.6 Business modelling or requirements elicitation (as part of early analysis work).

3.7
- They are used to model sequences of actions that are carried out by the system and that provide an observable result to someone or something outside the system, known as an actor.
- They provide a high-level view of what the system does and who uses it.
- They provide the basis for determining the human–computer interfaces to the system.
- They can be used to model alternative scenarios for specific use cases that may result in different sequences of actions.
- They use a simple diagrammatic notation that is comprehensible to end users and can be used to communicate with them about the high-level view of the system.
- They can be used as the basis for drawing up test specifications.

3.8 Generalization.

3.9 Generalization associations and «include» and «extend» relationships.

3.10 The include relationship means that the included use case will always occur as part of the use case that includes it. In the extend relationship, the extending use case may or may not occur.

3.11 A line joining the two model elements with a triangle icon at one end of the line, pointing at the supertype.

3.12 An open arrow head and a dashed line, with the arrow pointing at the included use case, with the stereotype «include» alongside the line.

3.13 An open arrow head and a dashed line, with the arrow pointing at the extended use case, with the stereotype «extend» alongside the line.

3.14 The point in the execution of a use case when another use case, which extends the functionality of the first, may or may not occur, depending on some condition. The name of the extension point is listed in a compartment in the use case.

3.15 The condition is shown in a comment enclosed in braces ({}), with a reference to the extension point in the use case. The comment is linked to the extend relationship.

3.16 The Requirements Workflow.

3.17 Find Actors and Use Cases, Prioritize Use Cases, Detail a Use Case, Structure the Use Case Model and Prototype User-Interface.

CHAPTER 4 CLASS DIAGRAM: CLASSES AND ASSOCIATIONS

4.1 Class diagrams consist mainly of classes and associations. Other symbols that you might see on a class diagram are notes (or comments) and objects. A diagram that consists solely of objects would more correctly be referred to as an object diagram though. See Chapter 7.

4.2   • They are used to document the classes that constitute a system or subsystem.
      • They are used to describe the associations, generalization and aggregation relationships between those classes.
      • They are used to show the features of classes, principally the attributes and operations of each class.
      • They can be used throughout the development life-cycle, ranging from the specification of the classes in the problem domain to the implementation model for a proposed system, to show the class structure of that system.
      • They can document how the classes of a particular system interact with existing class libraries.
      • They can be used to show individual object instances within the class structure.
      • They can show the interfaces supported by a given class.

4.3   A class represents the generic features and properties of a set of instances (objects) that exist in either the problem domain, or the solution that is implemented to support the problem domain. Classes have properties (shown in curly braces {...}), and features (attributes and operations).

4.4   The class name in a box.

4.5   The class pathname reflects the model management structures within which the class exists. This is also known as the namespace of the class.

4.6   A class in the **Accounts** package within the **Finance** package would have the class pathname **Finance::Accounts::Class**.

4.7   An attribute is a data item that a class is responsible for maintaining.

4.8   The most basic notation for an attribute is to show its name alone. Attribute names start with a lower-case letter and have no spaces within them. Each component word in an attribute name starts with an upper-case letter.

4.9   Other properties could include the data type, attribute properties, visibility, derivation, initial value and multiplicity.

4.10 In outline:

      • Data type is shown with **attributeName : type**.
      • Attribute properties are shown in curly braces ({...}).
      • Visibility is shown with −, + or # (or a user-defined symbol).
      • Derivation is shown by preceding the attribute name with '/'.
      • Initial value is shown with **attributeName [: type] = initialValue**.
      • Multiplicity is shown in the form `attributeName[lower..upper]`.

4.11 An operation is a functional responsibility that a class has. 'Fine-grain' operations on classes collaborate to provide some externally visible functionality (see chapters on interaction diagrams).

4.12 A parameter is a data item that is passed to an operation. The type of the data item could be either a standard library type (for example, String, int, Date) or a class type from the problem domain (for example, CarSharer).

4.13 Passing by reference passes the underlying memory location of a parameter. Any change to the parameter made by an operation is a direct change to the attribute that was passed as the parameter. Passing by value means that a copy value of the underlying attribute is taken. Changes to the parameter do not affect the underlying attribute.

4.14 The most basic notation for an operation is **operationName : type**. The operation could be annotated with its visibility.

4.15 A list of parameters is shown in brackets after the operation name. Each parameter in the list can be of the form `parameterName : type = defaultValue`. Type and initial value can be omitted either independently or together. The parameter type alone can be shown.

4.16 At a conceptual level, classes will reflect the problem domain. Such classes might arguably be more reflective of the data handling requirements of the system. Moving into the specification and implementation level, the emphasis shifts to functional responsibilities of the classes. Classes relating to the implementation of the system will be introduced and component operations of larger collaborations will be added to the (simplistic) **get** and **set** operations.

4.17 Initial value can be shown with attributeName [:type] **= initialValue**.

4.18 Default value can be shown in the form `parameterName : type = defaultValue` or `parameterName = defaultValue`.

4.19 An association specifies that two classes will pass messages to each other.

4.20 The most basic notation is a solid line between two classes. The label (name) of the association is suffixed or prefixed with a solid arrow-head to indicate the direction in which the label is intended to be read.

4.21 The role played by a class can be shown by adding a role name to the end of the association nearest the concerned class. The format of the role name is the same as the format of an attribute name.

4.22 In the context of attributes, multiplicity specifies the number of distinct values that the attribute can hold. In the context of associations, the multiplicity specifies the number of instances that may be involved in the appropriate end of an association.

4.23 Multiplicity is shown in the form `lowerBound..upperBound`. For an attribute the multiplicity is enclosed in square brackets. The lower bound can be any non-negative integer, including zero. The upper bound can be any non-negative integer that is equal to, or greater than the lower bound, or *. Several different multiplicity ranges can be specified as a comma-separated list.

4.24 Attributes and associations.

4.25 By taking either a data-oriented or a functionality-oriented approach. A data-oriented approach suits initial investigation and identification of data responsibilities. A functional approach builds a class diagram from the collaborations which should take place to fulfil some externally visible function.

CHAPTER 5 CLASS DIAGRAM: AGGREGATION, COMPOSITION AND GENERALIZATION

5.1 Aggregation implies that a 'whole' end of the association groups together instances of the 'part' end of the association. Furthermore, the 'whole' end is considered to be composed of instances of the 'part' end.

5.2 Semantically, aggregation associations imply a stronger coupling between whole and part than a normal association might.

5.3 Composition is a more strict form of aggregation where the 'part' instances have a life-cycle that is co-incident with the 'whole'. Parts cannot be created before the whole and are deleted when the whole is deleted.

5.4 In aggregation the part instances do not have a co-incident life-cycle with the whole. They are capable of independent existence alongside of, or instead of, their participation in the aggregation association.

5.5 Aggregation associations have an unfilled diamond annotation at the 'whole' end.

5.6 Either with a filled diamond annotation at the whole end of the association or by graphical containment,

5.7 'Normal' associations indicate that the operation of two classes is inter-related. Aggregation and composition clarify the nature of this inter-relationship as being one of 'whole–part'.

5.8 Generalization implies that objects of one class are 'a kind of' object of another class. The generic concept of generalization is well understood; for example, a banana is a kind of fruit. In a class diagram for a banking application it might be specified that a Debit and a Credit are both a kind of Transaction.

5.9 Generalization is shown with a solid line from the subclass to a triangular arrowhead at the parent class.

5.10 The path of a generalization relationship can be shown as a solid line with either separate or converging paths.

5.11 Generalization constraints can specify two things. First the inter-relationship between different generalization hierarchies that share the same parent class (either overlapping or disjoint). Second, the extent to which a generalization hierarchy in the problem domain is reflected in the class model (either incomplete or complete). The four generalization constraints are: overlapping, disjoint, incomplete and complete. A hierarchy showing a subset of different employee or customer types might be constrained as being **incomplete**. A parent type of Vehicle might have **disjoint** subclass hierarchies for fuel type and cabin type.

5.12 One example could be mapReferenceType to discriminate between OS, Tiger and Latitude–Longitude map references in the GeoLocation package.

5.13 By using Object Constraint Language (OCL).

5.14 If inappropriately used, aggregation and composition could be implemented too rigidly for the problem domain. Care should be exercised in their use.

5.15 In a top-down approach, likely parent classes in generalization structures may be identified by the analyst. The implications of introducing generalization can be explored and considered. This particular approach is usually based primarily on the experience of the analyst.

5.16 In bottom-up generalization the approach is to look for shared class responsibilities. Similar operations and attributes might well suggest the presence of an undetected generalization structure.

CHAPTER 6 CLASS DIAGRAM: MORE ON ASSOCIATIONS

6.1 The visibility indicator (-, +, # or user-defined) is prefixed onto a role name.

6.2 Changeability can be either {changeable}, {addOnly} or {frozen}. {frozen} means that instances cannot be added or deleted, {addOnly} means that instances can be added but not deleted, {changeable} means that both addition and deletion are permitted.

6.3 At a conceptual level the notation is {ordered}, or at a specification or implementation level {sorted}.

6.4 Navigability is shown with an arrowhead indicating the direction of navigability. Where it is standard practice to implement relationships of a given multiplicity combination in a particular way, then it may be necessary to specify explicitly that an association must be implemented so as to make it navigable in both directions.

6.5 Qualifiers allow the specification of the attribute(s) that can be used to identify occurrences of instances related by an association to be specified.

6.6 The names of both derived attributes and derived associations are prefixed with '/'.

6.7 UML provides the n-ary association, a diamond symbol linked by a solid line to the classes involved in the association.

6.8 The association class symbol can be used to show those attributes and operations. The notation for an association class is identical to the normal class symbol. An association class is connected to the association (either binary or n-ary) that it represents with a dashed line.

CHAPTER 7 CLASS DIAGRAM: OTHER NOTATIONS

7.1 Object diagrams can provide a useful way of illustrating points of discussion and to illustrate the effects of modelling classes in one way or another.

7.2 Permitted: association label, role names, interface specifier, visibility, navigability, aggregation, composition, qualifier. Not permitted: multiplicity. Multiplicity has no sense. The link is an instance of an association and relates the objects that it is seen to join.

7.3 The «realization» dependency is derived from the generalization relationship and the 'normal' dependency relationship. The generalization relationship provides the triangular arrowhead of the «realization» relationship. The dependency notation provides the dashed line. The notation of realization is one that combines generalization with dependency—one class realizes other class(es).

7.4 Class-scope features are underlined. This is arguably confusing since the UML notation for an object instance is to underline the class name. This could be seen as using the same annotation to indicate diametrically opposed concepts.

7.5 Instance-scope features are those which relate to individual objects. For example, an operation to add 10% to an attribute value of an object is operating upon the values of that attribute for that object. Class-scope attributes hold the same value across all instances of that class. Class-scope operations either operate upon class-scope attributes or operate upon instances of the class (for example, constructor operations).

7.6 Stereotypes can be shown using the stereotype name in guillemets («»), using a small icon of the stereotype in the upper right corner of the object/class name compartment or using the stereotype icon with the object/class name underneath it and no other object/class features or properties shown.

7.7 Enumeration classes provide a specified list of values that the enumeration class can hold.

7.8 Utility classes provide a notationally convenient way of collecting up system-wide attributes (global variables) and operations (utility functions) into one clearly identified place.

7.9 Provided interface classes can be shown using either the «interface» stereotype or as a small circle with the name of the class either just above or below the circle. Using the small circle notation no features or properties of the interface are listed. Required interfaces can be show using a half-circle that can be combined with a provided interface to give the ball-and-socket effect.

7.10 Provided interfaces are those interfaces that either a class or component will provide the attributes and operations to support. On the other hand a required interface is one that a class or component requires in order to perform part of its processing responsibilities.

7.11 A «type» class has operations and may have attributes and outward navigable associations. Those attributes and associations serve to support the specification of the operations of the class. The operations of a type class have no methods; they are place holders that ensure that another class that implements the type provides all the required operations. An «implementationClass» is a class that realizes a type class by implementing the methods of the type class.

7.12 By a «realize» dependency from the «implementationClass» to «type».

7.13 A template class is similar to the 'normal' class symbol with the addition of a box overlaid on the top-right corner of the class symbol. In the box, the parameters of the class are shown as a comma-separated list. The multiplicity and type of attributes in the template class and the return type of operations of the template class may be defined in terms of the parameters identified in the box.

7.14 Bound elements can be shown using either a «bind» dependency or a class named TemplateName <arguments>. If the bind dependency is used, the «bind» stereotype is suffixed with <arguments> to instantiate the parameters of the parameterized class.

CHAPTER 8 COMPONENT DIAGRAMS

8.1 A component («component») is a set of classes that provide a coherent unit of functionality in an application. Components may be as granular as individual classes (i.e. a component is a class) or they may represent a collection of classes (i.e. one component represents several classes).

8.2 Components can be shown using any of the other standard UML stereotype options; namely, by stereotyped name («component»), by iconized diagram element or by both stereotype name and iconized diagram element together.

8.3 Both required and provided interfaces can be used in component diagrams. They are used to show the interfaces of components. Using interfaces enables the boundaries of components to be described in terms of well-defined elements.

8.4 Required and provided component interfaces can be overlaid to form the ball-and-socket representation. Alternatively, they can be wired together with dependencies running from the required interface to the provided interface (showing that the required interface is dependent upon the provided interface).

8.5 Ports allow the specification of the internal class to the functionality that is delegated by the interfaces of the component. This can augment the interface definitions by defining the specific services that will support the port and hence interface definitions.

8.6 Ports can be linked to their internal classes with associations or by using «delegate» dependencies to link the port to the provided interfaces and from the internal required interfaces.

CHAPTER 9 INTERACTION SEQUENCE DIAGRAMS

9.1 An interaction is a specification of the way in which messages are sent between objects in order to perform a task.

9.2 Time is represented as running vertically down the page, so a message that is lower on the page is normally sent after one that appears above it, unless a parallel combined fragment is used.

9.3
- They are used to model the high-level interaction between active objects in a system.
- They are used to model the high-level interaction between subsystems.
- They are used to model the interaction between object instances that realize a use case.
- They are used to model the interaction between objects within an operation.
- They can be used to model reusable fragments of interactions that can be combined in other sequence diagrams or in interaction overview diagrams.

9.4 A rectangle with a heading area (a rectangle with the lower right-hand corner cut off) in the top left-hand corner where a keyword and other information, such as the name of an interaction and parameters, are shown.

9.5 A dashed line hanging from the rectangle or other shape that represents the object or other model element.

9.6 A white rectangle drawn on the lifeline of an object.

9.7 An arrow going from the lifeline or focus of control region of one object to another (or possibly to itself), with the message signature written (normally) above the arrow.

9.8 Using a dashed line with a closed arrowhead going from the object whose operation was called back to the object that invoked the operation. The line may have a message name above it with the assignment of the result to an attribute of the recipient of the return message.

9.9 All except (h) because it is underlined, which is UML 1.X notation.

9.10 Synchronous (or call), asynchronous, creation and reply (or return of control) from a call.

9.11 The first is a lost message (whose receive event is unknown), and the second is a found message (the origin of whose send event is unknown).

9.12 By a message arrow going to the rectangle representing the object, and the object's lifeline starting immediately below the rectangle. The arrow has a dashed line and an open arrowhead.

9.13 By a bold x-shaped cross at the lower end of the object's lifeline, at the point where it is destroyed.

9.14 An object running on its own thread of control.

9.15 A rectangle with a double line at each end.

9.16 Using a loop combined fragment: by placing a frame round the messages of the repeated interaction with the keyword loop and the condition that controls the iteration in square brackets in the heading compartment in the top left-hand corner of the frame.

9.17 Using an alt combined fragment: by placing a frame round the messages of the alternative interactions with the keyword alt in the heading compartment in the top left-hand corner of the frame, by separating the alternatives with dashed lines across the frame, and by placing conditions or the keyword **else** in square brackets at the top of each of the compartments created by the dashed lines.

9.18 Using an **opt** combined fragment: by placing a frame round the messages of the optional interaction with the keyword **opt** and the condition that determines whether the iteration takes place in square brackets near the top of the frame.

9.19 A fragment of a sequence diagram that can be used in other sequence diagrams by being referenced using a frame with the keyword **ref** in the heading and the name of the reused interaction occurrence in the content area of the frame.

9.20 To indicate that there are constraints on the time that is allowed to elapse either between the sending and receipt of a message (duration constraint), or between the send or receive event of one message and the send or receive event of another, often a response (timing constraint).

9.21
- Decide on the context of the interaction: system, subsystem, use case or operation.
- Identify the structural elements (classes or objects) necessary to carry out the functionality of the use case or operation. (There may already be a collaboration that defines these.)
- Consider the alternative scenarios that may be required.
- Draw sequence diagrams.
    - Draw a frame for the sequence diagram and name the sequence diagram.
    - Lay out the lifelines from left to right.
    - Starting with the message that starts the interaction, lay out the messages down the page from top to bottom. Show the properties of the messages necessary to explain the semantics of the interaction.
    - Include combined fragments where necessary.
    - Add the focus of control if it is necessary to visualize nesting or the point in time where an activation is taking place.
    - Add timing constraints and duration constraints if necessary.
    - Add state invariants to the diagram if required.
- If required, draw a single sequence diagram to summarize the combination of the alternative scenarios in the other sequence diagrams.

9.22 The Design Workflow and the Test Workflow.

9.23 Identifying the Participating Design Classes, Describing Design Object Interactions, Identifying the Participating Subsystems and Interfaces, Describing Subsystem Interactions and Capturing Implementation Requirements.

9.24 Designing Integration Test Cases, Designing System Test Cases, Designing Regression Test Cases and Identifying and Structuring Test Procedures.

CHAPTER 10 MORE ON INTERACTION DIAGRAMS

10.1 Sequence diagrams model an interaction in terms of the time-ordered sequence of messages that are sent, whereas communication diagrams show the messages in the context of the structural relationship among the object instances involved.

10.2 A set of participants, usually object instances, that work together to achieve some meaningful outcome in the context of the system.

10.3 A sequence of messages sent between instances to achieve a higher level of functionality.

10.4 It may result in the recognition of the need for new classes, attributes or, particularly, operations.

10.5
- They are used to model interactions between objects that deliver the functionality of a use case by showing the messages that are passed between lifelines.
- They are used to model interactions between objects that deliver the functionality of an operation by showing the messages that are passed between lifelines.
- They are used to model mechanisms within the architectural design of the system.

- They are used to model alternative scenarios within a use case or operation that involve the collaboration of different objects and different interactions.
- They are used in the early stages of a project to identify the objects (and hence classes) that participate in each use case. The objects in each communication diagram represent a partial view of a class diagram, and these partial models can be combined into a model of the whole system.
- They are used to show the participants in a design pattern (see Chapter 17).

10.6 They are all valid lifeline names apart from (b) because it is underlined, which is UML 1.X notation.

10.7 Operation calls and signals.

10.8 Synchronous, asynchronous, creation and reply.

10.9 The value returned from a procedural call that invokes an operation synchronously on another object.

10.10 An integer or name followed by an optional recurrence.

10.11 To represent the use case in which a message is sent, to represent the name of the object sending the message and to label alternative paths after a branch.

10.12 A conditional statement that must evaluate to true before the message is sent.

10.13
- Decide on the context of the interaction: system, subsystem, use case or operation.
- Identify the structural elements (objects, subsystems) necessary to carry out the functionality of this interaction.
- Model the structural relationships between those elements to produce a diagram showing the context of the interaction.
- Consider the alternative scenarios that may be required.
- Draw communication diagrams. (Alternatively, sequence diagrams can be drawn if the timing of messages is an important aspect of the interaction.)

10.14 **Actor**, **Worker**, **Case Worker**, **Internal Worker** and **Entity**.

10.15 Analysis Workflow and Design Workflow.

10.16 Identifying Analysis Classes, Describing Analysis Object Interactions and Capturing Special Requirements.

10.17 Flow of events analysis describes the interaction between classes internal to the system rather than between the system and external actors.

10.18 Identifying the Participating Design Classes, Describing Design Object Interactions, Identifying the Participating Subsystems and Interfaces, Describing Subsystem Interactions and Capturing Implementation Requirements.

10.19 State or condition timeline and general value lifeline.

10.20 Left to right.

10.21
- Reason about the time-related behaviour of objects, subsystems and systems.
- Specify the time-related behaviour of objects, subsystems and systems.
- Model the relationships between lifelines whose interaction depends on adherence to timing considerations.

10.22 Equal units of time.

10.23 Small vertical lines drawn on the bottom of the frame in which the timing diagram is drawn. This is known as the timing ruler. The tick marks may have a scale of time values associated with them.

10.24 Conditions.

10.25 Horizontal parallel lines with the name of a state written between them, followed by an X representing the crossing of the lines, and thus the change of state, and then another pair of parallel lines with the new state written between them.

10.26
- Decide on the lifelines to model.
- Decide on the type of timing diagram: whether to produce a timeline diagram or a general value lifeline diagram.
- Determine the states or conditions that should be shown.

- Identify the events that result in changes of state.
- Add timing and duration constraints with the necessary timing ruler and tick mark values.
- Review and elaborate the diagram.

10.27 Activity diagram notation.

10.28 Interaction overview diagrams are used to give a high-level overview of the flow of control within an interaction without showing all the detail of the lifelines and messages.

10.29 Decision node and merge node.

10.30 A diamond.

10.31
- Decide on the interaction to model.
- Break the interaction up into separate interactions and interaction occurrences.
- Replace alternatives, options, loops and parallel structures with the appropriate notation from activity diagrams.

CHAPTER 11 ACTIVITIES

11.1 Activities are used to describe business workflows (business processes), workflows within use cases, workflows between use cases and, for complex operations, the workflow within the operation.

11.2 Activities can be first used in business analysis, as a way of elaborating business use cases, or to support some other business workflow method.

11.3 Activities are a graphical two-dimensional illustration of the complicated flows that take place within a system, be it a business or a computer system. They are useful for describing systems to a range of stakeholders.

11.4 An action is a unit of work, not further subdivided in an activity. However, an action may be complex in its own right and can itself be described by an activity.

11.5 Complex actions can be described by activities, other workflow diagrams such as sequence diagrams, or textual descriptions.

11.6 An action can be instantaneous, or it can take place over an extended period.

11.7 A pin is an object used as input or output of an action, indicated by a rectangle on the side of an action, labelled with the name of the object and optionally its state.

11.8 An activity edge shows the movement between actions or between actions and objects.

11.9 An activity edge between two actions is known as a control edge.

11.10 If there are no guards on the edges, then two exit activity edges indicate that the flow runs in parallel down the two edges. This is known as an implicit fork.

11.11 When multiple control edges enter an action, the action only starts when all the flows from all the routes in are complete. This is known as an implicit join.

11.12 A merge node allows independent alternative activity edges to be merged into a single activity edge.

11.13 A decision node is a point in a workflow where the activity edge on exit from a state or activity may go in a number of alternative directions depending on a condition.

11.14 A guard is a condition on an activity edge. The activity edge can only be followed when the condition in the guard is satisfied.

11.15 A merge node can have two or more activity edges entering it.

11.16 A decision node can have two or more activity edges leaving it. Each exit activity edge must have a guard, and the guards from all activity edges leaving a decision edge must not overlap.

11.17 An activity partition is a column or row on an activity, used to indicate some organizational or technology unit that takes care of the actions in the column or row.

11.18 Activity partitions are useful for allocating actions to business units or technology areas.

11.19 A fork node is used to split an activity edge and open up parallel workflows.

11.20 A join node is used to synchronize multiple parallel flows into a single activity edge.

11.21 Objects can be placed on activities, and dependencies used to indicate how activities affect the states of the objects. This is known as an object flow.

11.22 You can keep state information about an object on an object flow.

11.23 An interruptible region is part of an activity that can be interrupted. It is shown by a dashed, round-cornered rectangle.

11.24 Activities can be attached to business use cases, system use cases, activities, objects and operations.

11.25 Signals are visual icons to indicate the point on a diagram where events are triggered or responded to.

CHAPTER 12 STATE MACHINES

12.1 Activities, communication diagrams and sequence diagrams.

12.2 The states that entities in the system can take and their changing state, defined by the transitions from one state to another.

12.3 A state is a condition that an object can enter, and remain in for a period of time.

12.4 A state lasts for an indefinite period of time, but it can be very brief.

12.5 Events can either trigger an action in a state or trigger the exit from a state.

12.6 A state machine is usually used to model objects, but it can be used to model actors, use cases and occasionally operations.

12.7 No.

12.8 On Entry: these actions are triggered as soon as the state is entered; Do: these actions take place during the lifetime of the state; On Event: these actions take place in response to an event; On Exit: these actions take place just before the activity completes.

12.9 action-label / action
where action-label is one of entry, do, exit, include, or the name of an event.

12.10 trigger-name(arguments) [constraint] / action
where arguments is a comma-separated list of arguments supplied by the trigger, and constraint is a condition that must be true for the event to trigger the action.

12.11 By dividing the state into two compartments and listing the actions in the second compartment.

12.12 Just one, or none.

12.13 A composite state is a state that can be viewed as having substates, and for which those substates are defined.

12.14 Composite states can either be depicted by using a separate state machine, or by drawing the subflows on the same diagram nested inside the state.

12.15 A composite state may have parallel workflows. Thus a composite state may be in multiple substates at any one time.

12.16 Forks allow the splitting of a flow to represent parallel flows between states, and the subsequent merging of those parallel flows is done by a join.

12.17 The entry actions for the composite state are fired. The subflow starts at its initial state, or if there are concurrent subflows then each of the subflows start at their initial states. The exception to this is when there is a history state, and the subflows resume at the point they exited.

12.18 Any substate in the composite state terminates, applying exit actions. The composite state terminates, applying its exit actions.

12.19 The subflow starts at the substate indicated by the transition. The entry actions for the composite state and the substate are fired.

12.20 A transition triggered by an event may take a number of routes depending on a condition. A choice or junction pseudostate can be introduced to indicate the alternative routes.

12.21 History states containing H mean that a composite state resumes at the point in the top-level flow where it last exited. H* indicates that the composite state resumes at the point in any nested composite state where it last exited; the point of resumption will be at whatever level of nesting is defined.

CHAPTER 13 OBJECT CONSTRAINT LANGUAGE (OCL)

13.1 A constraint is a rule about the values in a model, expressed as a restriction on the values.

13.2 They are used to define the behaviour of the model, and to define the legal use of the model.

13.3 OCL is the object constraint language, which is a language for the rigorous definition of constraints.

13.4 Natural language can be ambiguous. Models ultimately need unambiguous descriptions of their behaviour.

13.5 A pre-condition is a statement that defines the legal conditions under which an operation or use case can function. If the pre-condition is met, then the system is obliged to perform according to specification.

13.6 A post-condition is a statement about the model that defines the state of the model after an operation or use case has completed, given that it was invoked with the pre-conditions met.

13.7 An invariant is the property of an object or operation that must remain true at all times.

13.8 Design by contract involves specifying the behaviour of systems in terms of pre-conditions and post-conditions. The constraints form a contract.

13.9 The context of a constraint is a class or operation.

13.10 Boolean, integer, real and string.

13.11 Sets, and types defined in the model.

13.12 2.

13.13 Sets, sequences and bags.

13.14 a -> first

13.15 Bag{2,2,3,3,4}

13.16 true

13.17 Not usually. At the time of defining the use cases, the objects will not be adequately defined.

13.18 The ^ operator returns true if the message it prefixes has arrived during the operation. The ^^ operator returns a collection of the messages that have arrived during the operation that match the message it prefixes.

13.19 A tuple is an unordered collection of named items. The elements of the tuple can be accessed by putting the name after a full-stop (.) at the end of the tuple, for example **person.name** if the **person** tuple has a **name** element, and **person.address** if the **person** tuple has an **address** element.

CHAPTER 14 DEPLOYMENT DIAGRAMS

14.1 Deployment diagrams can be used to model physical hardware elements and the communication paths between them, to plan the architecture of a system, or to document the deployment of software artefacts onto hardware nodes, devices or execution environments.

14.2 Nodes are the hardware elements that make up a system. They are shown as a shallow three-dimensional cuboid on deployment diagrams.

14.3 A device («**device**») is a specific subelement of a node that has its own processing capability.

14.4 An execution environment is an environment on a node into which code artefacts can be deployed. Some typical execution environments might include: «**J2EE Container**», «**Application Server**», or «**IIS**».

14.5 A communication path is a channel of communication between two different nodes. Communication paths can be stereotyped to indicate the particular kind of communications that the path supports. Illustrative communication path stereotypes might include «**odbc**», «**TCP/IP**» or «**http**».

14.6 First, artefacts can be shown as being deployed to a particular node by graphical containment (drawing the deployed artefact inside the boundary of the node upon which it is deployed). Second, an artefact can be linked to a node using a «**deploy**» dependency.

14.7 Examples can include «**artefact**», «**component**», «**device**», «**J2EE Container**», «**deployment spec**».

14.8 Software components are mapped to artefacts using a «manifest» dependency from the artefact to the component. The artefacts can then be deployed to nodes using graphical containment or a «deploy» dependency.

CHAPTER 15 EXTENDING UML

15.1 A profile is a special kind of package that contains extensions to the UML metamodel that can be used to tailor UML to particular domains or platforms.

15.2 Profiles are packages that are linked to packages in a model using the «apply» dependency. Model elements in the model packages can then use features that are in the profile, typically stereotypes.

15.3 It is a means of specifying that a model element conforms to the well-understood pattern of behaviour or existence of the specified stereotype. Stereotypes are specified in guillemets («...») or as graphical icons.

15.4 Stereotypes extend metaclasses in the UML metamodel. For example, a new stereotyped class can be defined that extends the Class metaclass and adds particular properties to instances of that stereotyped class in the form of tagged values, or constraints on it in the form of UML constraints.

15.5 Stereotypes are shown in the profile package to which they belong, linked to the metaclass that they extend by an Extension association. Attributes of the stereotype become tagged values in the model.

15.6 As an icon; by placing the name of the stereotype in guillemets in the class above the class name; by placing an icon in the class above and to the right of the class name.

15.7 Classes from Bruce Conallen's web extensions, such as the «ServerPage» class.

15.8 A stereotyped message arrow for use in sequence diagrams.

15.9 A tagged definition is an attribute of a stereotype that defines a property that all instances of model elements that conform to that stereotype must have.

15.10 Tagged definitions are shown in a profile as attributes of stereotypes.

15.11 It is a pair, usually represented as {tag = value}, associated with a model element such as a class, where tag is a name that indicates the property (from the tagged definition), and value is an arbitrary value expressible as a string. The name and type are defined in the stereotype to which it applies as a tagged definition.

15.12 As {tag = value} alongside the model element to which the tagged value applies.

15.13 A constraint defines a relationship between model elements or on a model element that must be true, otherwise the system described by the model ceases to be valid.

15.14 As {constraint} alongside the model element to which the constraint applies, where the actual constraint is placed in the braces, usually as an OCL expression. Where a constraint applies to the relationship between two objects, they can be joined by a dependency and the constraint written alongside the dependency. They can also be shown in a comment.

15.15 {age <= 21 years}.

15.16 Object Constraint Language (OCL).

CHAPTER 16 SOFTWARE TOOLS FOR UML

16.1 No. Software tools support all aspects of the software engineering process, not just those involving UML. Modelling tools may also incorporate other modelling notations.

16.2 UML provides a common notation and common semantics for models developed in different software tools, and provides an interchange standard so that models can be exchanged between tools.

16.3 XMI stands for XML Metadata Interchange. XML stands for eXtensible Markup Language. XMI is the standard definition for a textual language to describe UML models, defined to enable interchange of models between different modelling tools.

16.4 The repository is where all the model elements are stored. Additional elements over and above UML may be stored in the repository.

16.5 It is a pair {tag = value}, associated with a model element such as a class, where tag is a name that indicates the property and value is an arbitrary value expressible as a string.

16.6 Tagged values are important because they permit UML to be extended.

16.7 Round trip engineering is where the software modelling tool can both generate program code and reverse engineer code, managing updates to software models and program code.

CHAPTER 17 DESIGN PATTERNS

17.1 The simplest notation is a dashed oval with the name of the collaboration inside or below it. A collaboration can also be shown with the classes that participate in it linked to it by lines. It can also be shown as a large dashed oval with a compartment containing the participants.

17.2 A collaboration may have a «trace» dependency on a use case or a «represent» dependency on an operation.

17.3 A pattern can be shown as a template collaboration. The name of the template collaboration is written in the oval, and the names of parameterized roles are written in the rectangle. The template represents the pattern, and when it is applied to a particular domain, the names of the classes that play the parameterized roles are linked to the collaboration oval by lines labelled with the roles, or shown in a compartment inside it with the names of the roles written alongside the class names.

17.4 A design pattern is a solution to a common problem in the design of computer systems. It is a solution that has been recognized as worth documenting so that other developers can apply it to solve the same problem when they come up against it.

17.5 A framework is more comprehensive than a pattern and is a partially completed application that can be applied to a specific domain.

17.6 An idiom is a set of guidelines for how to implement aspects of a software system in a particular language.

17.7 Using a template in a pattern catalogue.

17.8
- *Name*—The name of the pattern, ideally describing the solution in some way.
- *Problem*—The question that the pattern helps to resolve.
- *Context*—The context of the application of the pattern: architectural or business context and the critical success factors for the pattern that will make it work in a particular situation.
- *Forces*—The constraints or issues that must be resolved by the pattern.
- *Solution*—The solution that balances the conflicting forces and fits the context.
- *Sketch*—Symbolic sketch of the forces and how they are resolved.
- *Resulting context*—The context as it is after being changed by the solution.
- *Rationale*—The reason and motivation for the pattern.

17.9 Creational, structural and behavioural.

17.10
- *Creational*—Concerned with the creation of object instances, separating the way in which this is done from the application.
- *Structural*—Concerned with the structural relationships between instances, particularly using generalization, aggregation and composition.
- *Behavioural*—Concerned with the assignment of the responsibility for providing functionality among the objects in the system.

17.11 A collaboration is a structure of collaborating elements also known as roles, each of which performs a specialized function, and which together accomplish some desired functionality.

17.12 A composite structure diagram can show a collaboration with its name in the top compartment stereotyped as «collaboration», a sequence diagram or a reference to an interaction occurrence in the second compartment, and a class diagram showing the roles of the participants in the collaboration in the third compartment.

17.13 A dashed oval with a dashed rectangle superimposed on the top right-hand quadrant of the oval. The name of the template collaboration is written in the oval, and the names of parameterized roles are written in the rectangle.

17.14 Template collaboration, collaboration diagram, class diagram, sequence diagram.

17.15
- Read the pattern to get a complete overview.
- Study the structure, participants and collaborations of the pattern in detail.
- Examine the sample code to see an example of the pattern in use.
- Choose names for the pattern's participants (i.e. classes) that are meaningful to the application.
- Define the classes.
- Choose application-specific names for the operations.
- Implement operations that perform the responsibilities and collaborations in the pattern.

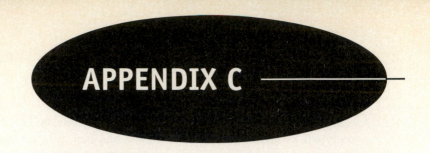

APPENDIX C

UML Common Notational Conventions

C.1 COMMON DIAGRAM ELEMENTS

Many UML diagrams have features in common. Within the notation there are a number of standard ways of representing the things that are of interest to the system developer, and these standard elements were set out early in the UML Specification (Object Management Group, 1999). The UML 2.0 Specification (Object Management Group, 2004a) no longer includes this information, but we feel that it is still useful in explaining the things you will find in diagrams, and so we have moved it from the body of the book to this appendix and updated it.

C.1.1 Graphs

Most diagrams in UML are *graphs*. A graph in this sense is not something like a histogram or an x-y graph used to represent statistical information graphically. A graph is a collection of nodes joined together by paths. Graphs are used to represent information about many kinds of problems. Often the term vertex is used instead of node, and edge or arc is used instead of path. Figure C-1 shows an example of a graph used to represent the travelling salesperson problem (in which a salesperson wishes to visit each of a number of locations by the shortest route, visiting each location once and only once). The locations at the nodes are represented by letters. The numbers labelling the paths represent the distances between nodes.

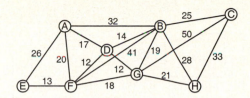

Figure C-1: Example graph representing a travelling salesperson problem

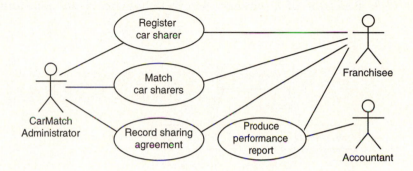

Figure C-2: Example of a graph—a use case diagram

Graphs are used extensively in UML. Figure C-2 shows a use case diagram in which there are two different kinds of nodes—actors and use cases—and paths connecting them.

C.1.2   Visual Relationships in Graphs

In most graphs in UML, it is the relationships among symbols that are important rather than their size: the fact than one class is drawn larger than another in a class diagram is not intended to convey information. The one exception to this is in some sequence diagrams where the time axis is drawn to scale—for example, to show one second as one centimetre.

There are three kinds of visual relationships in UML diagrams that are important:

- connection (usually symbols and two-dimensional shapes connected by lines);
- containment (usually of symbols by two-dimensional shapes);
- visual attachment (text or a symbol being close to a symbol on a diagram).

These relationships can be represented by graphs. In Chapter 2 we said that UML is a visual language. If you parse the visual representation into an internal representation using the rules of the UML grammar, then the result is a graph. Figure C-3 shows examples of these three kinds of visual relationships in a package diagram.

Figure C-4 shows the relationships among the elements of the diagram in Figure C-3 as a graph. (The notation used here is an adaptation of UML notation, but it has no formal meaning and is simply used to show the relationships as a graph.)

Note in particular that something being contained within something else and something being visually attached to something else (in this case as a label) can be converted into paths in the graph. Software modelling tools use some kind of internal representation such as this to hold the details of the

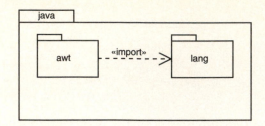

Figure C-3: Example of a package diagram showing visual relationships

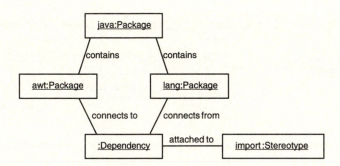

Figure C-4: Graph of visual relationships between elements of Figure C-3

relationships between pairs of model elements. For most software modelling tools, it will be the UML metamodel that is used for this purpose (see Chapter 2).

There are four kinds of element used in UML notation: icons, two-dimensional symbols, paths and strings. These are explained below.

- *Icons.* An icon is a graphical element of a fixed size and shape. It does not change shape to hold other elements. In UML, icons are often used as stereotypes for classes (see Section 15.2.2). Icons can be used as standalone elements in diagrams, within other elements or as terminators of paths (see below).

- *Two-dimensional symbols.* Two-d symbols can be used to contain other symbols and will change their size accordingly. They can be divided into separate compartments. Paths connect two-d symbols to each other and to icons. In a software modelling tool, if you move a two-d symbol, all its contents and all the paths connected to it move with it.

- *Paths.* Paths are used to connect together two-d symbols and icons. A path is made up of a sequence of lines whose endpoints are attached. Paths may not have dangling ends—they must always be attached at both ends to some other element. Paths may have *terminators* at their ends (where they attach to other symbols), and these terminators convey meaning about the path symbol.

- *Strings.* Strings are used to present a range of information in textual form. It is not necessary for them to be formally parsable within UML, but UML assumes that they are written in some language with a syntax that can be parsed into information within the model.

C.1.3   Icons

Icons are used to represent stereotyped graphical elements in UML. The stick-person symbol used to represent actors is an example of an icon. The Unified Software Development Process profile uses icons to represent three different kinds of classes: boundary classes, control classes and entity classes. (See Chapter 15 for more on profiles.) These are shown in Figure C-5.

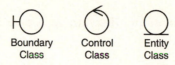

Figure C-5: Examples of icons from the Unified Software Development Process

Icons are also used on the *terminators* of paths. The triangle used to represent the generalization relationship, as shown in Figure C-6, is an example of this.

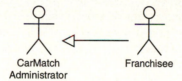

Figure C-6: Example of an icon as a terminator on a path

C.1.4   Two-dimensional Symbols

Two-dimensional symbols are used to represent many elements within UML. The obvious example is the class in class diagrams. Figure C-7 shows an example of a class divided into compartments for the class name, attributes and operations.

```
┌─────────────────────────────────────────────┐
│                 MapReference                 │
├─────────────────────────────────────────────┤
│  - externalForm : String                     │
│  - internalForm : Coordinate                 │
├─────────────────────────────────────────────┤
│  «abstract» # convertToInternal(String) : Coordinate │
│  «abstract» # convertToExternal(Coordinate) : String │
└─────────────────────────────────────────────┘
```

Figure C-7: Examples of a class as a two-dimensional symbol with compartments

As well as containing strings, two-dimensional symbols can also contain other symbols, including icons and other two-dimensional symbols. Figure C-8 shows a deployment diagram with two-dimensional symbols (components) to represent executables deployed on the **Web-server** node.

Of course, the symbol that represents the node designated **Web-server** is a two-dimensional projection of a three-dimensional symbol. Currently UML expects diagrams to be presented in only two dimensions. Until three-dimensional software modelling tools become widespread, it is likely that such symbols will stay two-dimensional!

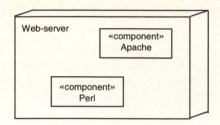

Figure C-8: Example of a deployment diagram as a two-dimensional symbol containing icons

C.1.5 Paths

Paths are used to represent all the many links among other symbols on UML diagrams. A path is made up of line segments for graphical display. It may be possible in a software modelling tool to manipulate an individual segment, for example to drag it around on the diagram, but an individual line segment cannot exist without the rest of the path. As mentioned above, paths must always be attached to some symbol at both ends. It is not possible to have a path that is left with a dangling end in a diagram. (They are attached logically, but do not always touch.) Paths may have icons as terminators at the point where they join onto another symbol.

Figure C-9 shows two paths each of which is made up of three line segments and terminated with an icon that signifies generalization.

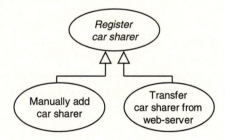

Figure C-9: Example of paths made of line segments terminated with icons

Some paths may be combined into branching tree structures as in Figure C-10. However, the physical appearance of the paths in the diagram hides the fact that these are conceptually still two separate paths.

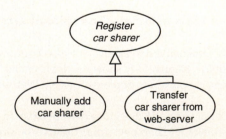

Figure C-10: Example of branching paths

The choice of how paths are laid out on diagrams is a presentation issue, and may be configurable within a software modelling tool. Figure C-11 shows some possible options. Normally only a single style will be used in a model.

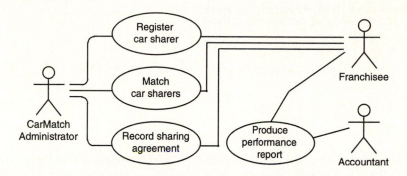

Figure C-11: Different path styles

Paths should be drawn to avoid crossing wherever possible, but where crossing line segments cannot be avoided, a small 'jog' can be included, to make it clear that the lines cross but do not join. An example of a jog is shown in Figure C-12 (although this diagram could be redrawn to eliminate the need for a jog).

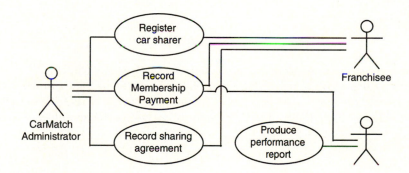

Figure C-12: Jog introduced to show where paths cross

C.1.6   Strings

Strings are sequences of characters in a particular character set that are used to display information about the model. The character set that is used need not be limited to Roman characters. UML assumes that the character set is capable of handling multi-byte characters. Eight-bit character sets such as ASCII (American Standard Code for Information Interchange) cannot handle more than 256 distinct character codes, and so cannot represent the full range of characters used by human languages. Unicode would provide this capability, although it is not singled out as a likely candidate in the UML Specification.

Strings are displayed in UML as text string graphics. Printable characters should be printed directly. Non-printable characters (control codes) are platform-dependent. Strings may be printed out as single lines or as paragraphs with line breaks. The choice of font or typeface can be used to indicate properties of the model. For example, in UML, italic typeface is used to indicate an abstract class name. Figure C-13 shows the use of different types of string.

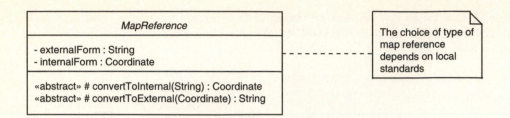

Figure C-13: Examples of strings in UML

C.1.7   Names

Strings are used as *names* to identify model elements. Model elements are uniquely identified within a particular scope. The scope may be a system, it may be a package, or it may be a class. For example, different classes may contain attributes or operations with the same name, but they can be distinguished from one another by the name of the class to which they belong. The term *namespace* is used to identify the scope of a name.

Pathnames can be used explicitly to show the scope of a name. In UML, packages are the normal mechanism for defining namespaces (see Chapter 2), and package names can be linked together using pairs of colons as delimiters, for example java::awt::Applet or CarMatch::Insurance::Policy.

C.1.8   Labels

Strings are also used as *labels* on diagram elements. Labels are attached graphically to another symbol on a diagram, either by being contained within or displayed adjacent to them. In a software modelling tool, if a symbol is moved, then any label attached to it will move with it. Figure C-14 shows examples of labels that are contained in and adjacent to other symbols, including the names of two classes qualified by paths.

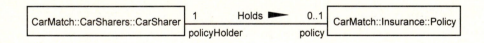

Figure C-14: Examples of labels and names in UML

C.1.9   Keywords

Keywords are used in places within UML to distinguish model elements that do not have a distinct visual representation. For example, there are a number of types of dependency in models, all of which are represented by a dashed arrow with an open arrowhead. The use of keywords in guillemets distinguishes these different types of dependency. Figure C-15 shows two different kinds of relationship in a use case diagram distinguished by the use of keywords.

Appendix B of the UML Specification lists a number of keywords as *standard elements*. These are reserved words within UML and should not be used except for their defined purpose. Other words can be used by modellers as stereotypes to extend the use of UML (see Section 15.2.2).

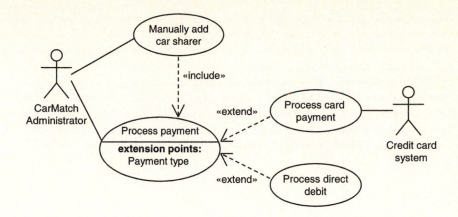

Figure C-15: Examples of keywords in UML

C.1.10　Expressions

An *expression* is a string that is displayed in a particular language. It is assumed that the expression can be evaluated appropriately or analysed to produce a meaningful result. It may be that the expression is in a language that will be used by a software modelling tool to generate code, and will be placed directly into the generated code, it may be in some specification language that will be translated into an expression in the target language, or it may be used by the tool at run-time to simulate some element of the running system.

The choice of language is dependent on the user and the options available in the software modelling tool being used. Expressions can be used in the specification of operations, as default values for attributes, as constraints (see Section 15.2.4) or as code fragments in comments (see Section C.1.11). Figure C-16 shows examples of some expressions. The comment contains a short piece of Java code to calculate the commission for an insurance policy.

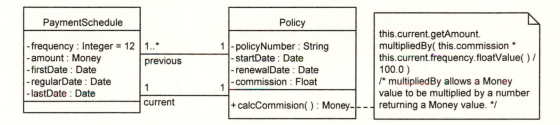

Figure C-16: Examples of expressions in UML

Expressions can be defined in Object Constraint Language (OCL), which is explained in detail in Chapter 13. The specification for OCL is part of the UML Specification. OCL is used particularly for expressing constraints such as pre-conditions and post-conditions for operations.

C.1.11　Comments

Already in this chapter you have seen the use of *comments* in diagrams. A comment is a two-dimensional symbol containing a string. The string can be a constraint, a code fragment in some language or a comment about the model in natural language. Figures C-13 and C-16 show examples of the use of comments in class diagrams. Comments are drawn using a rectangle with a 'turned down' top right-hand corner. They are joined to the thing they are documenting by a dashed line. Note the distinction between the endpoint of the line in Figure C-13, where the comment describes the class, and Figure C-16, where the comment describes the operation. Strictly speaking, the line should be a dependency arrow (with an open arrowhead), but because the dependency is always from the comment to the model element, the arrowhead can be omitted without loss of information. A comment placed on a diagram with no dashed line usually describes the diagram in some way, for example to provide details of the author, the date on which it was produced or the source of information for the model. The term *note* was used for comments in UML 1.X and may still be used.

C.1.12   Classifiers

Classifiers is a term that we have tried to avoid using in this book, although it is used extensively in the UML Specification, because it is central to the semantics of UML. However, it is so abstract as to make explanations of how UML works more difficult to understand. A classifier is a model element that describes behavioural and structural features of a model. Classifiers include classes, actors, use cases, data types, components, interfaces, signals, nodes and subsystems. In the UML metamodel, classifiers are specializations of both **GeneralizableElement** and **NameSpace** which are both specializations of **ModelElement**. As namespaces, classifiers may have features, such as attributes and operations that are uniquely identified by belonging to their particular classifier. As generalizable elements, classifiers may be further specialized in an inheritance hierarchy; stereotypes (see Section 15.2.2) provide a mechanism for this. The Boundary, Control and Entity Classes of the Unified Software Development Process are stereotyped specializations of Class. Some things that apply in general to classifiers can be applied to all the specializations of classifier. For example, classifiers can participate in associations or own state machines.

Some things are not classifiers. These include collaborations, interactions, relationships and states.

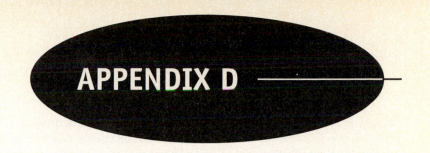

UML Metamodel

D.1 INTRODUCTION

The rules about how the elements of the Unified Modeling Language (UML) can be combined are set out and explained in the UML Specification (Object Management Group, 2004a). To be conformant with UML, a model (or a modelling tool that is used to build UML models) must conform to the *abstract syntax*, the *well-formedness rules*, the *semantics*, the *notation* and the *XMI Schema*. The abstract syntax is expressed as diagrams and natural language (English), the well-formedness rules in Object Constraint Language (OCL) (see Chapter 13) and English, and the semantics in English with some supporting diagrams, the notation in English with example diagrams, and the XMI Schema in XML. The rules that are expressed as diagrams use a subset of the notation of UML itself to specify how the elements of UML can be combined. This is an important feature of UML, but not one that you really need to understand in detail. It is called the *Four-Layer Metamodel Architecture* of UML and is summarized here.

D.2 FOUR-LAYER METAMODEL ARCHITECTURE

UML can be viewed as four layers. Each layer is an abstraction of the one below it, and each layer is defined in terms of the one above it. The lowest layer consists of *user objects*. These are the run-time instances of objects that are in the system, for example: <Insurance_Policy_2123434>, 21.34, set_premium and <Insurance_Quote_Server_213>. Note that these are not the same as object instances modelled in UML diagrams, which are part of the model layer. The next layer up consists of the *model*. These are the modelling concepts that define the user objects in the particular modelling domain, such as classes and attributes: InsurancePolicy, monthlyPremium, setPremium and InsuranceQuoteServer. (Much of the work of systems analysis and design lies in determining what the elements of the model are.) The layer above the model is the *metamodel*. The metamodel defines the elements of the model. (A meta-something is a higher-order something. So metadata is data that describes data, a metamodel is a model that describes another model.) The elements of the metamodel are the elements of UML, for example Class, Attribute, Operation, Component. The top layer is the OMG Meta Object Facility's (MOF) *meta-metamodel*. This defines the language for defining metamodels. Its elements are Class, Property and Operation. Strictly speaking, these are MetaClass, MetaProperty and MetaOperation. However, because the MOF is defined using UML, these are the elements defined in the UML Infrastructure Specification. These layers are sometimes referred to as M0, for the run-time instances, M1 for the model, M2 for the metamodel and M3 for the meta-metamodel. Figure D-1 shows this layered structure.

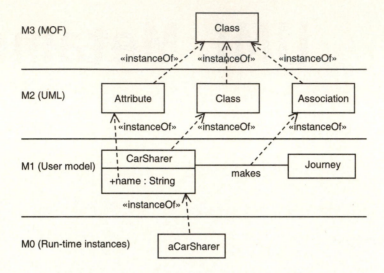

Figure D-1: Layered architecture of UML

In the same way as the UML metamodel can be applied to produce models of different domains—air-traffic control, banking, volunteering, libraries, car sharing, robotics, telecommunications and many others—the meta-metamodel can be used to specify many different metamodels—if you wanted to define other visual specification languages. For the purpose of understanding the abstract syntax of UML, it is the metamodel layer that is important.

D.3   UML ARCHITECTURE

The architecture of UML is modelled using packages. Each package contains definitions of the elements that make up UML. However, unlike UML 1.4, in which every metaclass was defined in one package, metaclasses are defined in multiple packages in UML 2.0. A complex structure of inheritance between elements in different packages and of dependencies between packages means that it has become far more difficult to track down the full definition of any metaclass.

The Infrastructure consists of two packages: **Core** and **Profiles**. The **Core** has been designed as a complete metamodel and is used (as a meta-metamodel) to define UML and the MOF as well as the Common Warehouse Model (CWM) and the **Profiles** package. These dependencies are shown in Figure D-2.

The **Core** package contains other packages, and these are shown in Figure D-3.

Of these packages, the **PrimitiveTypes** packages is the simplest. It contains no further packages within itself, and contains only four metaclasses, stereotyped as «primitive»: **Integer**, **String**, **Boolean** and **UnlimitedNatural**.

The **Abstractions** package on the other hand contains a further twenty packages within it in a hierarchy of dependency, at the top of which is the package **Elements**, which contains the single abstract metaclass *Element*. This metaclass represents an element that is a constituent of a model. Every other metaclass

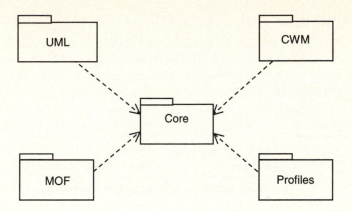

Figure D-2: Dependencies on the Core package

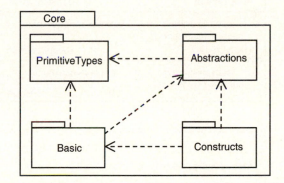

Figure D-3: Packages in the Core package

in the Infrastructure specification (and hence also the Superstructure specification), apart from the primitive types, is a subclass of *Element* (that is, a kind of *Element*).

The specifications are difficult to navigate through, as all packages and classes within packages are listed in alphabetical order rather than order of dependencies. While this is no doubt easier to maintain, as it does not require the order of sections to be changed if dependencies change, it does mean that the sequential reader reads definitions of elements that are dependent on other elements that have not been defined yet.

The UML Superstructure contains a further set of packages, all of which are dependent on packages in the Infrastructure.

D.3.1 Definition of Model Elements

We stated earlier that the rules that a model must conform to include the abstract syntax, semantics, well-formedness rules and notation. Each model element in the Superstructure has a definition that consists of these and other subsections: Description, Attributes, Associations, Additional Operations, Constraints, Semantics, Semantic Variation Points, Notation, Presentation Options, Style Guidelines, Examples, Rationale and Changes from previous UML. Some of these are optional and are not included for every model element.

D.3.2   Abstract Syntax

The abstract syntax of UML is specified using the notation of the metamodel. This is the core of the UML notation, using the UML class diagram to specify the elements of UML models and the relationships among them. Figure D-4 shows the diagram that expresses the abstract syntax of **Operations** in the Superstructure **Kernel** package.

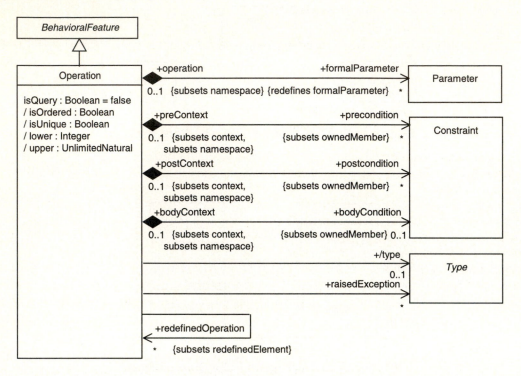

Figure D-4: Abstract syntax of Operations in the Superstructure Kernel package

This diagram uses the notation of class diagrams, explained in Chapters 4 to 7. The diagram shows that the metaclass **Operation** is a subclass of the abstract metaclass **BehavioralFeature**, and that an **Operation** can have zero or more **Parameters** associated with it. An **Operation** can be associated with **Constraints** in three different ways, as **preconditions**, as **postconditions** or as **bodyConditions**. An **Operation** may have a **Type** associated with it, as the type of the operation (that is, the type of its return value), and may also be associated with **Types** as exceptions that it raises. An **Operation** may also redefine other **Operations**.

The specification of a **Operation** and its attributes and associations is also provided in natural language in the UML Superstructure Specification (Object Management Group, 2004*c*), as follows.

> *An operation is a behavioral feature of a classifier that specifies the name, type, parameters, and constraints for invoking an associated behavior.*

There is a similar definition of every other metaclass in the metamodel.

D.3.3   Well-formedness Rules

The well-formedness rules apply to instances of metaclasses (that is, to operations, methods, classes and so on in the model layer). They provide the rules that instances of the metaclasses must conform to as a set of *invariants*. Invariants are constraints that cannot be broken: they must always be true for the model to be meaningful. They are specified in Object Constraint Language (OCL), which is explained in detail in Chapter 13. For example, the specification for the metaclass **Operation** states that if the operation has a body condition, then the operation must be a query. This constraint is written in OCL.

bodyCondition->notEmpty() implies isQuery

These constraints on the metamodel can be applied to check that the model conforms to the rules of UML and is well-formed.

Note that OCL is used **within** UML in order to document constraints within a model. For example, if one of the rules in the CarMatch system is that every journey that is linked to a sharing agreement must belong to a different car sharer, this could be documented in OCL as follows.

context SharingAgreement
inv: self.sharedJourney->forAll (i, j | (i.carSharer = j.carSharer)
    implies i = j)

What this says in English is that in the context of the **SharingAgreement** class there is an invariant rule as follows. If you take every possible pair of links between an instance of **SharingAgreement** and instances of **Journey** based on the association **sharedJourney**, and for each member of the pair you follow the link based on the association **carSharer** to an instance of the class **CarSharer**, then if the two **CarSharers** are the same, then the two journeys must be the same. Because they must be the same, it follows that two different journeys belonging to the same car sharer cannot be shared in the same sharing agreement.

D.3.4   Semantics

The semantics of UML are documented in English. For example, the following is part of the description of the metaclass **Operation**.

> *An operation is invoked on an instance of the classifier for which the operation is a feature.*
>
> *The preconditions for an operation define conditions that must be true when the operation is invoked. These preconditions may be assumed by an implementation of this operation.*
>
> *The postconditions for an operation define conditions that will be true when the invocation of the operation is completed successfully, assuming the preconditions were satisfied. These postconditions must be satisfied by any implementation of the operation.*
>
> *The bodyCondition for an operation constrains the return result. The bodyCondition differs from postconditions in that the bodyCondition may be overridden when an operation is redefined, whereas postconditions can only be added during redefinition.*

Note how these descriptions in the semantics relate to the aspects of the class diagram in the abstract syntax section.

D.3.5   Notation

The notation section of the specification of each metaclass describes the notation of UML elements in English with supporting diagrams. However, because English is used, the notation is ambiguous in places, and it is sometimes necessary to refer to the other sections of the specification.

In the UML 1.4 Specification the Notation Guide was an entire section in the document, which contained the specification of all model elements and diagrams. This included a useful section on common elements of the UML notation. Although this is no longer part of the UML 2.0 Specification, and indeed some of the concepts described are not defined in UML 2.0, it is a useful general introduction to elements of models, and we have included it as Appendix C.

The UML 2.0 Specification is organized by packages, and the notation part of each element's specification is included together with the other sections that define the element. The notation description explains the notation for the element and optionally provides examples of its use, style guidelines and presentation options. Presentation options are possible alternative ways of representing aspects of the notation that are not inherently part of the notation, for example the use of colour to distinguish different types of message.

The notation section for **Operation** begins with the format of the operation signature.

An operation is shown as a text string of the form:
`visibility name ( parameter-list ) : property-string`

It then goes on to explain each term within the string, as we do in Chapter 4.

Glossary

Action: A step in a workflow in an activity, used to represent where work is taking place; an executable statement, commonly associated with a state or transition in a state machine.

Active Object: An object represented by a lifeline in an interaction that has its own thread of control and so may carry out actions concurrently with other lifelines.

Activity: A workflow, comprising actions and flows between actions.

Activity Diagram: A means of describing workflows, linking activities and states. Used to describe business and system workflows.

Activity Edge: A flow between elements of an activity.

Activity Final Node: The final node in an activity that terminates all actions within that activity.

Activity Partition: A column or row in an activity used to indicate an area of responsibility for the actions.

Actor: External user of a system or an external system, shown in a use case diagram, which communicates with a system or subsystem being modelled.

Aggregation: Specifies that the nature of an association is one of 'whole–part'. One class is part of the other class.

Ancestor: Any superclass of a class regardless of the number of generalizations between the class and the superclass.

Artefact («artefact»): Artefacts are bundled collections of source code that can be deployed onto a node as a coherent set of functionality.

Association: A relationship between two or more classes. Specifies that the classes concerned collaborate with each other.

Association Class: The representation of an association as a class. Allows the association to have data and functional responsibilities (attributes and operations).

Association End: An association end is the binding of an association to a class that participate in that relationship. The association end can have properties such as *isDerived* and visibility.

Attribute: A data item for which a class is responsible.

Behaviour Specification: Description of the behaviour provided by a use case.

Bound Element: A class that is specified in terms of an instantiation of a parameterized class. (See *Parameterized Class.*)

Class: A generalized type representing a collection of objects which share the same data items and functional responsibilities.

Class Diagram: Shows the static structure of a set of classes. This static structure can include, but is not limited to, classes, attributes, operations, associations and generalization.

Class-scope [Feature]: An attribute or operation that exists on the class itself, rather than the instances of the class. A class attribute would hold the same value across all instances of that class.

Classifier: An umbrella term used for a model element that describes behavioural and structural features in a model. Classifiers include classes, actors, use cases, data types, components, interfaces, signals, nodes and subsystems.

Collaboration: A set of participants, objects or roles, that work together to achieve some meaningful outcome in the context of the system.

Combined Fragment: A way of representing an expression in a sequence diagram, which has an operator, such as loop, and one or more operands, which are fragments of sequence diagram that are combined according to the context of the operator.

Comment: A text string attached to a model element to provide additional information about it. In previous versions of UML, this was known as a *Note* and may still be described as such.

Communication Diagram: A type of interaction diagram that shows the objects that participate in an interaction with links between them that represent associations between classes or temporary connections needed to pass messages. (Called Collaboration Diagrams in previous versions of UML.)

Communication Path: Association between nodes in a deployment diagram, normally stereotyped with the communication mechanism or protocol.

Component («component»): A class or collection of classes that form a coherent functional unit of software for the system.

Component Diagram: Diagram to show components and the relationships between them.

Composite Structure: A set of associated classes or components that collaborate in order to achieve some defined, overall functionality.

Composite Structure Diagram: Shows the internal structure of a composite element (a class or component). Can also be used to relate collaboration occurrences to the composite structure of a classifier.

Composition: A more strict form of aggregation where the 'part' class has a lifecycle co-incident with the 'whole' class. (See *Aggregation.*)

Connectable Element: Represents a set of instances that are owned by a containing classifier and can be linked by connectors.

Connector: Represents a link between connectable elements.

Constraint: A restriction on the model, expressed as a condition, used to specify pre-conditions, post-conditions and invariants.

Decision Node: A point in an activity where the flow may branch according to certain conditions.

Dependency: A stereotyped relationship between two modelling elements. The stereotype indicates the nature of the relationship. Typically dependencies reflect process-oriented concepts. For example, «realize» or «refine».

Deployment Diagram: Diagram to show the implementation of the run-time system in terms of nodes (processors), communication paths among nodes and the components that are deployed on the nodes.

Deployment Specification («deployment spec»): A specific kind of artefact deployed to a node in order to configure the other artefacts deployed to the same node.

Design by Contract: Design using pre-conditions and post-conditions to specify the behaviour of parts of a system.

Device: A specific type of node used to show how specific processing devices are used in the implemented system.

Enumeration Class: A class that groups a set of defined members.

Event: A notable occurrence at a particular point in time. In activities or state machines these can trigger activity.

Event Occurrence: The point on a lifeline in a sequence diagram where a message is sent or received. The moment in time with which an action is associated.

Execution Environment: A distinct area within a node that can be used to show specific aspects of the implementation environment or to provide a more specific platform upon which an artefact can be deployed. Illustrative execution environments might include «container», «sandbox» or «J2EE Container».

Expression: A string in a particular language that can be evaluated to produce a result.

[Class] Feature: An attribute, operation or other user-specified concept (e.g. event) for which a class is responsible.

Flow Final Node: The final node within a particular flow in an activity that terminates all actions within that flow but leaves other flows unaffected.

Focus of Control: Small rectangular area shown on a lifeline in a sequence diagram to indicate that the object represented by the lifeline is executing an action.

Fork Node: A point in an activity or state machine where flow is split into multiple parallel routes.

Frame: Rectangle with a heading used to contain diagrams or fragments of diagrams referenced elsewhere. Mainly used for interaction diagrams.

Generalization: The abstraction of the shared common features of model elements (often classes) into an appropriate supertype. (See *Specialization*.)

Guard: A condition that must be satisfied for a flow to take place through a transition in a state machine or an activity edge in an activity.

Icon: Graphical representation of a stereotyped model element.

Initial Node: The entry point to the flow in an activity.

Instance: An occurrence of a class.

Instance-scope [Feature]: The normal scope of an attribute or operation. An attribute whose value relates to only one instance of a class or an operation whose method acts upon the attributes of that same instance as opposed to the attributes of the class as a whole.

Interaction Overview Diagram: A type of interaction diagram that combines the notation of sequence diagrams and activity diagrams. Combines interaction occurrences in sequence diagram format with the control structures of activity diagrams to provide an overview of an interaction.

Interaction Diagram: Generic term for sequence, communication, interaction overview and timing diagrams, which can be used to show the interaction between collaborating lifelines.

Interaction Occurrence: A fragment of an interaction drawn in a separate sequence diagram and reused by referring to it in a sequence diagram or interaction overview diagram.

Interface: A way of organizing a set of attributes and operation signatures that can be implemented by a model element such as a class.

Invariant: A condition on a class or use case that must always be true.

«J2EE Container»: A particular type of execution environment. (See *Execution Environment*.)

Join Node: A point in an activity or state machine where flows of multiple parallel routes are synchronized and flow continues down a single route.

Lifeline: Object in an interaction diagram that indicates the existence of an object, subsystem or other classifier that is participating in the interaction.

Link: An occurrence of an association.

Message: The specification of the communication sent between objects or roles in a collaboration. Defined in terms of its name, the types of its parameters and the type of its return value.

Method: The implementation of an operation.

Model: Abstraction of a physical system for a specific purpose. Used of the various views of a system that are developed at different stages of a project.

Multiplicity: The range of occurrences that may be found in the model element. One typical example is the multiplicity of an association end, that is, how many instances of a class could be associated with an instance of the source class.

N-ary Association: An association that links three or more classes.

Node: Processor in the implementation of a system, shown in a deployment diagram.

Object: An occurrence of a class.

OCL: Object Constraint Language—a formal language for the expression of constraints.

Operation: A functional or behavioural responsibility of a class.

Operation Signature: A collective reference to the name, parameter list and return type of an operation.

Package: Mechanism for organizing the different views of a project or system.

Parameter: An attribute or object passed as an argument to an operation or in a message.

Parameterized Class: A class definition consisting of attributes and operations specified in terms of parameters that are passed to the parameterized class in order to instantiate it. Also known as a template. (See also *Bound Element*.)

Parent Class: The class immediately above another class in a generalization is known as its parent class.

Pattern: A documented solution to a common problem in computer system design.

Port: For classes, a port provides a means of exposing a subset of class properties to support a particular interface to other classes. For components, the purpose of a port definition is to indicate that the component itself does not supply the required or provided interfaces. Instead, the interface requirement is delegated to an internal class of the component.

Post-condition: A condition that must be true if an operation or a use case has been legally executed.

Pre-condition: A condition that must be true for an operation to be legally executed, or for a use case to be legally applied.

Profile: A package that organizes stereotypes, tagged definitions and constraints in order to extend the UML metamodel for a particular purpose.

Provided Interface: An interface specification (see *Interface*) that is provided by a class or component.

Reflexive: Used of messages in an interaction diagram that are sent by a lifeline to itself.

Relationship: In UML, a generic name for some kind of semantic and notational join between two model elements. Associations, generalizations and dependencies are all specific types of relationship.

Repository: A facility for storing UML elements and diagrams, and associated documents.

Required Interface: An interface specification (see *Interface*) that is required by a class or component.

Role: A named behaviour of a model element in a particular context, typically the part played by an object in an association or a collaboration.

Sequence Diagram: Interaction diagram that shows the interactions among the participants in a collaboration or an operation. Shows the passage of time, usually on the vertical axis of the diagram.

Signal: An asynchronous message sent between instances in an interaction. In an activity, signals are visual icons to indicate the point on a diagram where events are triggered or responded to.

Signal Object: An object in an activity that represents an event that occurs outside the activity or an event raised by the activity for another activity to respond to.

Specialization: The inverse of generalization. A specialized class is one which differs from the superclass and any other sibling specializations of the same superclass in terms of its attributes, operations or methods. (See *Generalization*.)

State: A collective term for the attribute values of an object and the relationships it has with other objects at an instant in time. Objects may be in multiple states at any one time. States are terminated by events.

State Machine: A means of depicting how elements of a model move from state to state. Changes of state are the result of transitions.

Stereotype: In UML, a means of specifying that a model element conforms to the well-understood pattern of behaviour or existence of the specified stereotype. Stereotypes are specified in guillemets («...») or as graphical icons.

Structure Diagram: See *Composite Structure Diagram*.

Subclass: A specialized class in a generalization hierarchy.

Subflow: Activities may be broken down into subflows.

Subsystem: A meaningful division of a system into parts.

Subtype: See *Subclass*.

Superclass: A generalized class in a generalization hierarchy.

Supertype: See *Superclass*.

Tagged Definition: An attribute of a stereotype in a profile that is used to define permitted tagged values of instances to which the stereotype applies.

Tagged Value: Mechanism for attaching (name, value) pairs to model elements. One of the ways of extending UML.

Template: See *Parameterized Class*.

Timeline: A classifier shown in a timing diagram, typically an object or subsystem.

Timing Diagram: A type of interaction diagram that shows the lifelines of objects in terms of how the objects change state over time in response to events in a particular interaction.

Transition: A relationship between states in a state machine. When one state terminates, the transition indicates the next state.

Use Case: Sequence of actions carried out by the system to achieve some purpose that is meaningful for an external user or system. Graphically represented in a use case diagram and defined by behaviour specifications.

Use Case Diagram: Diagram showing use cases and actors and the associations between them. Provides a high-level model of the functionality of a system.

Utility Class: A collection of globally available attributes and operations. Specified using the «utility» stereotype.

Workflow: In UML, a generic term for modelling tasks in terms of a sequence of activities. In the Unified Process, a grouping of activities to carry out a particular system development task.

Visibility: Typically applies to attributes and operations, but may also apply to an association end. Specifies the accessibility of the model element to other associated model elements. UML specifies four options for visibility, public (+), private (-), protected (#) and package (~).

BIBLIOGRAPHY

Alexander, C., Ishikawa, S., Silverstein, M., Jacobson, M., Fiksdahl-King, I. & Angel, S. (1977), *A Pattern Language: Towns, Buildings, Construction*, Oxford University Press.

Beck, K. (2000), *Extreme Programming Explained*, Addison-Wesley.

Beck, K. & Cunningham, W. (1989), 'A laboratory for teaching object-oriented thinking', *Proceedings of OOPSLA 89. SIGPLAN Notices* **24**(10), 1–6.

Bennett, S., McRobb, S. & Farmer, R. (2002), *Object-Oriented Systems Analysis and Design using UML*, McGraw-Hill.

Booch, G. (1991), *Object-Oriented Analysis and Design with Applications*, Benjamin/Cummings.

Booch, G., Rumbaugh, J. & Jacobson, I. (1999), *The Unified Modeling Language User Guide*, Addison-Wesley.

Coad, P. & Yourdon, E. (1990), *Object-Oriented Analysis*, Yourdon Press; Prentice-Hall.

Coad, P. & Yourdon, E. (1991), *Object-Oriented Design*, Yourdon Press; Prentice-Hall.

Cockburn, A. (2000), *Writing Effective Use Cases*, Addison-Wesley.

Cockburn, A. (2003), `http://alistair.cockburn.us/usecases/usecases.html`.

Conallen, J. (1999), 'Modeling web application architectures with UML', *Communications of the ACM* **42**(10), 63–70.

Conallen, J. (2002), *Building Web Applications with UML*, Addison-Wesley.

Constantine, L. (1997), 'The case for essential use cases', *Object Magazine, May, 1997*.

Coplien, J. O. (1992), *Advanced C++: Programming Styles and Idioms*, Addison-Wesley.

Coplien, J. O. & Schmidt, D. (1995), *Pattern Languages of Program Design*, Addison-Wesley.

Crupi, J., Malks, D. & Alur, D. (2003), *Core J2EE Patterns: Best Practices and Design Strategies*, Prentice Hall PTR.

Douglass, B. P. (1998), *Real-Time UML: Developing Efficient Objects for Embedded Systems*, Addison-Wesley.

Evitts, P. (2000), *A UML Pattern Language*, MTP.

Fowler, M. & Scott, K. (1999), *UML Distilled: Applying the Standard Object Modeling Language*, *1st ed.*, Addison-Wesley.

Gamma, E., Johnson, R., Helm, R. & Vlissides, J. (1995), *Design Patterns: Elements of Reusable Object-Oriented Software*, Addison-Wesley.

Gomaa, H. (2000), *Designing Concurrent, Distributed and Real-Time Applications with UML*, Addison-Wesley.

Jacobson, I., Booch, G. & Rumbaugh, J. (1999), *The Unified Software Development Process*, Addison-Wesley; ACM Press.

Jacobson, I., Christerson, M., Jonsson, P. & Övergaard, G. (1992), *Object-Oriented Software Engineering: A Use Case Driven Approach*, Addison-Wesley.

Jacobson, I., Ericsson, M. & Jacobson, A. (1995), *The Object Advantage: Business Process Reengineering with Object Technology*, Addison-Wesley.

Kobryn, C. (1999), 'UML 2001: A standardization odyssey', *Communications of the ACM* **42**(10), 29–37.

Object Management Group (1999), OMG Unified Modeling Language Specification 1.3, Technical report, Object Management Group.

Object Management Group (2003*a*), OMG UML 2.0 OCL Specification, Technical report, Object Management Group.

Object Management Group (2003*b*), UML Profile for Schedulability, Performance, and Time Specification 1.0, Technical report, Object Management Group.

Object Management Group (2004*a*), OMG Unified Modeling Language 2.0 Specification, Technical report, Object Management Group.

Object Management Group (2004*b*), OMG Unified Modeling Language Infrastructure Specification 2.0, Technical report, Object Management Group.

Object Management Group (2004*c*), OMG Unified Modeling Language Superstructure Specification 2.0, Technical report, Object Management Group.

Pressman, R. S. (2004), *Software Engineering: A Practitioner's Approach*, McGraw-Hill.

Rosenberg, D. & Scott, K. (1999), *Use Case Driven Object Modeling with UML: A Practical Approach*, Addison Wesley.

Rumbaugh, J., Blaha, M., Premerlani, W., Eddy, F. & Lorensen, W. (1991), *Object-Oriented Modeling and Design*, Prentice Hall.

Rumbaugh, J., Jacobson, I. & Booch, G. (1999), *The Unified Modeling Language Reference Manual*, Addison-Wesley.

Shlaer, S. & Mellor, S. (1988), *Object-Oriented Systems Analysis: Modeling the World in Data*, Prentice-Hall.

Warmer, J. & Kleppe, A. (1999), *The Object Constraint Language: Precise Modeling with UML*, Addison-Wesley Longman Inc.

Wirfs-Brock, R., Wilkerson, B. & Wiener, L. (1990), *Designing Object-Oriented Software*, Prentice-Hall.

INDEX